Social Security Outside the Realm of the Employment Contract

Social Security Outside the Realm of the Employment Contract

Informal Work and Employee-like Workers

Edited by

Mies Westerveld

Faculty of Law, University of Amsterdam, the Netherlands

Marius Olivier

Law School, University of Western Australia, Perth and Faculty of Law, North-West University, South Africa

Edward Elgar PUBLISHING

Cheltenham, UK • Northampton, MA, USA

Published by
Edward Elgar Publishing Limited
The Lypiatts
15 Lansdown Road
Cheltenham
Glos GL50 2JA
UK

Edward Elgar Publishing, Inc.
William Pratt House
9 Dewey Court
Northampton
Massachusetts 01060
USA

A catalogue record for this book
is available from the British Library

Library of Congress Control Number: 2019930597

This book is available electronically in the **Elgar**online
Law subject collection
DOI 10.4337/9781788113403

MIX
Paper from
responsible sources
FSC
www.fsc.org
FSC® C013056

ISBN 978 1 78811 339 7 (cased)
ISBN 978 1 78811 340 3 (eBook)

Typeset by Columns Design XML Ltd, Reading
Printed and bound in Great Britain by TJ International Ltd, Padstow, Cornwall

Contents

Contributors

Pablo Arellano Ortiz is Labour Law Specialist at the Labour Law and Reform Unit, Governance and Tripartism Department, International Labour Office and Researcher at the Faculty of Law, Pontificia Universidad Católica de Valparaíso, Chile.

Catherine Barnard is Professor of European Union Law and Employment Law and Senior Tutor at Trinity College, Cambridge. Her expertise lies in the field of European Union law, especially migration law, and employment law.

Alysia Blackham is Associate Professor and Australian Research Council Discovery Early Career Research Fellow at Melbourne Law School, University of Melbourne. Her research focuses on the intersection of employment law, equality law and public law, using empirical evidence to cast new light on legal problems.

Elmarie Fourie is Senior Lecturer and Head of the Department of Public Law at the Faculty of Law at the University of Johannesburg. She has been part of various task teams preparing legal opinions to government departments and drafting legislation for South African Development Community (SADC) countries.

Avinash Govindjee is Executive Dean of the Faculty of Law at the Nelson Mandela University in Port Elizabeth, South Africa. He is a Consulting Attorney to the firm Cliffe Dekker Hofmeyr, a part-time Senior Commissioner of the Commission for Conciliation, Mediation and Arbitration (CCMA) and an associate of the International Institute for Social Law and Policy (IISLP).

Tamás Gyulavári is Professor and Chair of Labour Law at Pázmány Péter Catholic University in Budapest. He is author and co-author of several books and articles on European and Hungarian labour law in Hungarian and in English.

Li Jianfei is Professor of Renmin University of China Law School, Deputy Dean Research Institute for Disabled Persons' Enterprise Development, Director Labour and Social Law Institute and Director Institute for Maritime and Insurance Act.

Lucie Lamarche is a professor of law at University of Québec in Montreal, Canada and an Associate Professor at the University of Ottawa, Canada. She teaches international, regional and national labour and social law as well as human and women's rights. She also is a member of the Quebec Bar in Canada and a Fellow of the Royal Society of Canada.

Jing Li is Assistant Professor of China University of Labor Relations, Law School.

Juliana Masabo is Law Lecturer at the University of Dar es Salaam, Tanzania. She holds a PhD in Law from the University of Cape Town, South Africa, an LL.M and LL.B (Hons) from the University of Dar es Salaam. Her research interests are in international labour migration, social security law, citizenship, refugee law and human rights law.

Marius Olivier is Extraordinary Professor at the Faculty of Law, Northwest University, Potchefstroom, South Africa, Adjunct-Professor at the School of Law, The University of Western Australia, Perth, Australia, and Director of the International Institute for Social Law and Policy (IISLP).

Amir Paz-Fuchs is Senior Lecturer in Employment Law at the University of Sussex in the UK. His interests lie in the fields of labour and employment law, jurisprudence, social rights and social justice, and legal aspects of privatisation.

Mies Westerveld is Professor Social Insurance Law and Professor by Special Appointment Access to Justice at the Law Faculty of the University of Amsterdam, the Netherlands. She has done research on the position of (dependent and independent) self-employed workers in labour law and social security.

Annamaria Johansson Westregård is Associate Professor and Senior Lecturer in Business Law at the School of Economics and Management, Lund University, Sweden. She has done research on employee privacy and drug testing in working life, the Sickness Insurance System and rehabilitation, and on self-employment and crowdworkers in the collaborative economy.

Michael Wynn is Professor of Labour Law at the Group for Employment Law and Policy, Law Department, Kingston University, UK. He has written widely on labour and employment law topics including the contract of employment, temporary agency workers, maritime labour law and collective bargaining.

Preface

This book aims to build a bridge between policy makers and researchers who are working on similar issues within different frameworks and from varying perspectives. The central theme of the book is the organisation of social security for workers for whom the organisational device of the labour contract is missing. The theme is global, but the challenges governments are facing differ, if not from country to country then from region to region. In countries in the global south the main obstacle appears to be that the majority of work takes place in the informal economy, which is by nature hard to reach for formal institutions and remains largely uncovered from a social security perspective. Countries in the global north face the fact that the standard employment contract, originally a useful device for social insurance arrangements, is in retreat. Some researchers even claim that the labour contract is 'dead'. This development is especially troublesome for social security given its close connection with the concept of employment insurance. Countries that have built their systems on the concept of resident-related insurance, on the other hand, must acknowledge that residency has become fluid, perhaps even more so than in the past.

The fact that the ultimate goals of social security are not being met has not gone unnoticed. In 1999 the International Labour Organization (ILO) called for an expansion of social security coverage also in poorer countries. Over the years the realisation that this target is complicated, if not illusionary, in countries where informal economy work is the standard way of income generation has found its way into ILO instruments, as indicated below.[1] In the European Union (EU) a somewhat comparable development can be observed. In 2018 the European Commission (EC), in principle averse to initiate proposals of social policy, launched a Proposal for a Council Recommendation to support people who, due to the type of employment relationship or form of self-employment, are left without sufficient access to social protection.[2]

---

[1] ILO (2018). See also Vonk (2013).

[2] EC (2018).

The challenge has, in other words, been identified and recognised. The question how to deal with this systemic flaw in social security coverage is another matter. This question was the driving force behind this book and constitutes the book's central theme.

But before we turn to this theme and the book's architecture, two issues have to be raised, the one with respect to terminology, the other with considering the topic's legal underpinning.

TERMINOLOGY

Different from what one might assume concerning the frequent use of 'social security', a real consensus about its exact meaning, and its historical setting, is lacking. Eichenhofer places the origin of the term in 1941 when President Roosevelt introduced the 'freedom of want' concept in his annual message to the Congress.[3] Soon thereafter the concept appeared in the Atlantic Charter (1941),[4] the British Beveridge Report (1942) and the Canadian Marsh Report (1943). From a human rights perspective, social security can be classified as a foundation for an economically independent life, and when one is exposed to contingencies, which are beyond one's control.[5]

The second concept that deserves attention is the word 'informal', in combination with 'sector', 'economy' or 'economy worker'. The qualification 'informal sector' was coined in an ILO research paper that was drafted for the Kenyan context.[6] At that time (1972) no specific definition was attached. Rather, the qualification was used as an analytical term to describe the duality in the labour market. It has been suggested that the term 'informal sector' be replaced with the term 'informal economy'.[7] However, both these phrases fail to fully encapsulate the nature of what they are explaining. Activities within the 'informal sector' fall into a variety of sectors, often with no similarities, whilst 'informal economy' fails to illustrate the significant grey areas between the informal and formal economy.[8] The emphasis, it is suggested, should be on informality, encapsulating those activities falling *de facto* (factually or in practice)

---

3 Eichenhofer (2015) p. 5 with reference to F D Roosevelt, *The Annual Message to the Congress,* January 6, 1941.

4 https://en.wikipedia.org/wiki/Atlantic_Charter

5 Id. p. 6.

6 ILO (1972).

7 Reynaud (2002).

8 Olivier (2009).

or *de jure* (legally) outside the reach of law, in particular the current social security (legal and institutional) frameworks.[9] It has therefore been suggested that the informal economy is not 'an individual condition but a process of income-generation characterized by one central feature: *it is unregulated by the institutions of society, in a legal and social environment in which similar activities are regulated*'.[10]

Mention should also be made of the influential definition adopted by the International Conference of Labour Statisticians (ICLS). In 2003 the 17th ICLS moved from an *enterprise-based* to an *employment-based* definition. The focus is no longer on the formality of the enterprise; instead, using an employment-based definition, informality is defined in relation to the employment characteristics of the individual. Therefore, individuals are considered to be in informal employment if their employment relationship is, in law or in practice, not subject to national labour legislation, income taxation, social protection or entitlement to certain employment benefits. According to the 19th ICLS, in 2013, work is defined irrespective of its formal or informal character or the legality of the activity. Informal work/employment has effectively been mainstreamed in the notion of 'work'.

In the global north the qualification 'informal' is equally complex. US economist Restrepo-Echavarria observes the absence of a unique definition, while suggesting that a generally accepted approach is to imply individuals and their employers who engage in productive activities that are not taxed or registered by the government.[11] In this approach 'informal' is, in other words, associated with illegal, if not criminal, activities, such as tax evasion, evasion of immigration laws and – relevant for our topic – avoidance of social insurance contributions.

At EU level attempts have also been made to define 'informal employment'. The term has been described in a 2012 European Commission document in the following terms:

> The two main categories of informal employment, wage employment in jobs without social protection and self-employment in unincorporated enterprises, can be further disaggregated into different categories of employment relationships. Self-employment consists of own-account workers and employers of informal enterprises who hire other workers. The conditions of these two categories are often very different. Wage-employment includes informal employees of both formal and informal firms, subcontracted workers, wage

---

[9] ILO (2008).

[10] Castells and Portes (1989: 12); ILO (2008: 12), emphasis in the original.

[11] Restrepo-Echavarria (2017).

workers for households (domestic workers), and wage workers with no fixed employer (casual day workers).[12]

However, there is a vast and growing range of other forms of work that cannot be regarded as either self- or wage-employment. Much of this (informal) work takes place in supply chain contexts, and may not have a relationship with an employer, but at best with a 'provider' or 'user' of work. Others may be working in the care economy.[13]

The last concept that needs clarification is that of 'worker'. In some contexts this term is equivalent to an employee, in others it resembles an employee or an entrepreneur, and in some legal schemes a 'worker' occupies a middle category between an employee and a self-employed person.

With authors from so many parts of the world contributing to this book and terminology that is inherently multifaceted, it is all but impossible to create uniformity of terms. Rather than attempting to achieve uniformity, we have invited all authors to present 'their' system of social security employing its own unique terminology and conceptual framework.

LEGAL UNDERPINNING: GLOBAL AND REGIONAL STANDARD SETTING

The recognition of social security as a human right raises the question about the underpinning of social security *law* in the international standard setting, with specific reference to the book's target group. The description is, necessarily, succinct. The aim is no more than to give an inventory of rules and regulations that may have consequences for *national* standard setting. Given the African setting of some of the contributions in this book, a special section briefly deals with some of the African (continental) instruments. Also, since the majority of contributions about the global north originate from researchers in EU Member States, a special section is reserved for European standard setting.

Global Standard Setting

The oldest international standard setting in social security is of ILO origin. Ever since its foundation in 1919, social security was at the centre of ILO's activities. Among the many conventions and recommendations,

---

12 EC (2012: 1–2, emphasis added); see also Lund (2012: 12–15).
13 Lund and Srinivas (2000: 3).

Convention 102 of 1952 (Social Security (Minimum Standards)) was the first that included 'all' (nine) branches of social security. Later conventions set higher standards.

Over the years the assumption of completeness of the social risks of Convention 102 has been subject to some critique. It has been argued that the social risks in Convention 102 are individual-centred, while the risks that threaten the livelihood of informal economy workers more often than not are *collective* risks, such as war, crop failure or natural disasters.[14] In 2012, the position of informal economy workers received formal recognition in *ILO Recommendation 202* (*National Floors of Social Protection*).[15] This Recommendation mentions, as one of the principles to be applied, 'social inclusion including of persons in the informal economy' (paragraph 1(e)). Paragraph 15 in turn suggests that '[S]ocial security extension strategies should apply to persons both in the formal and informal economy'. ILO *Recommendation 204* (2015) (*The Transition from the Informal to the Formal Economy*) went further, by making a number of pertinent suggestions in the context of affirming that the transition from the informal to the formal economy is essential to achieve inclusive development and to realise decent work for all.[16] With particular reference to employment policies, the Recommendation confirms that countries should pay special attention to the needs and circumstances of those in the informal economy and their families (paragraph 19). Coverage of social insurance should progressively be extended to those in the informal economy, and administrative procedures, benefits and contributions should be adapted in accordance with the contributory capacity of those in the informal economy (paragraph 20).

Returning to the (post-war) international setting, the *UN International Covenant on Economic, Social and Cultural Rights* (ICESCR 1966)[17] is important for informal economy workers for two reasons. Firstly, by far the majority of countries, including developing countries have ratified this instrument. Secondly, General Comment No. 19 (on Article 9 ICESCR) requires a ratifying country to cover informal economy workers, and expects governments to respect and support social security schemes developed within the informal economy, such as micro-insurance schemes. Despite limited financial capacity, countries should consider lower-cost and alternative schemes to provide for marginalised

[14] Olivier (2011: 424). See also Sankaran (2012). Italics added.
[15] ILO (2012).
[16] ILO (2015).
[17] ICESCR (1966), Art. 9 (right of social security).

groups, and they should ensure the progressive inclusion of informal economy workers in social security arrangements.[18]

African (Continental) Standard Setting

Aligned with the *Social Policy Framework for Africa* (2008), the African Union (AU) *Social Protection Plan for the Informal Economy and Rural Workers 2011–2015* (SPIREWORK) focuses on the extension of social protection coverage to workers in the informal economy, with reference to existing and innovative models for extension, the development of a minimum package of social protection and ways to facilitate such a package. As such, this forms a part or subset of a broader AU initiative, namely the *Programme on Upgrading the Informal Economy* (2010). The draft *Protocol to the African Charter on Human and Peoples' Rights on the Rights of Citizens to Social Protection and Social Security* (2019) comprehensively deals with the social security position of informal workers, and suggests among others the adoption of a regulatory framework promoting appropriate and adequate social security of informal workers, through the inclusion of these workers in general social security schemes adapted to suit the context of these workers as well as the provision or recognition of appropriate formal and informal social insurance and micro-insurance mechanisms, universal schemes, social assistance measures and dedicated savings instruments.[19]

European Standard Setting

From a European perspective, EU standard setting, as well as the *European Social Charter* (ESC, 1961) and the *European Code of Social Security* (ECSS, 1964) may be relevant.

EU standard setting commenced with the foundation of the European Economic Community (EEC) in 1957. The 'Community' was predominantly economic: social security was considered the exclusive domain of the Member States (rule of subsidiarity).[20] However, in an open market

---

18 UN Committee on Economic, Social and Cultural Rights (CESCR), *General Comment No. 19: The right to social security (Art. 9 of the Covenant)*, 4 February 2008, E/C.12/GC/19.

19 Draft Protocol African Charter (2018), p. 5.

20 Art. 5(3) Treaty of the European Union (TEU): in areas that do not fall within its exclusive competence, the Union shall act only and in so far as the objectives of the proposed action cannot be sufficiently achieved by the Member States.

without impediments for free movement of workers, some Community rules are inevitable. The EEC founding fathers were well aware of this: one of the first EEC instruments was a regulation about social security rights (of migrant workers).[21] Less foreseen was the effect of the equal pay clause (men/women)[22] on social security law. This obligation for employers would have implications for equal treatment law, an area of the law that is both extensive and complicated, especially with respect to social security.[23] Over the years, the rule on subsidiarity was mitigated. As long as there is unanimity of votes, the Council may adopt minimum requirements, including in this politically sensitive domain.[24]

Also for non-EU countries, Article 12 ESC establishes the right to social security as a specific human rights instrument. Contracting states that are members of the European Council are to establish and develop a system of social security that complies with ILO standards embedded in Convention 102. The requirements are expanded in the European Code of Social Security, requiring provisions for at least six (instead of three) branches of social security. Another expansionary clause is the provision that a system of social security is to be developed progressively.[25] In practice – and in view of economic and demographic developments – this 'progressive development' is to be interpreted as an obligation to make the social security system of each country keep pace with the development of the society at large.[26]

Article 34 ESC explicitly states a *right* to social security. This provision was from the very beginning controversial. The wording is, consequently, somewhat of a compromise.[27] The right is to be guaranteed – both by the EU and its Member States – to everyone, which makes it, according to Eichenhofer, dubious that a selective protection, for instance confined to employment status, is permissible. The conventional explanation for this selection is that it finds its justification with reference to different levels of vulnerability, which in some cases imply self-sufficiency. However, in a labour market where self-employed workers

---

[21] Reg. 3/1958 OJ 30 of 16 December 1958 on the Coordination of Social Security Systems.

[22] Art. 119 EEC Treaty, Art. 157 Treaty on the Functioning of the European Union (TFEU).

[23] Burri (2015), Westerveld (2015). See also Chapter 4.

[24] Art. 153 TEU.

[25] Art. 12 section 3 ESC.

[26] Mikkola (2010: 298, 313, 320).

[27] Eichenhofer (2015: 28).

are – or can be – just as economically vulnerable as their counterparts in a formal employment relationship, this justification is losing ground.[28]

That realisation has become relevant for EU policy makers as well. In September 2015 EU President Juncker presented a 'vision' for a European Pillar of Social Rights implementing the EC's ten priorities.[29] Two years and several consultation rounds later, the vision had been entrenched in a document holding 20 principles and rights: 'from the right to fair wages to the right to health care; from lifelong learning, a better work-life balance and gender equality to minimum income'.[30] For our topic the 12th principle is relevant: all workers and, under comparable conditions, the self-employed have the right to adequate social protection, regardless of the type and duration of their employment relationship. The principle was translated into a Proposal for a Council Recommendation, which was presented in March 2018. Under this Proposal Member States must ensure that the self-employed have access to social protection by extending formal coverage:

a) On a mandatory basis for sickness and healthcare benefits, maternity/paternity benefits, old age and invalidity benefits as well as benefits in respect of accidents at work and occupational diseases, and
b) On a voluntary basis for unemployment benefits.[31]

As of yet, this is but a proposal, but bearing in mind the possible implications of Article 34 ESC, it may not be long before the intended access has become a reality, either as a result of EU decision making (unanimity of votes), or through EU case law.

BOOK ARCHITECTURE

All authors – with the exception of the contributors to the introductory part – were asked to either reflect on a pressing issue with respect to social security and workers outside employment, or present a telling case study from the country or region they are familiar with. As social security

---

[28] Ibid.

[29] State of the Union 2015, 9.9.15 (http://europa.eu/rapid/press-release_SPEECH-15-5614_en.htm). Fifth priority: We have to step up the work for a fair and truly pan-European labour market.

[30] https://ec.europa.eu/commission/priorities/deeper-and-fairer-economic-and-monetary-union/european-pillar-social-rights_en

[31] Art. 8 and 9 EC (2018).

schemes are very diverse, the request also included presenting a description of the relevant social security scheme. In the end the various themes and topics were brought together under four categories, reflected in the structure of the book.

1. General Reflections
2. Thematic Reflections
3. Regional Overviews
4. National Case Studies

In general reflections the central theme is analysed from two perspectives. Firstly: who is the target group and why is its position problematic for the architecture of social security? Secondly: what do we know of the target group in terms of race and gender? Olivier (informal economy workers) and Wynn and Paz-Fuchs (new economy workers) analyse the first question. Fourie (informal economy) and Barnard and Blackham (EU race and gender equality law) look into the racial and gender dimension.

Thematic reflections (2) are presented by Jing Li and Li Jianfei (workers in the shared economy) and Govindjee (vulnerable work). The chapters by Ortiz (Latin America), Gyulavári (Central and Eastern Europe) and Masabo (East Africa) present regional approaches, (3) while Westregård (Sweden), Westerveld (The Netherlands) and Lamarche (Canada) describe country case studies that are, with regard to the central topic, telling (4).

At the end a short epilogue is added containing a few overarching observations.

We conclude with expressing the wish that the reader will extract as much inspiration from the contents of the book as we have had in its compilation.

Mies Westerveld
Marius Olivier

BIBLIOGRAPHY

Books and Articles

Atlantic Charter (1941) accessed 11 February 2019 at https://en.wikipedia.org/wiki/Atlantic_Charter

Burri S (2015) 'Equal treatment: The EU approach', in Pennings F and G Vonk (eds), *Research Handbook on European Social Security Law*, Cheltenham, UK and Northampton, MA, USA: Edward Elgar Publishing, pp. 231–257.

Castells M and A Portes (1989) 'The world underneath: The origins, dynamics, and effects of the informal economy', in Portes A, M Castells and L A Benton (eds), *The Informal Economy: Studies in Advanced and Less Developed Countries*, Baltimore: Johns Hopkins University Press.

Eichenhofer E (2015) 'Social security as a human right: a European perspective', in Pennings F and G Vonk (eds), *Research Handbook on European Social Security Law*, Cheltenham, UK and Northampton, MA, USA: Edward Elgar Publishing, pp. 3–31.

Lund, F (2012) 'Work-related social protection for informal workers', *International Social Security Review*, 65 (4), 9–30.

Lund, F and S Srinivas (2000) *Learning from Experience: A Gendered Approach to Social Protection for Workers in the Informal Economy*, Geneva: ILO.

Mikkola M (2010) *Social Human Rights of Europe*, Helsinki: Legisactio.

Olivier, M (2009) *Informality, employment contracts and extension of social insurance coverage*, ISSA Project on 'Examining the existing knowledge of social security coverage', working paper, no 9, Geneva: International Social Security Association.

Olivier M (2011) 'Informality, employment contracts and extension of social insurance coverage: Rights-based perspectives in a developing world context', *International Journal of Comparative Labour Law and Industrial Relations*, 2 (4), 419–443.

Olivier M (2017) *Expanding the boundaries of social security protection for informal economy workers in developing countries*, presented at LLRN, working paper.

Pennings F and G Vonk (eds) (2015) *Research Handbook on European Social Security Law*, Cheltenham, UK and Northampton, MA, USA: Edward Elgar Publishing.

Restrepo-Echavarria P (2017) *What is the Informal Labor Market?* https://www.stlouisfed.org/on-the-economy/2017/april/informal-labor-market

Reynaud E (2002) *The extension of social security coverage: The approach of the International Labour Office*, Social Security Policy and Development Branch, ESS Paper No. 3, Geneva: International Labour Office, p. 2.

Sankaran K (2012) 'The human right to livelihood: Recognizing the right to be human', *Comparative Labor Law & Policy Journal,* 34 (1), 81–94.

Vonk G (2013) 'The 2012 Recommendation concerning national floors of social protection (No. 202): The human rights approach to social security in ILO wrapping paper 2013', *International Journal of Social Security and Workers Compensation*, 4 (1), 49–59.

Westerveld M (2015) 'Women and social security', in Pennings F and G Vonk (eds), *Research Handbook on European Social Security Law*, Cheltenham, UK and Northampton, MA, USA: Edward Elgar Publishing, pp. 257–281.

Policy Documents (Chronological)

Beveridge Report, *Social Insurance and Allied Services*. Presented to Parliament by Command of His Majesty, November 1942.

Marsh Report, Report for Social Security in Canada, 1943.

ILO 1972, *Employment, Incomes and Equality: A Strategy for Increasing Productive Employment in Kenya*, Geneva, ILO.

ILO 1999, *Decent Work,* Report of the Director-General, International Labour Conference, 87th session, Geneva, ILO.

ICLS 2003, International Conference of Labour Statisticians, 17th Conference.

AU *Social Policy Framework for Africa* (2008)

ILO 2008, International Labour Organisation, S*trategies to Promote Transition to Formality in Africa*, Contribution to the joint AU/ILO workshop on the informal economy in Africa, Dakar.

AU *Social Protection Plan for the Informal Economy and Rural Workers 2011–2015 (SPIREWORK)* (2011)

ILO 2012, *Recommendation No 202 on National Floors of Social Protection*, Geneva, ILO.

EC 2012, *Empowering People for Inclusive Growth: The Perspective of the Working Poor in the Informal Economy*, EC Concept Note – High Level Panel, Brussels.

ICLS 2013, International Conference of Labour Statisticians, 19th Conference

ILO 2015, *Recommendation No 204 Concerning the Transition from the Informal to the Formal Economy*, Geneva, ILO.

ICESCR (*International Covenant on Economic, Social and Cultural Rights*) 1966.

EC 2017, Recommendation on the European Pillar of Social Rights, C(2017) 2600 final, and Communication of 26 April 2017 establishing a European Pillar of Social Rights, COM(2017) 250 final.

EC 2018, Proposal for a Council Recommendation on access to social protection for workers and the self-employed, Strasbourg, 13.3.2018 COM(2018) 132 final.

ILO 2018, *Women and Men in the Informal Economy: A Statistical Picture*, Geneva, third edition.

Draft Protocol to the African Charter on Human and Peoples' Rights on the Rights of Citizens to Social Protection and Social Security 2019.

PART I

General reflections

1. Social security protection for informal economy workers: developing world perspectives

Marius Olivier

1. INTRODUCTION

Focusing primarily on informal economy workers in developing countries, this contribution critically reflects on, firstly, salient aspects of the conceptual and demographic framework relating to informal employment; secondly, the exclusion or limited application of social security for those who work in the informal economy; and, thirdly, a range of recent, innovative mechanisms to effect expansion of coverage regarding these workers, based on social security conceptual and instrumental innovation, and supported by a progressive appreciation of the social security values domain and human rights dispensation in developing countries. In the section preceding the conclusions, examples of coverage extension in four countries, that is, China, India, Tunisia and Ghana, are separately reflected on.

Different from what the position might be in the so-called developed economies, informal employment is not generally regarded as illegal or irregular in the developing world, but as a standard way of life and income-generation. Informal employment represents a significant share of non-agricultural employment in developing regions. The result is extremely low levels of social security coverage, both quantitatively and qualitatively. This flows from a variety of reasons, including restricted conceptual frameworks, absent or deficient institutional structures and instruments, inappropriate eligibility criteria, lack of or non-involvement of representative institutions, exclusionary contributory and benefit regimes, and limited administrative capacity and enforcement ability. Also, social insurance laws are restricted to those who work within the confines of the traditional employment relationship, who are employees in the narrow sense of the word, and who work for an identifiable and equally narrowly defined employer – thereby definitionally excluding most informal workers from protection. Finally, with some exceptions, international standards have limited impact on these workers.

And yet, especially in the last few decades, pronounced and unprecedented steps have been taken in several developing countries to extend social security coverage to informal workers. The contribution critically reflects on the rationale for and nature of these extension modalities. These developments have largely been informed by economic considerations and shifting social, cultural and conceptual perceptions; a new appreciation of the human rights debate in the provisioning of social security; and the social contract between the state/government and its citizens. Conceptual and regulatory adjustments in areas affecting the very notion and purpose of social security, the so-called contingencies covered by (traditional) social security, and some of the actors involved (e.g. a redefined understanding of "workers" and "employers") have been paramount. Also, there has been a dedicated construction of appropriate institutional frameworks, while new forms of representative structures have been operative in this domain.

These adjustments and developments challenge the traditional boundaries of the social security notion, aims, structures and mechanisms. The contribution adds to the developing scientific discourse on these matters, also by reflecting on the foundational values informing social security and alternative perspectives on social security.

2. SIZE AND CHARACTERISTICS[1]

In its recently published global overview of the magnitude of the informal economy, the International Labour Organization (ILO) indicates that two billion of the world's employed population aged 15 and over work informally, representing 61.2 per cent of global employment:[2]

> The proportion of informal employment varies in different regions. Among the five main regions, the vast majority of employment in Africa (85.8 per cent) is informal. Asia and the Pacific (68.2 per cent) and the Arab States (68.6 per cent) have almost the same level of informality. In the Americas (40.0 per cent) and Europe and Central Asia (25.1 per cent), less than half of employment is informal. Excluding agriculture, the global level of informal employment falls to 50.5 per cent, but non-agricultural informal employment remains high in three regions (Africa, the Arab States, and Asia and the

---

1 This part relies partly on Olivier, Andrianarison and McLaughlin (2013).

2 ILO (2018), references omitted.

> Pacific). Emerging and developing countries have higher shares of informal employment than developed countries. Emerging and developing countries represent 82 per cent of world employment, but 93 per cent of the world's informal employment is in these countries.

Those involved in agriculture, women, the young and the old, as well as those with no education and living in rural areas, are in particular affected.[3]

The lack of social protection is one key characteristic of the informal economy, as are low productivity, poor working conditions and an absence of legal protection and rights. It has been suggested that:[4]

> The two main categories of informal employment, wage employment in jobs without social protection and self-employment in unincorporated enterprises, can be further disaggregated into different categories of employment relationships. Self-employment consists of own-account workers and employers of informal enterprises who hire other workers. The conditions of these two categories are often very different. Wage-employment includes informal employees of both formal and informal firms, subcontracted workers, wage workers for households (domestic workers), and wage workers with no fixed employer (casual day workers).

While this distinction is valid, it needs to be said that there is a vast and growing range of other forms of work which cannot be regarded as either self- or wage employment, but which are also associated with the absence of or weak social security protection. Many of these (informal) workers do their work in supply chain contexts, and may not have a relationship with an employer, but at best with a "provider" of work. Others may be working in the care economy, and could hardly be regarded as being self-employed in the sense used above.[5]

In fact, one should be careful to rely on standard classifications in this area; as has been noted: "Informal sector heterogeneity continues to defy easy generalizations."[6] In their 2012 contribution, based on a representative sample from seven capital cities in francophone West Africa, Grimm, Knorringa and Lay commented on the needs experienced by a sizeable group of informal economy entrepreneurs, who generally lack access to capital, insurance and productive infrastructure. Appropriate social protection policy interventions would therefore require addressing these

---

3 ILO (2018) pp. 20, 26, 29–30.
4 EC (2012). See also Lund (2012).
5 See also Lund and Srinivas (2000).
6 Grimm, Knorringa and Lay (2012) p. 28.

shortcomings, including the provision of insurance to cover important household-related risks, such as health shocks and death.[7]

Also, the borderlines between formal and informal have increasingly become fluid and blurred as formal employment has decreased worldwide, and as people tend to move out of formal into informal and non-traditional employment, and vice versa, more readily than in the past. There is, therefore, both a continuum and a fluidity or mobility between the formal and informal economy.[8] This may make the development of suitable social security responses exceptionally complex.

Different from what the position might be in the so-called developed economies, informal employment is not generally regarded as illegal or irregular in the developing world, but as a standard way of life and income-generation.[9]

3. LIMITED ACCESS TO CONTRIBUTORY AND NON-CONTRIBUTORY SOCIAL SECURITY ARRANGEMENTS[10]

Informal economy workers' limited access to social insurance and social assistance arrangements partly emanates from the very concept of social security as it has found its way into national legal systems and policy frameworks, and largely also in international and regional instruments. Traditionally, as is the case with social security schemes established in most developing countries, the social security concept draws a relatively strict distinction between formal employment-based social insurance and poverty-related social assistance instruments.[11] Social insurance instruments rarely apply to informal workers,[12] while social assistance arrangements are often, in developing countries, restricted to specific categories of vulnerable persons (the old, the young and the disabled) and therefore not available to the majority of informal workers. As a result of this, and the inherent bias towards the formal economy, social security systems

---

7 Grimm, Knorringa and Lay (2012) pp. 27–28.

8 Barrientos and Barrientos (2002) pp. 18–19; Fudge (2012) pp. 7–8.

9 Lund (2012) p. 13–14.

10 Adapted from Olivier, Andrianarison and McLaughlin (2013).

11 ILO (1989) pp. 3–5; Pieters (1993) p. 5.

12 Subject to some exceptions, social insurance laws essentially cover those in the formal economy, who work within the framework of an identifiable employment relationship: ILO (2008) p. 19.

reach only a small percentage of the population in developing countries.[13] As noted by Meknassi:[14]

> ... Yet both the potential offered by and the needs of informal and small-scale activities remain excluded from any organized social protection. Social security law places them on the margins of a legal and institutional framework that is designed exclusively for the industrial economy. It could not be extended to the majority of workers without root and branch reform, given the predominance of 'atypical' forms of work and pay.

Secondly, the nine (ILO-indicated) traditional categories of contingencies,[15] including among others retirement, sickness, unemployment, employment injuries and diseases and maternity, which essentially inform international and regional social security standards and which form the basis of social security schemes in many developing countries, are largely incompatible with the realities in these countries.[16] While these risk categories may be helpful in identifying more common life experiences and the situations to which human beings are generally exposed, they are not suited to extending social security to informal economy workers – also because they prioritise state-regulated and formal social security as opposed to non-formal and non-state-regulated social security arrangements which service the majority of the workers in the informal economy. As noted by a renowned Indian scholar working in this area, Professor Kamala Sankaran:[17]

> The economic right to obtain gainful employment with the safety net provided by social security in the form of income security and health benefits has been at the center of the social security systems in the developed world. Over the last thirty years this paradigm of social security has been increasingly questioned, and an alternative conception of preventive and promotional forms of social security has been put forward. Economic security has usually meant the maintenance of existing levels of income. *For the self-employed in the informal economy, the loss of assets, loss of access to markets, and exposure to risks are often reasons for their economic insecurity.* A comprehensive right to economic security as a form of social security would require a comprehensive safety net against such risks.

---

13 Olivier (2009) pp. 3–4.
14 Meknassi (2006), p. 214.
15 See ILO Convention 102 of 1952 on Social Security (Minimum Standards).
16 Jutting (1999) p. 2.
17 Sankaran (2012a), pp. 89–90 (emphasis added).

Thirdly, the risks enumerated in the ILO definition are individual-centred, concentrating on protecting the individual from insecurity that may affect him or her. They largely ignore the common collective risks which normally befall informal economy workers in many developing countries such as war, crop failure, natural disasters and other calamities.[18] And yet risks such as these experienced by people in the developing world are often of a collective and covariate nature,[19] and require interventions that go beyond traditional individual-oriented social security responses.

In the fourth instance, there is a wrong presumption that the members of society have already reached an acceptable standard of living which has to be protected.[20] The reality in developing countries, Africa in particular, indicates that the majority of people live in abject poverty and they need to be uplifted to an acceptable standard of living.[21]

As a fifth consideration, the reach of international standards remains limited. Apart from the fact that the ratification record of developing countries as regards ILO social security standards is exceptionally limited, with some exception, it can hardly be said that these standards were generally developed with the informal economy in mind.[22]

Finally, informal workers may be excluded from coverage because:[23]

- a national social insurance scheme covering a particular benefit – such as pensions – does not exist, while participating in the private or occupational scheme alternatives may not be affordable for or otherwise attractive to informal workers;
- informal workers may not be compelled to take up membership of an existing national scheme; or
- little incentive exists to join a scheme which may be open to informal workers – this may be the result of the fact that
    - o (self-employed) informal workers are often required to pay a double contribution,[24] or

---

[18] Olivier (2011) p. 424; Jutting (1999) p. 2.
[19] Holzmann (2002) par III; Olivier (2011) p. 424; Jutting (1999) p. 2.
[20] Olivier (2009), p. 5.
[21] Kaseke (2005) p. 91.
[22] Meknassi (2006).
[23] Olivier (2011).
[24] This applies in particular to sub-Saharan countries (e.g. Ghana (in terms of earlier arrangements), Namibia, Rwanda, Tanzania and Zambia).

- o informal workers who employ others may be barred from participating in a social insurance scheme,[25] and
- o no incentives to join a national scheme, in the form of flexible contribution modalities and targeted or tailor-made benefit packages exist.

Overall the effect of all of the above is that dealing with and managing the risks to which informal economy workers and their dependants are exposed, due to the absence of labour law and social security protection, are effectively shifted onto such workers and their families, and ultimately to other social security schemes (such as health care schemes) and state-provided social assistance. A pronounced focus on social protection interventions which recognise the context of informal workers as (category/categories of) workers in need of protection is required – suggesting that formalisation of informal workers/informal activity will provide appropriate responses may be unrealistic, as the tendency in many parts of the developing world is towards increased informalisation.[26]

4. COMPARATIVE EXPERIENCES[27]

Comparative developments indicate that several innovative attempts have been made, especially in recent years, to extend coverage to informal workers in developing countries.[28] The attempts embrace both conceptual and regulatory developments, institutional initiatives, as well as tailor-made design options. In addition, supportive arrangements, including a focus on stakeholder consultation, communication and an informal sector-friendly enabling framework, are important. These developments discussed below cover employment-related protection, that is, that part of the system mainly captured by contributory arrangements, as well as social assistance provisions.

---

25 See, for example, section 20(2) of the Namibian Social Security Act, 1994.

26 See, among others, Lund (2012); for the statistical picture, see ILO (2018) 13–14.

27 See also Olivier (2017).

28 See in particular Olivier (2014).

4.1 Conceptual and Regulatory Developments

Some countries have addressed exclusion by redefining the concept of employee/worker in legislation governing social security coverage.[29] Developing countries are increasingly seeking innovative conceptualisation to widen the application of social security beyond the traditionally envisaged groups. In India, for example, in an attempt to ensure social security provision for the huge informal economy, the Unorganised Workers' Social Security Act (Act 33 of 2008) adopted a deliberately extensive notion of what is comprehended by the term "unorganised sector", and of who is intended to be an employer and a worker for the purposes of covering those embedded in a relationship of work in the informal economy.[30] Corresponding innovations are also found in some countries. In Tanzania, the Social Security (Regulatory Authority) Act, defines the "informal" as the sector that includes workers who work informally and who do not work in terms of an employment contract or another contract contemplated in the definition of employee.[31] The definitional extension could also occur on an industry basis. For example, in the beedi industry (hand-rolled cigarettes), the Beedi and Cigar Workers (Conditions of Employment) Act in India[32] covers a person employed directly or through any agency who is given raw materials by an employer or a contractor: in this way, outworkers and home workers are included.[33]

In a range of developing countries, labour laws (which often have social security consequences as well), achieve extended protection through a deliberate widening of the employee concept. In Swaziland, for example, an "employee" includes a person who works for pay or other remuneration not only under a contract of service but also "under any other arrangement involving control by, or sustained dependence for the provision of work upon, another person".[34] Similar developments have been discerned in Caribbean countries.[35]

Innovative conceptualisation is an area that lends itself to significant further development. For example, adopting appropriate regulatory techniques to comprehensively cover *supply chain scenarios* would support

---

29 See Olivier (2014), on which the rest of this sub-paragraph is based.
30 Unorganised Workers' Social Security Act (Act 33 of 2008), section 2(k).
31 Social Security (Regulatory Authority) Act 8 of 2008, section 3.
32 Act 32 of 1996.
33 Sankaran (2012a) p. 44.
34 Swaziland Industrial Relations Act 1 of 2000.
35 Taylor (2003).

extension of protection,[36] while a widening of the "trade union" membership concept in the legal systems of many developing countries (currently usually restricted to employees only) would enable trade unions to officially represent informal worker members.

4.2 Institutional Initiatives

Note should further be taken of institutional initiatives which have occurred world-wide. Developing countries have been adopting a wide range of complementary mechanisms to effect coverage extension to excluded categories, impacting in particular on self-employed and informal workers.[37]

- **Extending the reach of social assistance arrangements**:[38] In the search for effective poverty alleviation and sustainable development measures, several middle-income countries have introduced large-scale non-contributory programmes that transcend the concept of residual social assistance schemes, such as the *Bolsa Familia* and similar schemes in Brazil, *Opportunidades* in Mexico, and the social assistance grant system in South Africa, covering almost one-third of the population. Similarly, the Chinese Di-Bao programme is the largest unconditional cash transfer programme in the world, reaching about 78 million individuals.[39] The direct and distributional impact of these programmes has reportedly been comprehensive, as they are invariably linked with complementary social welfare programmes, and thus successfully address poverty at the individual and household levels, enhance educational, food and health care access and promote entrepreneurial activities.[40]

  Elsewhere, especially in most Asian and African countries, until recently, social assistance interventions have been weakly developed. And yet, means-tested and universal programmes have increasingly been established for certain risk areas, particularly

---

[36] Lund (2012) pp. 23–24. Important developments in this area have occurred in developed countries' jurisdictions, such as Australia, although even here the developments are still piecemeal and sector-focused: see Rawling (2006).

[37] Hu and Stewart (2009). See generally Olivier (2014), as well as Olivier, Andrianarison and McLaughlin (2013) pp. 81–82.

[38] See Olivier (2014), on which the rest of this sub-paragraph is based.

[39] World Bank (2014) p. 11.

[40] OECD (2009) pp. 24, 31; Woolard and Leibbrandt (2011).

pensions, for example, in Nepal and Namibia.[41] Given their universal focus, they are accessible to informal economy workers as well. To this should be added the recent focus on introducing cash and conditional cash transfer schemes even in poor countries, often on a pilot basis, with a view to transforming these into scaled-up programmes, for example in several sub-Saharan African countries.[42] And yet, as suggested above, these social assistance arrangements are often restricted to certain categories of persons only and are, therefore, not generally of benefit to informal workers.

- **Extension of existing schemes to the informal sector, and making participation compulsory**: In some cases existing contributory schemes have been extended to include at least some informal worker categories. For example, unemployment insurance and labour law arrangements (impacting on social security as well) have been extended to domestic workers in South Africa.[43] Of particular importance is extension of coverage on a compulsory basis to the self-employed, in particular in several Latin American countries, but also in the Philippines.[44] Traditionally, in developing countries, there was little incentive for the self- and informally employed to join existing contributory schemes, which were accessible to them on a voluntary basis. In an attempt to increase coverage, certain Latin American countries have commenced making participation in these schemes compulsory, supported by incentives such as eligibility for/access to other social security benefits (for example, family allowances) and lowering the contribution rate

---

41 Samson (2012) "Nepal".

42 Monchuk (2014); Olivier, Andrianarison and McLaughlin (2013) pp. 30–31.

43 Lund, (2012), p. 26; Olivier (2009) pp. 23–27.

44 Regarding the Philippines, see MacKellar (2009) pp. 26–28. MacKellar remarked (on p. 27): "The new social security law enacted in 1997 mandated compulsory social security coverage of self-employed persons, regardless of their trade, business or occupation, with an income of at least 20.1 USD a month and not over 60 years old. As a result, the coverage of informal sector workers has tripled over the last 10 years, from 1.7 million in 1997 to 5.6 million as of September 2006. As of June 2006, out of the 26.5 million individuals that were registered with the social security system in the Philippines, around 21% were informal sector workers, up from 8.8% in 1997."

for low-income self-employed persons.[45] As remarked by Mesa-Lago,[46] the few Latin American countries that require compulsory membership have better and more effective coverage.

- **Embracing the whole informal economy**: Some governments have extended existing arrangements to the entire informal market. India[47] and Indonesia[48] are examples of countries that adopted overarching framework legislation aimed at extending social protection to the whole of the informal economy and to informal workers generally. Also, establishing universal schemes has become the hallmark of achieving extended coverage. Risk-category schemes based on a dedicated legal mandate and/or policy framework have been introduced, including universal health insurance schemes in Ghana, Rwanda and Thailand[49] among others and, as indicated later in this contribution, comprehensive pension schemes have been introduced for rural and urban workers in China.[50] All of these schemes have achieved remarkable coverage in a short space of time.

  Another example of this approach concerns the creation of targeted schemes for informal workers. The Ghana Informal Sector Fund[51] and the Kenya Mbao Pension Scheme[52] serve as useful

---

[45] For example, in Chile the self-employed were meant to be fully mandatorily included in the national pension system by 2015, and in the health system as from 2016: see Mesa-Lago (2008) p. 394; see also Calvo, Bertranou and Bertranou (2010) p. 230.

[46] Mesa-Lago (2008) p. 389.

[47] Unorganised Workers' Social Security Act, Act 33 of 2008. See also par 5.2 below.

[48] National Social Security Law of Indonesia, Act 40 of 2004.

[49] Regarding Thailand, see Damrongplasit and Melnick (2009) p. 457; Olivier (2009) pp. 27–29. Other African countries that have decided to go this route (although implementation may still be absent, or not fully realised) include Benin, Côte D'Ivoire, Gabon and Nigeria.

[50] The voluntary rural and urban pension schemes were introduced in 2009 and 2011 respectively, and are (co-)funded by government via matching contributions. By the end of the first quarter of 2012, 376 million people were already participating in the two schemes, despite weak incentives to contribute above the minimum (see Dorfman, Wang, O'Keefe and Cheng (2012); Servais (2012), p. 14). See also par 5.1 below.

[51] Informed by an extensive consultative process initiated by a presidential commission, the Fund provides for flexible contribution modalities and a two-tier tailor-made benefit arrangement, which ensures both long-term benefits and the opportunity to utilise funds for a range of core needs; in a short space of time 90,000 informal workers have joined the Fund (Olivier, 2009). See par 5.4 below.

[52] Njuguna (2012) pp. 86–88.

examples, having attracted (also as the result of informal workers-sensitive design features) sizeable memberships in the few years since they were established.

- **Adopting a sector-by-sector-approach**: In some countries informal workers have been included sector by sector, usually on the basis of separate or dedicated schemes. Rather than attempting to solve the problem on an informal economy-wide basis, policy-makers have chosen key sectors to increase coverage. One example is the welfare funds established in India. They are financed through levies collected from selected employers and manufacturers,[53] and provide a range of benefits, including social security-related benefits such as medical care and maternity assistance. Also at a state level, a tax (cess) is imposed by state governments on the aggregate output of selected industries (for example, the Beedi Welfare Fund is financed by a tax on beedis).[54] Another prominent example is the establishment of gradualist sector-by-sector schemes embedding tailor-made solutions, provisions and prescriptions for particular groups of workers in the informal economy in Tunisia. This latter approach is among others based on the introduction of realistic income scales which determine the lowest income bracket (for purposes of contributions) relevant to the occupation of the insured person (physician, architect, shopkeeper etc.) and the size of the firm or farm, supported by educational and promotional programmes regarding the value of income protection.[55] Sector-based approaches have also been used in South Africa's domestic worker environment.
- **Self-initiated and government-supported arrangements for specific beneficiary groups**: Approaches to benefit specific beneficiary groups may have a home-grown basis – as is the case with the Self Employed Women's Association (SEWA) in India, which arranges among others social security protection for its 1.33 million members in the informal economy. Operating both as a trade union and cooperative, and through its links with formal insurance schemes, SEWA has managed to provide its members with wide-ranging services including credit, training, child care, health care, pension, life insurance (death and disability) and insurance against loss of work equipment; it has become an influential actor at both the

---

53 Lund (2012) p. 23.
54 Olivier (2009) p. 15.
55 Chaabane (2002). See par 5.3 below.

national and international level.[56] In Tanzania, a hybrid model is being implemented through the Community Health Fund (CHF), a voluntary government-introduced insurance-based hybrid scheme administered at district level and co-financed by the community (household) and the government.[57]

- **Micro-health insurance schemes**: Micro-health insurance schemes exist in many (West) African and Asian countries. However, due to lack of scale and other reasons few of these arrangements seem viable, unless they are consolidated and eventually linked to national initiatives. This is apparent from envisaged interventions in Senegal, and the recent experience of Ghana and Rwanda.[58]

4.3 Tailor-made Design Modalities

Design characteristics, in the form of specialised contribution modalities, relaxed entitlement criteria and context-sensitive benefit packages, for the informal economy as a whole, or for particular sectors, have assisted in addressing the challenge as to why informal workers were unwilling, if not unable, to participate in the past.[59] Contribution modalities include: (1) allowing informal workers to contribute to the extent of their ability at a frequency that suits their particular context and contributory capacity, for example in Ghana and the Philippines;[60] (2) adopting realistic income

---

56 Lund (2012) pp. 21–22; Routh (2013) pp. 15–17.

57 Mtei and Mulligan (2007) p. 2.

58 Olivier (2009) pp. 11, 29, 34–35; see also WHO (World Health Organization) (2010), pp. 12–14.

59 See Olivier (2009) pp. 15–17; Servais (2012) p. 4.

60 Regarding Ghana, this is provided for within the framework of the Ghana Informal Sector Fund, referred to above and in par 5.4 below. In the Philippines, in addition to compulsory arrangements, the Philippines Social Security System has adopted several flexible approaches to meet the requirements of informal sector workers who do not have access to formal banking arrangements and who are only able to contribute irregularly, by introducing the following programmes and (in the process) partnering with organised informal sector groups (ISGs) and Local Government Units (LGUs) (see Mines (2015)):

1) AlkanSSSya Program for the self-employed in the services sector;
2) Servicing and/or Collecting Partner Agent Agreement for cooperatives and microfinance institutions;
3) Contribution Subsidy Program for farmers and workers in the agricultural sector;

baselines for the calculation of contributions, for example in Tunisia; and (3) topping up small contributions of poor workers by way of government subsidies, for example in India[61] and Tanzania. Relaxed entitlement criteria allow informal workers to access benefits without complying with lengthy periods of contribution or other onerous conditions. Dedicated, context-sensitive benefit arrangements are addressing the key short- and long-term needs of informal workers. They may not include all the traditional social security benefit categories, but simultaneously provide for the use of benefits towards other core needs, such as education.

4.4 Supportive Arrangements: Consultation, Communication and an Enabling Framework

Extending coverage to and enhancing social security-related protection of the informally employed cannot be achieved in isolation. It is suggested that there are at least three areas of intervention that are required to ensure that a suitable context of coverage and protection is in place.

- **Stakeholder consultation**: Firstly, there is need to ensure that appropriate stakeholder consultation takes place, to determine concrete options – and consider challenges and solutions – in relation to extending coverage to the informally employed and developing suitable protection modalities for them.

  Relevant options, dealing among others with appropriate contribution rates and payment modalities, eligibility criteria and dedicated benefit regimes, have to be considered and, once revised and adopted, submitted for implementation. World-wide experience has shown that successful coverage extension and suitable forms of protection in social security terms for those who work informally have been preceded by thorough consultation with stakeholder groups and institutions.

  Also, while consultation would have to involve the targeted groups themselves, at times even at grass-roots level, the consultative team itself has to have a high-level status, and preferably

---

4) Coverage Program for government job order and contractual (JO/C) workers; and
5) MuniSSSipyo-Collect Program for unbanked areas or provinces.

[61] Both the Union Government and State Governments in India contribute comprehensively to top up small informal worker contributions in relation to social security schemes which focus on including informal workers: see among others Dorfman et al. (2013) pp. 99, 125. See also par 5.2 below.

reflect stakeholder group representation. In some countries the introduction of suitable arrangements for covering the informally employed was preceded by a thorough consultative process conducted by a presidential[62] or government-appointed[63] commission.

- **Communication**: Secondly, as supported by evidence emanating from other countries where the self- and informally employed have been included in social security schemes, there has to be thorough communication of envisaged new arrangements. In particular, those who are affected by the new arrangements, including informally employed workers and, where relevant, their providers of work, have to be properly informed. Given the national relevance of such arrangements, awareness-raising interventions targeting the general public also have to be introduced.
- **Enabling framework**: Thirdly, extending coverage and enhancing protection would require that a proper enabling framework has been established and is operational. The meaningful participation of the informally employed implies that they should be supported to do so – from both a broader policy and operational perspective they have to be strengthened and enabled.

  Among others, steps that would enhance the ability, in particular of those operating and working in the informal economy, to contribute to and access the new system have to be considered and introduced. Fixing the minimum wage at a level that would enable them to contribute would be one such matter to be considered.

  In addition, those operating in the informal sector are in need of access to credit, tailored banking services, transport, training and skills development packages, mentoring and appropriate business opportunities. Some of these matters are currently being addressed in, for example, the Indian context – among others through the linking of the so-called Aadhaar biometric identification card facility to bank accounts in order to enhance financial inclusion. Also, overcoming supply- and demand-side constraints, and access to markets are some of the core priorities to be addressed.

  In essence then, government and other stakeholders would have to play a crucial promotional and development role to support those involved in the informal economy and enhance their capacity to participate meaningfully in the reformed social security framework. Of course, it is necessary to consider and weigh up costs and

---

62 E.g. Ghana.
63 E.g. India.

benefits. A government has to prioritise actions and spending and ask where the attention should most crucially be focused.

5. SELECTED COUNTRY CASE STUDIES

5.1 Extension of Social Protection to Informal Workers: China[64]

The informal sector in China is considered as one of the main driving forces beyond economic growth in China. This heterogeneous sector is highly mobile, dynamic and competitive, and has close links with internal migration. Its growth in China has been associated with several factors, including economic restructuring, rural–urban migration, labour market segmentation, weak formal safety nets and a social protection system which incentivises informal sector growth.[65]

In 2007, an Organisation for Economic Co-operation and Development (OECD) study noted that, depending on the definition used, even in urban areas in China informal work constitutes 50 per cent of all urban employment, fuelled in particular by internal migration.[66] However, more recent data indicate that the share of informal employment has been decreasing rapidly, from a high of 65.2 per cent in 2001 to 40.3 per cent in 2010 – this is largely due to China's economic growth, market-oriented reform and labour market regulation, which effectively extended labour (law) protection to more informal workers.[67] Migrants account for more than one-third of urban workers,[68] thereby contributing to the shared fate of internal migrants (also migrant workers) and informal urban workers for social security coverage purposes. In fact, these categories remain poorly covered in terms of retirement-related social insurance provisioning. Poor coverage is the result of several overlapping factors, in particular:[69]

- the occupation-oriented nature of public pension scheme coverage;
- the lack of enforcement of labour regulations;

64 See Olivier (2017) from where this has been taken.
65 See Jütting and Xenogiani (2007).
66 Ibid.
67 See Gao (2015); Yang (2010).
68 Gao (2015).
69 Jiang, Qian and Wen (2018).

- the voluntary nature of membership of urban (and also rural) pension schemes for urban and rural *residents* respectively (as opposed to *workers*, who are compelled to enrol);
- self-selection, as a result of the fact that: (1) even those who opt out of social insurance coverage remain covered under the basic social assistance programme (e.g. the Minimum Livelihood Guarantee Scheme (Di Bao)); and (2) employers are more likely to opt out, as they think that the social insurance programmes emphasise re-distributive functions and provide unattractive benefits.

In addition, the inability of migrant workers who are not registered to work in cities, due to the operation of the Hukou system, further contributes to the absence of formal social protection.[70]

Informal workers are therefore served by old age-related social insurance schemes only to a limited extent, particularly in rural areas, and as they do not generally participate in urban old-age insurance systems.[71] In fact, as has been indicated, the weak social protection position of informal workers, in particular migrant workers, also extends to their family members, many of whom remain in rural areas.[72]

Nevertheless, important changes to this scenario are discernible, mainly for two reasons. Firstly, the Chinese government has strengthened labour market regulations, as is apparent from the range of new labour-related laws that have been enacted: it seems that stricter regulations have positive effects on increasing coverage rates. Secondly, the changes in main labour market outcomes (e.g. increased formal employment and increased earnings for unskilled workers) facilitate the improvement in coverage modalities.[73] Despite this, a considerable wage gap still exists between informal and formal workers, which enhances labour income inequality in urban areas: a recent study indicated that informal employees' earnings were 67 per cent of those of formal employees, and this large earnings gap raised the Gini coefficient to 0.42 in 2005.[74]

One of the critical tasks ahead is to take steps to reduce and overcome the inherited inequality. From a social protection perspective, also as far as social insurance-based retirement provisioning is concerned, it appears

---

70 Jütting and Xenogiani (2007).

71 Dorfman et al. (2013) pp. 3–4, 26, 35; see also Jütting and Xenogiani (2007).

72 Jütting and Xenogiani (2007).

73 Yang (2010).

74 Gao (2015).

necessary to take steps to integrate different components of the system.[75] The envisaged unification of public urban and rural pension systems, and the granting of urban residence permits to an increasing number of permanent urban residents are important steps towards integration, equal treatment and extended coverage.[76]

5.2 Comprehensive and Innovative Arrangements in India

5.2.1 Background

Despite attempts over several years by Central and State governments to extend social security coverage to marginalised groups of workers, the current state of affairs is still wholly unsatisfactory. In a study undertaken for the ILO, Srivastava (2013) indicates:[77]

- only 1 per cent of agricultural workers reported coverage in terms of employer-arranged social security in the form of a provident fund scheme;
- almost the entirety of casual workers did not avail of any social security benefit, while the share of those receiving at least one benefit among regular workers was only 55 per cent; only about one-fourth of regular workers had all three benefits (Provident Fund/Pension; Gratuity; Health care and maternity benefit);
- wage workers in the unorganised sector too had almost no social security benefit, except 1 per cent who had access to a provident fund/pension benefit. Even within the organised sector, nearly 33 per cent had all benefits and 10 per cent had access to a provident fund/pension benefit, while 47 per cent were not eligible for any benefit.

By 2010, the percentage of all wage workers covered under any social security provision had declined from 32.6 per cent in 1999–2000 to 28.6 per cent in 2004–2005 and further to 26.4 per cent in 2009–2010. This coincided with a casualisation of the workforce and the increased informalisation of regular employees in the government sector and in public limited companies.[78] According to the 2016 Economic Survey, the share of informal employment in the organised sector had increased from

---

75 Yang (2010).
76 See Olivier (2017) for further details.
77 Srivastava (2013) pp. 21–22.
78 Id., pp. 22–23.

48 per cent to 54.6 per cent from 2004–2005 to 2011–2012.[79] Srivastava further referred to the estimates of the National Commission for Enterprises in the Unorganised Sector (NCEUS) regarding coverage of workers in the unorganised sector, indicating that the Commission's estimates showed that the existing models covered only a small proportion – around 8 per cent – of the country's vast army of informal workers.[80] He concludes as follows:[81]

> Our brief review shows that governmental and non-governmental initiatives to address the social security needs of the working poor in India are woefully inadequate. In the organized sector, the proportion of workers covered has fallen due to informalization of the workforce. The poor, who eke out an existence through various types of informal employment in the unorganized sector, are among the most vulnerable in any society. A shock that has a relatively small impact on the non-poor can be a cause for great concern for the poor, since even marginal downward fluctuations in income can push them to destitution levels. Social security measures which address the contingent risks faced by them are woefully inadequate, except in certain parts of the country.

5.2.2 Recent developments – framework provided by the Labour Code on Social Security

The recently published 2018 Draft Labour Code on Social Security[82] (hereafter referred to as the Draft Code), prepared by the Ministry of Labour and Employment, Government of India, aims specifically at extending coverage of social security to informal economy workers. This follows an earlier largely unsuccessful legislative attempt to achieve such coverage extension. The Draft Code evidently foresees extensive coverage of those who work in the informal economy. This appears from the following:

- **Comprehensive sphere of application**: The Draft Code is said to apply among others to all "entities" as well as to "workers that are employed by any entity" as well as a worker "who may also be the

79 Ministry of Finance, GOI (2016).
80 Id., p. 25.
81 Id., pp. 25–26.
82 See the Draft Code of March 2018, published on the website of the Government of India's Ministry of Labour and Employment – http://www.labour.nic.in/sites/default/files/draft%20Labour%20Code%20on%20Social%20Security%20%26%20Welfare.pdf, accessed on 2 November 2018.

owner or the proprietor of an entity or a self-employed unit" (see clauses 1.4 and 1.5).

- o Extended application is achieved on the basis of the wide-embracing scope of both the concepts of "entity" and "worker", in addition to use being made of a distinction between "organised sector" and "unorganised sector" (see below).
- o "Entity" is defined with reference to both an "enterprise" and a "household".[83] "Enterprise" includes a project, undertaking or business carried out *also* by a cooperative society, a self-help group, and an association of persons or body of individuals whether incorporated or not.[84] "Household" in turn denotes "a group of occupants or a family regarded as a unit including individuals who comprise a family unit and who live together under the same roof, dwell in the same place, and are under control of one domestic head"[85] – the household may or may not encompass domestic help.
- o The "worker" concept is cast deliberately wide to encompass as wide a range of people who work as possible. This term is defined to include a person who performs work for an entity, or who provides services, whether regular or part-time to an entity, whether directly or through an agency, for wage, profit or gain, in cash or kind, whether under a contract of employment, or other contract where an individual undertakes to do or to provide personally the work or services, whether the contract is expressed or implied. The term is said to include all employees of an entity irrespective of the nature of work performed by them and, importantly, persons performing voluntary services for an entity and receiving honorarium shall be deemed to be workers.[86]
- o The term "worker" explicitly includes both "an employee" and "a non-employee".[87] "Employee" is an extensive concept, even though it is "limited" with reference to the requirement that wages must be earned by the person so employed by an entity. Nevertheless, this term encompasses all kinds of employment

[83] Clause 2.46.

[84] Clause 2.45.

[85] Clause 2.58. See also clause 2.43, which defines "employer" also with reference to the head of a household, in the case of a household or an enterprise undertaken by a household.

[86] Clause 2.140.

[87] Ibid.

contracts and includes among others extensively formulated employee categories, such as a part-time worker, a piece rate worker, an outworker, a seasonal worker, a domestic worker and a home-based worker.[88] A "non-employee" comprises a "self-employed worker" and an "owner-cum-worker".[89] The definition of "owner-cum-worker" is crafted in a way that includes a person who simultaneously works in two capacities – as owner, head or proprietor and as worker, in that establishment.[90]

- o "Unorganised sector" is defined to mean (1) establishments which employ workers, and the number of such workers is less than the threshold; (2) own account enterprise; and (3) households that employ domestic workers for carrying out the activities of the household.[91]

- The extensive categories of persons covered by the "worker" concept is then used, at least partly, as a basis for formulating registration and contribution-paying obligations. Registration of workers will be effected in any of the different categories; there is a general obligation on every worker to register/to be registered.[92]
- Contribution payment reflects and builds on the distinctions indicated above. Contributions are payable by employers and workers;[93] provision is also made for government contributions,[94] although not specified.
- Differentiated contribution payment obligations are imposed on workers depending on, in particular, the socio-economic category to which the worker belongs. No contribution is required by a worker who falls within the lowest socio-economic category.[95]

5.2.3 Other specialised arrangements to achieve informal economy worker inclusion

In serving the overarching goal that a transformed social security system should address the underlying structural and material basis of social exclusion, as well as multi-dimensional poverty, social security policy and system design should be sensitive to the fact that for informal

---

88 Clause 2.42.
89 Clause 2.77.
90 Clause 2.95.
91 Clause 2.133.
92 Clause 11.
93 Clause 20.
94 See in particular clause 25.1
95 Clauses 20.3 and 20.4.

economy workers, meeting immediate needs, and not merely future contingencies, is a priority.[96] Apart from the needed emphasis on sufficient health protection, there is evidently a need to provide for, and protect, the *means by which informal workers earn a livelihood.* It is significant to note that several Indian state governments (e.g. Karnataka and Odisha) make provision in their social security schemes for among others assistance for the purchase of working tools, which (at least in the case of Karnataka) has resulted in considerable take-up.[97]

5.3 Tunisia: Social Security for Informal Economy Workers[98]

Tunisia has employed an innovative gradualist approach that has achieved high levels of social security coverage, especially within the informal economy. In 1996, Tunisia implemented a social security system which combined proper enforcement with the creation of a more accurate income estimation system for the self-employed. These two aspects, combined with education programmes, have seen high levels of growth in coverage, with 80 per cent of Tunisia's employed population covered by some form of social security in 1999, in comparison to just 60 per cent ten years earlier. Coverage has been extended for health care, old age pensions, maternity and employment injury. The expansion of social security in Tunisia has been successful at targeting large portions of the informal economy, including: craftspeople, petty traders and small farmers although levels of coverage still remain low in these industries in comparison to other industries. The first part of the approach saw changes to the social security system, with new legislation enacted in 1995 which unified the two existing social security schemes – one for self-employed agricultural workers and one for self-employed non-agricultural workers. The two schemes had been differentiated by the scope and the amounts of benefits, the level of contribution rate and the basis taken for calculating contributions. The unification of the two schemes led to an increase in the amount of agricultural self-employed and an increase in the scope and benefits of the scheme. The second change to the system was the extension of the bracket on which the flat-rate income on contributions was calculated. To coincide with this, efforts were made to avoid minimal contributions by the self-employed based on the lowest income brackets. A realistic income scale which

---

96 Ahmad, Drezé, Hill and Sen (1991) p. 43.

97 In the case of Odisha, one of the schemes also provides for the purchase of a bicycle.

98 Chaabane (2002); Olivier (2009) (from where this part has been taken).

determines the lowest income bracket relevant to the occupation of the insured person (physician, architect, shopkeeper etc.) and the size of the firm or farm was introduced. Through the application of this scale, each insured person must contribute equal to the bracket employed on the scale, unless they can prove that their real income is lower, while they are free to contribute on a higher scale. These changes to the social security system had a positive influence which resulted in coverage extension. Educational and promotional programmes have also coincided with a change in attitude by many Tunisians which has seen them embrace income protection for old age, and protection against illness as a priority. This change in attitude is borne out of rising medical costs, an educational role played by trade unions and the government, and positive experiences of the benefits of social security. These aspects have combined to legitimise social security. The new measures combined with the awareness and education campaigns had led to almost 70,000 new affiliations in 1996 and 1997 alone. However, the reforms to the social security system have not been successful in extending coverage to everyone in the informal economy.

5.4 Ghana Informal Sector Fund[99]

Ghana provides an illustration of an initially less than successful attempt to use an existing public fund to extend social security coverage to the informally employed. However, innovative measures were introduced in 2010 to cover informally employed workers. This entailed the creation of the Informal Sector Fund, and dedicated arrangements relating to both contributions and benefits. Contributions to this Fund need not be fixed, but could be based on their ability to pay on a basis preferred by them, be it daily, weekly, monthly, annually or seasonally. Informal workers contribute to two accounts: (1) a retirement account (to provide benefits on retirement); and (2) a personal savings account with rules for withdrawals before retirement (e.g. for education and business enhancement). Within three years since the establishment of this Fund, 90 000 members have joined on this basis. It currently has 150 000 members.

---

99 See Arku and Akagbo (2012); Adombila (2016).

6. CONCLUSIONS

As indicated elsewhere,[100] it is submitted that the political commitment which underlies the recent extension of social security entitlements to and coverage of those operating in the informal economy is reflective of economic considerations and shifting social, cultural and conceptual perceptions. Changing values in Asia, Latin America and Africa confirm a new appreciation of the import of social security, and the social contract between the state/government and its citizens, based on dialogue, serving the welfare interests of the people and moving away from an exclusive focus on economic growth; and a realisation that welfare enhancement is good for economic growth.[101] Modernising society in emerging economies and its interest in appropriate social security arrangements imply that the state is no longer able to rely on the assumption that familial and community support would fill the void left by inadequate social security provision and regulation. Simultaneously these developments are seemingly informed by human rights considerations, which came to question increasingly the social security-concerned exclusion and marginalisation of the overwhelming majority of workers in most of the developing world.

The developments described in this contribution are indicative of a conceptual understanding and operational framework of social security which transcend traditional approaches and boundaries. And yet, challenges remain. One such area relates to the representative capacity of stakeholder institutions in the informal economy to exert appropriate influence on social security policy development to the advantage of informal workers. In this, the area of agency, voice and representation, there is some indication of innovative attempts to ensure that cooperatives, trade unions and other (often community-based) institutions represent the interests of informal workers.[102] However, the efficiency of these interventions remains limited due to (at times) lack of scale, and the absence of recognition in the regulatory and policy realm of the status, role and capacity of these institutions – both in domestic and international systems.

A second challenge relates to identifying the workers concerned and their registration. Another concerns the determination of their income. And as already mentioned, a fourth challenge has to do with the need to

---

100 See Olivier (2014), from where this and the next paragraph have been taken.

101 OECD (2012).

102 Routh (2013), pp. 21–22; Fudge (2012), pp. 8–9, 21–22.

involve, consult and liaise with these workers/persons – in the wake of weak representation and voice.

BIBLIOGRAPHY

Adombila, M "Contributions under SSNIT Informal Sector fund rises to GH ¢75m" (22 June 2016), accessed at https://www.graphic.com.gh/business/business-news/contributions-under-ssnit-informal-sector-fund-rises-to-gh-75m.html on 2 November 2018.
Ahmad, E, Drezé, J, Hill, J and Sen, A *Social Security in Developing Countries* (Oxford: Clarendon Press, 1991).
Arku, J and Akagbo, E "90,000 Join SSNIT – from the Informal Sector" (2012), accessed at http://www.graphic.com.gh/dailygraphic/page.php?news=14354 on 8 May 2012.
Barrientos, A and Barrientos, S *Extending social protection to informal workers in the horticulture global value chain* (Social Protection Discussion Paper Series No 0126, Washington, DC: World Bank report, 2002).
Calvo, E, Bertranou, F and Bertranou, E "Are old-age pension system reforms moving away from individual retirement accounts in Latin America?" *Journal of Social Policy*, 2010, vol 39(2) pp. 223–234.
Chaabane, M *Towards the universalization of social security: The experience of Tunisia* (Extension of Social Security, ESS Paper, no 4, Geneva: ILO, 2002).
Damrongplasit, K and Melnick, G "Early results from Thailand's 30-baht health reform: Something to smile about" *Health Affairs*, 2009, vol 28 (3) pp. 457–466.
Dorfman M, Wang, M, O'Keefe, P and Cheng, J "China's pension schemes for rural and urban residents" in R Hinz, R Holzman, D Tuesta and N Takayaka (eds) *Matching Contributions for Pensions* (Washington, DC: The World Bank, 2012) pp. 217–241.
Dorfman, J et al. *China's Pension System: A Vision* (Washington, DC: World Bank, 2013).
EC (European Commission) *Empowering people for inclusive growth: The perspective of the working poor in the informal economy* (EC Concept Note – High Level Panel, Brussels, 2012).
Fudge, J "Blurring legal boundaries: Regulating for decent work" in J Fudge, S McCrystal and K Sankaran (eds) *Challenging the Legal Boundaries of Work Regulation* (Oxford and Portland, Oregon: Hart Publishing, 2012).
Gao, W "Informal employment and its effect on the income distribution in urban China" (presentation, Brussels, 2015) *Journal of Social Policy*, 2015, vol 47 (2), accessed 2 November 2018 at file:///C:/Users/user/Downloads/Session%204%20-%20Gao%20Wenshu%20(1).pdf, pp. 335–357.
Grimm, M, Knorringa, P and Lay, J *Constrained gazelles: High potentials in West Africa's informal economy* (Working Paper No. 53, The Hague: International Institute for Social Studies (ISS), 2012).

Holzmann, R "Risks and vulnerability: The forward-looking role of social protection in a globalizing world" in E Dowler and P Mosely (eds) *Poverty and Social Exclusion in North and South* (London and New York: Routledge, 2002).
Hu, Y and Stewart, F *Pension coverage and informal sector workers: International experiences* (Working Papers on Insurance and Private Pensions, no 31, Paris: OECD, 2009).
ILO *Introduction to social security* (Geneva: ILO, 1989).
ILO *Strategies to promote transition to formality in Africa* (Contribution to the joint AU/ILO workshop on the informal economy in Africa, Dakar, 2008).
ILO *Women and men in the informal economy: A statistical picture* (3rd edn, Geneva: ILO, 2018).
Jiang, J, Qian, J and Wen, Z "Social Protection for Workers in the Urban Informal Sector in China: Institutional Constraints and Self-selection Behaviour" (2018), accessed at https://www.researchgate.net/publication/318831285_Social_Protection_for_the_Informal_Sector_in_Urban_China_Institutional_Constraints_and_Self-selection_Behaviour on 11 January 2019.
Jutting, J *Strengthening social security systems in rural areas of developing countries* (ZEF Discussion Papers on Development Policy, Bonn: Centre for Development Research, 1999).
Jütting, J and Xenogiani, T "Informal Employment and Internal Migration: The Case of China" (Beijing: OECD, Nov 2007), accessed at https://slideplayer.com/slide/8361611/ on 11 January 2019.
Kaseke, E "Social security and older people: An African perspective" *International Social Work*, 2005, vol 48 (1), pp. 89–98.
Lund, F "Work-related social protection for informal workers" *International Social Security Review*, 2012, vol 65 (4), pp. 9–30.
Lund, F and Srinivas, S *Learning from experience: A gendered approach to social protection for workers in the informal economy* (Geneva: ILO, 2000).
MacKellar, L *Pension systems for the informal sector in Asia* (Social Protection Discussion Paper, no 0903, Washington DC: World Bank, 2009).
Meknassi, R "Extending social security in the developing countries: Between universal entitlement and the selectiveness of international standards" *Comparative Labor Law and Policy Journal*, 2006, vol 27, pp. 207–223.
Mesa-Lago, C "Social protection in Chile: Reforms to improve equity" *International Labour Review*, 2008, vol 147 (4), pp. 377–402.
Mines, J "Moving toward inclusive growth: Philippine Social Security System" (Philippine Social Security System, 2015), accessed at https://www.sss.gov.ph/sss/DownloadContent?fileName=2015_Updated_ISSA_Report_on_ISCoverage_FINAL.pdf on 11 January 2019.
Ministry of Finance, GOI *Economic Survey 2016 (volume 1)* (New Delhi: Ministry of Finance, Government of India).
Monchuk, V *Reducing poverty and investing in people: The new role of safety nets in Africa* (Washington, DC: World Bank, 2014).
Mtei, G and Mulligan, J *Community health funds in Tanzania: A literature review* (Dar es Salaam: Ifakara Health Institute, 2007).
Njuguna, A "Critical success factors for a micro-pension plan: An exploratory study" *International Journal of Financial Research*, 2012, vol 3 (4), pp. 82–97.

OECD *Promoting pro-poor growth: Social protection* (Paris: OECD, 2009).
OECD *Rethinking the welfare state: Asia's next revolution* and *Asian welfare states: New cradles to graves* (*The Economist*, 8 September 2012).
Olivier, M *Informality, employment contracts and extension of social insurance coverage* (ISSA Project on 'Examining the existing knowledge of social security coverage', Working Paper, no 9, Geneva: International Social Security Association (ISSA), 2009).
Olivier, M "Informality, employment contracts and social insurance coverage: Rights-based perspectives in a developing world context" *International Journal of Comparative Labour Law and Industrial Relations, 2011, vol 2 (4), pp. 419–433.*
Olivier, M "Work at the margins of social security: Expanding the boundaries of social protection in the developing world" in W van Oorschot, H Peeters and K Boos (eds) *Invisible Social Security Revisited: Essays in Honour of Jos Berghman* (Leuven: Lannoo Publishers, 2014) pp. 215–230.
Olivier, M "Social protection innovation and challenges in China and Africa: Selected comparative perspectives" *Frontiers of Law in China*, 2017, vol 12 (3), September, pp. 429–472.
Olivier, M, Andrianarison, F and McLaughlin, M *Study on social protection in Sub-Saharan Africa* (Report commissioned by the European Commission, Brussels, 2013).
Pieters, D *Introduction to the Basic Principles of Social Security* (Deventer: Kluwer, 1993).
Rawling, M "A generic model of regulating supply chain outsourcing" in C Arup, P Gahan, J Howe, R Johnstone, R Mitchell and A O'Donnell (eds) *Labour Law and Labour Market Regulation* (Sydney: Federation Press, 2006).
Routh, A *Forms of solidarity for informal workers in India: Lessons for future?* (Paper presented at the Labour Law Research Network: Inaugural Conference, Barcelona, 13–15 June 2013).
Samson, M "Nepal senior citizens' allowance: A model of universalism in a low-income country context" in S Handayani and B Babajanian (eds), *Social Protection for Older Persons: Social Pensions in Asia* (Asian Development Bank, 2012) pp. 214–245.
Sankaran, K (2012a) "Flexibility and informalisation of employment relationships", in J Fudge, S McCrystal and K Sankaran (eds) *Challenging the Legal Boundaries of Work Regulation* (Oxford and Portland, Oregon: Hart Publishing, 2012) pp. 29–47.
Sankaran, K (2012b) "The human right to livelihood: Recognizing the right to be human" *Comparative Labor Law & Policy Journal*, 2012, vol 34 (1), Fall, pp. 81–94.
Servais, J "The new ILO Recommendation on social security" *E-Journal of International and Comparative Labour Studies*, 2012, vol 1 (3–4), pp. 1–26.
Srivastava, R S *A social protection floor for India* (New Delhi: ILO, 2013).
Taylor, O "The Jamaican labour relations and industrial disputes act (LRIDA): A critical assessment" in N Cowell and C Branche (eds) *Human Resource Development and Workplace Governance in the Caribbean* (Kingston: Ian Randle Publishers, 2003) pp. 426–450.

Woolard, I and Leibbrandt, M *The role of cash transfers in reducing poverty and inequality in South Africa over the post-apartheid period* (Unpublished paper produced for the National Planning Commission, Southern Africa Labour and Development Unit, University of Cape Town, 2011).

World Bank *The state of social safety nets 2014* (Washington, DC: World Bank, 2014).

WHO (World Health Organization) "World health report 2010 – Health systems financing: The path to universal coverage (Executive summary)" (2010), accessed at http://www.who.int/whr/2010/10_summary_en.pdf on 11 January 2019.

Yang, D "Improving social protection system in China: Key trends and policies" (OECD, 2010), accessed at https://www.oecd.org/els/emp/45276885.pdf on 2 November 2018.

2. Flexicurity outside the employment relationship? Re-engineering social security for the new economy

Michael Wynn and Amir Paz-Fuchs

> Many persons working on their own account are poorer and more in need of state insurance than employees.
>
> Beveridge (1942)

> Insuring a population means classifying it with a scale of degrees of risk and an analysis of behaviours, thresholds and marginal categories which are excluded …
>
> Defert (1991)

> The general welfare state will only survive if it imposes a limit on itself and does so generally; the discriminatory welfare state will not survive.
>
> Buchanan (1998)

What types of normative or regulatory frameworks of social protection are needed for labour markets to function effectively in countries with developed systems of labour law and social insurance? This issue will be addressed here, in four stages. The first section provides an overview of the theoretical structure that underpinned social security in the second half of the 20th century. The second section will discuss the effects of these changes in the labour market on the inclusiveness of the social security structure. The third section will develop proposals for policy and practice for re-engineering social security in a new labour market. The fourth and final section will suggest some proposals, whilst reflecting on some recent policy initiatives.

1. FROM BEVERIDGE TO A FLEXIBLE LABOUR MARKET

Articulating the aims, institutions, policies and practice of social security institutions will provide the backdrop towards understanding what has changed, how that change took place, and what needs to be done to recalibrate the original theoretical and institutional structure to the new types of employment relationship.

Setting the scene for the 'new' economy requires familiarising with the post-Beveridge era. The starting point for debate is that new risks in the labour market demand a different approach to the management of risk. The existing social insurance model, as conceptualised during the Beveridge era, was premised on 'male breadwinners' and full-time employment. Social insurance covered risks associated with the labour market, including unemployment, retirement, sickness and disability, and the premature death of the breadwinner. Correspondingly, eligibility conditions were also associated with employment, through contributions, work history, and the assertion that able-bodied persons should actively seek work before relying on benefits.

This structure suited the labour market that was in place from the industrial revolution to the second half of the 20th century. The first shift occurred with the transformation of focus from the production of goods to the service sector. In Britain, the share of the workforce employed by manufacturing industry dropped from 40 per cent in 1952, to 8 per cent in 2012;[1] indeed, that share dropped from 4.5 million workers in 1997 to 2.5 million workers in 2010. The manufacturing beasts of yesteryear – in shipbuilding, railway, motor vehicle and aircraft, for example – are gone, and replaced by the service sector: in 1961, 49 per cent were employed in the service sector, climbing to 81 per cent in 2011.[2] This shift is not without consequences: the service sector tends to be more exposed to booms and busts, thus producing uncertainty; more likely to move workers from full- to part-time (in the UK, a rise of 7.9 per cent since 2008[3]); from employment to self-employment (in the UK, from 3.3 million in 2000, or 12 per cent of the workforce, to 4.6 million in 2016, constituting 15 per cent of the workforce;[4] in the EU, 32 million self-employed constituted 14.9 per cent in 2009[5]); and particularly in part-time self-employment (in the UK, a rise of 46.6 per cent since 2008, and of 88 per cent from 2000);[6] and less likely to offer employment benefits. In the US, the share of workers who receive benefits dropped from 80 per cent to 40 per cent between 1947 and 1995. Moreover, the

---

1 Comfort (2013).
2 Chartered Institute of Personnel and Development (2013).
3 Wales and Amankwah (2016).
4 Ibid; Social Security Advisory Committee (2014), 8.
5 Wales and Amankwah (2016), 15; Taylor et al. (2017), 24.
6 Ibid.

nature of 'self-employment' is no longer easily identifiable. Thus, the International Labour Organization (ILO) has recently estimated that 47 per cent of the self-employed, amounting to 4.3 per cent of total employment, are 'dependent self-employed', defined as those who do not meet three criteria (more than one client; power to hire and fire employees; autonomy in decision making).[7]

But it is not only the type of employers that has changed. Perhaps more significantly, the type of workers involved in producing the work has changed as well, that is, the redistribution arrangement necessitated by transitions in the labour market from dependent to self-employment and by a change in the *ideological* mind-set and the focus on 'personal responsibility'. US Senator Newt Gingrich, for example, quipped that 'social responsibility is a euphemism for individual *irresponsibility*', thus implying that we should revisit social and economic problems and view them as fragmented, rather than structural.

Arguably, the UK has undergone a transformation that is akin to the one experienced across the Atlantic. Jacob Hacker refers to the Great Risk Shift, a regressive conversion of welfare state institutions, epitomised in transferring the burden of economic and social risks back onto workers and their families, in a manner that chimes with pre-war society and economy.[8] This chapter does not, however, focus on welfare state *institutions*, but rather on changes in the labour market that have created, for many, a fragile employment status and far less access to those institutions that still exist. There are notable new social risks outside the world of work. Perhaps most prominent amongst them is the need to cater for long-term care arrangements, particularly for older family members, but also for children with disabilities. This chapter, however, refers to such risks only tangentially. Instead, it focuses on new social risks that derive from the changing nature of the institutions of work and the economy. In other words, our aim is to re-examine social security aspects of the work/security formula to recalibrate the scope of social protection in developed economies to benefit all labour market participants.

---

7 Williams and Lapeyre (2017).

8 Hacker (2006).

2. FROM INTENTIONAL LABOUR REFORM TO UNINTENTIONAL SOCIAL SECURITY REFORM

The move towards a flexible labour market justified the need for significant reform and, according to some authors, was driven with a clear intention to erode the standard employment relationship and to support a rise in self-employment and other entrepreneurial forms of work.[9] But the same cannot be said about the consequent changes to the social security regime and, in particular, the extent of its inclusivity. As eligibility criteria for social security benefits are attached to, or parasitic on, employment status, the rise in self-employment and in 'atypical' employment relationships resulted in unintended, and perhaps unwanted, consequences for the ability of millions of workers to access social security benefits. Unlike labour market reforms, here the change was not from a putative 'rigidity' to 'flexibility', but rather from increased to decreased coverage of individuals. This transformation, however, took place without serious discussion as to its consequences. For example, do the rationales that justify access to unemployment benefits or sick leave cease to apply if a worker is employed on a 'zero hour' contract, through an employment agency or is even formally self-employed?

To the extent that one views these changes as intentional, and even justified, they would signify a shift in the balance of social security rationales, from one that is supposedly grounded in 'solidarity' to one that is based on 'freedom'.[10] This approach would assume that the multitude of workers who have moved from traditional to 'atypical' forms of employment, and to self-employment, prefer the 'freedom' to choose whether or not to take part in the social insurance pool and, consequently, gain some protection from risks such as unemployment, sickness and long-term disability, and lack of earning due to maternity/paternity and old age. This approach raises two concerns, the first, ideological and the second, pragmatic. The ideological reservation relates to the fact that social security schemes are avowedly paternalistic, and are designed to protect individuals from short-sighted and irrational choices and behaviour.[11] Pragmatically, this solution cannot be viewed as an honest and a real one for the vast majority of 'atypical workers', who are offered no such choice. The recent, local example of Uber offering its drivers access to sickness coverage for those who are willing to pay £2 a

[9] Freedland and Davies (2007).
[10] Schmid and Gazier (2002).
[11] Ariely (2008); Sunstein and Thaler (2008).

week[12] is the exception that proves the rule: very few companies offer access to benefits *outside* employment status.[13] Interestingly, responding to the criticism levelled against Uber for the denial of rights to their drivers, Uber UK regional manager responded that most Uber drivers 'love the freedom of being their own boss and choosing if, when and where they drive'.[14] Perhaps this is so. But it would be far more difficult to argue that drivers prefer the freedom not to enjoy maternity coverage or unemployment benefits. Moreover, while these private initiatives cover some traditional social risks (in this case, sickness) they are far removed from a comprehensive coverage for all workers, against all social risks. Arguably, the private sector cannot be expected to fill this gap entirely, and it is for the public sector to address these concerns.

Even prior to the trendy gig economy, 'atypical' work, including zero hour contracts and agency work, fragmented the labour contract and denied workers employment status. The social insurance system, however, has adapted to these changes in a manner that is only piecemeal, and not comprehensive. Thus, different countries have elected to award some, but not other, benefits to workers outside the standard employment contract.[15]

In particular, we focus on four central social insurance schemes that are closely related to the world of work: pensions, unemployment benefits, sickness and long-term disability pay, and maternity/paternity leave and pay. This choice necessarily excludes other, highly important schemes, which cannot be addressed within the confines of this chapter. And yet, we find that the four schemes cover the rationales underpinning 'social risks' with which the original Beveridge model was intended to cope. It is thus important to assess them against the new employment reality and the risks it poses.

- **Pensions**: Pensions are, in effect, annuities that 'insure against biometric risks – in particular, longevity – and thus protect retired

12 Booth (2017).

13 Important caveat: the workers are 'outside workers' status' only in the way the company views it, and contrary to the Employment Tribunals, and Court of Appeals' decisions which confirmed their worker status – Uber v Aslam [2018] EWCA Civ 2748.

14 Booth (2017).

15 See Table 1 – Entitlement of self employed to social benefits, July 2015 in Williams and Lapeyre (2017), 12.

individuals from outliving their savings'.[16] And yet, there is a significant gap between employees and the self-employed in this respect, as only 27 per cent of the self-employed have pension savings (down from 33 per cent in 2006–7), compared to 50 per cent of employees.[17]

Prior to the introduction of the first pension schemes in the late 19th century, labourers 'worked until death or disability'.[18] In most countries, the term 'pensions' refers to a dual-layered structure of the income support for old age. These 'layers' were developed separately in the latter part of the 19th century in different countries, and were later merged in many countries.[19] The first, universal, layer was developed in Britain[20] and Denmark as the extension of the poor laws, emphasising poverty relief and the maintenance of minimal living standards. Somewhat confusingly, this residual layer is sometimes (e.g. in the UK) referred to as 'state pensions' or 'old age pensions' and sometimes (e.g. in the US) as 'social security'.

The second layer, developed in Bismarck's Germany, was based on a social insurance paradigm that sought to ensure that workers maintain a proportion of their income and, correspondingly, living standards to which they were accustomed, following retirement.[21]

For present purposes, it is important to note two crucial aspects of the pension system, each bearing a different evaluative force. First, the pension system already includes a non-contributory (i.e. tax funded) layer. Thus, there is no need, in this case, to wage an ideological and political campaign to establish the *principle* that support for individuals in their old age can be disconnected from their employment status. Second, and on the other hand, this basic and universal layer is minimal, and guarantees a standard of 'living' that is well below the poverty line.[22] Age UK estimates that 14 per cent of UK pensioners (1.6 million) live in poverty, and a further

---

16 Hinrichs and Lynch (2010), 353, 355.
17 D'Arcy (2015).
18 Stearns (1975)
19 Hinrichs and Lynch (2010) 363.
20 Old Age Pensions Act 1908 (UK).
21 Orenstein (2008), 22; Bonoli (2000) 10–11.
22 The poverty line in the UK, for example, is 60 per cent of the median income. As the median income in 2016 was £26,300, the poverty line stood at £15,780, or £303 per week for two adults (Wells 2017). Meanwhile, state pension was £122.30 per person.

10 per cent (1.2 million) have incomes just above the poverty line.[23] And the Office for National Statistics (ONS) estimates that 40 per cent of pensioners experienced poverty between 2010 and 2013.[24]

- **Unemployment**: 'Given its impact on the labour market, unemployment insurance was the last of the four classic social risks to be introduced in most European welfare states.'[25] And yet, the concept of unemployment has transformed with the changed understanding of job, and employment, security. Workers are more likely to move in and out of employment, as corporations are no longer willing to serve as a buffer against economic ebbs and flows. In addition, the rise of self-employment, and within this group – of bogus self-employment and enforced self-employment (as is common in the gig economy, for example) – has changed the nature of the risk.

  In a manner that is analogous, but not identical, to the pension structure, many countries offer two layers of benefits for those temporarily out of work: a means-tested (income based), non-contributory benefit, at a very low level; and a contribution-based, non-means-tested benefit, that is at a level proportionate to prior earnings, but is time limited (in the UK, for example: 182 days). Only a few countries (Czech Republic, Denmark, Estonia and Hungary) offer social insurance cover for self-employed workers in the event of unemployment.[26] Again, as in the case of pensions (albeit with different eligibility criteria, crucially concerning means-testing) we find a 'social insurance' paradigm which is layered on a residual, or 'poverty relief' paradigm. Correspondingly, here too we find a structure that could be expanded and reformed to accommodate individuals in a less traditional work status.

- **Sick pay**: In the UK, only 'employees' are entitled to Statutory Sick Pay at a rate of ~£90 per week, from the fourth day of absence to the 28th week. And over half of employers pay more than this sum through Occupational Sick Pay.

  This is not to say that the self-employed do not have access to illness and disability benefits. In fact, 25 of the 27 European member states award some form of this type of benefits for the self-employed. In the UK, for example, self-employed workers are eligible for both types of the Employment and Support Allowance

23 McGuinness (2018).
24 Office for National Statistics (2015).
25 Ebbinghaus (2010), 196, 206.
26 OECD (2015), 181.

(ESA) – contribution-based and means-tested. A self-employed worker is eligible for the former if she has paid National Insurance contributions for the past two years, and may receive ESA for 12 months. If one is not entitled to contribution-based ESA, or if that benefit has expired, it is possible to apply for means-tested ESA.

- **Maternity/paternity pay and leave**: Analogous to sick pay, the right to maternity pay is based on strong social and medical rationales. There is a consensus amongst medical professionals that the first months of a child's life are crucial for his or her development; that a relaxed environment, conducive to breast-feeding, is beneficial both for the mother and for the child, and that a mother should be subject to minimal stress and physical demands during the first three to six months following childbirth. These aims cannot be fulfilled, of course, if a mother who has just given birth is forced to return to work immediately because she cannot afford not to do so. And, indeed, the vast majority of developed nations (the US being a notable outlier) entrench a statutory right to maternity pay (and not only to protected leave) ranging from 14 weeks in Japan to 16 weeks in France, the Netherlands and Spain and on to a full year in Canada and Denmark, and 420 days in Sweden.

We find, then, that while these categories cover a range of social security rationales, are correspondingly different in their precise implementation, and developed in different fashions, they have a common structure. Notwithstanding their differences, the structure for these benefits already includes the ability to bolster a universal layer which is contingent on links to the labour market but indifferent to employment *status*. This structure may be conducive to address changes to labour markets and employment relations and, in particular, the new social risk of workers remaining with insufficient funds in retirement, for unemployment, or for time off work due to illness or the welcoming of a new child.[27] Moreover, whereas pensions and unemployment have always offered a two-tiered approach, sick pay and maternity leave included a universal, residual layer only recently. This is an interesting development, reflecting the awareness that social security rights should be guaranteed to all, and that the traditional employment/self-employment divide should no longer be a determinant in this respect. But now that the principle is settled, its effectiveness will be a matter of degree and the political reality may make this difficult.

---

[27] Hinrich (2001), 77–101.

3. RECALIBRATING SOCIAL SECURITY

Having outlined the changes in labour markets post-Beveridge, we can now develop proposals for policy and practice for re-engineering social security in a new labour market. The transformation of social and employment policy to manage the risks in the new economy will require a reconfiguration of the institutions of social protection to re-align techniques of intervention with the nature of the risks they are intended to cover.

The proposed solutions cannot be solely 'technical', or institutional, just as the shift from *social* security to the cult of personal responsibility was not solely technical or institutional. Rather, it was a shift from 'we're all in this together' to 'you get what you deserve'. Indeed, while this chapter does not aim to explain *why and how* these changes to the social security fabric came about, when considering the way to address their consequences, it is worth noting that 'historical and sociological neo-institutionalists have come to view ideas and discourses as factors that can drive or prevent institutional change'.[28] Revisiting the new 'frontiers of insecurity' requires reminding the public, legislators and policy makers that workers are currently excluded, and convincing them that it is unfair to demand that individuals face the new risks alone.

But *what* changes and reforms are necessary to bring about these changes? An overview of European paradigms reveals approaches across different axes. Thus, one can identify three types of institutional approaches: first, provision through occupational and sectoral schemes, as in Austria, France, Greece, Italy, Luxembourg and Spain. Second, a separate, dedicated and comprehensive social insurance scheme, as in Belgium. And third, provision for the self-employed through the expansion of the social security schemes.[29] In addition, and as observed above, one may address the *types* of schemes provided. Here we find two main groups: countries that provide basic allowances that may be supplemented through voluntary contributions (e.g. Denmark, Finland, Germany, the Netherlands, the UK); and countries that provide income-based benefits (e.g. Austria, Greece, Italy, Luxembourg, Portugal and Spain).[30]

---

28 Blyth (2007); Campbell (2010), 87.

29 Social Security Advisory Committee (2014), 28.

30 Mutual Information System on Social Protection (2013).

3.1 Setting the Framework: Ideology and the Welfare State

The process of reclassification will begin with a consideration of the underlying values or ideology for the redistribution of rights and then proceed to outline the new risks to be covered. One of the central assumptions of the chapter is that social security law is not separate from labour law – rather the two are indissolubly intertwined as they both concern the protections afforded to working people in work and out of work. Social security and labour law perform a redistributive role in that they act as a counterbalance to the power of capital. Developed and developing nations have off-loaded social risks onto the individual, the former through welfare reform and the latter through market liberalisation and structural adjustment programmes.[31] Williams notes that in a socially constructed labour market which has often alienated and subordinated waged work, the worker/non-worker distinction is itself highly ideological as the state defines the identity of the worker and then leaves social welfare to construct deserving and undeserving claimants.[32]

Hugo Sinzheimer recognised the redistributive nature of social insurance as collective law based on universal human rights that guarantee participation in the production and distribution of society's welfare.[33] According to Sinzheimer, social insurance created a new type of law 'no longer based on legal capacity to be a subject of legal rights and duties but rather also on people's capacity to make a living'. The new model would then involve the state redistributing property rights according to the new risks created in the flexible labour market.

Social insurance was designed as an economic mechanism enabling contributions to fund redistribution on an intergenerational scale through social pooling of risk. Ideologically, and perhaps even philosophically, social insurance may be seen to rest on the idea of fairness, or more concretely in welfare state terminology – the idea of reciprocity.[34] Now, whilst the idea that 'something for nothing' rings hollow for many, understanding where reciprocity is relevant, and moreover, what are its concrete implications, are far more problematic issues. Increasingly, reciprocity is seen as related to a 'social', and then to a concrete, 'contract'. At times, this 'formalised contract' has been seen (e.g. by the British House of Commons Employment Committee) as signed between

---

[31] Klare (2004).

[32] Williams (2004).

[33] Hugo Sinzheimer, (1976 [1928]) *Arbeitsrecht und Rechtssoziologie, Gesammelte Aufsatze und Reden*, Vol 2, quoted by Schmid (2008).

[34] White (2003); White (2010), 19, 22.

a claimant and 'the taxpayer'.[35] Here we find the financial aspect of reciprocity, which perhaps is the closest to the idea of social insurance. For, as a matter of strict practicality, if individuals do not contribute to the general pot, there will be no source from which to redistribute. But the idea of reciprocity becomes even more relevant when we consider that by far the most common civic obligation that is posited as a precondition for social entitlements is work.[36] In part, this phenomenon can be grounded in institutional history as, since the late 19th and early 20th centuries, only workers were eligible for benefits that addressed risks and needs:

> The welfare state's key contribution was the mobilization of solidarity in those 'legitimate' circumstances in the life of a worker in which the successful commodification of his labour power could no longer be expected. It thereby helped to institutionalize a 'Fordist' life course consisting of three main stages – education, employment, retirement – providing financial support for its first and especially last phase and protecting its middle phase against unforeseen or short-term vulnerabilities (sickness, accidents, disability, and short-term unemployment).[37]

Developments in employment relations have led to a decrease in the percentage of those who are employed in traditional settings, and the blurring of lines between employed and self-employed individuals. And yet, regardless of their inherent soundness, the moral underpinnings of reciprocity support the eligibility of some self-employed individuals, who are forced to take part in the labour force outside the traditional employment relationship. The financial and welfare institutions should thus adapt accordingly.

3.2 Reformulating the Criteria for Social Protection

What criteria should inform the development of new social security protections for a flexible economy? These criteria need to address the central issue of how workers should be supported in making transitions in a flexible labour market, for example from full-time to part-time and from employee to self-employed status.

---

[35] House of Commons Sessions 1995–6, Employment Committee Second Report, *Right to Work/Workfare* (HMSO, 13 February 1996), xxiv cited in King (1998), 248.

[36] Paz-Fuchs (2008).

[37] Zutavern and Kohli (2010), 169, 175.

Gunther Schmid identifies four criteria by which new structures may promote 'good' transitions.[38] *Freedom* involves providing choice to workers to adopt risks in the labour market; *solidarity* involves collective risk-sharing; *effectiveness* and *efficiency* require appropriate coordinative instruments in allocation of resources, including possible public/private mixes. Central to Schmid's schema is the notion that the traditional Beveridgean solidarity should be combined with freedom as a basis for a redistributed security of workers in transition (see above). We would add a word of caution: freedom in the labour market should serve not just economic purposes such as mobility and flexibility but should support workers in their decisions to refuse low-paying or dangerous jobs, to seek financially secure work or not be penalised for accepting financially insecure employment, to take entrepreneurial risks or set up potentially risky business projects, to work for one or many employers, and to learn new skills and competences or to leave or combine work with reproductive facility. We would also note that the social elements of the equity/efficiency trade-off that Schmid envisages can be bolstered by adding further solidarity factors.

Thus, *security* should be promoted by identifying the economic risks associated with new flexibilities in the labour market. The new flexible workers face economic uncertainty, in relation to irregular income streams with the loss of secure jobs. In the words of the 2017 Taylor Report, commissioned by the British government, flexibility in the labour market is actually 'one sided', and consists of employers transferring risks to workers.[39] Where employment policy encourages workers to take low-paid and insecure jobs and to take on self-employed economic activity, protection is needed in the form of transparent and non-conditional benefits. *Equality* is a prerequisite and aim of all universal systems of security.[40] The drawbacks of traditional Beveridgean models of welfare are that they often include a gender and even a race bias.

3.3 Coverage: New Risks, New Needs

What would be the scope of any new scheme? The scope of coverage will be determined first by identifying the contingencies or risks to be covered and, second, by identifying basic needs of the population and then determining the level and type of benefits to cover these risks.

---

[38] Schmid (2002), 398.
[39] Taylor et al. (2017), 42.
[40] White (2003), 23–27.

How might this extension be achieved? The first step is to outline the new types of risk associated with flexible labour markets. The following typology is suggested by the logic of transitional labour market theory (TLM) outlined by Schmid.[41] The key aspect of TLM theory is to identify more precisely the types of life cycle risk that occur endogenously in a flexible labour market, where stable employment is no longer the norm. The assumption is that the borders between the labour market and other social systems must become more open to accommodate transitory states between employment and other productive non-market activities, for example private households, education, retirement and unemployment.

To facilitate this, Schmid suggests that risks should be classified with reference to the critical transitions that occur during the life course and identifies five main types of risks. The first and most important is to guarantee *income security* during critical transitions between employment relationships, for example, part-time and full-time work, and dependent employment and self-employment; second, *income maintenance* during transitions between employment and unemployment; third, *income replacement* where capacity is reduced through sickness or retirement; fourth, *income capacity* during transitions between education/training and employment; and finally, *income support* during life course phases when income capacity is reduced through child care and other social obligations.[42]

Risks one, two and four are key areas of reduced income in future labour markets. The life cycle concept[43] is prominent in many European systems and indeed the 'flexicurity' method[44] has been instrumental in promoting appropriate insurance interventions to support transitions in the new labour market. The fine-tuning of social security to supplement uneven income streams in a labour market where there are more jobs but fewer permanent or well-paid jobs is a key challenge for the future. One result of the new digital economy is that jobs generally pay less as more work is digitised, outsourced or re-cast into new evolving employment relationships. The Beveridge model never contemplated the fact that people can remain poor even when in paid employment. Fluctuating incomes can arise as a direct result of many of the new types of atypical work promoted in the flexible economy.

---

41 Schmid and Gazier (2002) 395 and see ch 5.

42 Ibid.

43 For an extended discussion of life cycles and welfare, see Hills (2015).

44 See, for example, Wilthagen (1988).

How might labour market policy be adapted to enable the new risks to be addressed? The broad aim of this chapter is to set out a forward-looking agenda for social security system in a new flexible labour market. The idea of a dynamic social security whereby social security can encourage individuals to find and remain in work and help people to reduce the severity of risk events that may impede capacity to work will appeal to individual self-interest and promote long-term collective financial sustainability.[45]

Both TLM and flexicurity theory envisage flexibility so that institutions can adapt to new risks. One way of achieving this would involve tailoring social security with flexible lifetime employment rather than linking it to particular jobs.[46] For example, simple unemployment insurance (UI) can be extended so that instead of covering external risks, it will cover internal risks in the labour market such as employability, mobility and flexibility. Advocates of extended employment insurance (EI) argue that it encourages individuals to assume responsibility for risky transitions thus enhancing employability, whereas others claim that extension may reduce unemployed workers' job search efforts.[47]

New types of extended insurance will require both new hybrid work/security arrangements which facilitate transitions across the spectrum of employment and self-employment. Working time may need recalibrating; insurance schemes will evolve to cover the risk of volatile income streams; mobility between employment and self-employment can be encouraged by insurance against business failure.

Activating insurance schemes for the self-employed will involve adaptation of social security at multiple levels. In many countries the self-employed have favourable treatment for tax and social security, involving lower tax rates, reduced social security contributions and off-setting of expenses. The support of entrepreneurial sections of the economy may, however, lead to disguised self-employment, so methods need to be found to protect vulnerable solo-self-employed without increasing tax avoidance. There are different approaches to the extension of social security to the self-employed: inclusion in general schemes, for example UK, Brazil, Mexico; separate schemes for self-employed, for example Belgium, Algeria; separate schemes for different categories of self-employed such as the liberal professions, for example France,

---

[45] McKinnon (2007), 149.

[46] Schmid and Gazier (2002), 396.

[47] Ibid, 397.

Germany and Spain, or simple exclusion.[48] However, there are significant challenges as a result of the heterogeneity of self-employed persons as a group and their variability of income and activity, thus different bases for benefits and contributions may be required.

Activating transitions between education, training and work is crucial in the new global economy. Concrete measures to link training with work might include converting unemployment benefit into vouchers for training, legal rights to request training and educational leave and progressive tax treatment.[49]

Transitions between domestic work in the household and paid work in the labour market involve measures to adapt work organisation to family organisation and the re-conceptualisation of parental leave as an income maintenance issue.[50]

Finally, transitions into retirement will require a variety of measures to promote income replacement for the self-employed, for example the introduction of compulsory enrolment onto pensions or government-backed Individual Savings Accounts (ISAs).[51]

3.4 Issues in Extending Coverage

One method of extension would simply be to introduce a non-contributory basic income to all. The attraction of this method is that it would avoid the problems associated with differentiating the gradations of employment status, for example the problematic employee/self-employed distinction which has proved so elusive. In addition, as Guy Standing argues, it would be the most effective way to reduce poverty as it would be direct and transparent with low administration costs.[52] While this may come up against arguments of affordability, moral objections concerning giving people something for nothing (see the discussion of reciprocity above), and that it would reduce work and support the 'bad', Standing argues convincingly that a basic income system, by benefiting those on low incomes most, would 'twist the structure of aggregate demand towards more basic goods and services … increasing demand and boosting growth and jobs'.[53]

---

48 International Social Security Association (ISSA) (2012).

49 Schmid and Gazier (2002), 399.

50 Ibid, 408. See also the Taylor et al. (2017), which recommended measures to extend shared parental leave to the self-employed.

51 Dellot and Reed (2015).

52 Standing (2017).

53 Ibid.

In contrast, a number of theorists[54] recognise that a complete break in the connection between social security and work on the basis of universal social benefits may be problematic. Replacing social insurance with a basic income may be politically unacceptable to governments and polities that view participation in the labour market as axiomatic and a precondition for entitlements.

A second issue is geographic. While this chapter deals primarily with social security in developed economies, it is arguable that the developed/developing economy dichotomy is a false one. Global competition results in a possible race to the bottom in all economies as all fight for survival. Developed economies may import cheap labour *and* disband social safety nets to regain advantage. The UK and US economies are good examples of this radical 'right' phenomenon. Globalisation therefore necessitates both developed and developing nations to adopt minimum standards to maintain social justice and counter precariousness. The World Commission argues that 'A global commitment to deal with insecurity is critical to provide legitimacy to globalisation.'[55]

If the idea of a basic globalised floor[56] is not accepted, the problem remains of identifying a basis for extended coverage that can be directly related to work. If the very concept of 'work' and the 'worker' has become problematic in the globalised digital economy, the contributory principle is also in jeopardy. This perhaps is the nub of the problem we face in re-engineering social security for the new economy. For many workers, employability itself is the issue. If the worker cannot find a standard job and the only jobs available are atypical jobs where employment status is denied, a significant share of workers become disenfranchised and are unable to find an employment link to access contributory schemes.[57] This means that the Bismarckian principle of contribution will need to be fine-tuned so that the genuine self-employed, the casual workers, the digital platform workers and the many false self-employed can gain protection against the new transitional risks.

There is a financial issue related to contributory schemes. For contributory social insurance schemes, the coverage rate is the number of contributing members (persons protected) as a percentage of the labour force.[58] Particularly in the case of pensions, benefit levels are based on previous earnings. The irregularity of earnings of many atypical workers including

---

54 See for example, Bergman et al. (2005).

55 World Commission (2004).

56 See Cichon and Hagemejer (2007).

57 Kannan (2007).

58 Van Ginneken (2007), 41.

the self-employed means that contribution records are patchy at best. Such workers may not qualify for eligibility on a number of grounds. For example, they may not build up continuity of employment because they lose their job or abandon economic activities or simply because they stop making contributions and join the informal economy without actually declaring this.

4. POLICY CHOICES

Now that we have considered the basis for the extension of the coverage of social insurance, we can start to formulate some proposals. The final section will provide a general framework for discussion and then make some brief detailed recommendations.

4.1 Schematising a New Formula for Security and Freedom: Labour and Welfare Perspectives

The formulation of policy for the future might be schematised along two dimensions, which we will term labour and welfare perspectives. The *labour* perspective involves a reformulation of the definitional elements of the employment relationship to provide a more inclusive relationship which would accommodate new types of employment status. The *welfare* perspective involves a reconfiguration of the coverage of social security to make it less dependent on particular types of employment status or type of activity in the labour market.

From a *labour perspective*, it is logical and practical to think about a more inclusive definition of work which will accommodate both dependent self-employment and other hybrid categories[59] of entrepreneurial worker. The issue of false self-employment also needs addressing, particularly in view of the increasing numbers of self-employed workers in the gig economy.[60]

One way of breaking down the binary division of employment and self-employment is through Freedland and Countouris' concept of the 'personal work relation' or 'nexus'.[61] If traditional notions of subordinate

59 See Wynn (2016), 826 and the concept of 'entreployee'.

60 Taylor et al. (2017), 25.

61 Defined as 'A connection or set of connections, between a worker and another person or persons or an organisation or organisations, arising from an engagement or arrangement or set of arrangements for the carrying out of work

employees associated with the contract of employment are revisited when considering eligibility for employment rights, it is surely appropriate to construct a much wider family of interconnecting work relationships which might include freelancers and other entrepreneurial workers who may still be dependent on single employers for the purposes of social security legislation. A 'purposive' approach would buttress this approach.[62] Similarly, the 2017 Taylor Report suggests revisiting and revising judicial tests for worker status, placing more emphasis on the ability of a company to control its workers, and less on exculpating clauses (e.g. the substitution clause) that allow employers to avoid categorising workers as such.[63] Such a change could have an immediate effect on workers in the gig economy, agency workers and workers on zero hour contracts. We should also acknowledge the dynamic and transitional nature of work relations which may evolve towards more commercial relationships in the network economy where security is reduced and risk is transferred to the worker.

Freedland's work nexus idea is taken further in Alain Supiot's idea of 'social drawing rights'.[64] While Freedland is explicitly concerned with the relational scope of labour law, Supiot's project is more related to the interrelationship between labour law and social security. His concept of 'labour force membership' encompasses all types of work including both paid and unpaid work, periods of unemployment and training, employment and self-employment.[65] If workers can draw on a reserve of social rights to protect their livelihood in key transitional phases of work activity, they can actively manage their participation in a flexible labour market.

With Supiot, we gain a more expansive view of social security as an active rather than a passive mechanism whereby the notion of risk is modified by the exercise of choice. If workers can choose which risks/contingencies they need to insure against and when they want to exercise their rights, social security becomes a process of active risk management tailored to individual need. Flexible transitions are also managed by reformulating working time for the purposes of social security.[66] The continuity of labour force membership can be maintained

---

or the rendering of service or services by the worker personally' (Freedland and Countouris (2011), 31).

62 Davidov (2016).

63 Taylor et al. (2017).

64 Supiot (2001).

65 Ibid, 55.

66 Ibid, 56.

both inside and outside the labour contract to allow access to social security in periods of non-work between short engagements or training or spells of self-employment. Alongside more active participation in labour markets, stakeholders in the labour relationship – employers, workers and the state – can develop new ways of paying for social benefits through public/private mixes.

What lessons can we learn from these expanding definitions of work and social security? First, we can distil new motifs to guide our search for a recalibration. According to Supiot, the new worker combines freedom with security,[67] whereas Freedland envisages a tripolar scheme converging around the poles of security, autonomy and precarity.[68] Perhaps, a new framework can be drawn from these baselines with two major axes. The first axis consists of a *freedom/security* polarity whereas the second axis consists of a *flexibility/mobility* axis. On the first axis, social protection can be modified according to the degree of freedom that a worker chooses. More entrepreneurial workers may trade more freedom for less security or vice versa. On the second axis, the type and level of benefits may be conditioned on the type of transition or work mode required by the market. In this way, social rights are adapted to the degree of discontinuity or displacement caused in the worker life cycle by new forms of work.

However, a note of caution is warranted here, following the call from Deliveroo, a gig economy platform/employer, to change the law that currently 'prevents it from offering enhanced rights' such as sick leave, to its riders.[69] The company argued that, while it would like to provide such benefits, it cannot do so as it wishes to retain the ability to define its riders as self-employed. In other words, the company is advocating a move away from the all-or-nothing, status-driven approach. Instead, it would prefer an approach that would allow companies to view individuals as entitled to some benefits, but not entitled to others. This approach is embraced by the courts in some countries (e.g. Israel), but has been criticised as breaking down employee status and creating a strong sense of uncertainty.

The *welfare perspective* assumes a modification of tax and insurance structures to extend social security coverage to wider categories of labour market participation and narrow the gap in non-wage labour costs between employees, dependent self-employed and self-employed. The

---

67 Ibid, 57.
68 Freedland and Countouris (2011), 346.
69 Ahmed (2017).

Beveridge Report recognised the need to support the self-employed, as they are likely to be poorer and more in need of state insurance than employees.[70] The real question for today is whether the self-employed should gain parity of social rights with employees. If employees gained security in return for subordination, should the self-employed who gain independence from control by employers and benefit from lower contributions and tax advantages, gain similar security?[71] Complicating the picture is the fact that the current financial gain by employing workers on a self-employed basis due to lower National Insurance contributions has led to a significant rise in 'false' or 'bogus' self-employment for, according to one estimate, 460,000 workers in the UK.[72] This term refers to the situation in which workers are told – and at times their contract states explicitly – that they are self-employed, but the legal tests would characterise them as workers. These workers are thus denied employment rights either because they are not aware of their true legal status or because they are afraid to challenge their employers.

If we return to the four schemes identified in Section 2 of this chapter, we find that there are noticeable developments, in tune with the welfare perspective.

Thus, insofar as *pensions* are concerned, the introduction of the Single Tier Pension in the UK, in 2016, includes the self-employed as one of its main beneficiaries, as it will treat their National Insurance contributions in the same way as those of employees when calculating pension entitlement. However, while it is welcomed in principle, as this move affects only the basic (state) pension (raising it by about £30 per week), 'it will not provide enough for many people to have a standard of living similar to that of their working life, meaning additional income sources will be required'.[73] Noting that only 4.2 per cent of self-employed people between the ages of 25 and 34 are enrolled in pension schemes, the Taylor Review calls on the government to improve pension provision amongst the self-employed, inter alia by auto-enrolling them into pension schemes, and to incentivise savings through the tax system.[74]

As self-employment is typically prone to ebbs and flows, it is notoriously difficult to determine when a period off work should qualify as *unemployment* for the purposes of benefit entitlement. Traditionally,

70 Beveridge (1942), Para 4.
71 Deakin (2001).
72 Citizens' Advice (2015); Social Security Advisory Committee (2014), 31–33.
73 D'Arcy (2015), 6.
74 Taylor et al. (2017), 78,

periods of unemployment are far easier to ascertain in the traditional employment relationship. While this is still true, to a large extent, this assertion is not as obvious as it was in the past. Many 'gig economy' workers, for example, supplement their income with various 'gigs'.[75] And workers in the current economic climate tend to work in more than one job. In other words, a degree of flexibility and realism is necessary when addressing the needs of unemployed workers as well. So what can be done? While far from an ideal solution, the approach adopted by the UK in the form of Universal Credit is one possible route. It works on an *assumption* that the income from self-employment reaches, at least, a 'minimum income floor', based on a set number of hours per week, and the minimum wage. Exemptions to the minimum income floor are given to single parents, people with disabilities and individuals who have been self-employed for less than 12 months. The interesting aspect about this approach is the conflation of concepts associated with the employment relationship – primarily, here, the minimum wage and working time – within the boundaries of self-employment. This requires, as noted, some assumptions, which may be controversial and contested. But, perhaps, while the details may be negotiated, creating entitlements for the self-employed for benefits that were solely granted to those in traditional employment relationships requires some imagination, and a price to pay.

The Uber and Deliveroo examples, noted above, highlight the importance of ensuring that workers are able to take time off due to ill health, in a manner that will not impact on their income in a serious manner. The fact that a special arrangement was needed also indicates, however, that, in its absence, only employees with an acknowledged status are entitled to this benefit. In this respect, *sick pay* diverges from pensions and unemployment benefits. The rationale behind delivering sick pay is straightforward: apart from their own severe discomfort, individuals who come to work sick are likely to prolong their illness and, in the interim, pose a risk to the health of others – colleagues, clients and consumers, as the case may be. There is, thus, a clear and strong reason to allow individuals to recuperate fully before returning to work. And yet, the fact that this benefit is reserved to those who enjoy formal, employee status effectively bars a growing number of self-employed, agency and gig economy workers, for example, from accessing the benefit. Therefore, we would support expanding the scope of the right to workers (including

---

[75] Taylor et al. (2017).

agency workers and workers in the gig economy) and expanding its breadth, to start from day one.[76]

Until recently, no parallel maternity/paternity benefits and leave rights were awarded to self-employed mothers. In 2010, an EU Directive was adopted to provide (non-compulsory) maternity leave for self-employed mothers for 14 weeks, along with a maternity allowance.[77] The Directive has been implemented, inter alia, in the UK, so women will be entitled to a full maternity allowance if they have been self-employed and paid Class 2 National Insurance contributions within the 66 weeks before the baby is due. As of June 2017, the full rate of maternity allowance is set at a flat rate of £140.98 or 90 per cent of average earnings, whichever is less. Women who have not paid enough National Insurance will not be entitled to the full maternity allowance, but will still receive £27 for 39 weeks. Parental rights for fathers have been established and expanded only recently, by comparison, in most countries. Initially awarding only protected, but unpaid, leave for a birth of a child, many countries have now moved towards allowing parents to decide whether to, essentially, transfer the mother's right to paid leave to the father. Unsurprisingly, take-up for this right has been minimal, indicating that there is little pressure to expand this right to self-employed fathers.

Finally, and most ambitiously, the World Employment Confederation suggested implementing an 'individual social account' that accrues benefits for a worker throughout her life, applying to all forms of employment or work, pro rata (related to income earned, time worked or jobs completed).[78] This account would comprise all social rights – including unemployment benefits, pension, training, sick pay, maternity and paternity – and would be available for the individual to use when needed.

4.2 The Tax Question

While a detailed discussion of tax is outside the scope of this chapter, the importance of tax arrangements in the overall economy of the welfare state necessitates a brief *discursus*.[79]

So far, we have argued for some extension of social security rights to the self-employed. However, the earlier discussion regarding reciprocity

---

[76] Taylor et al. (2017), 99.

[77] Directive on self-employed workers and assisting spouses (2010/41/EU).

[78] Williams and Lapeyre (2017), 40.

[79] For an extensive treatment of tax and workers in the UK, see Freedman (2001).

has highlighted issues of fairness concerning relative contributions to the pot. It would seem axiomatic, from both fiscal and ethical perspectives, that the self-employed should not gain financial advantages from their different legal status. On the other hand, it is also recognised that some social security benefits are delivered through the tax system. Prominent amongst them is the Negative Income Tax (known as Earned Income Tax Credit in the US and Working Tax Credit (WTC) in the UK), which is supported by progressives and libertarians alike. And, indeed, we find that the UK has expanded WTC (incrementally replaced by Universal Credit) to include self-employed individuals who (if aged between 25 and 59) work at least 30 hours a week and have an hourly income that is below the minimum wage. Indeed, in 2012–13, about 770,000 families with at least one member who identified as self-employed benefited from WTC.[80]

If a new welfare settlement is to be constructed, a starting point might be the alignment of taxation of income across different legal forms. A recent failed attempt in the UK to increase National Insurance contributions (NICs) for the self-employed in the 2017 Budget indicates how politically contentious this issue is likely to be.[81] In the UK, the self-employed pay income tax and NICs on their earnings but are charged a lower rate of NICs and face no equivalent to employer NICs.[82] The result of this differential is that whereas employees face a tax rate of 30 per cent, the self-employed pay 22 per cent and company owner–managers pay just 18 per cent. The size of the differential is not justified by the small differences in access to benefits, particularly in the UK where the self-employed have gained rights to the same single tier pension since April 2016. Apart from the feelings of unfairness (whether justified or not) and the loss of income to the Treasury (estimated between £3.5 and £5.1bn annually in the UK, and at $149bn in the US[83]), there is a real danger that these differences create strong incentives for employers to categorise workers as self-employed, rather than employees.[84]

---

[80] Hansard, *Parliamentary debates: written answers* (2014, question from Guto Bebb MP) (202509).

[81] Philip Hammond was forced to withdraw the measure after serious opposition. See Budget 2017: 'Philip Hammond faces row over tax rises for self-employed, as it happened', *The Guardian*, 8 March 2017.

[82] Miller (2017).

[83] Bruckner (2016).

[84] Social Security Advisory Committee (2014); Taylor et al. (2017), 66–70.

In terms of reform, the proposal that the tax treatment of employed and self-employed might be aligned would deal with the fairness issue and would also mean that definitional problems regarding the classification of worker status would be reduced. However, classification for purposes of tax law and employment law is not straightforward and problematic distinctions will always remain.[85] Another proposal suggested is a complete merger of tax and NICs.[86] This would not necessarily align the treatment of employed and self-employed as they could still pay different rates, but it has long been the case that NICs have been treated as a form of indirect taxation, so that some consolidation would reduce the possibility of governments using the National Insurance fund to subsidise cuts in income tax and remove distortion in the fiscal system.

5. CONCLUDING, AND THE WAY FORWARD

We have identified some key themes in mapping out the contours of a future welfare state and how it might adapt to a flexible labour market of the future. Many of the policy choices are ultimately dependent on political and ideological choices and each type of welfare state will adapt accordingly. However, it is imperative that changes are made if the welfare state is to survive. As Ewald has correctly identified: ‘In guaranteeing security, the state is equally guaranteeing its own existence, maintenance, permanence. Social insurance is also an insurance against revolutions.’[87]

The final shape of any social model will ultimately depend on finding the right balance between freedom and security, between efficiency and equity and between reciprocity and solidarity. Apart from a wholesale reconstruction of labour law and social security to make a more inclusive framework, or in the absence of a non-contributory universal basic income, it may be possible to make some less radical changes to adapt existing contributory frameworks to the new forms of non-standard employment.

One approach suggested in the paper is to analyse the key transitions in a worker’s life course to determine what new risks may lead to precarity or exclusion. The higher risks in terms of income volatility, unemployment and income security in old age demand a new technology

---

[85] See Leighton and Wynn (2011).

[86] Freedman (2001), 4.

[87] Ewald (1991), 197.

of insurance which is flexible, fair and efficient. One necessary adjustment might be to decouple social insurance from specific jobs and link it with lifetime employment. In this way, the contributory principle is still linked to work but more in terms of labour force membership. Another possibility is to implement a form of employment insurance which, unlike unemployment insurance, is designed to cover internal rather than external risks in the labour market and thus encourage the more entrepreneurial workers to make transitions between different employment statuses.[88] A further reform which would address the problem of uneven contributions in atypical employment might be to subsidise social security contributions where income remains low or volatile and then build up progressive contributions in times of high earnings.[89] Another aspect which needs consideration is the gendered division of work and home which often impacts unfavourably on women. How far one goes in the marketisation of care work is another difficult political question but it remains true today that 'at the end of the day the welfare state and the family are the foundations of the labour market'.[90]

In sum, the overview of recent trends suggests that, against the background of increased precarity and insecurity in the labour market, there is a growing understanding, in the public and in the private sector, that social security schemes need to respond. This suggests, at the very least, that it is unlikely that the welfare state itself will be replaced at any time in the near future by the market principle.[91]

BIBLIOGRAPHY

Ahmed, Kamal. 2017. 'Deliveroo opens the door to benefit win for gig economy workers' BBC (7 July) http://www.bbc.co.uk/news/business-40524377

Ariely, Dan. 2008. *Predictably Irrational: the Hidden Forces that Shape our Decisions* (HarperCollins)

Bergman, Jos, D'Haeseleer, Steven, et al. 2005. *Social Protection, Globalised* (Leuven University Press).

Beveridge, William. 1942. Social insurance and allied services (HM Stationery Office).

Blyth, Mark. 2007. Powering, puzzling, or persuading? The mechanisms of building institutional orders, *International Studies Quarterly* Vol 51, 761.

Bonoli, Giuliano. 2000. *The Politics of Pension Reform* (CUP).

---

88 Schmid and Gazier (2002), 397.

89 Schmid (2010).

90 Deakin (2001), quoting Alain Supiot.

91 Ibid.

Booth, Robert. 2017. 'Uber to offer UK drivers sickness cover in return for £2-a-week fee' *The Guardian* (27 April) https://www.theguardian.com/technology/2017/apr/27/uber-to-offer-uk-drivers-sickness-cover-in-return-for-2-a-week-fee

Bruckner, Caroline. 2016. Shortchanged: The Tax Compliance Challenges of Small Business Operators Driving the On-Demand Platform Economy (Kogod Tax Policy Centre,)

Buchanan, James. 1998. The Fiscal Crisis in Welfare Democracies: with Some Implications for Public Investment, in Toshihiro Ihori and Hirofumi Shibata (eds) *The Welfare State, Public Investment, and Growth* (Springer).

Campbell, John. 2010. Institutional Reproduction and Change in G. Morgan et al. (eds) *Oxford Handbook of Comparative Institutional Change* (OUP).

Chartered Institute of Personnel and Development, 2013. *Megatrends: the trends shaping work and working lives.*

Cichon, M and Hagemejer K. 2007. Changing the development policy paradigm: investing in a social security floor for all, *International Social Security Review* Vol 60, 2–3, 169.

Citizens' Advice Bureau. 2015. 'Neither one thing nor the other: how reducing bogus self-employment could benefit workers, business and the Exchequer' https://www.citizensadvice.org.uk/Global/CitizensAdvice/Work%20Publications/Neither%20one%20thing%20nor%20the%20other.pdf

Comfort, Nicholas. 2013. *The Slow Death of British Industry: a 60-year Suicide, 1952-2012* (Biteback).

D'Arcy, Conor. 2015. *Pensions and the Self-Employed* (Resolution Foundation).

Davidov, Guy. 2016. *A Purposive Approach to Employment Law* (OUP).

Deakin, Simon. 2001. Labour Law and Social Insurance in the New Economy, in David Marsden and Hugh Stephenson (eds) *The New Economy: A Debate on the Supiot Report* (Centre for Economic Performance).

Defert, Daniel. 1991. 'Popular Life' and Insurance Technology, in Graham Burchell, Colin Gordon and Peter Miller (eds) *The Foucault Effect: Studies in Governmentality* (University of Chicago Press, 211).

Dellot, Benedict and Reed, Howard. 2015. *Boosting the Living Standards of the Self-employed*,(RSA Action and Research Centre).

Ebbinghaus, Bernhard. 2010. Unions and Employers in Francis G. Castles et al. (eds) *The Oxford Handbook of the Welfare State* (OUP).

Ewald, François. 1991. Insurance and Risk, in Graham Burchell, Colin Gordon and Peter Miller (eds) *The Foucault Effect: Studies in Governmentality* (University of Chicago Press) 197–210.

Freedland, Mark and Countouris, Nicola. 2011. *The Legal Construction of Personal Work Relations*, (OUP).

Freedland, Mark and Davies, Paul. 2007. *Towards a Flexible Labour Market: Labour Regulation and Legislation Since the 1990s* (OUP).

Freedman, Judith. 2001. 'Employed or self-employed, tax classification of workers and the changing labour market' (Tax Law Review Committee, IFS), https://www.ifs.org.uk/comms/dp1.pdf

Hacker, Jacob. 2006. *The Great Risk Shift* (Yale UP).

Hills, John. 2015. *Good Times Bad Times, The Welfare Myth of Them and Us* (Policy Press).

Hinrich, Karl. 2001. Elephants on the Move: Patterns of Public Pension Reform in OECD Countries, in Stephen Leibfried (ed.) *Welfare State Futures* (CUP).
Hinrichs, Karl and Lynch, Julia. 2010. Old Age Pensions, in Francis G. Castles et al. (eds) *The Oxford Handbook of the Welfare State* (OUP).
International Social Security Association (ISSA). 2012. *Handbook on the Extension of Social Security Coverage to the Self-employed*, (Geneva).
Kannan, K.P. 2007 Social security in a globalising world, *International Social Security Review* Vol 60, 2–3, 30.
King, Desmond. 1998. *In the Name of Liberalism* (OUP).
Klare, Karl. 2004. The Horizons of Transformative Labour and Employment Law, in J. Conaghen, R.M. Fischl and K. Klare (eds), *Labour Law in an Era of Globalisation: Transformative Practices and Possibilities* (OUP).
Leighton, Patricia and Wynn, Michael. 2011. Classifying employment relationships – more sliding doors or a better regulatory framework? *Industrial Law Journal* Vol 40, 5-44.
McGuinness, Feargal. 2018. *Poverty in the UK: Statistics* (Briefing Paper 7096, House of Commons).
McKinnon, Roddy. 2007. Dynamic social security: A framework for directing change and extending coverage, *International Social Security Review* Vol 60, 149.
Miller, H. 2017. Tax in a changing world, *Tax Journal* (April) https://www.taxjournal.com/articles/tax-changing-world-work-20042017
Mutual Information System on Social Protection (MISSOC) (2013), *Social Protection of the Self-employed*
OECD. 2015. *In it Together: Why Less Inequality Benefits All* (OECD Publishing).
Office for National Statistics. 2015. *Persistent Poverty in the UK and EU: 2008–2013* https://www.ons.gov.uk/peoplepopulationandcommunity/personalandhouseholdfinances/incomeandwealth/articles/persistentpovertyintheukandeu/2015-05-20
Orenstein, Mitchell. 2008. *Privatising Pensions: The Transnational Campaign for Social Security Reform* (Princeton University Press).
Paz-Fuchs, Amir. 2008. *Welfare to Work: Conditional Rights in Social Policy* (OUP).
Schmid, Gunther. 2002. Transitional Labour Markets and the European Social Model: Towards a New Employment Compact in Gunther Schmid and Bernard Gazier (eds) *The Dynamics of Full Employment: Social Integration Through Transitional Labour Markets* (Edward Elgar).
Schmid, Gunther. 2008. Sharing Risks, On Social Risk Management and the Governance of Labour Market Transitions, in Ralf Rogowski (ed.) *The European Social Model and Transitional Labour Markets* (Ashgate Publishing).
Schmid, Gunther. 2010. *Non-standard Employment and Labour Force Participation: A Comparative View of the Recent Development in Europe* (Discussion Paper Series, The Institute for the Study of Labour (IZA) DP No 5087).

Schmid, Gunther and Gazier, Bernard (eds). 2002. *The Dynamics of Full Employment: Social Integration through Transitional Labour Markets* (Edward Elgar).
Social Security Advisory Committee. 2014. *Social Security Provision and the Self-Employed* (Occasional Paper 13).
Standing, Guy. 2017. *Basic Income: And How We Can Make it Happen* (Pelican Books).
Stearns, Peter. 1975. *Lives of Labor: Work in a Maturing Industrial Society* (Croom Helm).
Sunstein, Cass and Thaler, Richard. 2008. *Nudge* (Yale University Press).
Supiot, Alain. 2001. *Beyond Employment, Changes in Work and the Future of Labour Law in Europe* (OUP).
Taylor, Matthew et al. 2017. *Good Work: The Taylor Review of Modern Working Practices* (Department for Business, Energy and Industrial Strategy).
van Ginneken, W. 2007. Extending social security coverage: concepts, global trends and policy issues, *International Social Security Review* Vol 60, 2–3, 41.
Wales, Philip and Amankwah, Andrew. 2016. *Trends in Self-employment in the UK: 2001 to 2015* (Office of National Statistics).
Wells, Claudia. 2017. *Household disposable Income and Inequality in the UK: Financial Year Ending 2016* (Office of National Statistics).
White, Stuart. 2003. *The Civic Minimum: On the Rights and Obligations of Economic Citizenship* (OUP).
White, Stuart. 2010. Ethics, in Francis G. Castles et al. (eds) *The Oxford Handbook of the Welfare State* (OUP).
Williams, Lucy. 2004. Beyond Labour Law's Parochialism: A Re-envisioning of the Discourse of Redistribution, in J. Conaghen, R.M. Fischl and K. Klare (eds), *Labour Law in an Era of Globalisation: Transformative Practices and Possibilities* (OUP).
Williams, Colin and Lapeyre, Frederic. 2017. *Dependent Self-employment: Trends, Challenges and Policy Responses in the EU* (ILO, Working Paper No 228).
Wilthagen, Ton. 1988. *Flexicurity: A New Paradigm for Labour Market Policy Reform?* (WZB Discussion Paper, No. FS 1 98–202).
World Commission. 2004. *A Fair Globalisation: Creating Opportunities for All*, February.
Wynn, Michael. 2016. Chameleons at large: entrepreneurs, employees and firms – the changing context of employment relationships, *Journal of Management and Organisation* Vol 22, 6, 826.
Zutavern, Jan and Kohli, Martin. 2010. Needs and Risks, in Francis G. Castles et al. (eds) *The Oxford Handbook of the Welfare State* (OUP).

3. Gender and race in the informal economy: the South African framework

Elmarie Fourie

3.1. INTRODUCTION

The informal economy is now a reality and a growing acknowledgement of this exists. Vulnerable or precarious employment[1] account for 1.4 billion people across the world.[2] In developing countries four out of five workers are in a form of vulnerable employment.[3] Globally, 586 million women are own account or contributing family workers.[4] Women workers are disadvantaged due to market relationships within the informal economy, as members of groups defined by race, class, ethnicity or caste and as women due to gender norms in societies.[5] The feminisation of poverty together with gender and racial discrimination contribute to their vulnerabilities.

Work in the informal economy is characterised by insufficient labour and social protection measures or no coverage at all. It is important to identify and analyse the scope of existing labour laws and social protection provisions and to provide ways, where appropriate, to extend existing legislative provisions to provide protection to these vulnerable women workers. However, in many instances a mere extension of existing legislative provisions will not be adequate and innovative tailor-made solutions will be more appropriate to deal with the specific needs of these women workers. Creating gender awareness within the informal

---

1 Vulnerable employment is described by the International Labour Organization (ILO) as work associated with limited access to social protection (ILO 2017) 2.

2 ILO (2017) 2.

3 Ibid.

4 ILO (2016a) xii.

5 WIEGO <https://www.wiego.org> accessed 20 May 2017.

economy will require a critical analysis of how various identities are shaped through unequal hierarchies. A new paradigm is needed, to move from practices that reinforce gender, race and class hierarchies, to a paradigm that promotes substantive equality. In other words, a framework that recognises the vulnerabilities of women and addresses the challenges accordingly.

The chapter will reflect on the precarious position of categories of women workers in the informal economy, in South Africa, that are particularly vulnerable, as a result of gender and racial inequalities. Although the chapter reflects on these women workers in South Africa, their particular vulnerabilities are representative of the majority of women workers in the informal economy.

3.2. WOMEN IN THE INFORMAL ECONOMY

In the Southern African region, many workers, in particular women, do not enjoy decent work or a quality life. In most developing regions, more workers in the informal economy are women (Table 3.1).

Table 3.1 Informal employment as a source of non-agricultural employment

Country	Female workers (%)	Male workers (%)
South Asia	83	82
Sub-Saharan Africa	74	61
Latin America and Caribbean	54	48

Source: Vanek et al. (2014) 8.

In 2004, the following key assumptions were published in respect of the linkage between informality, gender and poverty, namely that:

1. the poor are more likely to work in the informal economy;
2. more poor women than non-poor women work in the informal economy; and
3. there is a gender gap in the earnings in the informal economy, as women are earning less than their male counterparts, and are less likely to be organised and have social protection.[6]

[6] UN Women <https://www.un.org> accessed 20 May 2017.

According to Kalula et al.[7] women in Africa are located in work that resembles cultural stereotyping of their roles and as such men are more likely to be representative in activities such as construction and mining and women in activities that involve more domestic chores such as cooking, weaving and cleaning. These women workers are also often engaged in under-recognised and undervalued work, such as unpaid care work and domestic work. Within the informal economy, gender hierarchies exist. Men are predominantly employers or regular wage workers with higher average wages and lower poverty risks.[8] Women are more prevalent as casual wage workers, homeworkers, industrial outworkers and unpaid family workers. Their wages are irregular and low and their poverty risks are high. In the South African Development Community (SADC) region, inequalities are reflected in income, access to employment and access to social protection measures.[9] The colonial past of many countries in the region contributed to the fact that these inequalities are also structured along racial lines.

Studies indicate that these women are exposed to cultural and social injustices at various levels, such as macro or societal level,[10] meso or enterprise level[11] and micro or interpersonal level.[12] These women are vulnerable and face discrimination on multiple grounds and levels. This varies and can be linked to the position or location of the woman worker in the informal economy (sectoral location), their status as worker (class and race) and then their status as a woman in society, the community or the household (gender).[13] Gender inequalities in the informal economy cuts across race and class lines.[14]

---

[7] Kalula et al. (2011) 20.

[8] Chen (2012).

[9] Kalula et al. (2011) 19.

[10] These workers are excluded from labour and social protection as they are not recognised as 'workers' and their work is not valued. They also suffer from cultural injustices as they are marginalised and excluded from a social and political life. Injustices at this level are mostly generated from institutionalised forms of exclusion and exploitation (Hill 2010: 59).

[11] Economic empowerment or the lack thereof plays an important role at this level, as these workers do not have access or have limited access to resources, such as markets, credit and industry information (Hill 2010: 60).

[12] At this level injustices occur as a result of direct forms of exploitation and intimidation at a personal level. Intimidation at this level results in a culture of fear and weakened productivity (Hill 2010: 59).

[13] Ibid.

[14] Dias stated: '... in many societies there is a clear association between racial structures of oppression with such kinds of labour being allocated by

3.3. SOUTH AFRICA AND WOMEN IN THE INFORMAL ECONOMY

South Africa is categorised by the World Bank as an upper middle income country and is one of the largest economies in Africa.[15] In 2016, the population was estimated at 55.9 million and more than half were women.[16] The country held its first democratic elections in 1994, and adopted one of the most progressive constitutions in the world, with a Bill of Rights entrenched with values such as human dignity, equality and freedom.[17] However, inequality and poverty still represents its apartheid past, as African women are particularly vulnerable.[18] The apartheid legacy has a profound effect on the inequalities in the country, and slow employment creation and high unemployment remains a reality. In June 2017, unemployment reached its highest levels in 13 years.[19] South Africa is one of the countries in the SADC region with a relatively small informal economy; however, earnings from informal employment account for 14% of the income that allows households to exist above the poverty line.[20]

Table 3.2 provides an overview of the labour force in South Africa from 2017 (Quarter 3).

---

gender, class, caste, race and ethnicity' (Dias and Ogando 2015). In South Africa, this is clearly illustrated when considering categories of work in the informal economy such as domestic workers, street traders and waste pickers. The majority of these women are black and from poor communities. Waste pickers also represent one of the most vulnerable categories of workers within the informal economy.

15 STATS SA (2016).

16 Ibid.

17 See Chapter 2 of the Constitution of the Republic of South Africa.

18 It is estimated that more that 7 million people live with HIV/AIDS and the prevalence is nearly twice as high among women (STATS <https://www.statssa.gov.za> accessed 10 August 2017).

19 In May 2018, official unemployment was 26,7%. Women are more likely to be in long term unemployment (STATS SA Quarterly Labour Force Survey 2018).

20 Rogan and Cichello (2017). According to this report, approximately a third of the workforce is in informal employment.

Table 3.2 Work in the Informal Economy in South Africa

	Weight			% of Weight		
	Male	Female	Total	Male (%)	Female (%)	Total (%)
Formal sector (non-agricultural)	6 494 273	4 803 462	11 297 735	57,4	42,6	100
Informal sector (non-agriculture)	1 759 667	1 049 432	2 809 099	62,8	37,2	100

Source: STATS SA: Quarterly Labour Force Survey 2017 (Quarter 3).

In South Africa, the majority of domestic workers are African women workers. The apartheid government's exclusion of African people, and particularly African women, from the formal economy, means that informality and race are inextricably linked. During the apartheid regime, racist laws incorporated the ideology that African people's contribution was to provide unskilled, cheap labour to white business owners. Africanisation and feminisation of sectors such as domestic work can be seen as a direct consequence of this ideology. As a result of these exclusions African women display different levels of education and often form part of a large group of unskilled labourers that enter the informal economy.

Categories of workers in the informal economy, such as women street traders[21] and waste pickers,[22] are amongst the most vulnerable workers as they are excluded from labour laws and social protection measures,

---

[21] Street traders sell a variety of goods from fresh produce to fashion accessories and can also provide services, such as hairdressing. Gender hierarchies exist within this category as women are more likely to trade from a mobile stand and men are more likely to have a permanent stand (Roever 2014).

[22] Waste pickers work in various public spaces, including streets, landfills and dumping sites. Their livelihood is based on the collecting, sorting, recycling and selling of waste. Their contributions to the environment, waste management systems of local authorities and economies are undervalued.

including most social security schemes.[23] Globally, women waste pickers represent previously disadvantaged groups, and in South Africa, waste collection is highly gendered and women are mostly excluded from formal waste management systems, leaving them on the edges of the waste management system.[24] Street traders and waste pickers are excluded from labour laws and social security measures in South Africa.[25]

With reference to categories of informal employment, Table 3.3 provides the most recent statistics in the informal economy in South Africa and clearly illustrates the gender and racial dimension of work within categories, such as domestic work and street vending.

---

[23] These exclusions can be ascribed to the lack of legal recognition as workers, narrow conceptual frameworks and the lack of a distinct employer–employee relationship. In South Africa, the court has recognised the vulnerabilities of African street traders and stated: 'However, apartheid layered poverty over race. The degree of coincidence or intersectionality of race with socio-economic status results in the greatest impact being on Africans. As the population with the largest component of poor people the impact is deeper and more expansive than on any other race group. As street traders their discrimination is ostensible and direct on the grounds of their socio-economic status. However, subversively and indirectly race remains an additional ground of discrimination in appropriate instances. Recognising race acknowledges that for black people and Africans in particular discrimination is doubly compounded.' See *Makwickana v eThekwini Municipality*.

[24] As an occupation waste picking does not require high levels of education or skill, and allows for easy entrance into the informal economy. Dias and Ogando (2015) 54.

[25] The regulatory framework often falls within the sphere of local authorities and regulation is fragmented as comprehensive national legislation is lacking. As own account workers, these women are in a precarious position, and this can be ascribed to gender and racial inequalities. Inequalities include barriers with reference to access of education and skills training, cultural and patriarchal practices within societies, lack of economic and legal empowerment, and their responsibilities with regard to unpaid care and domestic work (Ogando et al. 2017: 437,438).

Table 3.3 Occupation, gender by population group for weight, employed

Categories of work in the informal economy	African/ Black	Coloured	Indian/ Asian	White	Total
Domestic helpers and cleaners					
Male	41 474	1 555	0	0	43 029
Female	876 434	73 484	665	0	950 583
Total	917 908	75 039	665	0	993 612
Street vendors and related workers					
Male	91 889	3 035	1 988	0	96 912
Female	224 515	1 918	0	0	226 433
Total	316 404	4 953	1 988	0	323 345
Street vendors: non-food products					
Male	93 666	2 459	10 062	938	107 125
Female	100 294	4 069	0	0	104 363
Total	193 960	6 528	10 062	938	211 488
Garbage collectors (waste pickers)					
Male	30 410	4 951	0	3 945	39 306
Female	15 633	0	0	0	15 633
Total	46 043	4 951	0	3 945	54 939

Note: Obtaining accurate statistics for workers in the informal economy is challenging and these figures may be much higher.

Source: STATS SA: Quarterly Labour Force Survey 2018 (Quarter 1).

3.4. SOCIAL PROTECTION IN SOUTH AFRICA

Women workers in the informal economy in South Africa do not enjoy adequate social protection as many of them do not have access to benefits, including maternity, retirement and health benefits.

A number of countries such as South Africa, Malawi and Zambia have, however, taken steps to extend protection to vulnerable women workers and various policies and programmes are in place.[26]

[26] Van de Meerendonk et al. (2016). Malawi represents one of the least developed countries in the world. The majority of the workforce, 89%, are in

For workers in the informal economy the concept of social protection as a wider concept than social security is preferred.[27] This is also in line with the ILO Decent Work Agenda. Social protection is not linked to a specific employment relationship and it is preferable to extend protection to workers in the informal economy as they are often not recognised as

informal employment, and women are more likely to be engaged in the informal economy. Nearly 82% of domestic workers are women. Malawi's Growth and Development Strategy II 2011–16 supports the objectives of poverty reduction, the reduction of food insecurities as wells as social protection measures for the poor and vulnerable.

In 2014, in Zambia, 88,6% of the employed persons were informally employed and the majority of these workers were women. The social security system, as in most SADC countries, is based on the formal employment relationship and the employment contract. Employers are responsible for maternity benefits, in terms of the Employment Act of 1965. Zambia has not ratified Convention 102; however, the government aims to ratify all social protection related instruments. The current social security system is fragmented and the government is currently developing a comprehensive national social security system. The legal framework of this system will be based on the Social Protection Bill. This bill will provide for the gradual extension of social protection measures to workers who are currently excluded from protection. Challenges in extending social protection measures to workers in the informal economy have been identified and include: irregular and low income; lack of trust in the institutional framework; lack of knowledge about existing provision, institutions and procedures; absent or weak workers' organisations; isolation, fragmentation and current exclusion from systems. With reference to workers in the informal economy, a national approach is envisaged that can be adapted to the needs of categories of informal workers, such as self-employed or domestic workers. A unique benefits package is proposed based on a unified contribution. For many of these workers, immediate needs, including immediate expenditure, are often prioritised, and maintaining contributions to a scheme can be challenging. Allowing these workers to withdraw benefits in cases of emergencies can be useful. The system aims to overcome the challenges with reference to contribution by introducing a flat rate contribution for the self-employed based on the number of household members. With reference to workers in the informal economy with irregular incomes, strategies are proposed to introduce a levy on a specific job or project (Goursat and Pelterano 2016: 1–4). The government aims to implement a national maternity protection programme by 2018 (National Social Protection Policy 2014: 28).

27 This is also in line with the ILO Decent Work Agenda <https://www.ilo.org/legacy/english/lib/century/sources/sources1999.htm> and <https://www.ilo.org/public/libdoc/ilo/P/09605/09605(1999-87).pdf> accessed 17 June 2017. See the SADC Code on Social Security (2007), the SADC Protocol on Gender and Development (2008) and the SADC Charter of Fundamental Social Rights (2003).

employees and are not in traditional employment relationships as defined by legislative provisions. Olivier states:

> It could be argued that the term social protection also encapsulates elements and rights and ancillary to social security itself. Together with social security, the presence of these elements ensures adequate social protection. From a constitutional rights perspective, it is clear that there is a close interrelationship between the concept of social security and several other related concepts which constitute the bases of specific fundamental rights, such as the right to have access to land[28], to housing[29] and to health care services, and sufficient food and water.[30]

The starting point of the social protection framework in South Africa must be evaluated against the constitutional framework in section 27:

> (1) Everyone has the right to have access to –
> (a) health care services, including reproductive health care;
> (b) sufficient food and water; and
> (c) social security, including, if they are unable to support themselves and their dependants, appropriate social assistance.
> (2) The state must take reasonable legislative and other measures, within its available resources, to achieve the progressive realization of each of these rights.
> (3) No one may be refused emergency medical treatment.

However, it must be noted that other fundamental rights are also relevant to these workers with reference to social protection and includes the right to equality,[31] the right to human dignity,[32] the right to property,[33] the right to housing,[34] children's rights,[35] the right to education,[36] the right to just administrative action[37] and right to have access to courts.[38]

---

[28] Constitution of the Republic of South Africa (1996) Section 25(5).
[29] Section 26(1).
[30] Olivier (2003) 26. See also *Government of the Republic of South Africa v Grootboom*.
[31] Constitution of the Republic of South Africa (1996) Section 9.
[32] Section 10.
[33] Section 25.
[34] Section 26.
[35] Section 28.
[36] Section 29.
[37] Section 33.
[38] Section 34.

Social security in South Africa and also in other developing countries in the SADC region is premised on a formal based employment relationship, and most women workers in the informal economy are excluded. Work in the informal economy is diverse and it is submitted that the nine classic risks as initially identified by the ILO do not include the specific risks and vulnerabilities that these women experience.[39] The risks experienced by these workers can also be linked to the specific categories of work in the informal economy. Moreover, for example, waste pickers may be exposed to specific risks associated with the work that they do as a result of the hazardous circumstances that they are exposed to. Due to the diverse nature of the work it is envisaged that social protection measures may even vary from category to category of work in the informal economy. Women workers in the informal economy are often marginalised, and excluded from social insurance schemes, because these schemes are linked to the traditional formal employment relationship.

In South Africa, the social security framework is administered by the Department of Social Development, the Department of Labour and the South African Social Security Agency (SASSA).[40] In respect of South Africa, social security schemes comprise social insurance, social assistance and social relief.[41] A limited social security enquiry is considered below, including: occupational health and safety, unemployment insurance, social assistance and health care.

3.4.1. Occupational Health and Safety

In developing and middle income countries women workers are exposed to greater risks in respect of occupational health and safety at the place of work, often because of limited resources. The poor working conditions experienced by women in the informal economy are exacerbated by poverty, illiteracy, gender and race inequalities, and low socio-economic status within societies. In respect of certain categories of workers in the informal economy, such as domestic workers, street traders and waste pickers, the lack of recognition as workers by governments and policy makers often transcend into the lack of regulation in respect of occupational health and safety at the place of work.

---

39 Olivier et al. (2012).

40 See also Malherbe (2013) 117.

41 In terms of the Non-Profit Organisation Act 71 of 1997, social relief refers to 'alleviation of need of persons by means of the temporary tendering of material assistance to them'. See also Olivier (2003) 26.

In respect of statutory provisions, the Occupational Health and Safety Act 85 of 1993 and the Compensation for Occupational Injuries and Diseases Act 130 of 1993 (COIDA) provide provisions in respect of occupational health and safety at work. Domestic workers are covered by the Occupational Health and Safety Act; however, street traders and waste pickers, as own account workers, do not enjoy this protection.[42] Domestic workers, employed in private households in South Africa, although included under labour legislation remain excluded from the scope of the COIDA.[43] As the majority of domestic workers are black this exclusion is a form of racial discrimination. South Africa has a constitution that supports substantive equality and it is of the utmost importance to recognise the fundamental values of freedom, human dignity, social justice and non-discrimination when considering the protection of poor women workers in the informal economy.[44] Arguments

---

[42] Informal economy workers are also excluded from employment injury protection in most SADC countries. In Lesotho domestic workers are excluded from the Workmen's Compensation Act 13 of 1997. Street traders and waste pickers are excluded, as the status of an employee status is linked to a contract of employment. Malawi is currently addressing challenges in respect of employment injury protection, including the specific regulation of workers in the informal economy. In Zimbabwe, informal economy workers, including domestic workers, are expressly excluded from the Factories and Works Act 20 of 1948 (Mpedi and Nyenti 2016).

[43] The act aims to provide compensation for disabilities caused by employment injuries and diseases during employment. Section 1 excludes domestic workers from the definitional scope of employee. In 2018, the Minister of Labour published the Compensation for Occupational Injuries and Diseases Amendment Bill. The Bill now seeks 'to provide coverage to domestic employees'.

[44] The Constitution of the Republic of South Africa, 1996, Section 1. Section 9(1) provides that everyone is equal before the law and has the right to equal protection and benefit of the law. Section 9(2) states that equality includes the full and equal enjoyment of all rights and freedoms. When considering the extension of protection to vulnerable women workers in the informal economy it is important to acknowledge that the constitutional concept of equality includes both formal and substantive equality, and that substantive equality will require an analysis of the social and economic conditions of these women. See also van Niekerk et al. (2015) 117–119. The Constitutional Court have on a number of occasions confirmed the concept of substantive equality and gave meaning to the concept. See also *South African Police Service v Solidarity obo Barnard* (2014) par 29: 'At the point of transition, two decades ago, our society was divided and unequal among the adamant lines of race, gender and class. Beyond these plain structures there were indeed other markers of exclusion and oppression, some of which our Constitution lists. So clearly it has a transformative nature … In so

for the exclusion, namely the intimate nature of the relationship and the problematic nature of enforcement and compliance, are no longer valid. Domestic workers constitute a particular vulnerable group of workers[45] and represent a previously disadvantaged group, and this exclusion is unconstitutional and represents a discriminatory practice.[46] This exclusion also contravenes our international obligations in terms of conventions, as domestic workers are treated less favourably in this regard compared to other workers.

3.4.2. Unemployment Insurance

From 2003, domestic workers were included within the scope of the Unemployment Insurance Act 63[47] (hereafter UIA) and the Unemployment Insurance Contributions Act 4[48] (hereafter UICA). The purpose of the UIA is described in the following terms:

> The purpose of this Act is to establish an unemployment insurance fund to which employers and employees contribute and from which employees who become unemployed and their beneficiaries, as the case may be, are entitled to benefits and in so doing to alleviate the harmful economic and social effects of unemployment.[49]

The UIA and the UICA provide for provisions on contributions to be made to the fund by employers and employees, therefore demonstrating a

---

many words, it enjoins us to take active steps to achieve substantive equality, particularly for those disadvantaged by past unfair discrimination.' See also *Minister of Finance & another v Van Heerden* (2004).

45 The ILO highlighted the health and safety risks of domestic work in its report about decent work as follows: 'The work tends to involve a great deal of repetition, bending and reaching, lifting of heavy objects, extremes of heat (cooking, ironing), sharp objects (knives), handling potentially toxic cleaning products and prolonged exposure to dust' (ILO 2010: 62).

46 If the *Grootboom* test in respect of reasonable state measures, namely whether it provides for: 'those whose needs are the most urgent and whose ability to enjoy all rights therefore is most in peril is applied', the exclusion by COIDA is unconstitutional and cannot be described as reasonable measures by the state (*Government of the Republic of South Africa v Grootboom* 2000).

47 2001.

48 2002. In terms of the act: 'Domestic worker means an employee who performs domestic work in the home of her employer, and includes a: (a) gardener; (b) persons employed by a household as a driver of a motor vehicle; and (c) person who takes care of any person in that home.'

49 Section 2.

most straightforward form of social protection for workers, when they become unemployed through dismissal, disease or disability. Employers and employees are mandated to make contributions and the determination of the contribution to be made is 1% of the remuneration that an employee receives on a monthly basis.[50] By contributing, employees who become unemployed are entitled to a range of benefits which are listed in section 12 of the UIA, namely unemployment benefits, illness benefits, maternity benefits,[51] adoption benefits[52] and dependants' benefits. The act makes specific provision for domestic workers who work for multiple employers and provides that in instances of dismissal by one employer, the worker is entitled to benefits, despite still being employed by other employers.[53] This provision is important as it takes specific cognisance of the nature of domestic work and the reality that these workers often work for multiple employers. Specific provision is also made for domestic workers to claim unemployment benefits in the case of the death of the employer. This specific regulation once again recognises that domestic work is unlike other work.

Benefits are calculated on a sliding scale and may vary between 60% for lower income earners and at a lower rate for high income earners.[54] This provision provides additional benefits for women workers during maternity leave; however, it is submitted that it is still not sustainable and many women return to work prior to the end of the four month period due to financial restraints. Maternity benefits do not affect a women's entitlement to other categories of benefits; however, in cases where they have claimed benefits, such as unemployment, this may affect an unlimited claim in respect of maternity benefits.[55]

The Unemployment Insurance Amendment Act 10 of 2016 aims to extend coverage,[56] and endeavours to bring South Africa in line with its international and regional obligations.[57] Specifically important for

---

[50] Section 6 in the UICA.

[51] Section 12(1)(c). The maternity leave period is 17,32 weeks. Special provision is made for cases of miscarriage or stillborn children during the third trimester.

[52] Section 12(1)(d). Adoptions must occur in terms of the Child Care Act 74 of 1983.

[53] Section 12(1A).

[54] Section 12(3)(b).

[55] Section 13(5)(a), (b) and (c).

[56] Civil servants and learners are included.

[57] See ILO Social Security (Minimum Standards) Convention 102 (1952), ILO Maternity Protection Convention 183 (2000), ILO Social Protection Floors Recommendation 202 (2012), the International Covenant on Economic, Social

domestic workers is the amendment of section 12. This section now provides for maternity benefits to be paid at a rate of 66% of the earnings of the applicant, with reference to the maximum threshold. Unfortunately no provision is made for own account workers, including the waste pickers and street traders that represent a particularly vulnerable group of women.

The UIA provisions in respect of maternity benefits are not in line with the ILO Maternity Protection Convention 183 of 2000. The convention requires that member states ensure that the majority of women within the scope of the convention are able to meet the conditions,[58] and member states must provide adequate benefits for the women that are excluded, through social assistance.[59] The amendment act introduces a limitation in respect of the period of employment prior to the application and requires a minimum period of at least 13 weeks.[60] Women workers who apply for benefits and have not been in employment for a period of 13 weeks before the application will be without protection. This qualification does not ensure that a large majority of women meet the requirements for benefits as required by the convention. In terms of the convention, these women must then be provided with means tested social assistance. Maternity benefits are the only category of benefits that require a minimum employment period and the provision appears to be discriminatory against women during a very vulnerable time and therefore disregards any notion of solidarity in respect of this social responsibility born by women.[61] Section 24(4) provides for a maximum period of benefits of 17,32 weeks, and the actual benefit amount seems to be dependent on the period of contributions. The question arises whether these minimum periods provide adequate protection to these workers during maternity, and if not, whether social assistance is available?

Challenges with regard to domestic workers, in respect of unemployment insurance, furthermore include compliance and enforcement measures. Although domestic workers are included under the scope of coverage, receiving benefits is dependent on registration with the fund by

---

and Cultural Rights (1996), UN Convention on the Elimination of All Forms of Discrimination against Women (1979). Regional instruments include the SADC Protocol on Employment and Labour (2014) and the Code on Social Security (2007) in SADC.

58 Article 6(5).

59 Article 6(6).

60 See section 24 as amended.

61 Olivier and Govindjee (2015) 2747.

employers. In respect of waste pickers and street traders it is recommended that the UIA provides for these own account workers to contribute to the fund. It is submitted that the collection of contributions in this regard is challenging as their income is low and often irregular; however, measures must be introduced to accommodate these own account workers and other workers in the informal economy that are excluded.[62] The exclusion increases the vulnerabilities of these women and contributes to their marginalisation. The majority of women workers in the informal economy identified by this contribution includes black women, and many of these women, as own account workers, are engaged in survivalist activities such as waste picking and street trading. In addition to that, statistics also indicate that black women in South Africa have the highest birth rate.[63]

Due to the inequalities, stereotyping and prejudices that still exist within these communities, many of these women do not have control over their reproduction choices and the apartheid legacy of migrant labour strategies means that a large number of them are single mothers. These vulnerable women require state intervention with specific reference to maternity benefits. The South African Law Reform Commission invited submissions in 2017 with reference to the inclusion of self-employed persons in respect of maternity and paternity benefits with reference to South Africa's constitutional, international and regional obligations.[64] The research proposal by the South African Law Reform Commission identified important challenges with respect to the extension of coverage to these workers, namely the challenges in respect of contributions from low income and irregular wage earners, and administrative challenges, such as maintaining and updating information.

3.4.3. Social Assistance

There are a number of grants administered in terms of the Social Assistance Act 13[65] (hereafter SAA), namely the child support

---

[62] Social insurance schemes that cover self-employed or own account workers are more prevalent in the European Union (South African Law Reform Commission Research Proposal Paper Project 2017: 7).

[63] Ibid 14.

[64] Ibid.

[65] 2004. See also the South African Social Security Act 9 of 2004. In terms of section 5 of the Social Assistance Act, the criteria for social assistance include: 'that applicants meet the specific requirement of each grant and must reside in South Africa. The Minister may prescribe additional requirements in

grant,[66] foster child grant,[67] care dependency grant,[68] disability grant,[69] a grant in aid,[70] a war veteran's grant[71] and the older person's grant.[72] Social relief is also available for persons in dire need who require temporary assistance.[73]

The majority of grant recipients are women and specifically African women when race, gender and class join as remaining legacies of apartheid.[74] Grants are means tested, except for the foster child grant and the grant in aid. Applicants in most instances must be South African citizens, permanent residents[75] or refugees currently residing in South Africa. Most domestic workers will qualify for social assistance as their minimum incomes provided for by the sectoral determination complies with the means test. Street traders and waste pickers that comply with the

---

respect of means testing; age limits; disabilities; various measures of proof; and measures to prevent fraud.'

66 Section 6. The value of the grant is R380 per month.

67 The value of this grant is R920 per month. This grant is not means tested. See also section 8.

68 The value of this grant is R1 600 per month and the grant is means tested. This grant is provided to the caregivers of children with disabilities and who cannot be cared for by a state institution. See section 7 of the SAA and regulation 8.

69 The value of the grant is R1 600 per month and recipients must be between 18 and 59. The person must be unable to work and a medical officer must make the determination. See section 9 of the SAA and Regulation 3.

70 The value of the grant is R380 per month. The recipient must require care and attendance due to a physical or mental condition See section 12 and regulation 5.

71 The value of the grant is R1 620 per month and recipients must be over 60 or disabled. See section 11 of the act and regulation 4.

72 The value of this grant is R1 600 per month if you are 60 years and older. Persons older than 75 receive an additional R20 per month. See section 10 and regulation 2.

73 Temporary assistance includes assistance while awaiting the child care grant to be processed, the occurrence of a crisis or disaster, you do not qualify for a grant but need assistance, and where a disability lasts for less than six months and the breadwinner in the family has died. Beneficiaries cannot simultaneously receive a grant and social relief. Social relief is granted for three months and may be extended for another three if so required. See section 13 of the act and regulation 9. See also SASSA <http://www.sassa.gov.za> accessed on 10 October 2017.

74 Section 27(1)(c) of the Constitution provides for social assistance if people are unable to support themselves and their dependants.

75 See *Khosa v Minister of Social Development; Mahlaule v Minister of Social Development* (2004).

criteria will also be eligible for social grants. These women workers can qualify for the child support grant and, in 2016, 98% of recipients were women.[76] This grant does have an impact on the well-being of the children, reduces income poverty, specifically for the very poor and women headed households, but also provides the recipients with decision-making ability within the household.[77] All three categories of workers may also qualify for the foster grant and this grant is not means tested. In instances where these workers care for a disabled child, they may apply for the care dependency grant. In respect of these workers, care will often then be provided by a third party as the domestic worker, street trader or waste picker is working. These cash transfers do provide relief; however, they do not automatically affect the redistribution of labour.[78] Quality public services, including health care, access to education, access to resources and child care will provide these women with improved agency to participate in all aspects of productive life.[79]

Domestic workers, waste pickers and street traders are excluded from the COIDA; however, they may benefit from the disability grant if they are no longer able to work due to a mental or physical disability.[80] This is also applicable to waste pickers and street traders.

The older persons grant is particularly important for women who are 60 years and older as South Africa does not have a national retirement funding scheme.[81] Statistics indicate that 71,9% of older persons receive the grant and 94,5% of poor women received the grant in 2015.[82] These workers are vulnerable, low income earners and there is no statutory obligation for them to join and contribute to a pension or provident fund. Employers of domestic workers are also not obliged to contribute to a retirement fund in respect of these workers. They will have to meet the criteria of the means test; however, it is submitted that most of these

---

76 Patel et al. (2016).

77 WIEGO <https://www.wiego.org/core-programmes/socialprotection> accessed 10 June 2017.

78 Ibid.

79 Ibid.

80 See also Malherbe (2013: 131). The current value of this grant is R1 600. In terms of COIDA, the highest percentage of previous income is 75%; a domestic worker would have to earn R2 133,33 to receive an amount equal to the grant.

81 See also Malherbe (2013: 132). Retirement funds in South Africa can be categorised in two ways, namely defined benefits or defined contributions.

82 Poverty Trends in South Africa an Examination of Absolute Poverty between 2006 and 2015 STATS SA (2017) 36 <https://www.statssa.gov.za/publications/Report-03-10-06> accessed 10 August 2017.

workers will qualify as the earnings are below the single limit of R73 800 (monthly income of R 6 150) and combined income of not more than R147 600 (monthly income of R12 300). These women workers in all three categories have limited access to other retirement benefits and this older person's grant plays an important role in alleviating poverty amongst these women. Even if these workers were to contribute to retirement funds, their low and irregular wages would result in limited benefits.

In 2012 the Department of Labour invited submissions in respect to the establishment of a retirement fund for domestic workers and farm workers.[83] This decision was based on the recognition that these workers are unique and require specific provisions. Although this would provide for domestic workers and farm workers, other workers in the informal economy, such as street traders and waste pickers, will remain excluded from any coverage, whilst public role players focus on a specific category of worker in the informal economy.

3.4.4. Health Care

Health care is an important component of social protection. Women workers in the informal economy who suffer from ill health will not be able to earn a livelihood. Section 27(1) of the Constitution provides that everyone has the right to have access to health care services.[84] Particularly important for these women is adequate maternity health care. Before 1994, South Africa's fragmented health care system mostly benefited the white population in the country. After 1994, attempts were made to address the inequalities created by apartheid. Free primary health care was available for pregnant women, children under six and people with disabilities.[85] Health facilities were extended to rural areas through the infrastructure of clinics and community based services were launched in poorer areas.[86]

Health care services in South Africa are divided between public and private health care, where a small percentage of middle and high income

---

83 GN 736 in *GG* 33480 of 20 August 2010.

84 Section 27(2) obliges the state to take reasonable measures, including legislative measures within its available resources to give effect to these rights. Section 27(3) states that no one may be refused emergency medical treatment. See also *Soobramoney v Minister of Health, KwaZulu-Natal* (1998).

85 See the White Paper on National Health Insurance No 123 *GG* 39506 11 December 2015 5.

86 Ibid.

earners enjoy private health care and the poor are dependent on the public system funded by the State. This illustrates the persistent inequalities in South Africa along racial and gender lines. Social and cultural norms within societies contribute to the fact that the health needs of women are not adequately addressed in South Africa and specifically in respect of women workers in the informal economy.

South Africa is currently realising universal coverage through the National Health Insurance (NHI) Scheme.[87] This fund aims to cover all South Africans, irrespective of their income or unemployment status, and will contribute to the alleviation of poverty and the promotion of equality with reference to gender and race. Public and private health care providers will be included and the current disparities between public and private care will be eliminated to promote equality. The fund will mostly be funded through taxes, and low income earners will not contribute directly to the fund; however, persons earning above a threshold amount will be legally obliged to contribute. Individuals may continue to contribute to their private medical schemes, but will also have to contribute to the NHI. NHI payments will be higher for high income earners. Employers will match the contributions of the employees and ensure that contributions are made by employees, similarly to UIF contributions. The fund will cover all South Africans, legal residents, refugees and asylum seekers with valid permits. All workers in the informal economy will benefit from the fund and low income earners will thus not contribute directly to the fund, supporting a notion of solidarity. It is submitted that this fund will provide equal opportunities for all in respect of adequate health services in South Africa and will promote the constitutional values of equality and human dignity as well as social justice, and supports section 27(1)(a).

3.5. OTHER MEASURES

Other social protection measures do exist. It must be noted that these workers are included under the scope of the Road Accident Fund Act 56

---

[87] The NHI, a non-profit public entity, aims to provide access to comprehensive quality, affordable health services for all South Africans irrespective of their socio-economic status. Reasons for the establishment of this fund include the inequality between private and public health care services, the quality of care in public services, the high cost of health care in South Africa and the increase of out of pocket payments in the country. See the White Paper on National Health Insurance No 123 *GG* 39506 11 December 2015.

of 1996 (as amended) in respect of traffic accidents. South Africa also launched an Expanded Public Works Programme (EPWP) in 2004. The goal of this programme was to target specific vulnerable categories and women were identified as the largest beneficiaries.[88] The National Development Plan of 2012 aimed to provide a framework for decent work, sustainable livelihoods and to alleviate poverty and eradicate income inequality. The recommendations for women included:

(a) public employment must include a focus on women;
(b) women should participate in the transformation of the economy and be empowered;
(c) women must be supported as leaders in society;
(d) all barriers such as cultural and educational challenges must be adequately addressed; and
(e) quality early childhood education can relieve women of their unpaid care duties and allow them to enter the labour market.[89]

Unfortunately, studies have indicated that public works programmes do not offer sustainable long term solutions and the designs often do not allow for improving workers' employability. A more integrated approach is required.[90]

3.6. CONCLUDING REMARKS

When we consider social protection for women workers in the informal economy, certain important factors must be considered. These factors include the feminisation of poverty,[91] the impact of poverty affecting women more adversely, the burden placed on women in respect of care and domestic work, that more women are prevalent in atypical work, and their limited access to resources. It is imperative that strategies and policies aimed at addressing the decent work deficits and vulnerabilities of women recognise the structural inequalities at all levels and aim at the empowerment of these women to ensure equality and decent work for them.

---

88 Parenzee and Budlender (2016) 11, 12, 13.

89 Ibid. 23.

90 Ibid. 30.

91 Women are also more likely to work in low skilled jobs, specifically in the informal economy.

Coordination between social protection objectives and measures and gender equality and empowerment strategies are required. Social protection measures for these women must promote substantive equality.

If we consider the extension of labour and social protection measures, conceptual exclusions in existing legislative provisions, policies and regulations must firstly be addressed. Conceptual presumptions as to the notion of an 'employee' will probably not benefit street traders or waste pickers as own account workers.

Innovative and tailor-made provisions in respect of social protection measures must include specific benefit packages compatible with the need of women workers in the informal economy and allow for contribution structures to accommodate their irregular and low income.[92]

Social protection measures aimed at providing protection to women workers must address specific gender issues to be successful. Policies must focus on the disadvantages suffered by these women and a gender neutral approach will be inadequate to address their specific disadvantages in line with substantive equality.

Accordingly, when one considers the South African position it appears to provide an adequate regulatory framework in respect to the regulation of certain workers; however, in practice there are various challenges, including the enforcement of the legislative provision and the disregard for the notion of substantive equality. These provisions do not consider the social–economic circumstances of these workers and therefore cannot provide adequate protection. A mere extension of an existing legislative framework runs the risk to promote only formal equality and does not support transformative constitutionalism. This approach can be perilous for all women workers in the informal economy as they often present a previously disadvantaged group due to race, caste and gender, and their circumstances require scrutiny to adequately regulate their positions and to ensure equality.

BIBLIOGRAPHY

Books and Chapters

Banik D (ed) *The Legal Empowerment Agenda Poverty, Labour and the Informal Economy in Africa* (Ashgate, 2011).

Becker U et al. (eds) *International Standard-Setting and Innovations in Social Security* (Kluwer 2013).

92 Olivier et al. (2012) 12.

Becker U, Pennings F and Dijkhof T (eds) *International Standard Setting and Innovations in Social Security* (Wolters Kluwer 2012) 25.

Du Toit D et al. (eds) *Exploited, Undervalued – and Essential: Domestic Workers and the Realisation of their Rights* (PULP 2013).

Dupper O and Garbers C (eds) *Equality in the Workplace: Reflections from South Africa and Beyond* (Juta 2009).

Hill, E *Women Identity, Agency and Economic Development Women's Empowerment in the Indian Informal Economy* (Routledge 2010).

Kalula E et al. 'Towards an Effective Regulatory Framework for Labour Rights and Social Protection in Southern Africa' in Dan Banik (ed), *The Legal Empowerment Agenda: Poverty, Labour and the Informal Economy in Africa* (Ashgate, 2011).

Malherbe K 'Implementing Domestic Workers' Social Security Rights in a Framework of Transformative Constitutionalism' in Darcy du Toit et al. (eds), *Exploited, Undervalued –and Essential: Domestic Workers and the Realisation of their Rights* (PULP, 2013).

Mpedi L and Nyenti M *Employment Injury Protection in Eastern and Southern African Countries* (SunMeDIA 2016).

Olivier M 'The Concept of Social Security' in Marius Olivier and other (eds), *Social Security: A Legal Analysis* (LexisNexis, 2003).

Olivier M and other (eds), *Social Security: A Legal Analysis* (LexisNexis 2003) 26.

Parenzee P and Budlender D (eds) *Who Cares? South Africa's Expanded Public Works Programme in the Social Sector and its Impact on Women* (Heinrich Böll Stiftung 2016).

Van Niekerk A et al. (eds) *Law@work 3rd edition* (LexisNexis 2015).

Journals and Papers

Chen M 'The Informal Economy: Definitions, Theories and Policies' (2012) WIEGO Working Paper No 1.

Dias S and Ogando A 'Rethinking Gender and Waste: Exploratory Findings from Participatory action research in Brazil' (2015) 9 Work Organisation, Labour & Globalisation 54.

Ogando A, Roever S and Rogan M 'Gender and Informal Livelihoods: Coping Strategies and Perceptions of Waste Pickers in Sub-Saharan Africa and Latin America' (2017) 37(7/8) International Journal of Sociology and Social Policy 435–451.

Olivier M and Govindjee A 'A Critique of the Unemployment Insurance Amendment Bill, 2015' (2015) 18(7) Potchefstroom Electronic Law Journal 2739–2776.

Vanek J et al. 'Statistics on the Informal Economy: Definitions: Regional Estimates and Challenges' (2014) WIEGO.

International Instruments

Convention on the Elimination of all forms of Discrimination against Women (1979)
Convention on the Elimination of all forms of Racial Discrimination against Women (1965)
Convention on the Rights of Persons with Disabilities (2006)
Convention on the Rights of the Child (1989)
Declaration of Commitment on HIV and AIDS (2001)
Declaration of Philadelphia
Domestic Work Convention 189 (2011)
Domestic Workers Recommendation 201 (2011)
International Covenant on Civil and Political Rights (1966)
International Covenant on Economic, Social and Cultural Rights (1996)
International Covenant on the Protection of the Rights of all Migrant Workers and Members of their Families (1990)
Maternity Protection Convention 183 (2000)
Occupational Safety and Health Convention 155 (1981)
Recommendation 204 of 2015 Concerning the Transition from the Informal to the Formal Economy
Social Protection Floors Recommendation 202 (2012)
Social Security (Minimum Standards) Convention 102 (1952)
Universal Declaration of Human Rights (1948)

Regional Instruments

African Charter on Human and People's Rights (1981)
Charter of Fundamental Social Rights (2003)
Code on HIV and AIDS and Employment in SADC (1997)
Code on Social Security (2007)
Declaration on Gender and Development (1997)
Draft Protocol on the Facilitation of Movement of Persons (2005)
Protocol on Education and Training (1997)
Protocol on Employment and Labour (2014)
Protocol on Gender and Development (2008)
Protocol on Health (1999)
Protocol on the Rights of Women in Africa (2003)
SADC Treaty (1992)
The Social Protection Plan for the Informal Economy and Rural Workers 2011–2015

Other

Goursat MP and Pelterano L ILO 2016 Extension of Social Protection to Workers in the Informal Economy in Zambia Lessons Learnt from Field Research on Domestic Workers, Small Scale Farmers and Construction Workers (2016) (ILO Geneva) 1–41.

ILO *Decent Work and the Informal Economy* (2002) International Labour Conference 90th Session 1.
ILO Decent Work for Domestic Workers Report IV (2010) 62.
ILO *General Survey concerning Social Security Instruments in the Light of the 2008 Declaration on Social Justice for a Fair Globalization* (2011) International Labour Conference, 100th session.
ILO *Social Protection for Domestic Workers Key Policy Trends and Statistics* (2016b) Social Protection Policy Papers (ILO Geneva).
ILO *Transitioning from the Informal to the Formal Economy* (2014) (ILO Geneva).
ILO *Women at Work Trends 2016* (2016a) (ILO Geneva).
ILO *2017 World Employment Social Outlook* (2017) (ILO Geneva).
ILO *World Social Security Report* 2014-2015 (2014) (ILO Geneva).
National Social Protection Policy (2014) (Minister of Community Development, Mother and Child Health) republic of Zambia.
Patel L et al. 'Gendered Social Protection and Economic Outcomes of Social Protection in South Africa' (2016) International Conference: Comprehensive Social Protection in the SADC, SASPEN Friedrich Ebert Stiftung.
South African Law Reform Commission Research Proposal Paper Project *143 Maternity and Paternity Benefits for Self-Employed Workers* (2017).
Van de Meerendonk A et al. 'Towards a Malawian Social Protection Floor: Assessment of Social Protection Programmes in Malawi' (2016) ILO Report 8 (ILO Geneva) 25, 28.
White Paper on National Health Insurance no 123 *GG* 39506 11 December 2015 5.

Legislation

Child Care Act 74 of 1983
Constitution of the Republic of South Africa, 1996
Compensation for Occupational Injuries and Diseases Act 130 of 1993
Factories and Works Act 20 of 1948
Non-Profit Organisation Act 71 of 1997
Occupational Health and Safety Act 85 of 1993
Road Accident Fund Act of 1996
Social Assistance Act 13 of 2004
Social Security Agency Act 9 of 2004
Unemployment Insurance Act 63 of 2001
Unemployment Insurance Amendment Act 10 of 2016
Unemployment Insurance Contributions Act 4 of 2002
Workmen's Compensation Act 13 of 1997

Cases

Government of the Republic of South Africa v Grootboom 2000 11 BCLR 1169 (CC)

Khosa v Minister of Social Development; Mahlaule v Minister of Social Development 2004 (6) BCLR 569 (CC)
Makwickana v eThekwini Municipality 2015 (3) SA 165 (KZD) par 115
Minister of Finance & another v Van Heerden 2004 12 BLLR 1181 (CC)
Soobramoney v Minister of Health, KwaZulu-Natal 1998 (1) SA 765 (CC)
South African Police Service v Solidarity obo Barnard 2014 6 SA 123 (CC)

Internet Sources

African Union 2016 https://www.au.int.
Budlender D 2011 *Measuring the Economic and Social Value of Domestic Work* https://www.ilo.org/global/topics/domestic-workers.
ILO Report VI 2009 *Gender Equality at the Heart of Decent Work* https://www.ilo.org/wcmsps/groups/publicwcms_105119.
ILO Report 2013 *Domestic Workers across the World: Global and Regional Statistics and the Extent of Legal Protection* https://www.ilo.org/global publications/books/WCMS.
Olivier M et al. 'Informality, Employment and Social Protection: Some Critical Perspectives for/from Developing Countries' (2012) <http://www.ilera2012.wharton.upem.edu> accessed 17 June 2017.
Poverty Trends in South Africa an Examination of Absolute Poverty between 2006 and 2015 STATS SA (2017) 36 https://www.statssa.gov.za/publications/Report-03-10-06.
Roever S (2014) *Informal Economy Workers Monitoring Study Sector Report: Street Vendors* (WIEGO) <https:// wiego.org/publications/iems-sector-report-street-vendors> accessed 17 June 2017.
Rogan M and P Cichello P 'Can Informal Employment actually Reduce Poverty?' 16 February 2017 WIEGO <http://www.wiego.org/blog/can-informal-employment-actually-reduce-poverty> accessed 23 October 2017.
SASSA https:// www.sassa.gov.za.
STATS SA Quarterly Labour Force Survey 2016 <https://www.statssa.gov.za> accessed 10 June 2017.
STATS SA Quarterly Labour Force Survey 2017 <http//www.statsa.gov.za> accessed November 2017.
STATS SA Quarterly Labour Force Survey 2018 <https://www.statssa.gov.za> accessed 5 June 2018
UN Resolution on Transforming our World, the 2030 Agenda for Sustainable Development https://sustainabledevelopment.un.org/post2015.
UN Treaties https://treaties.un.org.
UN *Trends in Maternal Mortality: 1990-2013 Estimates by WHO, UNICEF, The World Bank and the United Nations Population Division* https://www.who.int.
UN Women https://www.un.org
WIEGO *About the Informal Economy* https://wiego.org/informal-economy/about informal.
World Economic Forum *Why We Need Better Social Safety Nets in Cities* https://www.weforum.org.

4. The self-employed and the welfare state in the EU: insights from gender and race equality law

Alysia Blackham and Catherine Barnard

1. INTRODUCTION

The growth in self-employment in European Union (EU) Member States has the potential to fundamentally challenge the existing scope and implementation of welfare structures. In the EU28, the self-employed formed 16.1 per cent of total employment in 2015.[1] At the domestic level in the UK, there has been an increase from 3.8 million self-employed in 2008 to 4.6 million in 2015.[2] This rise is seen as one of the 'defining characteristics of the UK's economic recovery' following the 2008 financial crisis.[3] However, the growth in self-employment is part of a longer-term trend in the UK economy, with self-employment increasing from 11.9 per cent of all employment in 2000 to 14.9 per cent of all employment in March 2016.

The growth in self-employment is accompanied by a breaking down of the traditional binary divide between 'employees' and the 'self-employed'. Jobs that would have traditionally been performed by 'employees' are now being done by 'sole-traders': in some cases, companies are even asking employees to incorporate themselves as sole traders, so that employers can avoid paying benefits such as statutory maternity pay or sick pay.[4]

The UK government is closely attuned to the complex challenges posed by an increase in self-employment. The Taylor Review of Modern

---

1 OECD (2019).
2 Office for National Statistics (2016).
3 Ibid.
4 Elgot (2017).

Working Practices, launched in November 2016, inquired into the modern labour market – including the gig economy – and considered the implications of new forms of work for workers' rights and responsibilities. It concluded that there was a need to improve the rights and entitlements of the self-employed, including by government encouraging the self-employed to 'plan for the future'.[5] In the 2017 spring budget, the UK Chancellor announced a tax rise for self-employed workers, with national insurance contributions increasing from 9 per cent of earnings to 10 per cent in April 2018, and then to 11 per cent in 2019. In exchange for this, it was announced that there would be a consultation on improving maternity allowances for the self-employed, which could potentially reduce existing differences between state benefits for the employed and the self-employed. These proposed reforms were later abandoned, at least for the present, due to public and political backlash.

This incident provides two key lessons: first, that governments are attuned to the need to review social welfare provision for the self-employed, to secure their access to some social security benefits, and are aware of the challenges facing the self-employed; and, second, that introducing reform in this area is highly political, and likely to encounter substantial resistance in practice.

The UK is not alone in struggling to address the problems posed by an expansion of self-employment and sometimes false self-employment. Some jurisdictions, including the UK, have adopted a tripartite approach to classifying work relationships, with a second 'worker' category to accommodate this blurring of boundaries between employment and self-employment. So, a tripartite system covers: (1) employees; (2) (self-employed) workers; and (3) self-employed (entrepreneurs). The first category concerns those who are the usual subject of employment law. The second 'worker' category includes those who are self-employed but who are largely dependent on one particular 'employer' or work provider. The third category concerns those self-employed persons who are genuinely self-employed and work for a number of 'employers', more naturally called customers or clients. In some systems they might be covered by civil or commercial law and thus fall outside the realm of employment law altogether.

The use of a tripartite classification model helps to capture and extend some employment and welfare benefits to 'workers', who would traditionally have likely been employed as employees. However, it does not help to accommodate those who are working as genuine self-employed or

---

[5] Taylor (2017) 74.

entrepreneurs, who have generally been beyond the scope of employment and social protection. It is in this group that an increasing number of women now find themselves; among the self-employed, women are the most vulnerable (see Section 2).

It is in this lacuna that EU legislative provisions are increasingly seeking to operate. For example, the key provisions of the little known Directive 2010/41 on the application of the principle of equal treatment between men and women engaged in an activity in a self-employed capacity are aimed at ensuring social and maternity protection for the self-employed. The problem, however, with extending protection to the self-employed relates to the identification of the duty-holder (i.e. the person/institution responsible for delivering on the equality duties): if the duty-holder is the state, then extending protection does not pose any particular issues. However, if the duty-holder is an employer – as is the case with the right to equal treatment – then identifying the duty-holder becomes far more problematic. This may be why rights to equal treatment in Directive 2010/41 are limited to *access* to self-employment (enforceable 'vertically' against the state or professional regulatory bodies), not the *exercise* of self-employment (generally enforceable 'horizontally' against private individuals).[6]

In this chapter, then, drawing on insights from a gender-based analysis, we question the extent to which welfare provision extends to female 'entrepreneurs', as opposed to (dependent) 'workers'.[7] These results are compared with findings from an analysis of EU race equality law, particularly as it relates to social protection for the self-employed. We argue for a broad understanding of the term 'self-employed worker', so as to include the maximum number of workers possible within welfare structures. This may help to accommodate the new reality of work for many self-employed women but, as the British example shows, it comes with a price attached. We also flag the comparative neglect of issues of ethnicity as they relate to the self-employed at EU level, and consider why a racial lens is important for the future development of the welfare state.

6 Barnard and Blackham (2017).

7 This analysis is based on Barnard and Blackham (2015).

2. THE WELFARE STATE AND THE FEMALE SELF-EMPLOYED

The notion of the 'welfare state' is one means of capturing the political phenomena of state involvement in social provision.[8] The 'welfare state' could deploy instruments such as a minimum income; protection from the risks of old age, sickness, disability and unemployment; and providing services, such as education and healthcare; or some combination of these.[9] Increasingly, however, the modern welfare state also encompasses some protection from the economic risks of caring and parenting, including through maternity, paternity or parental leave, and carers' leave.[10]

There is a growing trend in academic scholarship to recognise the gendered dimensions of the welfare state. This scholarship focuses both on the relationship of women to the welfare state, and on how the welfare state creates and reinforces gendered relations for both women and men.[11] While a gender lens offers significant potential to advance research and analysis of the welfare state, particularly through critique of the breadwinner model underlying much social welfare provision, it is especially useful when considering new or increasing segments of the labour market, such as the self-employed.

There are fundamental gender differences between male and female self-employed. First, men are far more likely to be self-employed: in Organisation for Economic Co-operation and Development (OECD) economies, the rate of self-employment for women (10 per cent of total employment) is almost half that for men (18 per cent).[12] Further, self-employed men are far more likely to employ others (at 5.58 per cent of total employment) than self-employed women (at 2.15 per cent).[13] Further, in the majority of OECD countries, 70 per cent or more of self-employed women work in the services sector, compared with only 50 per cent for men.[14] Thus, women are less likely to be self-employed, less likely to employ others, and more likely to work in the services sector, which may be more likely to be associated with low pay.

---

8 Sainsbury (2008) 95.

9 Briggs (1961) 221, 228. See also Sainsbury (2008) 96.

10 Sainsbury (2008) 111.

11 Ibid., 100; Orloff (1996) 51. See further Orloff (2009) 317; Sainsbury (1994).

12 OECD (2016) 122.

13 Ibid.

14 Ibid.

This may mean that the female self-employed are generally more vulnerable than their male counterparts, and may have more need for the protection of the welfare state in undertaking their self-employed activity. Further, maternity and parental rights are particularly significant for the female self-employed (as women generally tend to take on a larger share of caring responsibilities, and are biologically more likely to require some maternity or parental leave). Thus, for them, the extent and coverage of the welfare state is a matter of some significance.

Indeed, some entrepreneurs generally may be equally vulnerable to the risks addressed by the welfare state as workers and employees. Not all self-employed are driven to their work arrangement by positive factors, such as increased income or flexibility. In the UK Labour Force Survey 2016 October to December, self-employed respondents were asked for the first reason they became self-employed in their main job. While 20.3 per cent (or 1117 respondents) cited better work conditions or job satisfaction as their main reason for becoming self-employed, 22.2 per cent were driven by the nature of their job or chosen career, implying that becoming self-employed was not an active decision, but related to the nature of their work. Further, 7.6 per cent were driven by redundancy, and 5 per cent as they could not find other employment.[15] Thus, not all individuals make a positive choice to be self-employed. Indeed, some self-employed undertake this arrangement as a measure of last resort.

Thus, some self-employed entrepreneurs may occupy a vulnerable position in the labour market, and deserve protection from the risks addressed by the welfare state. As the Taylor Review noted, there is significant diversity among the self-employed. Some have greater financial security than traditional employees. Many, though, are heavily dependent on the protection of the welfare state. For example, in the UK, median annual earnings from self-employment have been falling, from £14,535 in 2007/8 to only £10,800 in 2013/14.[16] Thus, the Taylor Review concluded that 'While many self-employed people would not expect sick pay, paid annual leave or automatic enrolment to a pension, for others, the availability of this safety net is essential to make sure they can pay their rent, put food on the table or plan for the future.' Thus, the scope of the welfare state becomes particularly important for this group of vulnerable self-employed.

---

15 Other reasons included: saw the demand of the market, better work conditions or job satisfaction, to maintain or increase income, job after retirement, other, and started or joined a family business. See further Wales and Amankwah (2016).

16 Taylor (2017) 75.

Drawing on data provided by the European Network of Legal Experts in the Field of Gender Equality, obtained as part of an analysis of the implementation of Directive 2010/41 on the application of the principle of equal treatment between men and women engaged in an activity in a self-employed capacity, we consider the scope and coverage of the 'welfare state' as it relates to female self-employed workers.

3. SCOPE AND COVERAGE OF THE 'WELFARE STATE' THROUGH A GENDER LENS

We have previously argued that, despite the title of the Directive 2010/41, which focuses on equal treatment, the main goals of the Directive are in fact:[17]

1. encouraging female entrepreneurship;
2. protecting 'assisting' spouses and life partners; and
3. providing maternity rights to female self-employed workers and spouses and life partners of self-employed workers.

Goals (2) and (3), which relate to the scope and coverage of the welfare state, are addressed by Articles 7 and 8 of the Directive.

Article 7, which concerns social protection, says:

> 1. Where a system for social protection for self-employed workers exists in a Member State, that Member State shall take the necessary measures to ensure that spouses and life partners referred to in Article 2(b) can benefit from a social protection in accordance with national law.
> 2. The Member States may decide whether the social protection referred to in paragraph 1 is implemented on a mandatory or voluntary basis.

Article 8, which relates to maternity benefits, says:

> 1. The Member States shall take the necessary measures to ensure that female self-employed workers and female spouses and life partners referred to in Article 2 may, in accordance with national law, be granted a sufficient maternity allowance enabling interruptions in their occupational activity owing to pregnancy or motherhood for at least 14 weeks.
> 2. The Member States may decide whether the maternity allowance referred to in paragraph 1 is granted on a mandatory or voluntary basis.

---

[17] Barnard and Blackham (n 6).

3. The allowance referred to in paragraph 1 shall be deemed sufficient if it guarantees an income at least equivalent to:
   (a) the allowance which the person concerned would receive in the event of a break in her activities on grounds connected with her state of health and/or;
   (b) the average loss of income or profit in relation to a comparable preceding period subject to any ceiling laid down under national law and/or;
   (c) any other family related allowance established by national law, subject to any ceiling laid down under national law.
4. The Member States shall take the necessary measures to ensure that female self-employed workers and female spouses and life partners referred to in Article 2 have access to any existing services supplying temporary replacements or to any existing national social services. The Member States may provide that access to those services is an alternative to or a part of the allowance referred to in paragraph 1 of this Article.

To consider the effectiveness of these provisions in extending welfare state coverage to the self-employed, we must first consider the personal scope of the Directive (i.e. who is entitled to these rights under the Directive).

A. Personal Scope of Directives Relating to Social Security

Equal treatment directives that relate to social security differ in their personal scope. For example, Article 6 of the General or 'Recast' Equality Directive 2006/54 contains a different personal scope for the purposes of equal treatment in occupational social security to other areas. It provides that:

> This Chapter [on equal treatment in social security schemes] shall apply to members of the working population, including *self-employed persons*, persons whose activity is interrupted by illness, maternity, accident or involuntary unemployment and persons seeking employment and to retired and disabled workers, and to those claiming under them, in accordance with national law and/or practice. (Emphasis added)

The broad scope, including the reference to the self-employed, is weakened by the exclusions in Article 8 and the deferral options in Article 11. Article 8, for example, excludes from the scope of the Chapter a range of schemes, including individual contracts for the self-employed; single-member schemes for the self-employed; insurance contracts to which the employer is not a party; optional provisions of occupational social security schemes; and occupational social security schemes financed by voluntary worker contributions. Article 11 provides deferral options for Member States in relation to pensionable age for old-age or retirement benefits; survivors' pensions; and actuarial calculation factors.

Reflecting the terms of Article 6 of the Recast Directive 2006/54, Article 2 of Directive 79/7 on equal treatment in social security also provides:

> This Directive shall apply to the working population – including *self-employed persons, workers and self-employed persons* whose activity is interrupted by illness, accident or involuntary unemployment and persons seeking employment – and to retired or invalided workers and self-employed persons. (Emphasis added)

Directive 2010/41 differs from other instruments in its personal scope. Article 2 – which is headed 'scope' – says:

> This Directive covers:
>
> (a) self-employed workers, namely all persons pursuing a gainful activity for their own account, under the conditions laid down by national law;
> (b) the spouses of self-employed workers or, when and in so far as recognised by national law, the life partners of self-employed workers, not being employees or business partners, where they habitually, under the conditions laid down by national law, participate in the activities of the self-employed worker and perform the same tasks or ancillary tasks.

The rights to social protection and maternity benefits in Articles 7 and 8 of the Directive apply to those listed in Article 2, that is, self-employed workers, their spouses or life partners. The language of Articles 7 and 8 expressly makes this link.[18] This raises the question as to who are 'self-employed *workers*'. Returning to the tripartite formula outlined above, does the phrase apply to only the second category (dependent 'worker') or does it also apply to the third category (entrepreneurs)?

The arguments against such a broad reading to include both the second and third groups are that the reference to 'self-employed *workers*' appears to limit the personal scope. The case law does appear to be coalescing around the *Allonby*[19] approach to 'worker', which is based on

---

[18] For example, Article 7 provides: 'Where a system for social protection for self-employed workers exists in a Member State, that Member State shall take the necessary measures to ensure that spouses and life partners referred to in Article 2(b) can benefit from a social protection in accordance with national law.'

[19] Case C-256/01 *Allonby v Accrington & Rosendale College* [2004] ECR I-873.

some form of subordination. *Allonby* concerned Article 4 of the Recast Directive 2006/54, which concerns the personal scope for equal pay provisions in the Directive. Drawing on its own definition of 'worker' developed in the context of the free movement of workers case law, the Court ruled in *Allonby* that:[20]

> For the purposes of that provision, there must be considered as a worker a person who, for a certain period of time, performs services for and under the direction of another person in return for which he receives remuneration (see, in relation to free movement of workers, in particular cases *Lawrie-Blum*,[21] and *Martínez Sala*[22]).

The Court added: 'The formal classification of a self-employed person under national law does not change the fact that a person must be classified as a worker within the meaning of that article if his independence is merely notional.'[23] Thus, the *Allonby* definition does not cover 'entrepreneurs' (category 3) but is likely to cover employees and self-employed workers (categories 1 and 2). This would suggest that only the second category of individual would benefit from the rights under Articles 7 and 8 – *not* self-employed entrepreneurs (category 3).

However, there are a number of arguments in favour of a broad reading of Article 2(a) to include (category 3) entrepreneurs. First, this would fill any gap which may have been left by the other directives. Second, this would fit with the agenda based on encouraging entrepreneurship. Third, this may have been the intention of the drafters: the original definition of self-employed workers in Article 2(a) of Directive 2010/41 said 'all persons pursuing a gainful activity for their own account, under the conditions laid down by national law, *including farmers and members of the liberal professions*' (emphasis added), thus suggesting that entrepreneurs would be covered. Finally, a broad reading would be compatible with the idea that equality is a universal value and so should be enjoyed by as many people as possible, a view supported by the reference to '*all persons* pursuing a gainful activity for their own account' in Article 2(a) (emphasis added). A reading of the Directive against Article 33 of the

[20] Ibid. paragraph 67.
[21] Case C-66/85 *Lawrie-Blum* [1986] ECR I-2121, paragraph 17.
[22] Case C-85/96 *Martínez Sala* [1998] ECR I-2691, paragraph 32.
[23] *Allonby* at paragraph 79.

Charter[24] might also indicate a broader understanding of the term 'self-employed worker'.[25]

Even if the Court of Justice favours a narrow *Allonby* style definition, as it may well do, the reference in Article 2(a) to 'under the conditions laid down by national law' gives the national systems the freedom to extend the protection to entrepreneurs (that is, to category 3) because in these cases the duty-holder – that is, the one paying the social protection or maternity benefits – is not the private party but the State, which may decide to assume greater responsibility. We would argue for this latter, broader scope for maternity and social security rights, which encompasses entrepreneurs, given the fact that, as we saw above, many female self-employed workers experience similar vulnerability to employees.

The question, then, is whether Member States have extended social protection and maternity benefits to all self-employed, or just the more limited group of employees and self-employed workers (categories 1 and 2). Further, we need to consider the extent to which the provisions of the Directive 2010/41 have been effectively implemented by Member States, as this will significantly affect the rights and entitlements of self-employed women. It is to these questions that we turn in the sections that follow, drawing on data provided by the European Network of Legal Experts in the Field of Gender Equality, obtained as part of an analysis of the implementation of Directive 2010/41.

B. Social Protection for the Self-employed

All EU countries have some system of social protection for self-employed workers. These systems vary considerably from country to country, with some being paid automatically on the basis of residence and financed via broad-based taxation (e.g. Norway, Sweden, the United Kingdom), some being mandatory and contribution-based (e.g. Belgium, Greece, Slovenia, Estonia, Finland, Hungary), some being voluntary (unemployment insurance), and others being provided in a highly differentiated structure of special legal provisions, independent social security systems, choice of private or statutory insurances and a variety of professional pension funds administered by professional or sectoral associations (e.g. Germany). Most schemes cover some combination of old-age and disability pensions and health benefits.

---

[24] 'Everyone shall have the right to protection from dismissal for a reason connected with maternity and the right to paid maternity leave and to parental leave following the birth or adoption of a child.'

[25] Case C-232/09 *Danosa v LKB Līzings SIA* [2010] ECR I-11405.

Unemployment protection for self-employed workers is provided in Croatia, Greece (where, however, the benefits are well below the poverty threshold and subject to a discriminatory condition: permanent residence), Hungary, the former Yugoslav Republic of Macedonia, and Sweden, but not in Cyprus, Ireland, Latvia, Portugal or the United Kingdom (except for share fishermen and volunteer development workers employed abroad), and is voluntary in Denmark, Spain and Romania (via private insurance). In some countries, the system is different for professionals compared with other self-employed persons, and in Germany there are not two separate systems but many different systems, which are quite different in practice. However, in some countries separate systems were very similar in practice (e.g. France, Italy) and in Greece separate systems were being merged into larger schemes. Many countries have voluntary supplementary social protection for self-employed workers, often available through private providers (e.g. Bulgaria, Iceland, Luxembourg; compare Malta, where there is no second pillar pension).

In most countries, the self-employed are responsible for their own contributions to the social protection system where required. However, in Portugal the beneficiary of 80 per cent or more of the activity of an independent worker is responsible for a small contribution to the social security system, despite the worker being classified as an independent worker.

In some countries there remain significant differences in social protection between the employed and the self-employed (e.g. Lithuania). This can be exacerbated where social protection is provided on a voluntary or semi-voluntary basis. For example, in Latvia, unlike employees (who have to make social protection contributions in proportion to their real earnings), the self-employed are required to make social insurance contributions related to the minimum statutory salary, irrespective of their real income (similar arrangements are in place in Estonia). Any additional contribution is voluntary. Similarly, in Spain, self-employed workers declare their own income for determining their monthly contribution. The vast majority (85.7 per cent) of self-employed workers declare the minimum wage, reducing their monthly contribution and their future benefits. Thus, the self-employed may receive significantly lower social protection than those in employment.

The self-employed are also exposed to other gaps in social protection: in Slovakia, the self-employed cannot be insured against employment injuries or occupational diseases, because these kinds of insurance only apply to employees, whose contributions are fully covered by the employer. In relation to sickness insurance, the self-employed are only eligible for sickness benefits if they have paid insurance contributions for over 270 days in the two years before the onset of the incapacity. Employees do not have such a pre-condition.

Thus, while all EU countries have some system of social protection for self-employed workers, there are likely to be substantial gaps in practice, potentially undermining the adequacy of social protection for the self-employed.

C. Social Protection for Spouses of the Self-employed

In some countries, spouses and life partners were covered by social protection systems prior to the adoption of the Directive, so specific implementation of Article 7 was not required (e.g. Austria). However, other countries have explicitly amended their law to comply with Article 7 (e.g. Estonia, France, Ireland, Romania).

Spouses and life partners are covered in three key ways in state laws: as dependent workers or employees of the self-employed (e.g. Cyprus, Finland, France, Malta, Slovenia); as assisting, participating, helping or collaborating spouses (e.g. Belgium, Bulgaria, Czech Republic, Estonia, Germany, Ireland, Italy, Poland, Portugal); or as members of a partnership (e.g. Ireland). This division was made explicit in France, where spouses were explicitly required to register one of these forms of activity. In Germany, assisting spouses are perceived as being dependent employees.

Social protection for spouses (and, sometimes, life partners) was mandatory in most countries, including Austria, Belgium, Croatia, Cyprus (not life partners), Czech Republic, Denmark, Finland, France (not for spouses of liberal professionals or for life partners), Germany, Iceland, Ireland, Italy, Liechtenstein, Luxembourg, the former Yugoslav Republic of Macedonia (not life partners), the Netherlands, Norway, Poland, Portugal, Spain and Sweden. In some countries, the social protection system is a mix of voluntary and mandatory provisions (e.g. Liechtenstein). However, this is generally the same for both the self-employed and their spouses. In other countries, this 'mandatory' system consisted of universal, residence-based benefits (e.g. in Finland, Iceland, Norway, Sweden), with spouses and life partners having no additional entitlements.

Voluntary systems are in place in Bulgaria, Estonia, Latvia, Lithuania (but with some residence-based entitlements), Luxembourg (voluntary if not in agriculture), Romania, Slovakia, Slovenia and the United Kingdom (though with some residence-based entitlements). In Belgium, a voluntary system of social protection for assisting spouses was found by most common consent to be 'insufficient'. The system has been compulsory since 1 January 2006. Indeed, under the voluntary system in Latvia, no spouse of a self-employed worker had contributed to the statutory social insurance scheme in 2013, despite approximately 7500 people being helping family members. Thus, there is a sizable group of spouses that lack social protection. Therefore, voluntary systems may have significant limitations.

Schemes that were mandatory for the self-employed worker but voluntary for his/her spouse or life partner existed in Estonia, Romania, Slovakia, Slovenia and the United Kingdom.

The reports explicitly noted that Greece had failed to implement Article 7; however, spouses (not life partners) are mandatorily covered as family workers or dependent family members.

Thus, while most Member States have ensured they comply with Article 7, this may not lead to adequate social protection in practice, particularly where voluntary systems are put in place. As a result, spouses and life partners may not receive adequate coverage from social protection systems in practice.

D. Maternity Benefits for the Self-employed

Few countries have amended their law to comply with Article 8. However, changes to secure compliance were noted in the reports from Greece (only in relation to self-employed women, not spouses or life partners), Croatia, Ireland (in respect of assisting spouses or civil partners), Poland and France.

The requirement of sufficiency in Article 8(3) caused issues for many countries. In some cases, the amount of the allowance was dependent on the self-employed worker's *declared* income, which could be significantly lower than their actual income.

Few countries provided temporary replacement services or national social services, meaning these did not need to be extended to the self-employed and/or their spouses or life partners. However, the lack of replacement services meant that many self-employed workers and their spouses/life partners returned to work before the end of the maternity period.

According to the reports, most countries provide a level of protection that is no greater than that required by the Directive. Where the protection is higher, this normally relates to the availability, length or amount of maternity benefits available. In other countries, the level of protection is less than that required by the Directive. The responses of the experts are summarised in Table 4.1.

Table 4.1 Summary of expert responses regarding the level of protection offered

Higher	Same/Not higher	Less
Belgium – *compulsory for spouses to join social protection scheme; adoption allowance*	Croatia	Cyprus – *self-employed not covered by Industrial Disputes Tribunal*
Bulgaria, Denmark, Iceland, Ireland, Norway, Poland, Romania, Sweden – *amount/length of maternity benefits*	Czech Republic	Germany
Finland – *stand-in service during family-related leave for agricultural entrepreneurs*	Lithuania	Greece
France	Luxembourg	Portugal – *coverage of spouses; length of maternity leave*
Italy – *coverage of maternity benefits*	The former Yugoslav Republic of Macedonia	Hungary – *gaps regarding spouses and life partners*
Latvia – *availability of parenting allowance*	Malta	
	the Netherlands	
	Slovakia	
	Slovenia	
	Spain	
	United Kingdom	

Source: Barnard and Blackham (2015).

Again, adequacy and sufficiency of maternity benefits for the self-employed may be a problem in practice.

4. ETHNICITY AND THE SELF-EMPLOYED

There is limited evidence or statistics relating to race or ethnicity among the self-employed, particularly at EU level. This is perhaps unsurprising, given the EU has traditionally had less of a focus on equality on the grounds of ethnicity than, for example, gender. It was only in 2000 that race equality law was included in EU directives, lagging behind Member States such as the UK.

However, there is some statistical data on self-employment and ethnicity available at the domestic level. For example, the 2016 UK Annual Population Survey (UK Data Service 2016) breaks down the self-employed by ethnicity (Table 4.2).

Table 4.2 UK self-employed by ethnicity

		Frequency	Percentage
Ethnicity	White	18388	90.3
	Mixed/Multiple ethnic groups	147	0.7
	Indian	441	2.2
	Pakistani	445	2.2
	Bangladeshi	90	0.4
	Chinese	79	0.4
	Any other Asian background	166	0.8
	Black/African/Caribbean/Black British	328	1.6
	Other ethnic group	260	1.3
	Total	20344	99.9
Missing	No answer	21	0.1
Total		20365	100.0

Source: UK Data Service (2016).

These statistics indicate that, at least in the UK, the vast majority of the self-employed are white (90.3 per cent). This is slightly higher than would be expected based on the ethnicity of the general population: in the 2011 Census, the white ethnic group accounted for 86 per cent of the population in England and Wales.[26]

Thus, the white ethnic group is slightly overrepresented among the self-employed. This may reflect the fact that those in the white ethnic group are also the most likely to be employed: according to the 2014 Labour Force Survey, the white ethnic group had an employment rate of 75 per cent.[27] In the 2011 Census, of minority ethnic groups, the Other

26 Office for National Statistics (2012).
27 Office for National Statistics (2014).

White ethnic group had the highest employment rate of all ethnic groups (at 77 per cent of those aged 16 to 64).[28] That said, of those actually in employment, Gypsy and Irish Traveller men (41 per cent) and women (18 per cent) represented the largest proportion of all ethnic groups who were self-employed: this was twice the average for other minority ethnicity groups.[29] Thus, the overrepresentation of the white ethnic group in self-employment may reflect the strong presence of Gypsy and Irish Travellers among the self-employed (as these groups are often subsumed under 'white'). This is understandable, given the Gypsy and Traveller culture and tradition that rejects wage-labour, creating an economic niche of 'mobile multi-/flexi-skilled family-based self-employment'.[30] However, it also implies that ethnicity discrimination could be a very live issue for some members of the self-employed, including those in the 'white' ethnicity group who are Gypsies or Irish Travellers. Thus, as with gender, it is important to consider the scope of the welfare state through a racial lens.

5. SCOPE AND COVERAGE OF THE 'WELFARE STATE' THROUGH A RACIAL LENS

The discussion above in relation to gender equality law, and the potential gaps in social protection for the female self-employed, may be compared with findings from an analysis of EU race equality law, particularly as it relates to social protection for the self-employed. Council Directive 2000/43/EC of 29 June 2000 implementing the principle of equal treatment between persons irrespective of racial or ethnic origin prohibits direct or indirect discrimination based on racial or ethnic origin (Article 2), and applies to 'all persons, as regards both the public and private sectors, including public bodies', including in relation to 'social protection, including social security and healthcare' (Article 1(e)). There is no further development of the personal scope of the Directive, though it does note that it extends to 'conditions for access to employment, to self-employment and to occupation' (Article 3(1)(a)).

While a gender lens is a common tool for analysing the welfare state, race and ethnicity are comparatively neglected. However, a more ethnically diverse population may pose particular challenges to the sustainability of the welfare state. First, as 'closed systems' that are designed to

---

[28] Ibid.

[29] Ibid.

[30] Clark (2002) 184.

protect 'members' (and, in most cases, membership is inextricable from citizenship), welfare states may exclude migrants,[31] who are often from ethnic minorities, undermining social protection. Indeed, immigration controls may make some workers even more precarious, including through exclusion from social welfare protection.[32]

Alternatively, multiculturalism policies that integrate and include ethnic minority groups in the welfare state may be seen as undermining the social solidarity that supports the redistributive role of the state embodied in many welfare structures.[33] For Kymlicka and Banting, this reflects two separate concerns: first, that racial and ethnic diversity (i.e. a greater presence of ethnic minorities as a proportion of the national population) may make it more difficult to sustain redistributive policies, as it is more challenging 'to generate feelings of national solidarity and trust across ethnic lines'; and, second, that multiculturalism policies adopted by government to accommodate diversity, such as multicultural education, legal exemptions, and funding of ethnic groups, can undermine national solidarity and trust.[34] Kymlicka and Banting find limited evidence to support these concerns, and argue that both are overstated.[35]

Second, workers of particular ethnicities (or 'nationalities') may be particularly sought after in some industries, such as domestic work and personal care,[36] which are often characterised by poor terms and conditions of employment, informal work and, as a result, limited social protection, and which tend to engage large numbers of the self-employed. Further, McDowell, Batnitzky and Dyer found that migrants of colour were typically concentrated into the least prestigious and lower level jobs within their occupation in their case studies of the UK service sector, indicating a 'hierarchy of inequality' within migrant labour according to ethnicity and skin colour.[37] These lower level jobs typically have the least access to the welfare state. Thus, workers of some ethnicities may be overrepresented in areas that are traditionally excluded from the protection of the welfare state, or in precarious jobs that do not benefit from welfare state coverage, emphasising the importance of a racial lens.

---

31 Freeman (1986) 51, 53.

32 Anderson (2010) 300.

33 Banting and Kymlicka (2006) 3–4; Kymlicka and Banting (2006) 281; Mau and Burkhardt (2009) 213.

34 Kymlicka and Banting (2006).

35 Ibid.

36 Anderson (2007) 247.

37 McDowell et al. (2009) 3.

Thus, as with gender, there needs to be an expansion of the personal scope of the welfare state, to include the vulnerable self-employed of particular ethnicities. However, unlike in relation to gender, there is comparatively little consideration of ethnicity and the welfare state in EU law. This is an area which would benefit from a deeper consideration by law-makers.

6. CONCLUSIONS

Under existing EU directives, there is limited protection on the basis of ethnicity to ensure the extension of the welfare state to the self-employed; on the basis of gender, there is more protection, though the personal scope of the directive remains unclear, and likely excludes the self-employed entrepreneur. We argue for a broad understanding of the term 'self-employed worker', such as to include the widest groups of workers possible within welfare structures, and a deeper consideration of the interaction between ethnicity, self-employed work and the welfare state at EU level. This may help to support and extend the welfare state, such as to accommodate the new reality of work for many self-employed.

However, the growth of self-employment and other forms of 'atypical' work may pose a more fundamental challenge to the existing notion of the 'welfare state', particularly in an era of increasing population diversity. The fundamental question remains: is the traditional 'welfare state' sustainable in this new, more diverse world of work? For the Taylor Review, the solution to this question lies in promoting self-reliance: 'Government should focus on encouraging self-employed people to plan for the future, reducing the potential that the taxpayer has to pick up additional costs associated with ill health or inadequate retirement saving',[38] including through private sector and technology-driven savings vehicles, and encouragement of private saving. However, in the context of very low earnings from self-employed activity, it appears unlikely that individuals will be able to protect themselves from employment risks. Thus, there is a compelling case for an extension of the welfare state, to cover the most vulnerable self-employed.

[38] Taylor (n 5) 74.

BIBLIOGRAPHY

Anderson B, 'A Very Private Business: Exploring the Demand for Migrant Domestic Workers' (2007) 14 European Journal of Women's Studies 247.

Anderson B, 'Migration, Immigration Controls and the Fashioning of Precarious Workers' (2010) 24 Work, Employment and Society 300.

Banting K and Kymlicka W, 'Introduction: Multiculturalism and the Welfare State: Setting the Context' in K Banting and W Kymlicka (eds), *Multiculturalism and the Welfare State: Recognition and Redistribution in Contemporary Democracies* (OUP 2006).

Barnard C and Blackham A, 'Self-Employed: The Implementation of Directive 2010/41 on the Application of the Principle of Equal Treatment between Men and Women Engaged in an Activity in a Self-Employed Capacity' (European Commission 2015) <https://www.equalitylaw.eu/component/edocman/?task=document.viewdoc&id=2732&Itemid=> accessed 17 January 2019.

Barnard C and Blackham A, 'Discrimination and the Self-Employed: The Scope of Protection in an Interconnected Age' in H Collins (ed.), *European Contract Law and the Charter of Fundamental Rights* (Intersentia 2017).

Briggs A, 'The Welfare State in Historical Perspective' (1961) 2 European Journal of Sociology 221.

Clark C, '"Not Just Lucky White Heather and Clothes Pegs": Putting European Gypsy and Traveller Economic Niches in Context' in S Fenton and H Bradley (eds), *Ethnicity and Economy: 'Race and Class' Revisited* (Palgrave Macmillan UK 2002).

Elgot J, 'PM Backs Plans to Overhaul Workers' Rights to Reflect Gig Economy', *The Guardian* (20 March 2017) <https://www.theguardian.com/uk-news/2017/mar/20/pm-backs-plans-to-overhaul-workers-rights-to-reflect-employment-practices> accessed 28 April 2017.

Freeman G, 'Migration and the Political Economy of the Welfare State' (1986) 485 The ANNALS of the American Academy of Political and Social Science 51–63.

Kymlicka W and Banting K, 'Immigration, Multiculturalism, and the Welfare State' (2006) 20 Ethics & International Affairs 281.

Mau S and Burkhardt C, 'Migration and Welfare State Solidarity in Western Europe' (2009) 19 Journal of European Social Policy 213.

McDowell L, Batnitzky A, and Dyer S, 'Precarious Work and Economic Migration: Emerging Immigrant Divisions of Labour in Greater London's Service Sector' (2009) 33 International Journal of Urban and Regional Research 3.

OECD (2016), *Entrepreneurship at a Glance 2016* (OECD Publishing, Paris).

OECD (2019), *Self-employment Rate (Indicator).* doi: 10.1787/fb58715e-en accessed on 17 January 2019,

Office for National Statistics, 'Ethnicity and National Identity in England and Wales' (Office for National Statistics, 11 December 2012) <https://www.ons.gov.uk/peoplepopulationandcommunity/culturalidentity/ethnicity/articles/ethnicityandnationalidentityinenglandandwales/2012-12-11> accessed 28 April 2017.

Office for National Statistics, '2011 Census Analysis: Ethnicity and the Labour Market, England and Wales' (Office for National Statistics, 13 November 2014) <https://www.ons.gov.uk/peoplepopulationandcommunity/culturalidentity/ethnicity/articles/ethnicityandthelabourmarket2011censusenglandandwales/2014-11-13> accessed 28 April 2017.

Office for National Statistics, 'Trends in Self-Employment in the UK' (Office for National Statistics, 13 July 2016) <https://www.ons.gov.uk/employmentandlabourmarket/peopleinwork/employmentandemployeetypes/articles/trendsinselfemploymentintheuk/2001to2015> accessed 28 April 2017.

Orloff A, 'Gender in the Welfare State' (1996) 22 Annual Review of Sociology 51.

Orloff A, 'Gendering the Comparative Analysis of Welfare States: An Unfinished Agenda' (2009) 27 Sociological Theory 317.

Sainsbury D (ed.), *Gendering Welfare States*, vol 35 (Sage modern politics series, Sage Publications, 1994).

Sainsbury D, 'Gendering the Welfare State' in G Goertz and A G Mazur (eds), *Politics, Gender, and Concepts* (Cambridge University Press, 2008).

Taylor M, *Good Work: The Taylor Review of Modern Working Practices* (July 2017) <https://assets.publishing.service.gov.uk/government/uploads/system/uploads/attachment_data/file/627671/good-work-taylor-review-modern-working-practices-rg.pdf> accessed 15 January 2019.

UK Data Service, *Annual Population Survey 2016* <beta.ukdataservice.ac.uk/datacatalogue/series/series?id=200002> accessed 17 January 2019.

Wales P and Amankwah A, *Trends in Self-employment in the UK: 2001 to 2015* (Office for National Statistics, 13 July 2016).

Cases

Case C-256/01 *Allonby v Accrington & Rosendale College* [2004] ECR I-873

Case C-66/85 *Lawrie-Blum* [1986] ECR I-2121

Case C-85/96 *Martínez Sala* [1998] ECR I-2691

Case C-232/09 *Danosa v LKB Līzings SIA* [2010] ECR I-11405

PART II

Thematic reflections

5. Labour relations and labour law in shared economy

Jing Li and Li Jianfei

The shared economy is evolving and is spawning new forms of economic and social development. It is difficult to accommodate the symbolic features of the shared economy such as "mass entrepreneurship", "sharing economy" and "borderless expansion" in traditional labour, labour relations and labour laws. Labour relations and labour law have faced unprecedented challenges along with the deep integration of the Internet and traditional industries.

In different disciplines, or from different perspectives, "labour relations" has different meanings. This chapter discusses the influence of the shared economy on labour relations and labour law at the legal level, and the definition of labour relations is also from the legal level and perspective. Therefore, strictly, the labour relations referred to in this chapter should be called labour legal relations, which focuses on the influence of the shared economy on the subject, object and content of the labour legal relationship.

I. THE OMNI-DIMENSIONAL IMPACT OF THE SHARED ECONOMY ON LABOUR RELATIONS

In his *Critique of Political Economy*, Marx pointed out that

> people participate in the social production of their own lives in certain inevitable relations that are independent of their own will, i.e. the production relations that are appropriate for the level of the development of material productivity at that time. The sum of these production relations constitutes the economic structure of the society, i.e. the realistic foundation based on which the legal and political superstructure are to be established and one that has a certain social ideology to go along with.[1]

[1] Central Compilation Bureau (1975) Vol. 2, p. 82.

"Labour relations" lies within the relations of production, and the change of relations of production determines the change of labour relations. Also, human beings cannot go without labour for a single day, nor can they go without production for a single moment, which means that the changes in production relations will be prominently and rapidly reflected in labour relations. As Engels concluded based on field investigations in the *State of British Working Class*: "The first invention to make a fundamental change in the situation of British workers is Spinning Jenny … Everything is totally involved in this mighty current."[2]

In traditional industries, capital accumulation is the only source of reproduction. After the Industrial Revolution, the reform of the traditional mode of production has mainly relied on invention, technological innovation and capital investment. Changes in these ways can change the mode of production, but such change is more of an incremental change that requires a slow accumulative process. As a result, the changes in labour relations are also slow and incremental ones rather than swift and brand new changes. Therefore, though the labour law accompanying traditional industry has had its moment of embarrassment and discomfort in the long journey of over 200 years, it is still able to cope with the changes in general. The incremental and pro forma changes in labour relations do not change the nature and the state of labour relations, which, when reflected in the labour law, means that the labour law only needs to be modified instead of being restructured.

When it comes to the shared economy, it is a completely different story. The shared economy does not invent, nor does it make any technological innovations. It does not even require any substantial investment – it works just by connecting the existing factors of production in the traditional production mode with the Internet! Therefore, in this sense, the "plus" of the Internet is neither the increase of its own capital investment nor the expansion or increase of the traditional factors of production, but rather the addition of the existing factors of production to the existing Internet. And, following this "plus", the resulting energy and influence is beyond the wildest imagination of the traditional mode of production, and is also not covered by the current labour law. As Richard B. Freeman wrote (in *The Labour Market in the New Information Economy*)

> the extension of information and communication technologies to economic activity is changing the labour market in important ways. The computerization and use of the Internet are associated with greater hours worked as well as

2 Central Compilation Bureau (1975) Vol. 4, p. 358.

> higher wages; IT occupations are rapidly increasing their share of employment; job search and recruitment are moving rapidly to the Web, with consequences for matching employers and employees; and possibly most important of all, trade unions have begun to use the Internet as a tool for servicing members and carrying their message to the public, raising the possibility of a major change in the nature of the union movement.[3]

These developments and changes are inevitable in economic and social development, and people will accept them either quickly or slowly. What aroused our concern was that they directly influenced and changed our labour relations and directly affected and changed our labour law. Take the online shops as an example, judging by their actual state, what they do is what the sales clerk does in traditional shopping malls, that is, delivering the goods chosen by the customers to the hands of these customers. They were merely the employees of the shopping mall in the old sense. Now, however, no one knows who they are, and no one needs to know who they are.

> The Internet has also fundamentally changed the way people work, and it frees people from the hierarchical type of management and centralized control mode in the traditional industrial era. The Internet devices and people who operate the Internet no longer need to work in sequential and linear ways, but rather work in a paralleled manner, and various transactions and production activities can be conducted in a scattered and decentralized manner. In particular, due to the innovative characteristics of information transparency and disorganization brought about by the Internet, the original enterprise management methods now tend to disintegrate.[4]

Thus, the object of traditional labour relations is now missing, and it has become difficult for traditional labour law to apply. In this sense, the changes rendered by the shared economy to labour relations are omni-dimensional, so are the challenges to the labour law.

II. CHANGES IN LABOUR RELATIONS IN THE SHARED ECONOMY

(i) Changes to the Subject

For a long time, labour legal relations has been adhering to an expressly identified "one-to-one" labour relationship, that is, a labour relationship

---

3 Freeman (2002).
4 Zheng (2015) p. 8.

between two sides: one employer facing an employee. Even when an employer has a lot of employees, in specific labour relations, it is always an employer facing an employee. In such a labour relationship, the labourer knows who his/her employer is, and the employer knows who its workers are. The relationship between the two is as simple and clear as marriage: one is an employer, and the other is a hired person or a labourer.

> According to the provisions of China's labour law, the labour relationship between the labourer and the employing unit should also be exclusive, i.e. the labourer who is a natural person can only sign the labour contract and establish the labour relationship with one employing unit at the same time. No worker can sign a labour contract and establish a labour relationship with two employers, otherwise, he/she will be liable for violating the provisions of Section 99 of the Labour Law.[5]

However, in a state of shared economy, a person that we call an employee or a labourer may have no idea who the employer is, or if there is a so-called employer at all. For example, Taobao has many online shops, where there are many goods sellers working, but who are their employers? Do they have an employer? Do those who ride "Jingdong" or "Tmall" delivery carts have labour relations with "Jingdong" or "Tmall"? Are they labourers of the latter?

> Obviously, the concept of "workers" needs to be redefined. In the mid-1920s, the word "workers" would conjure up images of men in blue shirts and helmets sitting around having lunch together. And they were the proud members of the Union. By the 1980s, people also use the term "workers" to refer to white-collar office clerks, which includes not only white-collar workers, but also lawyers, doctors, consultants and accountants. By the end of the 1990s, we have webmasters and program engineers. Today, the term "worker" is widely used to include anyone earning a paycheck.[6]

In this way, the "one-to-one" labour relationship becomes "0+1", "1+n" and "n+1", which leads to the embarrassment of labour relationship determination, and the difficulty of labour law application.

In the field of labour law, the principle that we have long adhered to is "whoever employs will be the responsibility bearer". As any labour is always accompanied by risk, the labour law not only clarifies that the employer not only shall be responsible for the labourer's labour process, but also shall be responsible for the living conditions necessarily required

---

5 Jianfei (2013) p. 53.
6 Cortada (2000) p. xiv.

for the subsistence of the labourer; the labour law not only emphasizes the employer's responsibility for the labourer's normal work, but also emphasizes that the employer shall bear no-fault liability of compensation for any labour risk encountered by the labourer in the labour. However, all of a sudden, the elements and principles of the labour law lose their playground in a state of shared economy, as there is no knowing who your employer is or even whether you have an employer or not. So, as the shared economy changes the subject of a labour relationship, the labourer no longer has an employer or otherwise cannot locate a specific employer. The labour laws are now naturally left off the table.

(ii) Changes to the Object

In traditional industry, even in the 200 and some years from the advent of the labour law to date, labour behaviour and labour results have at all times been expressly identified or even fixed at the legal level. We have identified different jobs pursuant to specialization and division of labour as well as production technology of the enterprises in accordance with the needs of labour management. For example, we have different labour positions, catering waiters, car maintenance workers, cattle and sheep slaughtering and processing workers, stevedores, maintenance workers and security guards. The nature, content, characteristics and requirements of such labour are relatively fixed, and the corresponding standards are also clear and specific. On this basis, we have long advocated that the worker should "love whatever job one takes up", emphasizing that this is not only professional ethics, but also the only way to success.

In the shared economy, the uncertainty of labour behaviour becomes the certain behaviour characteristic of the labourer. First and foremost, the continuation of labour positions and the inheritance of technology that are determined by the product stereotypes are no longer unalterable and everlasting principles. "Loving whatever job one takes up" is reversed to "taking up whatever job one loves". In the traditional production process, individual labourers, regardless of their work or position, are just small screws on a huge complex machine doing their jobs in the high-speed running of the machine equipment in order to ensure that the entire machine functions normally. After the advent of the shared economy, people are describing labourers as follows:

> Employees of the mobile Internet era are no longer screws forced to stay where they are under the carrot and the stick. They have enough information to grasp the core of the enterprise, enough capacity to attract a group of

> consumers, adaptive enough to respond to market changes, and sufficient knowledge to innovate independently.[7]

The change of labourers' labour behaviour will inevitably cause the change of the object character in labour relations, thus triggering the change of labour behaviour patterns, the nature of labour behaviour and the legality and rationality of labour behaviours.

Compared with the certainty of the labourer's labour behaviours, the fruits of labour produced by the labourer's labour is the iron law in labour law. "According to the principle of labour contract, the employee shall not claim ownership of the work result."[8]

> Where the employee is hired to engage in the work of invention, or where the invention of the employee is the result of the work expected to be performed by the employee in consideration of the compensations paid for such work, the invention so derived normally would belong to the employer.[9]

It is precisely due to the fact that the fruits of labour are entirely vested in the employer, that the law can compel the employer to bear many obligations and responsibilities to the labourer – the employer shall not only assume responsibility for the labourer while the latter is working, but also bear responsibilities for the labourer while the latter is off work or cannot work. The obligations and responsibilities of the employer to the labourer are directly manifested in the payment of labour remuneration to the labourer and the social insurance paid on behalf of the labourer. However, in the shared economy, the attribution of fruits of labour presents some fuzzy characters. Take the "dividend collection" prescribed in a company's "Chauffeured Car Guide" as an example: in the case of "user mark-up", the chauffeured car driver only gets to keep "80% of the Business Fee (which, in this case, includes the starting fare, kilometre fare, low-speed fee, extra mileage fare and night shift

---

7 Shangkuan (1967) p. xi. "A group of 2–3 MI Engineers are given decision-making power in the communication with the users, and 30% of the projects are defined and developed in such process of communication" (Chi Wang quoted in Wanqiang 2014). "Baidu Culture fully embodies an independent spirit of the staff, for example, in decision-making, Baidu requires the employees to 'listen to the opinions of the majority of people, to discuss with a few people, and to make your own decisions'" (Dicong and Xiaoqin 2015 p. 124).

8 Yueqin (2004) p. 181.

9 Changkuan (1978) p. 47.

fee)".[10] In addition, the driver will also be subject to a deduction of an Administrative Fee of 0.5 dollar for each single service trip. Under such a labour context, it seems to be a tough job for the proper determination of labour relations and the normal application of labour laws. In the environment of the shared economy, we see a type of employer who never assumes any labour risks but is able to possess the fruits of the labourers' labour, which has never before been the case since the birth of the labour law. Even if we retrospectively attribute the source of the labour law to the old civil code, the civil code principle of "He who benefits assumes responsibility" seems no longer applicable in the context of the shared economy!

(iii) Changes in the Content

In the changes that the shared economy has caused to labour relations, the change in content is the biggest of all and will inevitably lead to significant change to the labour law.

The first is labour time. One of the characteristics of the shared economy is the fragmentation of time. The original meaning of time fragmentation is that

> it is very convenient for consumers to receive information, whether they are taking the subway, waiting for friends, or having meals, they can take out the mobile phone anytime, anywhere, and send a piece of Wechat-message, or surf the Micro blog, or receive some messages.[11]

When these elements are combined with labour, be it transactions, deliveries, writings or programming, it has nothing to do with the "8-Hour Working System", nor is it related to the weekly/monthly working hours.

The second is the workplace. The mode of shared economy breaks through the boundaries of enterprises, forms spontaneous organizations with evolved cooperative modes, and thus changes the principles and preconditions of management. "Enterprise without Borders" is an often boasted advantage of shared economy: "Boundary-free is one of the characteristics of the Internet. The rules and regulations proved effective by the traditional enterprises are the boundaries of enterprises. And, to

---

10 "20% of Fare Collected for Drivers Joining with Their Own Cars", *IT Times* (Shanghai), 26 January 2015. http://tech.163.com/15/0126/10/AGSLH6oq000915BF.html. Access date: 10 December 2015.

11 Wang and Peng (2015) p. 14.

achieve the Internet transformation of the enterprises, one needs to think out of the box of such rules and regulations."[12] Such "boxes" can be replaced with various work-related communities or groups that are created based on the Web, transplanting the various types of "groups" already in place in social tools to the internal and external nodes of the enterprise. Thus, the special creative and productive capacity needed by the enterprises is generated.

The third is the labour remuneration. According to the definition in the Convention on the Protection of Wages of the International Labour Organization, a "wage" is a remuneration paid by an employer to an employee for the work completed or to be completed, or for the service provided or to be provided. This standardized definition that has been applicable over the past years has encountered a dilemma in the shared economy: the likelihood that an employer will pay for a job or service that the employee is "about to complete" or "about to provide" disappears, simply because the preconditions of the payment by the employer are not only the labourer who has already provided labour or service, but also the labour or service that the labourer has already realized. Take the Chauffeured Car Service as an example: after the driver has paid the fare from the passenger into the account, 20% of the fare goes to the platform owner; what is the nature of the remaining 80%? If it is remuneration, who will be the one paying it? If the platform embezzles the money and disappears, should the driver lodge a civil lawsuit or dispute over obligation in court, or submit a labour dispute for arbitration? Last but not the least, the most difficult issue is social security. In the era of the shared economy, if the workers of the online platform pay their own premiums for social security while the operators of such a shared economy do not assume the corresponding responsibility or do not bear the primary responsibility, can this be called social security? On the other hand, the State bears the overall responsibility for social security, and in this case, how should the State act as the "bearer of overall responsibility" of social security? As a matter of fact, wherever the State undertakes the responsibility, it means all members of the society are actually bearing it. Currently, these web-based companies are undergoing rapid development. For example, the Didi Chuxing is appraised at US$16.5 billion. Should these Internet companies be assigned with more social responsibilities?

---

12 Dicong and Xiaoqin (2015) p. 98.

III. THE CHALLENGES PRESENTED BY THE SHARED ECONOMY TO LABOUR LAW

When the proportion of the primary and secondary (material production) sectors of the economy declined and the proportion of the tertiary and quaternary sectors continued to rise, the labour laws, which have factory production as the source and norm, exhibited symptoms of discomfort. Now, facing the challenges of the shared economy, the scope of application and the authority of efficiency of labour law will be further suppressed.

Almost at the same time, judges in both the United States and China are confronted with cases of "confirming labour relations for dancers". Lilianna Chavez, a 32-year-old dancer, dances at the King Arthur Nightclub in Chelsea near Boston. The nightclub treats the dancers as independent suppliers, and the dancers get a fixed commission of US$35 each day, and an extra commission of 30% of the tip income from night-time solo dancing; other than that, no minimum wage or any labour protection is provided. To this end, Attorney Lis Riordan filed a class action for the nightclub's 70 dancers, demanding compensation from the nightclub for misclassifying their labour status. In August 2009, the court ruled that dancing services are an integral part of the nightclub service, and demanded the nightclub pay minimum wages to dancers and not to share tips from dancers.[13] In January 2011, Mrs Lu went to Zhangjiawan town Tongzhou District, Beijing, to serve as a waitress at the Xiang Hai Long KTV, where her wages would be a commission of a certain proportion of the customers' consumption; therefore her monthly wages were not fixed, and there was no labour contract between her and the KTV. On 1 July 2015, Mrs Lu was strangled to death by a criminal in her rented apartment. Mrs Lu's daughter believed that her mother's death should be identified as an occupational death as the victim worked at the Xiang Hai Long KTV before she was murdered and that the rented apartment where she died was provided by the KTV. The Xiang Hai Long KTV denied that Mrs Lu was employed as a waitress, saying that the KTV had around ten waitresses who received no wages from the KTV, the KTV didn't maintain social security insurance on their behalf, and that their wages were purely tips from the customers. On 16 October 2015, the Arbitration Commission decided to dismiss the daughter's request for arbitration. The daughter later sued the KTV in court.[14]

---

13 Jianfei (2011).
14 Zheng (2015), p. 20

Strictly speaking, to confirm labour relations in such cases is rather difficult. Under the Anglo-American law system, judges can find a way for the case through the construction of the law and create judicial precedents for similar cases to follow suit. However, in a code law country like China, to find out the legal basis for confirming the labour relationship between Mrs Lu and the KTV in the current Labour Law and the Labour Contract Act is tantamount to milking a bull, or possible only with far-fetched associations. As Vince Chabria (US Federal District Judge, also the presiding judge of the class action lawsuit against the chauffeured car service platform giant Lyft) put it, it would be "like driving a square tenon into a round mortise",[15] to use the labour law of the 19th century (a separate category of "Independent Supplier" was created in 1947) to try labour cases of the 20th century. The labour law experts believe that a lot of changes need to happen in the law system, from the reform of the administrative procedures of the United States Labour Relations Commission to the certification system or the dispute arbitration system that applies to the first contract.[16] US Senator Mark Warner proposes the establishment of a third category of labour between employees and independent suppliers, that is, the so-called "dependent contractor". Canada created such labour categories in 2008, and Germany also has similar practices. However, distant water cannot quench present thirst. Judges are having a hard time dealing with pending trials for cases arising from the shared economy.

In China, the Ministry of Transport has drafted the *Interim Measures for Administration of Online Booking Taxi Services (Exposure Draft)* to solicit opinions from the public. At a seminar, the labour law experts from Peking University, Tsinghua University, Renmin University of China and other universities, law firms and labour administrative departments pointed out that the content of "the labour contract signed between the platform and the driver" is inconsistent with the relevant provisions of the Labour Contract Law and should be amended. Due to the huge difference among the operating modes and models of the chauffeured car service operators, other than the business mode of using drivers by way of establishment of labour relations, there do exist some flexible business modes requiring only loose non-labour relationships. The employment form in the era of the shared economy is more pluralistic and flexible than that of traditional employment. It is inconsistent with the relevant provisions of the Labour Contract Law to make it a compulsory

---

15 Kirken (2008), p. 172.
16 Yueqin (2004), p. 172.

requirement for the chauffeured car service operators to sign a labour contract with drivers who use the platform.[17] At the same time, Mr Zhang Ping, professor and deputy dean of the Intellectual Property Institute at Peking University Law School, suggested that

> the intellectual property system in the big data era must be radically changed in terms of the ideology, and if requirement of prior permission is not changed on the matter of intellectual property, the humanity will be caught in its own traps in the future. If there is no escape from this system, there will be endless litigation cases, which consume the cost of social administration.[18]

The "Third Road" or "third type of labourer" advocated by American jurists, and the "loose type non-labour relationship" or "radical change of ideology" called for by Chinese jurists, are realistic descriptions of the transcendence of labour relations and challenge to the labour law of the shared economy. What we are looking forward to is that these responses and reflections can be more prompt and more effective, so that they can be linked seamlessly to the existing legislation in a more reasonable manner. And in this way, relevant social relations can be properly adjusted at the legal level, and the labour relations and labour law can achieve their metamorphosis and regeneration symbiotically with the shared economy, and continue to perform their sacred mission of safeguarding the legitimate rights and interests of the labourers in the new modes of labour and production.

IV. COUNTERMEASURES OF LABOUR LAW IN THE CONTEXT OF THE SHARED ECONOMY

Faced with the difficulties and predicaments of labour relations and labour law caused by the shared economy, there are but two strategies: one is to include them within the existing framework, that is, to "contain" and "dissolve" through the construction of law and trial cases. In this regard, case law countries have an advantage over code law countries. On 5 July 2015, the US Federal Labour Agency issued administrative explanations about how to distinguish between employees and independent suppliers. Peres, the Minister, reiterated that the current criteria for the division of labour relations are strict and will be strictly enforced, and government regulators will determine the status of workers by uniform

---

17 Bing (2015).
18 Zhang (2015), p. 47.

standards and will not be deliberately flexible despite the new economic model. The Agency also disclosed the law enforcement report for the year 2014, which shows that a total worth of US$79 million in compensation was recovered for workers with wrongly classified status, calling for active whistle-blowing of similar misconduct. An American judge quoted Abraham Lincoln's metaphor – "If you call a dog's tail a leg, the dog still has 4 legs as it does not make a dog's tail a leg by calling it a leg" – in sharp satire of the fact that FedEx tried to circumvent the employment relationship by calling drivers by a different name.[19] The judge forced FedEx to settle with the employees involved for compensation up to US$228 million.[20] However, in code law countries, neither administrative interpretations nor judges' rulings can have such extensive power. The relevant disputes may even encounter troubles regarding case filing at labour arbitration agencies, and they will not be smoothly dealt with at court. Therefore, new ideas and countermeasures, that is, the second way out, must be sought, including new countermeasures for labour law adjustment and new approaches to the social security levy.

(i) New Countermeasures For Labour Law Adjustment

After confirming the homogeneity of labour relations in the shared economic era, we must also face the great changes in the form of labour relations in the shared economic times, and take corresponding legal measures to carry out effective legal adjustments.

In light of "working online", labour legislation should address the work standards of intelligent terminals and mobile intelligent terminals, and pay attention to online working conditions, the work safety of online jobs, occupational injury to online workers' health, employers' compensation for the acquirement and use of online facilities and devices, and the various types of labour legal responsibilities that arise from these elements of online work.

In light of "time fragmentation", labour legislation should regulate labourers' labour time, both in terms of the labourers' unit working time

---

[19] It turns out that not all drivers who serve FedEx are real company employees. Instead, they are part of the contract ground staff established for certain routes. In the FedEx business model, FedEx Express and FedEx Ground are considered to be two completely separate entities. According to a report from Mental Floss, some routes will eventually be contracted with FedEx Ground. Here, people can buy routes from FedEx and then continue to hire their own driver team (see Sicilianmenniu 2015).

[20] Jianfei (2011).

and labourers' daily working time. In particular, drivers of chauffeured car services must still abide by the longest daily working hours, the longest working hours per service trip, and the farthest kilometres per service trip which have long been established by labour legislation, so as to effectively protect the health and safety of the workers.

In light of "boundless enterprises", labour legislation should expand its "labour place", virtualize the "labour place" in the field, and make the limited "labour place" into an infinite one. At the same time, under the premise of "rules and control", adhere to the labour law protection of "workplace" safety and health, adhere to labour law's standards with regard to the occupational safety and health for workers, adhere to the comprehensive protection for the workers in terms of labour safety and health, and uphold the fundamental principle of labour law – the employer assumes liability for all the labourers' labour risks.

In view of "working communities", labour legislation should be consistent in adopting the rule of thumb, "He who engages labourer assumes responsibility", the specific embodiment of which shall be the civil law principle of "He who benefits assumes responsibility". As for employers without a business licence or lawful registration, "units" lawfully revoked of their business licence or registration, and the "working communities" organized by such "units", the accountability mechanisms provided in the "Illegal Employment" section may be invoked, or qualified employers assume the relevant legal liabilities, or disqualified "units" undertake responsibility for illegal employment.

In light of "shared fruits of labour", labour legislation should draw up the minimum wage guarantee rules and paid rest and leave rules applicable under the condition of the shared economy; in particular, it needs to set up the wage payment guarantee rules for workers who cannot work due to circumstances outside their control, so as to guarantee a basic standard of living for labourers under the shared economy.

Finally, labour arbitration and the People's Court should accept the labour disputes which arise under the shared economy, and should apply the relevant regulations and rules of the labour law to effectively protect labourers' lawful rights and interests.

(ii) New Approaches to the Social Security Levy

Social security is the fruit of the civilized evolution of the human society, and is the rational choice following the social cognition of labour risk and labour after entering the industrial society. It rationally allocates social security responsibility and obligation among the individuals of social organizations, thus forming a risk-shared social security responsibility mechanism: the social care of the affluent to the impoverished, the sound and robust to the sick and handicapped, the young to the old, the strong to the weak, thereby achieving the social goal of harmonious coexistence. At the same time, via social security, social equity and social justice are achieved through the secondary allocation of personal wealth. Social security can not only reduce the unfairness of social allocation to a certain extent, but also eliminates, to a certain extent, unfairness among social members as a result of accidental disasters, competition failure, or illnesses or occupational injuries. It is in this sense that Roosevelt, the President of the United States, proudly declared that the Social Security Act was the cornerstone of his New Deal. The same Act is also called the security device of the American society.[21]

In stark contrast with the labourers "running naked" under the shared economy is the extremely wealthy "platform" owners, who in each minute acquire huge amounts of excess profits, that is, "profits beyond average profit, or additional profit acquired through the extra productivity of the labour exploited".[22] The Internet platform owners acquire profits far beyond normal ones by taking advantage of their leading adoption of new technologies and their entitlement to specific markets, and will have access to such excess profits following the formation of their monopoly. On the contrary, online shop owners or chauffeured car drivers without social security, whether they work full-time or part-time, are responsible for their own labour risk which they are hardly able to assume themselves. Therefore, the levy of Social Security Tax against the Internet platform owners must be put on the agenda.

Social Security Tax is a form of tax or tax payment levied by many countries in the world today to raise social insurance funds. China implements the social security premium levy system. This is a long-established and self-contained system. As a result, despite the constant claims on the levy of Social Security Tax, there is hardly any dominating consensus at the moment. At present, a "Dual Model" is adopted in China, that is, in some provinces the social security premiums are levied by the local tax bureau, and in some other provinces such premiums are levied by the human resources and social security departments. The levying of Social Security Tax under the condition of the shared economy not only helps to strengthen the levy of social insurance funds, but also overcomes the phenomenon of arrears and non-payment by taking

---

21 Jianfei (1989).

22 Central Compilation Bureau (1956), p. 220.

advantage of the mandatory and normative attributes of taxation, and such tax can be levied and managed by exploiting the institutional framework, material resources and human resources of the existing tax department, resulting in enhanced fundraising efficiency of the social insurance funds.

What is especially noteworthy is that, in China, the objects of the current social insurance premium levy are the employing units and workers, and the payment of social insurance premiums is determined based on the monthly average amount of the employee's entire wage income from January to December of the previous year, which will then be payable directly by the employer and be withheld by the employing unit on behalf of the employee. These methods are feasible in the traditional and normative mode of labour relations, yet hardly sustainable under the mode of the shared economy. Therefore, it is necessary to change the collection mode of social insurance funds, to set up a separate tax category where the Internet platform becomes a single type of taxpayer. The Internet platform operators will then serve as the taxpayer of Social Security Tax in accordance with the operating scale of the platform, the number of labourers, the amount of the platform commission and the amount charged in the name of administrative fees, thus fulfilling the legal obligation of payment of Social Security Tax for the labourers dependent on such platforms.

V. CONCLUSION

The sharing economy affects labour law and social security laws in many ways. Traditional legislation cannot cope with the new changes. The protection of the rights and interests of employees, especially the acquisition of the benefit of social security, has become increasingly blurred and difficult. However, no matter how the economic model changes, we must insist that employees always enjoy social security and, whether through national unified taxation or by labour relations parties' payment, employers must pay for employees and employees should get the benefit from the employers.

BIBLIOGRAPHY

Bing S, *8 Law Experts Questioned the New Car Policy. Is it against the Labor Contract Law?* 2015. http://news.163.com/15/1106/12/B7O47UT200014SEH.html. Access date: 31 October 2018.

Central Compilation Bureau, *The Complete Works of Marx and Engels*, Renmin Press, 1st Edition, December 1956.

Central Compilation Bureau, *Marx and Engels Anthology*, Renmin Press, 1st Edition, May 1975.

Changkuan S, *The Original Theory of Labour Law*, Zhengda Press, 1978.

Cortada J W, *21st Century Business: Managing and Working in the New Digital Economy*, Prentice-Hall, Inc. 2000.

Dicong W and Xiaoqin C, *Shared Economy in One Book*, Southern Publishing House, Guangdong Renmin Press, 1st Edition, August 2015.

Freeman R B, The Labour Market in the New Information Economy, NBER Working Paper No. 9254, October 2002. http://www.nber.org/papers/w9254. Access date: 16 January 2019.

Kirken T, The Transformation of American Industrial Relations, *China Labor and Social Security Press*, 2008.

Jianfei L, *Social Legislation in the United States, Reference Materials for American Studies*, the American Research Institute of the Academy of Social Sciences, China, Vol. 10, 1989.

Jianfei L, *Labour Issues: The Achilles Heel of Shared Economy*, huxiu.com, 2011. http://www.groundbreaking.cn/yanyi/laogong/4290.html?from=timeline&isappinstalled=0. Access date: 16 December 2015

Jianfei L, *Course Book of Labour and Social Security Law*, Renmin University of China Press, 3rd Edition, March 2013.

Shangkuan S, *The Original Theory of Labor Law*, Zhengda Printing House, 1st Edition, 1923, Shanghai, Reprint 1967, Taipei.

Sicilianmenniu, *Labor Issues: The Achilles Heel of Shared Economy*, huxiu.com, 11 November 2015. https://www.huxiu.com/article/130549/1.html. Access date: 12 December 2015.

Wang J and Peng D, *Shared Economy: Traditional Enterprise and Self-Subversion, Organizational Refactoring, Management Evolution, and Internet Transformation*, Mechanical Industry Press, April 2015.

Wanqiang L, *Sense of Participation: Xiaomi Word-of-mouth Marketing Internal Manual*, CITIC Publishing House, 2014.

Yueqin H, *The New Theory of Labor Law*, China University of Political Science and Law, 2004.

Zhang P, *If Intellectual Property Rights Still Require Prior Permission, Humanity Will Be Caught in Its Own Trap*, Financial Network, 19 November 2015. http://www.chinaiprlaw.cn/index.php?id=3045. Access date: 13 December 2015.

Zheng X, *Industrial Internet: The Industrial Transformation in the Era of Shared Economy*, China Machine Press, 1st Edition, May 2015.

Zheng Y, *A Woman in Nudity Suspected to Have Been Strangled to Death, Daughter of Victim Demands Compensations from KTV on Basis of Occupational Death*, China Daily Network (Beijing), 5 November 2015. http://news.163.com/15/1105/03/B7KLC3Q500014SEH.html. Access date: 12 December 2015.

6. Social protection and vulnerable workers in South Africa

Avinash Govindjee

INTRODUCTION

Sipho is 30 years old. A father of two, he lives in South Africa, and is unemployed. Following the completion of his schooling, Sipho managed to obtain one job in the automotive sector but was soon retrenched due to a downturn in the economy. Sipho lives with his mother and is dependent upon her social assistance grant (an older person's grant) for his survival. Dissatisfied with his situation, Sipho decides to try his hand at being a car guard outside a small beachfront restaurant complex. He relies on tips from motorists who park their vehicles at the complex in order to generate some income. The centre has employed its own security guards to ensure safety at the complex, and considers Sipho to be something of a nuisance. Nevertheless, he is permitted to continue with his "work" and manages to earn approximately R1000,00 per month as a result of his endeavours.

Atypical or non-standard forms of employment (including dependent self-employment, temporary agency work and employment on the basis of fixed-term contracts) are now a common feature of labour markets around the world.[1] For many workers, this development is associated with insecurity.[2] The ILO's recent report, *Non-standard employment around the world*, arrived at the following key findings in this regard:[3]

---

1 ILO (2016) 1. For example, nearly two-thirds of wage employment is casual in Bangladesh and India and one in three employees is a casual worker in Mali and Zimbabwe. For useful definitions of the notion, see IZA (2013) 13 and Yesuneh (2010) 15. Also see Theron (2002) 45.

2 A study conducted for the European Parliament suggests that dependent self-employment does not always place workers in a vulnerable situation, although this is often the case: IZA (2013) 9.

3 ILO (2016) 3–4.

- The greater the incidence of temporary employment in a country, the greater the likelihood of workers transiting between non-standard employment and unemployment, with the possibility of transitioning to better jobs less likely;
- Workers in non-standard employment face substantial wage penalties relative to comparable standard workers;
- Workers in on-call employment and casual arrangements typically have limited control over when they work, with implications for income security given uncertainty regarding pay;
- There are significant occupational health and safety risks due to a combination of poor training and supervision and injury rates are higher among workers in non-standard employment;
- Workers in non-standard employment may be excluded by law from social security coverage. Even when formally protected, lack of continuity in employment and short working hours may result in inadequate coverage or limited benefits during unemployment and retirement;
- Workers in non-standard employment may lack access to freedom of association and collective bargaining rights, also facing the dangers of forced labour and discrimination.

Various policy recommendations have been proposed in response.[4] In particular, the ILO proposes that "legislation also needs to address employment misclassification, restrict some uses of non-standard employment to prevent abuse, and assign obligations and responsibilities in multi-party employment arrangements". In respect of social protection, the suggestion is that "countries should strengthen, and sometimes adapt, their social protection systems to ensure that all workers benefit from social protection coverage … changes should be complemented by efforts to guarantee a universal social protection floor".[5]

South Africa's unemployment rate is presently 27,2%, with over 6.2 million persons classified as unemployed.[6] More than 2864 million persons are "discouraged work-seekers", being available to work or start a business but unable to take active steps to find work as a result of unavailability of jobs, lack of skill or loss of hope of finding any kind of work.[7] In 2013, of the 1.5 million persons running non-value-added

---

4 ILO (2016) 4–5.

5 ILO (2016) 4–5.

6 Statistics South Africa (2018). Unemployed persons are those (aged 16–64 years) who: a) were not employed in the reference week; and b) actively looked for work or tried to start a business in the four weeks preceding the survey interview; and c) were available for work; or d) had not actively looked for work in the past four weeks but had a job or business to start at a definite date in the future and were available.

7 Statistics South Africa (2017) 19.

taxation (VAT) registered businesses, as many as 1,4 million were in the informal sector. Predominantly run by black Africans, persons aged 35–44 years and those with the lowest levels of education, the businesses are survivalist in nature and most often are formed as a result of unemployment and the inability of the individual to obtain an alternative source of income.[8] Turnover levels and profit margins are small for most informal businesses in South Africa: in 2013, as many as 52,3% had less than a R1500,00 turnover (and only 14,6% had sales above R6000,00 in a month). In the month prior to the survey conducted by Statistics South Africa in 2013, 65% of businesses experienced profit below R1500,00.[9]

It is against this backdrop that debates such as the distinction between the notions of "employee" and "independent contractor", and social protection "outside the realm of labour law" ought to be construed in the South African context. Following a description of the legal position of non-standard workers in South Africa, a brief survey of key literature and comparative best practices, this contribution focuses on possible modalities for extending the social protection net in South Africa to include vulnerable, non-standard workers. It is submitted that there has been an over-emphasis on linking most labour and social security protection to "employment", particularly given the South African constitutional framework, and that "vulnerable workers", as a broader group, are deserving of enhanced focus and expanded social protection.

LEGAL POSITION OF NON-STANDARD WORKERS IN SOUTH AFRICA

Only persons defined as "employees" have recourse to the dispute-resolution provisions of the Labour Relations Act 1995 (LRA).[10] Furthermore, only persons classified as employees can be victims of unfair labour practices or be dismissed for purposes of the statutory definition

---

8 Statistics South Africa (2014) v.

9 Statistics South Africa (2014) v. For the most recent available information in relation to poverty trends in South Africa, see Statistics South Africa (2017).

10 Section 36 of the Constitution provides that (all) the rights of the Bill of Rights may be limited by a law of general application, to the extent that the limitation is reasonable and justifiable in an open and democratic society based on constitutional values. Applicants for employment are included only for purposes of unfair discrimination (in terms of the EEA) and alleged victimisation claims (in terms of the LRA).

of that term.[11] It is "employees" who are protected against unfair discrimination by the Employment Equity Act 1998 (EEA) (although applicants for employment are included in this regard)[12] and against victimisation in terms of the LRA.[13]

Certain employees are expressly excluded from the scope of labour legislation, even if they fall within the statutory definition of "employee".[14] These include members of the National Defence Force, the National Intelligence Agency, the SA Secret Service and the SA National Academy of Intelligence.[15] It is clear that in every labour dispute it is necessary to decide whether the referring party was an *employee* at the time of his or her alleged dismissal or unfair labour practice. Both the LRA and the Basic Conditions of Employment Act 1997 (BCEA)[16] contain the following definition of "employee":

> a) any person, excluding an independent contractor, who works for another person or for the state and who receives, or is entitled to receive, any remuneration; and
> b) any other person who in any manner assists in carrying on or conducting the business of an employer.

As is the case with many other jurisdictions, the major debate that has arisen from this definition relates to the dividing line between "independent contractors" and "employees" (also because the second part of the above-mentioned definition is apparently wide enough to encompass independent contractors in labour law protection). The courts have relied on tests developed under the common law when seeking to apply these definitions in particular (labour law-related) cases, in order to determine whether the contractual relationship between the parties is more in accordance with the requirements of *locatio conductio operarum* (the contract of work) or *locatio conductio operis* (the Roman law contract of service).[17] The application of these tests has resulted in the following

---

11 Grogan (2014) 16.

12 Section 6(1) read with section 9 of the EEA.

13 Section 5(2) and (3).

14 See, in general, Cheadle and Clarke (2000).

15 Section 2 of the LRA. See Grogan (2014) 17.

16 Act 75 of 1997.

17 Grogan (2014) 19. The tests applied by the courts include the "supervision and control test", the "organization" or "integration" test and the "dominant impression" test, which considers the relationship between the parties as a whole in order to decide whether the relationship amounts to one of employment or not. A number of judgments have focused on applying these tests in South African

workers being classified as *employees* by the courts: managing directors, freelance writers, fishing boat skippers, radio personalities, directors of companies and sole members of close corporations who hire out their labour through the close corporation. More recently, even *Uber* drivers have been considered (at least by a Commission for Conciliation, Mediation and Arbitration commissioner) to be employees.[18] By contrast, insurance salesmen, sales agents, consultants, and market-research field workers have been held to be *independent contractors*, and there have been conflicting judgments in relation to priests.[19]

To assist with the process of separating "employees" and "independent contractors", the legislature introduced a statutory "presumption of employment" in both the BCEA and the LRA, which applies to persons earning less than an amount (presently R205 433,30) specified from time to time by the Minister of Labour. A person earning below this amount and who renders service to another is presumed, regardless of the form of the contract, to be an employee if one or more of a number of "factors" are present.[20] In addition, the Department of Labour has issued guidelines (known as the "Code of Good Practice: Who is an Employee?") to which all persons determining whether a person is an employee must adhere.[21] The BCEA, in addition, permits the Minister of Labour to "deem" any category of persons as employees for purposes of this Act. The courts have also played their part, with judgments confirming, for example, that the definition of "employee" is broad enough to encompass

---

labour law: see, for example, *Smit v Workman's Compensation Commissioner* 1979 (1) SA 51 (A); *SABC v McKenzie* (1999) 20 *ILJ* 585 (LAC).

[18] *Uber South Africa Technological Services (Pty) Ltd v NUPSAW* [2017] ZACCMA 1.

[19] See, in general, Grogan (2014) 20–21.

[20] The factors include whether: "the manner in which the person works is subject to the control or direction of another person; the person's hours of work are subject to the direction or control of another person; in the case of a person who works for an organization, the person forms part of that organization; the person has worked for that other person for an average of 40 hours per month for the last three months; the person is economically dependent on the other person for whom he or she renders services; the person is provided with the tools of the trade or work equipment by the other person; or the person only works for or renders services to one other person" (LRA section 200A).

[21] GN 1774 in *GG* 29445 of 1 December 2006.

people due to commence work, and receive remuneration in the future,[22] and even persons employed in contravention of statutory prescripts.[23]

From the perspective of social security law, the Compensation for Occupational Injuries and Diseases Act 1993 (COIDA) covers casual workers, apprentices, labour broker/temporary employment services (TES) employees, but not domestic workers and categories of state employees. The Unemployment Insurance Act 2001 (UIA) has undergoing amendment so that public servants and foreign workers will be covered in future. Coverage is, nonetheless, restricted to "employees", traditionally defined, and special measures still need to be developed in order to incorporate the self- and informally employed. The effect of relying on the "employee" notion in order to signify coverage is that while fixed-term contract employees are covered under the UIA, atypical workers, including independent contractors, so-called dependent contractors, the self-employed and the informally employed, as well as the long-term unemployed, are excluded from protection.

The overwhelming focus on "employees" and "non-employees" in the legislation is questionable, given that section 23(1) of the Constitution provides that "*Everyone* has the right to fair labour practices" (own emphasis).[24] In addition, "everyone" has the right to have access to social security including, if they are unable to support themselves and their dependants, appropriate social assistance and the state must take reasonable legislative and other measures, within its available resources, to progressively realise this right.[25] Other rights in the Constitution, such as human dignity, equality, assembly, demonstration, picket and petition and freedom of association,[26] are also for "everyone", and rights may only be

22 *Wyeth SA (Pty) Ltd v Manqele* [2003] ZALC 60; [2005] ZALAC 1. In other words, people who have concluded employment contracts that are cancelled prior to their commencement of employment are considered to have been dismissed by their future employers.

23 *Discovery Health Ltd v CCMA* [2008] 7 BLLR 633 (LC). In this case, a foreign national working without a work permit issued under the Immigration Act, was nevertheless considered to be an "employee" for purposes of the LRA (interpreting, in the alternative, the definition of "employee" in section 213 of the LRA to not be dependent on the existence of a valid and enforceable contract of employment); also see *Kylie v CCMA* [2010] ZALAC 8, pertaining to a sex worker operating in contravention of the Sexual Offences Act 1957.

24 The section goes on to provide for worker and employer rights, as well as for rights applicable to trade unions and employers' organisations.

25 Section 27(1)(c) of the Constitution.

26 Sections 10, 9, 17 and 18 respectively.

limited by way of a law of general application, and only to the extent that such limitation is reasonable and justifiable.[27]

The past few years have also seen significant changes to labour law legislation, with the introduction of amendments to the BCEA, EEA, LRA and UIA. A new piece of legislation, the Employment Services Act 2014, has also been signed into law and amendments to the COIDA are also expected. The amendments to section 198 of the LRA, dealing with the regulation of "non-standard work", are arguably the most contentious of these developments, and are relevant for the present discussion.

Following significant negotiation amongst government, labour and business, the final version of this section attempts to strike a balance between the competing considerations of labour flexibility and employment security.[28] By permitting employment through Temporary Employment Service arrangements to continue, rather than banning this outright, the legislature appears to have acknowledged the need for flexibility in the realm of employment.[29] Similarly, work in terms of limited duration contracts and part-time work is now regulated. Measures have been introduced in order to ensure that non-standard employment is permitted only with reference to objective factors. The focus of the amendments is on preventing the abuse of workers considered to be "vulnerable", so that protection, in the form of enhanced employment security, is generally reserved for lower-income earners (those presently earning below the statutory threshold of R205 433,30).[30] In particular, employees engaged in work for a client (via a labour broker or temporary employment service provider) that does not amount to a "temporary service" may be considered to be employed on an indefinite basis by the *client*, and dismissal protection (including reinstatement) may also operate against the client. Similarly, low-earning employees employed on a fixed-term contract basis for longer than three months without a justifiable reason are "deemed" to be indefinitely employed.

---

27 Section 36 of the Constitution.

28 See, in general, Govindjee and van der Walt (2017) 101–108.

29 Temporary Employment Services are defined in section 198 of the LRA to mean any person who, for reward, procures for or provides to a client other persons who perform work for the client and who are remunerated by the temporary employment service. This arrangement is also referred to as "labour brokering" in the South African context. On the issue of whether the client of a labour broker is the sole or dual employer of the workers placed, see *NUMSA v Assign Services and others* [2018] ZACC 22.

30 See, in general in this regard, Govindjee and van der Walt (2017) 101–108.

Still, a significant number of categories of workers are effectively (and deliberately) either excluded by the current legislative framework, or enjoy rights only for a limited duration, despite the wording chosen by the drafters of the Constitution. For example, employees employed on fixed-term contracts working on "special projects" for longer than three months (which an employer would be able to define very widely) typically enjoy few benefits and no employment rights upon termination of the contract. Low-earning independent contractors and self-employed persons, including persons in Sipho's situation, are left outside the framework of "employment" protection. Problematically, workers in such situations are typically unable to obtain access to a range of social security benefits and may become dependent on social assistance in time to come. Although no social assistance grant is payable to unemployed persons of working age in South Africa unless they are suffering from a disability (in terms of the Social Assistance Act 2004),[31] an older person's grant is paid to men and women who qualify in terms of a means test at the age of 60. What the recent amendments to the legislation targeted at "vulnerable" employees have done, effectively, is to bring certain categories of workers into the fold of employment law protection (particularly via the "deeming provisions" discussed above). What they have failed to address is the multitude of work-seekers unable to obtain any standard employment, as well as the plethora of informal workers, independent contractors and self-employed workers who are in a vulnerable position as a result of their limited earnings. It is these workers and work-seekers that fall through the cracks of both the existing labour and the social security legislative frameworks in South Africa, at the risk of destitution.

THE VULNERABILITY OF INFORMAL WORKERS

The ILO's report, *Decent Work and the Informal Economy*, identifies the following broad range of informal workers:

> Own-account workers in survival-type activities, such as street vendors, shoe-shiners, garbage collectors and scrap- and rag-pickers; paid domestic workers employed by households, homeworkers and workers in sweat-shops

[31] Act 13 of 2004.

> who are "disguised wage workers" in production chains; and the self-employed in micro-enterprises operating on their own or with contributing family workers or sometimes apprentices / employees.[32]

According to Fudge, the important attribute these different groups of workers share is that "they are not recognised or protected under the legal and regulatory frameworks" and they are also characterised by a high degree of vulnerability.[33] Not only are these workers outside the scope of labour law, and thus deprived of legal and social protection and legal enforcement regimes, "they are rarely able to organise for effective representation and have little or no voice to make their work recognised and protected".[34]

As a result of the realities of externalisation, Fudge characterises work arrangements into three categories.[35] Firstly, knowledge workers at the high end of the spectrum, associated with the rise of the "new economy" and networked organisations and typically not needing labour protection. Secondly, an increasing number of workers, such as independent contractors, freelancers and franchisees, enjoying some control over, and independence in, their work process (in addition to some capital). Such workers are also exposed to a number of risks, such as illness and lack of work, that some may not be well-placed to meet, particularly given their limited bargaining power. Some of these workers are drawn from social locations that increase their vulnerability to exploitation while others have access to capital or professional qualifications, and are less vulnerable. Finally, "precarious" or vulnerable workers drawn from poorer social locations and associated with sub-contracted labour, poorly paid and employed in atypical and unstable jobs typically falling outside the scope of collective representation or legal regulation (including many women, people from ethnic minorities and workers with precarious immigration statuses).[36] ILO Recommendation 204 of 2015 deals specifically with the transition from the informal to the formal economy and applies to all workers and economy units (including enterprises, entrepreneurs and households) in the informal economy. The scope of application of this Recommendation extends to "... employees holding informal jobs in or for formal enterprises, or in or for economic units

[32] International Labour Conference 2 as quoted in Fudge (2012) 8.
[33] International Labour Conference 2 as quoted in Fudge (2012) 8.
[34] International Labour Conference 3 as quoted in Fudge (2012) 8.
[35] Fudge (2012) 12–13.
[36] For a definition of the term "precarious work", see IZA (2013) 14.

in the informal economy, including but not limited to those in subcontracting and in supply chains, or as paid domestic workers employed by households; and workers in unrecognized or unregulated employment relationships".[37]

Irrespective of categorisation, the ILO has clarified that the fundamental principles and rights at work, and the conventions with which they are associated, apply to *all workers*, and that "there should not be a two-tiered system or separate regulatory framework for formal and informal workers – although there may be a need for different modalities and mechanisms for guaranteeing them in the less regulated, less formal parts of the economy".[38]

Despite this, permitting employers to engage in contract labour via intermediaries and increased casualisation, for example, has afforded tremendous flexibility in various parts of the world. This, for example, typically relieves the principal employer of concerns relating to recruitment and supervision, results in irregular wage scales being applied, results in few benefits and allowances being available and, for various reasons, generally reduces the likelihood of workers receiving social security benefits.[39] Various responses directed at protecting the rights of workers and aimed at bridging the divide between the protection enjoyed by employees and the situation of workers classified as independent contractors or "contract labourers" have emerged.

The ILO's Employment Relationship Recommendation 2006[40] notes the challenges associated with establishing whether or not an employment relationship exists in certain situations and calls for a national policy to be formulated which should provide guidance as to who is considered to be a worker in an employment relationship and on the distinction between employed and self-employed workers.[41] According to the Recommendation, the determination of an employment relationship should primarily be guided by *facts* relating to the performance of work and the remuneration of the worker, notwithstanding how the relationship is characterised in any contrary arrangement, contractual or otherwise, that the parties may have agreed upon.[42] The National Policy for

---

37 ILO (2015).

38 International Labour Office (1972) 40.

39 Ahsan et al. (2008) 262 as cited in Sankaran (2012) 40.

40 ILO (2006).

41 Sankaran (2012) 46.

42 Art 9. "Consideration should be given to the facts and context within which the work is carried out, the manner in which wages are provided, the extent to which the employer benefits from the work performed, the place of

protection of workers in an employment relationship should not interfere with *true* civil and commercial relationships, while at the same time ensuring that individuals in an employment relationship have the protection they are due.[43]

Considering a different part of the developing world by way of example, Sankaran notes that courts in India have examined the facts of each case to decide if there was unity of ownership, management and control between the main enterprise and contract company to determine if they could be treated functionally as a single unit and for liability as an employer to be imposed on the main enterprise. The case of beedi workers suggests that "it is possible to recognise that economic dependence coupled with vulnerability are factors that transform a commercial relationship into an employment relationship".[44] The courts in that country have also played a role, being involved in a form of "de facto" regulation, reinterpreting labour law to introduce greater flexibility without the need for a legislative amendment of labour laws to remove perceived rigidities in the labour market.[45] Union membership is also permitted. The consequence is that certain social benefits for temporary incapacity or for work-related illnesses for occupations with a higher risk have been extended to self-employed workers. Significantly, protection in the form of unemployment benefits for self-employed workers at the end of their work activity has also been introduced.[46]

A VULNERABILITY-CENTRED APPROACH FOR THE FUTURE?

> The challenge for labour law in the 21st century is to protect and shelter workers during transitions in the labour market: from employee to state employee or to self-employment, through different life stages of the individual (from training, through social and political activism, to balancing work and family life) and from transitions regarding capacities, opportunities and jobs. This challenge does not mean that labour law should relinquish its traditional role of protecting workers in the first circle, the hard circle of the

work, working hours, provision of tools, availability of leave periods, etc.": as quoted in Sankaran (2012) 46).

43 Art 8. As Sankaran notes, this suggests that the veil could be lifted from commercial relationships that disguise or prevent an employment relationship from being legally noticed: Sankaran (2012) 46.

44 Sankaran (2012) 46.

45 Sankaran (2012) 40.

46 Landa Zapirain (2012) 164.

> industrial worker and trade unionist. But labour law's importance will diminish as history progresses if it is not capable of providing efficient responses, which attend to well-being and environmental sustainability, to emerging forms of work, and with the "other" economy.[47]

Work-seekers such as Sipho are part of the "dependent pole of the self-employed spectrum" because they:

- typically do not have the skills or the resources to establish a business themselves;
- are driven into self-employment because they have either lost their jobs or cannot find employment as employees; and
- acquire work through legal forms that place them outside the protection of the labour legislation in law and fact.[48]

Guy Standing has characterised such insecure and unstable workers as the "precariat", because of their association with casualisation, informalisation, agency labour, part-time labour, phoney self-employment and crowd-labour.[49] Importantly, the precariat has distinctive relations to the state, in having fewer rights than most others and suffering from "rights insecurity", increasingly being denied "the right to have rights" and struggling to attain the essence of proper citizenship.[50]

Legally speaking, such workers would typically fall within the notion "independent contractors" in South Africa, which results in the workers falling outside the ambit of the protective labour legislation, being "independent in legal form but dependent in practice".[51] Such workers also fall through the gaping hole in the social security net, usually being unable to qualify for any social assistance or social insurance benefits as a result of their situation.

Is it possible and justifiable to identify workable solutions for such workers/work-seekers by focusing on their vulnerability for purposes of categorisation, and in order to consolidate and expand upon available approaches? This idea resonates with Martha Fineman's "vulnerability

47 Landa Zapirain (2012) 168.

48 See Cheadle and Clarke (2000) 34. A practical test, according to these authors is to ask whether the worker would prefer to do the work that he or she is doing as an employee as opposed to doing so as an independent contractor.

49 Standing (2014) 9–24. As Standing notes, the precariat relies almost entirely on money wages, usually experiencing fluctuations and never having income security, facing a life of "unknown unknowns".

50 Standing (2014) 12.

51 Cheadle and Clarke (2000) 34.

theory", which is rapidly gaining momentum as a justification for (more) expansive social welfare laws.[52] Kohn, for example, has argued that although Fineman's theory of vulnerability does not indicate how to allocate resources among vulnerable individuals, vulnerability may nevertheless be a useful construct around which to design social policy.[53]

South African labour law already provides a legislative model for distinguishing amongst different categories of workers. The BCEA, for example, defines domestic workers and farm workers and differentiates between senior managerial staff and workers working less than 24 hours per month.[54] It would also not be the first time that income (as an indicator of vulnerability) is used in order to determine which categories of persons are to be beneficiaries of certain forms of protection. For example, and as alluded to above, the Minister of Labour has set an income threshold (presently R205 433,30) for purposes of aiding the determination of who is an employee[55] and also for deeming workers to be employees of the clients of TESs[56] and indefinitely employed.[57] A means test, based primarily on income, is also used in order to assess eligibility for social assistance grants and other forms of social protection (broadly construed, such as housing subsidisation, taxation status, and provision of various other state-provided services at discounted rates). In the context of higher education, the National Student Financial Aid Scheme utilises a household income of approximately R120 000,00 in order to advance loans to qualifying South African students. No taxation is payable in respect of working-age individuals earning less than R73 650,00.[58]

It is unnecessary, for present purposes, to enter the debate as to the precise level of individual income below which a person should be considered to be a "vulnerable worker". It is suggested that extending available social security benefits to such workers would form part of the basket of social protection presently provided to low-income earners by the state and would, utilising a purposive approach,[59] give effect to the

---

52 See Fineman (2008).

53 See Kohn (2014).

54 See Theron (2002) 42.

55 Section 200A of the LRA.

56 Section 198A of the LRA.

57 Section 198B of the LRA.

58 This figure applies for the 2016 tax year: https://www.westerncape.gov.za/service/paying-income-tax (accessed on 10 June 2017).

59 See Davidov (2012) 173. Davidov's "purposive" interpretation of labour law suggests that it is fallacious to consider one category of "employees" and

Constitution's promise of progressive realisation in respect of access to social security. At first blush, this may seem to be an over-simplistic solution to a complex problem, and that other criteria should be added to that of the proposed income threshold prior to extending social protection benefits. Practically speaking, however, it is suggested that a more flexible approach to linking existing social security benefits to vulnerable workers is necessary, particularly given the frequent absence of formal employment relationships and the inability of low-earning workers to contribute on a regular basis to social insurance funds.[60] The simplicity of the proposed approach would, at least as an opening gambit for social protection expansion to informal workers, certainly be advantageous for purposes of social security administration, which has historically been notoriously weak in the South African context.[61]

Applying this approach to Sipho's situation, it is conceivable that it would be fairly easy to cover Sipho against the risk of an "occupational" injury (which may well occur given the nature of his work) by levying a small margin on the assessment paid by each of the restaurants and commercial enterprises (in respect of their employees) to the Compensation Fund.[62] Should Sipho's work terminate (for example because the restaurant complex is closed down), he should be able to obtain a limited (flat rate) benefit from the surplus funds that have been accumulated by the UIF (e.g. an amount equivalent to a minimum wage for a three month period, upon proof of the loss of work, to assist in buffering against the adverse effects of the unexpected life-change), particularly given the

---

then to apply the entire gamut of "labour law" to this group. This line of thinking includes conceptualising a worker as an "employee" for one purpose and an "independent contractor" for another: Davidov (2012) 175. The main advantage of a purposive approach is that it avoids overly legalistic applications of tests that could be outdated, instead seeking the ultimate objectives behind the law in order to determine who should be protected. As such, according to Davidov, the approach is well-suited to dealing with new forms of work arrangements: Davidov (2017).

60 This appears to dovetail with Torres and Supiot's suggestion that there are various concentric circles of labour and social protection and that the largest circle encompasses universal and constitutional social rights for all kinds of workers, including the rights to dignity, equality and non-discrimination, together with individual rights to work: see Landa Zapirain (2012) 158.

61 See, for example, the saga relating to the payment of social grants, fully described by the Constitutional Court in *Black Sash Trust v Minister of Social Development and others* [2017] ZACC 8.

62 This notion resonates with the idea of workers forming part of a community in the "workplace": see Davidov (2014).

absence of any available social assistance in terms of the South African system.[63] In addition, linking people in Sipho's position to the UIF would have the added advantage of exposing such workers to the possibility of skills training, and assist them to formally register as work-seekers and be notified in the event that other work opportunities arise.[64] It is also possible to make participation in such activities a precondition for receipt of any financial benefit. Sipho should also be able to associate with other non-standard workers who work in the area, and this grouping should be capacitated to obtain the correct information, and to assist one another, in the event that a social security claim is necessary.[65] What is perhaps more difficult to achieve in practice, without exposing the restaurant establishments to the risk of abuse, is a guaranteed minimum wage.[66]

Nevertheless, piloting such an extension of social security benefits to categories of non-standard workers who are not employees (such as car guards and waste-pickers[67]) would enable policy-makers to consider the financial implications and take steps to eliminate the risk of abuse.[68] Arguments suggesting that an established social insurance fund, such as

---

63 Prior to the recent amendments, it was estimated that the Fund's surplus would reach R175 billion by 2019: City Press (2017).

64 The UIF has already been involved with a "Training Layoff Scheme", in partnership with the Commission for Conciliation, Mediation and Arbitration, for employees, which makes this suggestion a realistic proposition.

65 It has been noted, for example, that taxi proprietors have formed formidable taxi associations for the purpose of representing their interests to government. The right to freedom of association has been expressly extended in the Constitution to the right to assemble, demonstrate, picket and to present petitions, and this right has been extensively used by categories of self-employed workers in the past: Cheadle and Clarke (2000) 33.

66 Permitting such workers to obtain some, but not all, basic employment standards, has been contemplated previously: see Fudge (2010) 253, 254 as quoted in Landa Zapirain (2012) 165.

67 See Chikarmane and Narayan (2012) 65. In India, according to these authors, journeys from rag picker to recycling worker have involved a dignity-affirming realisation that informal work is real "work", accompanied by the very tangible benefits of an identity-card as proof of worker status, decrease in harassment, group life insurance, group medical insurance, access to credit at competitive rates of interest, access to sorting space and generally better work opportunities and agency.

68 Barnard and Blackham argue for a broad understanding of the term "self-employed workers", such as to include the widest number of workers possible within welfare structures, because this may help to accommodate the new reality of work for many self-employed persons, albeit at a cost to the state and others: see, in general, Barnard and Blackham (2015).

the UIF, should not be used to benefit workers who have not contributed to the Fund could be addressed in various ways, for example by considering the extension as another form of social solidarity/taxation on employers and employees, or by enabling such workers to make periodic, ad hoc contributions (possibly matched by government co-contribution), and de-linking the receipt of (flat-rate) benefits from the "credits" system presently applied to employer and employee contributors. The outcome of this is likely to be the formalisation of an intermediary category of social security benefits, straddling the boundary between social assistance and social insurance.

This kind of suggestion seems to accord with the findings of research conducted for the European Parliament, arguably providing more universal and appropriate social protection for all, by seeking to extend social insurance to self-employed or particular target groups/creating a specific social security regime for self-employed workers.[69] This development is consistent with the Supiot Report's call for movement "beyond employment", which concluded that labour law should be expanded to apply to all forms of work performed for others, and not merely to subordinate work.[70]

Significantly, such an approach also seems to have sprouted support in the South African context. Darcy Du Toit has, for example, and with reference to the ILO's "decent *work* agenda" and the need for social justice, recently questioned the exclusion of independent contractors from the broad definition of an "employee" as an overly "narrow interpretation of an important constitutional right" to fair labour practices.[71] Jan Theron, more than 15 years ago, lamented the manner in which the definition of an "employee" was being interpreted in South Africa and asked the following questions: "If the definition of employee is to be extended, are rights premised on an employment relationship still relevant? Must these rights

---

69 IZA (2013) 11.

70 See, in this regard, Benjamin (2012) 25. The Supiot Report suggested "redesigning the notion of security" to prevent the working world being split in two, and argued that employment status should be redefined to guarantee the continuity of employment status in order to protect workers during transitions between jobs: Supiot and Meadows (2001) 221. As Benjamin suggests, this broader focus also accords with the ILO Decent Work Agenda goal of promoting opportunity for all workers to obtain productive work in conditions of freedom, equality, security and human dignity: see Somavia (1999).

71 Du Toit (2017).

not be re-conceptualised to take account a broader set of relations than the employment relationship encompasses?"[72]

CONCLUSION

All workers are entitled to fair labour practices and to have access to progressive realisation of their right to social security (given the wording of sections 23 and 27 of the Constitution). Vulnerable workers, being workers earning less than a particular, stipulated, amount of income to be determined, are particularly in need of support, constantly at risk of their human dignity being violated as a result of the precarious position in which they find themselves.[73] These workers are unlikely to be in a position to contribute to available mainstream social insurance schemes, requiring their limited income for basic necessities such as food, water, shelter and the like. Such workers are also, at present, typically excluded from available social assistance (unless they qualify for a disability grant), but may receive some social protection support from the state in terms of subsidised access to services. Vulnerable workers would certainly benefit from various forms of protection typically associated with standard employment – such as safe working conditions, the ability to organise and bargain collectively, minimum levels of income, and safety nets in the event of loss of work, injury on duty and the like. The idea would be to combine some flexibility with a minimum level of work security directed towards providing social protection guarantees for the professional and economic needs of workers. Designing the social security structure in this way would serve the objectives of developing systems capable of adaptation to new patterns of work and of providing appropriate protection to people engaged in such work.[74]

BIBLIOGRAPHY

Books and Chapters

A Ahsan, C Pages and T Roy "Legislation, enforcement and adjudication in Indian labor markets: Origins, Consequences and the Way Forward" in

[72] Theron (2002) 43.
[73] Informal work and work conducted by entrepreneurs are characterised by a high degree of vulnerability: International Labour Conference (2002) 2.
[74] Landa Zapirain (2012) 168.

D Mazumdar and S Sarkar *Globalization, Labor Markets and Inequality in India* (International Development Research Centre, Ottawa, 2008)
P Benjamin "Labour law beyond employment" in A Rycroft and R le Roux (eds) *Reinventing Labour Law* (Juta, Cape Town, 2012)
P Chikarmane and L Narayan "Transform or perish: changing conceptions of work in recycling" in J Fudge, S McCrystal and K Sankaran (eds) *Challenging the Legal Boundaries of Work Regulation* (Hart Publishing, Oregon, 2012)
G Davidov "Freelanceers: An intermediate group in labour law?" in J Fudge, S McCrystal and K Sankaran (eds) *Challenging the Legal Boundaries of Work Regulation* (Hart Publishing, Oregon, 2012)
J Fudge "Blurring legal boundaries: Regulating for decent work" in J Fudge, S McCrystal and K Sankaran (eds) *Challenging the Legal Boundaries of Work Regulation* (Hart Publishing, Oregon, 2012)
A Govindjee and J A van der Walt "Legal position of atypical workers" in A Govindjee and J A van der Walt (eds) *Labour Law in Context* (2nd Ed) (Pearson, South Africa, 2017)
J Grogan *Employment Rights* (Juta, South Africa, 2014)
K Sankaran "Flexibility and informatlisation of employment relationships" in J Fudge, S McCrystal and K Sankaran (eds) *Challenging the Legal Boundaries of Work Regulation* (Hart Publishing, Oregon, 2012)
A Supiot and P Meadows *Beyond Employment: Changes in Work and the Future of Labour Law* (Oxford University Press, Oxford, 2001)
J Landa Zapirain "Regulation of dependent self-employed workers in Spain: A regulatory framework for informal work?" in J Fudge, S McCrystal and K Sankaran (eds) *Challenging the Legal Boundaries of Work Regulation* (Hart Publishing, Oregon, 2012)

Journal Articles

C Barnard and A Blackham "Self-employment in EU Member States: The role of equality law" *European Equality Law Review* (vol. 2, 2015)
G Davidov "The Status of Uber Drivers" *Spanish Labour Law and Employment Relations Journal* (vol. 1–2, 2017) 6–15
D du Toit "Are independent contractors protected by a standard of fairness" (unpublished, IR Network, 2017)
J Fudge "A Canadian perspective on the scope of employment standards, labour rights and social protection: The good, the bad and the ugly" *Comparative Labour Law & Policy Journal* (vol. 31, 2010) 253–266
M A Fineman "The vulnerable subject: Anchoring equality in the human condition" *Yale Journal of Law and Feminism* (vol. 20: iss. 1, article 2, 2008)
N A Kohn "Vulnerability theory and the role of government" *Yale Journal of Law and Feminism* (vol. 26, iss. 1, article 2, 2014)
G Standing "The precariat and class struggle" *Revista Crítica de Ciências Sociais* (103, May 2014) 9–24
J Theron "The erosion of workers' rights and the presumption as to who is an employee" *Law Democracy and Development* (2002) 27–56

A Yesuneh "The regulation of atypical/non-standard employment relations in Ethiopia" *Jimma University Law Journal* (vol. 3, iss. 1, 2010) 15

Legislation

Basic Conditions of Employment Act 1997
Compensation for Occupational Injuries and Diseases Act 1993
Constitution of the Republic of South Africa, 1996
Employment Equity Act 1998
Employment Services Act 2014
Labour Relations Act 1995
Social Assistance Act 2004
Unemployment Insurance Act 2001

Case Law

Black Sash Trust v Minister of Social Development and others [2017] ZACC 8
Discovery Health Ltd v CCMA [2008] 7 BLLR 633 (LC)
Kylie v CCMA [2010] ZALAC 8
NUMSA v Assign Services and others [2018] ZACC 22
SABC v McKenzie (1999) 20 *ILJ* 585 (LAC)
Smit v Workman's Compensation Commissioner 1979 (1) SA 51 (A)
Uber South Africa Technological Services (Pty) Ltd v NUPSAW [2017] ZACCMA 1
Wyeth SA (Pty) Ltd v Manqele [2003] ZALC 60; [2005] ZALAC 1

International Instruments

ILO *Non-standard employment around the world: Understanding challenges, shaping prospects* (2016)
ILO Recommendation 198: Employment relationship recommendation (95th Conference Session, Geneva, 2006)
ILO Recommendation 204: Recommendation concerning the transition from the informal to the formal economy (104th Session, Geneva, 12 June 2015)

Research Reports

H Cheadle and M Clarke *International Labour Office National Study on Workers' Protection: South Africa* (2000)
G Davidov "Indirect employment – should lead companies be liable" written for a *Symposium of the Comparative Labour Law and Policy Journal on David Weil, The Fissured Workplace* (Cambridge, MA, Harvard University Press, 2014)
International Labour Conference, 90th Session, *Decent Work and the Informal Economy: Report VI* (International Labour Office, Geneva, 2002)

International Labour Office *Employment, Incomes and Equality: A Strategy for Increasing Productive Employment in Kenya* (International Labour Office, Geneva, 1972)

IZA *Social Protection Rights of Economically Dependent Self-employed Workers* (Research Report 54) (2013)

Statistics South Africa (2017) *Poverty Trends in South Africa: An examination between absolute poverty and 2006-2015* (Report 03-10-06)

Websites

City Press "UIF gets a benefits revamp" (2017) accessed at www.fin24.com/Economy/Labour/uif-gets-a-benefits-revamp-20170113 (accessed on 18 June 2017)

J Somavia "Report of the Director-General: Decent Work" (1999) accessed at www.ilo.org/public/english/standards/relm/ilc/ilc87/rep-i.htm (accessed on 17 November 2017)

Statistics South Africa "Survey of Employers and the Self-employed 2013" (2014) accessed at www.statssa.gov.za/publications/P0276/P02762013.pdf (accessed on 8 June 2017)

Statistics South Africa "Quarterly Labour Force Survey: Quarter 2: 2018" (2018) accessed at www.statssa.gov.za/publications/P0211/P02112ndQuarter2018.pdf (accessed on 2 September 2018)

PART III

Regional approaches

7. Informal and self-employed workers in Latin America: from an excluded category to an example of innovative inclusive measures

Pablo Arellano Ortiz

Latin America is one of the places in the world where both labour and social security law is more developed, but at a lower level than Europe,[1] while at the same time employment status is more precarious than in the northern hemisphere. There are many reasons for this state of affairs. The informal working relationships and independent or self-employment work have a significant presence in Latin America among the most vulnerable categories of people.

This contribution will attempt to put into perspective the Latin American reality. It will do this by analysing how this region will continue to develop protective measures and also the possible relevance of these measures for other regions in the world. It will attempt to demonstrate that the principle that formalization is needed to protect is not a *sine qua non* condition to protect these workers. Another protection strategy is possible by analysing what has been done in Latin America.

The analysis begins with a section dedicated to providing the theoretical background about informality, with emphasis on the Latin American discussion. Then, some cases of measures that have tended to deliver social benefits to specific groups of informal workers will be reviewed. These cases have been chosen as representative of measures that consider the informal worker in his condition as such. Some measures we recognize can mean a formalization, but in our view, this is a partial formalization. Towards the end of this contribution we will see that forcing formalization is not always the best strategy to protect informal workers. The cases selected seem to demonstrate this position.

1 Arellano Ortiz (2017) 15.

1. INFORMALITY IN THE LATIN AMERICAN REGION: THEORETICAL BACKGROUND

The informal working relationship average rate in the region is about 50 per cent of the economically active population. In some countries, this figure even reaches 60 per cent; even in those countries where the rate is lower than 50 per cent, informal employment is nevertheless a significant dimension of the labour market and has a major impact on the measures taken to protect this category of workers and their families.[2]

A recent ILO report[3] states that in the Americas, 40.0 per cent of total employment is informal. In absolute numbers, 183 million people are in informal employment whether in formal or informal enterprises. These rates vary widely by sub-region, at 18.1 per cent in North America and 53.1 per cent in Latin America and the Caribbean (LAC). Within LAC countries, the highest shares of informal employment are in Central America (58.0 per cent) and the Caribbean (57.6 per cent). At the country level, the share of informal employment ranges from 24.5 per cent in Uruguay to close to 80 per cent in Honduras, Guatemala and Nicaragua, and above 80 per cent in the plurinational State of Bolivia. In LAC, the share of informal employment in total employment is higher for women (54.3 per cent) than for men (52.3 per cent), especially in Central America, where informal employment rates for women are 61.8 per cent compared to that of men, at 55.6 per cent. There is an inverted relation with the level of education. The informality rate decreases as education increases. The place of residence influences informality: 52.6 per cent of the employed population in rural areas and 35.8 per cent in urban areas are in informal employment. Informality accounts for 77.5 per cent of employment in agriculture, 38.4 per cent in industry and 35.5 per cent in services.

In general, social legislation tends to protect all workers and even all categories of workers. Nonetheless, distinctions must be made that do not make the issue of protection easy. The economic perspective must be separated from the legal dimension. Simultaneously, there is need to distinguish between remunerated and non-remunerated work. To this must be added the high degree of deregulation that exists in Latin America.

---

2 OIT (2016) 38.
3 See: ILO (2018).

In this context it should be mentioned that informality carries with it different nomenclature.[4] The doctrine for example speaks of the informal sector, the informal economy or the non-structured sector to refer to almost identical groups of workers.[5] This term has been introduced by the International Labour Organization (ILO),[6] pointing out that the

> term 'informal economy' refers to all economic activities by workers and economic units that are – in law or in practice – not covered or insufficiently covered by formal arrangements. Their activities are not included in the law, which means that they are operating outside the formal reach of the law; or they are not covered in practice, which means that – although they are operating within the formal reach of the law, the law is not applied or not enforced; or the law discourages compliance because it is inappropriate, burdensome, or imposes excessive costs.

The origins of this ILO concept can be found in the works of the Institution carried out in relation to labour markets on the African continent in the 1960s and 1970s.[7] However, today it is used on a global scale as its object is no longer specific to just that continent.

More recently, the ILO has given a definition of informal employment, which is usually understood to include the following types of jobs:[8]

(i) own-account workers employed in their own informal sector enterprises;
(ii) employers employed in their own informal sector enterprises;
(iii) contributing family workers, irrespective of whether they work in formal or informal sector enterprises;
(iv) members of informal producers' cooperatives;
(v) employees holding informal jobs in formal sector enterprises, informal sector enterprises, or as paid domestic workers employed by households;
(vi) own-account workers engaged in the production of goods exclusively for own final use by their household.

The doctrine also has tried to specify the scope of this category of workers. For Professor Marius Olivier[9] informal work relations comprise all those activities which are de facto or *de jure* outside the scope of the law, including social security. The informal economy is not an individual condition, but a process of generating income characterized by one

---

4 See: Tokman (2007b); Kucera and Roncolato (2008); Servais (1994).
5 See: Servais (1994).
6 See: ILO (2007); ILO (2002a); ILO (2002b).
7 ILO (1972).
8 ILO (2003).
9 Olivier (2014) 215.

central feature: it is not regulated by the institutions of the society, within a juridical and social environment where similar activities are regulated. According to Victor Tokman[10] two factors have probably contributed to the increasing interest in informality. The first one is the strong relation between informality, poverty and underemployment, as well as a strong absorption of the most vulnerable groups of society, including women and young people. The second factor is the concept's capacity of adapting to the economic and social changes happening in the world.

Formal working relationships are those that are formalized by contract and are subject to legal and contractual rules. They are governed by a professional legal status: irregular work relations, illegal work, work in black, relations work in facts and labour relations *infra* protected. In other words, informal working relationships are governed by more diffuse and hidden rules.[11] However, in our opinion, the existence of a particular status regulated by the legislation does not matter. This is because these relations are often included in the regulation of dependent and subordinate work; this reasoning makes general labour regulations and their protection applicable to these precarious relationships.

Bearing in mind that this is a complex category with multiple edges, and considering its characteristics and its consequences in relation to the status of the workers covered by this sector, two major forms of productive units can be defined:[12]

- The family enterprise, formed by a worker on his own account (the employer), and others working with him (not necessarily on a permanent basis), without any legal labour relationship of dependence, but including in fact determined, normal and regular remuneration.
- The microenterprise, of similar size and degree of organization as the family enterprise, but with the crucial difference that the owner provides salaried employment to third persons on a continuous basis.

Informal labour may include dependent or independent workers; the common feature is the precariousness in which they find themselves, and their lack of protection, both in terms of labour law and social security. In relation to the latter it is important to point out that if the social security system is based on contributions this leads to coverage gaps,[13] as not all members of the labour market can contribute, so one group will stay

---

10 Tokman (2007a) 2.

11 Monereo Pérez (2011).

12 Lacchini and Zuccotti (2009) 27.

13 Bertranou (2006).

outside. Also, it has to be considered that there is a growing tendency of deregulation of the labour market: a considerable number of workers of the formal sector have precarious contracts,[14] with all the risks that this implies.

An example may be the situation in the Southern Cone region of South America where independent workers represent 24 per cent of the active population and the majority of them are active within the informal economy.[15] The issue of independent workers can be addressed in different ways. On the one hand, there are structural limitations to the qualitative creation of paid employment. On the other hand, there are certain problems in the conception of social security programmes.[16] It is important to bear in mind what Queisser[17] stated, when she says that it is common in Latin American countries that in order to pay lower contributions people will declare a lower than actual income and only towards the end of their work life will they tend to declare a higher income.

Many efforts have been made by governments with a view to formalizing and incorporating these workers into social security. This is also the policy promoted by the ILO and its Recommendation No. 204. This instrument, the Recommendation about the transition from the informal to the formal economy, defines in Article 1.2 what is meant by the 'informal economy' for the purposes of the Recommendation:

(a) refers to all economic activities by workers and economic units that are – in law or in practice – not covered or insufficiently covered by formal arrangements; and
(b) does not cover illicit activities, in particular the provision of services or the production, sale, possession or use of goods forbidden by law, including the illicit production and trafficking of drugs, the illicit manufacturing of and trafficking in firearms, trafficking in persons, and money laundering, as defined in the relevant international treaties.

In our opinion Recommendation No. 204 and the logic behind the idea of a transition from informality to formality through various strategies, seems to be rather limited in scope. The ILO does not fully appreciate the complexity of the labour market reality, at least the Latin American market. It should be noted that many of the informal economy workers choose to be in this position. In some cases, entering the formal market implies a decrease in the social security benefits they receive. Thus the

---

14 Ibid., 28.
15 Bertranou (2007) 1.
16 Ibid., 3.
17 Queisser (1995) 29.

precarious context of these workers must be taken into account to protect them in their state and not force them to move to a state they do not wish to be part of. Public policies must adapt to the realities of the workplace and not vice versa.

However, these efforts have been met with certain limitations related to vulnerability and precariousness. Given this, creative mechanisms have been implemented that understand the complexities of informality and serve as vehicles to bring these workers within the coverage of the social security system. These examples should be highlighted as an ingenious way of extending social security to excluded groups. This contribution will try to highlight the main measure that has been taken.

It also needs to be taken into account that in this region inequality is very high. In this sense, the Gini coefficient shows that the highest level of inequality can be found in this region. Vulnerability and precariousness are two important features that characterize the labour market in Latin American countries.

In relation to this point it is interesting to be able to measure the levels of inequality existing in the region. For this, it is important to use the Gini coefficient, which is used to measure income inequality, within a country, but can be used to measure any form of unequal distribution. The Gini coefficient is a number between 0 and 1, where 0 corresponds to perfect equality (all have the same income) and where the value 1 corresponds to perfect inequality (one person has all the income and the other none). The Economic Commission for Latin America and the Caribbean (ECLAC) has recently published a study[18] that shows that the average Gini coefficient for the countries with recent information available fell from 0.497 in 2013 to 0.491 in 2014. When the most recent figures are compared with those from the start of the 2010s, a more substantial reduction is found. The regional index stood at 0.507 in 2010; by 2014 there had been a cumulative fall of 3.2 per cent, equivalent to 0.8 per cent a year. There were statistically significant changes in the Gini coefficient in nine of the 16 countries considered during this period. The largest reductions were in Uruguay (–2.7 per cent a year), Argentina (–2.3 per cent) and Ecuador (–2.2 per cent) (Figure 7.1).

The levels of inequality are important considering that if we compare the Gini coefficient of Chile and Mexico with the rest of the countries in the region it can be easily observed that the levels of inequality are very similar, although it is appreciated that at the regional level there is a slight decrease between 2012 and 2015.

---

[18] See: ECLAC (2016).

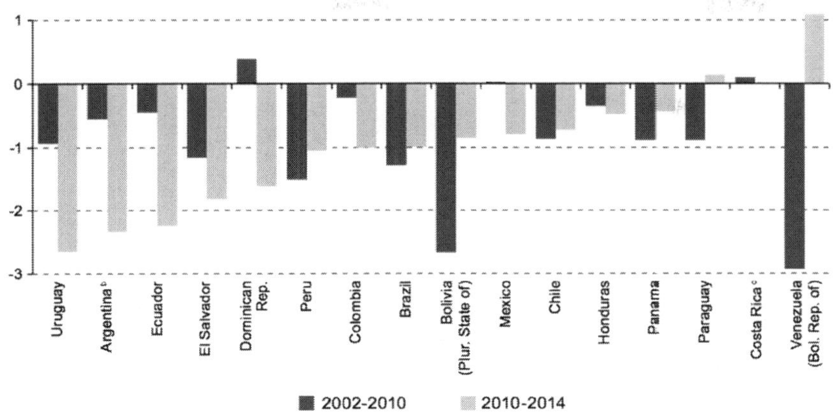

Source: *Social Panorama of Latin America 2015 (13)* by Social Development Division and the Statistics Division of the Economic Commission for Latin America and the Caribbean, © 2016, United Nations. Reprinted with the permission of the United Nations.

Figure 7.1 Latin America (16 countries): annual rate of change in the Gini coefficient, 2002-2010 and 2010-2014 (Percentages)

However, in analysing the presence of Latin American countries in the context of the Organisation of Economic Co-operation and Development (OECD), one can observe the true reality of inequality in the region in relation to the more developed countries (Figure 7.2). This is because it can be seen that Mexico and Chile are the most unequal countries of the OECD, with a level of inequality well above the average of OECD countries.

In addition to the above it should be mentioned that according to ECLAC and Oxfam, income and wealth concentration are at the heart of inequality in the region. The richest 10 per cent in Latin America and the Caribbean own 71 per cent of wealth and their tax rate is only 5.4 per cent of their income (Figure 7.3).[19]

[19] See the information at http://www.cepal.org/en/pressreleases/income-and-wealth-concentration-are-heart-inequality-region-according-eclac-and-oxfam

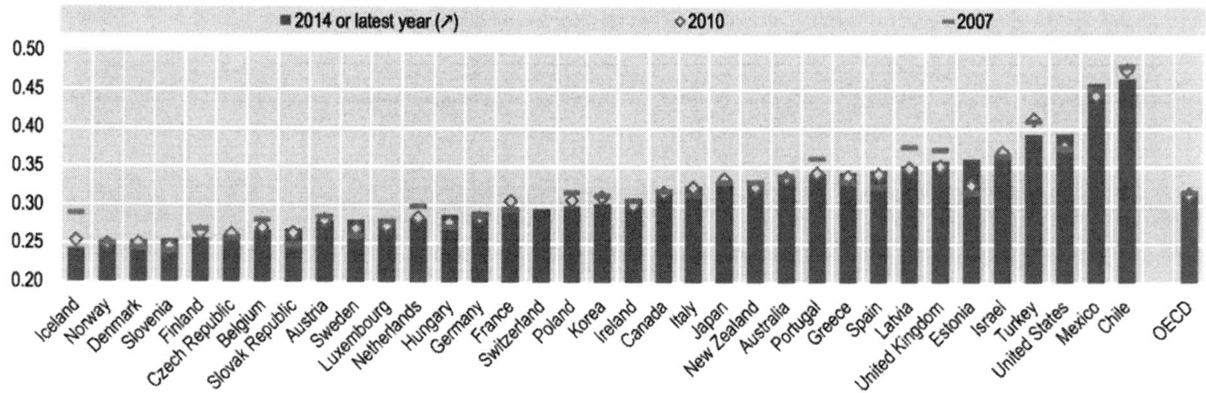

Source: OECD (2016).

Figure 7.2 Gini coefficient of disposable income inequality in 2007–14 (or latest year), total population

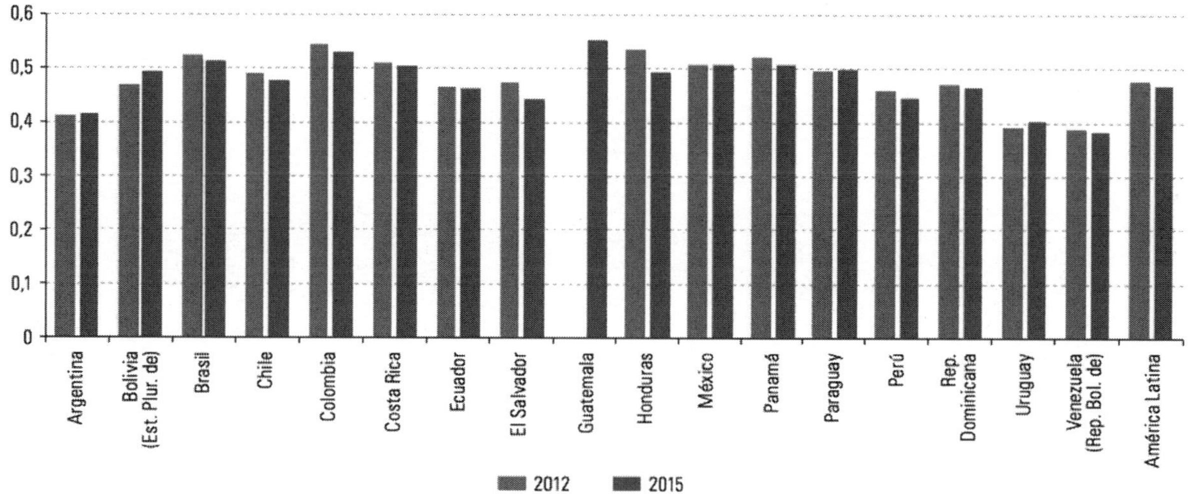

Source: *Social Panorama of Latin America 2016 (14)*, by Social Development Division and the Statistics Division of the Economic Commission for Latin America and the Caribbean, © 2017 United Nations. Reprinted with the permission of the United Nations.

Figure 7.3 Latin America (17 countries): Gini coefficient, around 2012 and 2015

Now if we situate the levels of informality, from a quantitative perspective, of the Latin American region in relation to other regions, we must indicate, for example, that in Mexico and Brazil about half of the jobs are in the informal sector, in comparison with 80 per cent in India and Indonesia. Informal jobs contribute to inequality in a number of ways, such as lower incomes than in formal jobs. In addition, they rarely offer workers training and promotion opportunities. And they are unpredictable, which means that workers can find themselves without income in a very short time.[20]

Recent figures indicate, according to the ILO, that in 2016 there was an increase in informality in the Latin American region compared to 2015. It is estimated that there are 134 million workers in the informal market, representing approximately 47 per cent of the labour market. The trend also suggests that these figures will continue to increase from the 2016 figures, and in greater proportion.[21]

In this way it can be indicated that it is a vulnerable group that has increased in number and that this increase has not been able to be stopped in the region. The traditional public policies have not been able to create an impact that allows a decrease of informality, as it has been verified that the opposite happened. In this way it is important to look for mechanisms that allow informal workers to be able to benefit from coverage of social risks, without forcing them to formalize, but allowing them to stay in the informal economy.

Whereas labour informality is not a uniquely Latin American phenomenon, the measures adopted in this region to extend social rights to this unprotected group should be considered. In this sense, the rights have been delivered through various measures and have tried to give the fullest possible protection to concerned (informal and self-employed) individuals. Protective measures have been introduced through trade union intervention, through changes to immigration laws, through social security measures, through developments in labour law and so on. The examples in the region are diverse and this chapter will try to develop a systematization that allows these measures to be considered as alternative solutions for other regions.

---

20 Keeley (2015) 28.

21 OIT (2016) 38.

2. SOCIAL SECURITY AND INFORMALITY: A VARIETY OF EXPERIENCES AND RESULTS

In general, in Latin America mechanisms reflect the major influence of a Bismarckian system, as a great percentage of the covered population is covered only because they belong to the formal market where they contribute to social security. However, the labour market structure in the region makes it necessary to reconsider the traditional principles of social security funding in the region with the aim of extending coverage in order to protect the marginalized part of the active population and it is also necessary that the State increases its participation in this context.[22]

Advances in coverage have taken place mainly through conditional cash transfer mechanisms. These programmes have had an important influence on improving social protection coverage in the Latin American region. At the same time, they have had an impact on the labour market, leading to a higher degree of affiliation in order to be able to contribute to social security systems.

An ECLAC and ILO document[23] states that public policies are focusing on money transfers through these programmes. The low amounts of the benefits paid by these programmes often do not lead to labour integration of adults but – as intended – of children. Labour integration, both for adults as well as young people who have just finished their education, is confronted with the lack of productive jobs, which is especially true for areas with elevated poverty figures. This must be brought into relation with the weakness of public support measures for children, the elderly and the disabled, having a negative impact on the participation of women living in poverty in the labour market. Hence it is important that transfer programmes are tightly coordinated with integral social protection schemes and active labour market policies increasing labour demand, among other objectives.

On the other hand, it can be concluded that the design of these programmes should be embedded in the idea of the 'passage' of their recipients through different stages of continuous intervention, so that eventually 'graduating' from the programmes does not imply the loss of rights, as this might discourage wanting to belong to the formal sector. So, there would be a close relation of these programmes with informality, stimulating the formalization of the beneficiaries. However, as this study also points out, such programmes do have limitations. We share this

---

22 Lacchini and Zuccotti (2009).

23 ECLAC and ILO (2014) 6.

assessment of the limitations of these types of programmes in the protection of the informal economy.

The different efforts of public policy to cover the informal population in Latin America more extensively has been marked by success and failure. Without any doubt, the focus of interest has been the classical effort to bring these groups into a formal work relationship, which, however, is not always desired. As a consequence, this region has a rate of informal workers of around 50 per cent, in some countries even higher, as we have already mentioned.

The Latin American region is diverse and the labour market in Central America is very different from the Southern Cone region. Thus, it is very difficult to make affirmations about trends in the Latin American region as a whole. There are informal workers in both sub-regions, but we think the reason of their existence as well as measures to protect them vary greatly. So, there are no measures to be applied as remedies for the whole region, nor can some of them be exported to other regions. But we do think that they can be adapted and their results are worth being studied.

In this context, we would like to share the results of a study[24] which explores the reasons for the important decrease of informal employment in Argentina after the 2001–2002 crisis, namely by 15 per cent from 49 per cent to 34 per cent. This study considers that this decrease corresponds to the net creation of formal employment and, to a lesser degree, to the net elimination of unregistered employment. According to the statistical evidence carried out by the study, the Argentine economy had started to show increased growth rates, with an average of 7.8 per cent until 2011. The economic activity was reflected in a reduced unemployment rate from 16.1 per cent in 2003 to 7.2 per cent in 2012. At the same time, unregistered employment decreased in all work categories during this period, although to a greater degree in the case of workers carrying out operational tasks (minus 18.8 per cent), followed by workers carrying out unqualified tasks (minus 12.3 per cent). The professional and technical categories remained practically unchanged. This study considers that the decrease was a consequence of the establishment of different strategies for the formalization of employment, such as the National Program of Work Regularization (Programa Nacional de Regularización del Trabajo; PNRT) implemented as of 2003, facilitating workers' registration, employers' identification and enforcement inspection. Among the measures, the incentive to register domestic work by way of deducting the contributions

[24] Bertranou et al. (2013).

paid under the Special Social Security System for Household Employees when determining the basis of income taxes stands out.

In general these measures trying, in different ways and to different degrees, to bring the informal worker closer to the protection offered by formality are varied. Different mechanisms can be found in the most varied contexts: in some cases the inclusion of trade unions, in others of public institutions as well as protection of specific categories of workers in the informal economy.

An example that can be mentioned is the one found in a study on migration policies in the Central American and Caribbean region[25] where the Dominican Republic is distinguished due to the effort of the unions in the fight against informality. It is important to bear in mind that in the Dominican Republic, as in other countries, one of the major challenges of the social security system is the incorporation of independent workers, in many cases migrant workers coming mostly from Haiti who are excluded from social security benefits. In order to address this problem, the Mutual Association of Solidarity Services (Asociación Mutual de Servicios Solidarios; AMUSSOL)[26] was created with the aim to incorporate workers of the informal economy into a more formal framework and provide them with social security coverage. It is the objective of this Association to represent workers so that they can join the Dominican Social Security System. In the end this Association sometimes functions as an employer so that informal workers have access to social security. It has more than 14,000 affiliates plus their dependent beneficiaries, covering more than 40,000 people in total. Among its members are a considerable number of street vendors and housekeeping staff, typically excluded from social security. Coverage is obtained by means of a voluntary insurance depending on the contributions paid. If the beneficiary does not pay contributions, there is no coverage. The most interesting feature of AMUSSOL is that it was created by the Autonomous Confederation of Workers' Unions (Confederación Autónoma Sindical Clasista; CASC). This makes this initiative even more remarkable, as it shows the importance union movements may have not only for dependent but also for informal workers. It also shows that informal workers do not have to radically change their way of work; it is the policies around them that change and adapt to their reality, in this case the approach of the unions.

25 Arellano Ortiz (2014).
26 See http://www.amussol.org.do/web/

Among the different realities found in the Latin American region we would like to highlight the case of the Monotributo Scheme in Uruguay. This mechanism consists of an optional unified tax package, which includes both the payment of social security contributions and the payment of taxes. It is mainly intended for micro and small enterprises involved in the informal economy. Implemented initially in 2001, due to the recognition that more than 80 per cent of Uruguayan independents were excluded from social security, it did not have much success until the incorporation of new criteria in 2006 when multiple companies were able to access the Monotributo Scheme.

The Monotributo Scheme came into being because in Uruguay independent employment occupies the second place in the labour market, as three out of ten workers earn their living this way. In early 2000, it was acknowledged that a significant section of own-account workers with limited economic activity was governed by inadequate rules which fostered their marginalization within the social protection system.

This provided the context for the second stage, which began with the creation of the Monotributo Scheme, established in terms of Article 590 of Law n.° 17.296, of February 21, 2001. The scheme consisted of a unified optional tax payment which replaced special contributions to social security generated according to economic activity, as well as all applicable national taxes in force (except for import taxes). Initially, this scheme focused on small one-person businesses developing business activities in the street or in public spaces. However, the system was modified in order to achieve the goal of increasing social protection coverage.

In 2006 the Monotributo Scheme was subject to substantial modification, initially promoted by the Banco de Protección Social (BPS)[27] Board and later – through minor modifications – by the Executive and then Parliament. The changes introduced through the Tax Reform Law[28] from 2006, in force as of July 2007, aimed to facilitate the withdrawal of at least 170,000 people from the informal economy, allowing for the taxation of their productive microenterprises, and increased access to social security benefits, mainly to health benefits.

It has been pointed out that the effects of the reform of the Monotributo Scheme on coverage of independent workers in the period following the reform (2007–2009) was that the annual average of contributing

---

[27] The Social Protection Bank, which is a public institution in charge of social security and social protection benefits; it is also regulated in the Uruguayan Constitution. See more at http://www.bps.gub.uy

[28] Law No. 18.083, of December 27, 2006 and the respective decrees.

one-person businesses registered rose to 68,588, which was 12,722 more that the annual average of contributing one-person businesses registered in the previous period (55,866). Nevertheless, in terms of average growth between periods, one-person businesses are the companies registering the most momentum (5.1 per cent), followed by small companies, with only 1.7 per cent. As a consequence, the relative share of one-person businesses in comparison with the total of contributing companies increased about 2.0 per cent.[29] It has been stated that the evolution was positive for most activities, and was particularly important in one-person businesses engaged in trade, repair of vehicles (cars and motorcycles), agricultural production, reforestation and fishing, which jointly absorb 52.2 per cent of the total number of companies of this type.[30]

These results show that the Monotributo Scheme has effectively reached a vulnerable group of workers (such as craftspeople, locksmiths, carpenters, grinders, weavers, photographers, blacksmiths, welders and car washers, among others), favouring their coverage and inclusion.

Although the evaluation of the 2006 reform has been positive, the system was again reformed in 2011 by law 18.874 incorporating the Monotributo Scheme. This system covers workers who produce goods or services and includes households under the poverty line or in a situation of social vulnerability. Their registration requires previous authorization by the Ministry of Social Development.

This new regime is a special system for personal and associative businesses for persons who live in households under the poverty line or in a situation of socio-economic vulnerability. It helps them to become included in the social security system by contributing a reduced amount of money to the BPS.

Contribution payment is progressive, starting with 25 per cent of the total contribution, later 50 per cent and then 75 per cent, until only after 36 months of activity, 100 per cent of the contribution needs to be paid.

One of the main lessons to learn from this system is that in contexts of diverse socio-economic profiles the designing of more flexible funding mechanisms may constitute a valuable tool to promote social inclusion protecting a wide range of economic activities.[31] In addition, the Uruguayan experience shows that it is possible to form strategic alliances

---

29 Duran-Valverde (2013).

30 Ibid.

31 Activities included in the Monotributo Scheme as at January 2015: http://www.bps.gub.uy/innovaportal/file/4660/5/actividades_incluidas_en_mono tributo_-_enero_2015_.pdf

between social security institutions and tax collection authorities. Uruguay's quest to include sectors of society previously excluded from social security coverage is well worth pointing out. These categories will keep their work in the form that they wanted and at the same time participate in a social protection scheme. In our view it is a partial formalization, an incentive to be protected but being informal at the same time. These reforms turn the country into a model to follow in Latin America by their efforts to extend coverage to informal workers through innovative mechanisms.

Another example is The Peasants' Social Insurance programme (Seguro Social Campesino; SSC) in Ecuador, which provides coverage to independent agricultural workers and local fishermen. The old age pension paid under this programme amounts to 75 per cent of the minimum wage. Affiliation can be individual or collective, although individual affiliation is given priority. Contributions are collected by the farmers' organization. The system is funded on a solidary basis with the involvement of the affiliates and employers who belong to the National Social Security System, contributions by the State and contribution payments by the protected workers. As can be seen, this scheme is based on the fundamental principles of any social security system: solidarity. However, the way the contributions are calculated is original due to the difficulties to determine the monthly income of agricultural workers and fishermen.

One of the features characterizing social security coverage in Ecuador is the high percentage of the rural population in the labour market and the important role of the SSC in the social security structure of that country. It has become a groundbreaking mechanism for the extension of social security to agricultural workers, a group traditionally excluded from social security due to its own characteristics.

The target population for the SSC are the rural workers and local fishermen who work on their own behalf and with their families. Due to its nature this population group mainly lives in the rural areas of the country. According to the Household Survey 2005, 48 per cent of the economically active population are considered independent workers. Moreover, 42 per cent out of this category work in the primary sector of the economy.[32] The great majority of agricultural workers who belong to a social security system do so through the SSC. According to data from the Household Survey 2005, an overall 262,986 workers are affiliated to the SSC, out of which 181,932 belong to the sector of private non-wage

[32] Duran-Valverde (2013).

earning workers, and 83 per cent of this population group (151,156) are independent agricultural or peasant workers.[33]

The SSC is characterized by an important service infrastructure, through which it achieves remarkable regional presence. By the year 2008 the system had some 600 dispensaries distributed in the 24 provinces of Ecuador, where beneficiaries have access to health services. Also, when more specialized medical assistance is required, affiliates have the option to turn to the hospital units of the General Individual and Family Health Insurance and other medical units having agreements with the SSC. In short, Durán Valverde[34] indicates that the SSC is characterized by operating under a model of geographical de-concentration and operative decentralization, under the hierarchy of SSC's management, which in turn reports to the Instituto Ecuatoriano de Seguridad Social's (IESS's) general management, and must submit its policies and programmes to the approval of that entity's board of directors.

The SSC has been affected by a series of situations that make clear that improvement still needs to be made. One of these improvements is the development of the affiliation rates over recent years, which is far from desired, in comparison with the many people in the rural areas who still are totally unprotected. SSC affiliation has been losing ground compared to the growth of the rural population. At the same time, predictions have referred to problems existing in the processing of information and registers, monitoring of the affiliated population and their contributions and the State's commitment, among others.

Nevertheless, the SSC stands out due to several factors mentioned above and still constitutes one of the major strengths of social security in Ecuador. In 2009 it covered 917,417 people, 227,694 families and a total of 34,729 pensioners. Hence this means important progress for a category of workers within the informal economy commonly excluded from protection. Its innovative character of universal coverage while respecting the typical features of the protected group makes it an example worth mentioning.

3. SOME FINAL THOUGHTS

We agree with Duran-Valverde[35] when he stated in a study on independent workers:

33 Duran-Valverde (2013).
34 Duran-Valverde (2008) 116.
35 Duran-Valverde (2008) 92.

> In practice countries take different approaches, reflecting the different specific national practices which vary even within one country or one social security system and which we have called – innovations. Such innovations make perfect sense in view of the numerous edges or dimensions forming part of the complex characteristics and needs of a highly heterogeneous group of difficult coverage as is the case of independent workers.

The same holds true for workers in the informal economy. Their heterogeneity calls for innovative solutions.

A new ILO international instrument that seeks to protect informal workers, that is, Recommendation No. 204, has recently been approved. It is now waiting on an action plan which must be submitted by the International Labour Office to the Council of Administration. The logic behind this recommendation is the transition from informality to formality through various strategies.

As different experiences show, public policies must not be rigid and reduced to the idea of formality being the only recommended structure of labour. For that matter, formalizing a work relationship does not seem to be the only solution. An alternative is trying to protect the informal worker in his/her informality. This is the challenge of public policy and this is where the Latin American experience may be useful.

The current conception of social security was born in Europe at the end of the nineteenth century and developed on that continent, North America and Australia, even before World War II.[36] But it also developed in Latin America in the same period. We must highlight the adoption of laws on social insurance in Brazil in 1923 and in Chile in 1925.[37] Both regions have a more advanced level of development in this regard than the rest of the world, but in Europe the level of coverage is more important.

In our opinion if we tried to characterize social security in the Latin American region we would find a strange mixture of social insurance mechanisms with purely private financial mechanisms; a mixture of universal coverage mechanisms with self-protection mechanisms or individual coverage; and a relevant protective culture within national legislations – each country has their own protective model. The Latin American region is very diverse and the labour market in Central America is quite different from the Southern Cone region. There are informal workers in both sub-regions, but we think the reason for their existence as well as measures to protect them vary greatly. So, there are no measures to be

---

36 Arellano Ortiz (2017) 15.
37 Durand (2005) 85.

applied as remedies for the whole region, nor can some of them be exported to other regions. But the principles and the logic behind these measures can be used as examples for other countries and regions.

Mechanisms used to protect informal workers are based on social insurance, social assistance and of course by social protection, in particular through conditional cash transfers programmes. Also it needs to be taken into account in relation to this region that the population is ageing very fast, there is an inverted population pyramid, and also it is necessary to highlight the appearance of new social risks and the need to cover them.[38]

In relation to the coverage of informal workers we can identify measures which involve the unions; are embedded in migration laws; are carried out through social security mechanisms, such as conditional transfer programmes; and are carried out through adjustments or new developments in labour law regulations.

It can be observed that inequality and informality are not decreasing in the region. In our opinion these factors should be studied together if we want to have a more homogeneous and better protected middle class. The fight against poverty is linked to the reduction of informality in the region. In some cases, it is clear that the poor stay poor even if they participate in these programmes. An alternative is trying to protect the informal worker in their informality. This is the challenge of public policy and this is where the Latin American experience may be useful. Innovative mechanisms that try to adapt to the changes in the labour market are the key to protect all workers, formal and informal.

BIBLIOGRAPHY

Pablo Arellano Ortiz, *Lecciones de seguridad social* (2nd edition, Librotecnia, Santiago, 2017)

Pablo Arellano Ortiz, *Identificación de acciones y estrategias para mejorar la protección de las trabajadoras y trabajadores migrantes y sus familias mediante la seguridad social, Políticas de Migración Laboral Sensibles al Género en los Corredores de Nicaragua-Costa Rica-Panamá y Haití-República Dominicana* (Organización Internacional del Trabajo, Oficina San José de Costa Rica, 2014)

Fabio Bertranou, Luis Casanova and Marianela Sarabia, *Dónde, cómo y por qué se redujo la informalidad laboral en Argentina durante el período 2003–2012* (1st edition, Documentos de trabajo, No 1 Oficina de País de la OIT para la Argentina, Buenos Aires, 2013)

---

[38] Arellano Ortiz (2017).

Fabio Bertranou, *Informal Economy, Independent Coverage in Argentina, Chile and Uruguay* (Oficina Internacional del Trabajo, Santiago, 2007)
Fabio Bertranou (ed.) *Envejecimiento, empleo y protección social en América Latina* (Organización Internacional del Trabajo, Santiago, 2006)
CEPAL, *Panorama Social de América Latina* (División de Desarrollo Social y División de Estadísticas de la Comisión Económica para América Latina y el Caribe, CEPAL, Naciones Unidas, Santiago, 2016)
Paul Durand, *La politique contemporaine de Sécurité Sociale* (Dalloz, Paris, 2005)
Fabio Duran-Valverde (ed.) *Innovaciones en la extensión de la cobertura del seguro social a los trabajadores independientes. Experiencias de Brasil, Cabo Verde, Colombia, Costa Rica, Ecuador, Filipinas, Francia y Uruguay* (Organización Internacional del Trabajo, Ginebra, 2013)
Fabio Duran-Valverde, *Diagnóstico del sistema de seguridad social del Ecuador* (Organización Internacional del Trabajo/Oficina Subregional para los Países Andinos. Lima, 2008)
ECLAC, *Social Panorama of Latin America 2016* (Social Development Division and the Statistics Division of the Economic Commission for Latin America and the Caribbean, Santiago, 2017).
ECLAC, *Social Panorama of Latin America 2015* (Social Development Division and the Statistics Division of the Economic Commission for Latin America and the Caribbean, Santiago, 2016).
ECLAC / ILO, *Los programas de transferencias condicionadas y el mercado laboral*, (Conyuntura laboral en América Latina y el Caribe, Número 10, Mayo 2014, Naciones Unidas, Organización Internacional del Trabajo, Santiago de Chile, 2014)
ILO, *Women and Men in the Informal Economy: A Statistical Picture* (3rd edition, International Labour Office, Geneva, 2018)
ILO, Transition from the Informal to the Formal Economy Recommendation, 2015 (No. 204)
ILO, Social Protection Floors Recommendation, 2012 (No. 202)
ILO, *L'économie informelle: permettre une transition vers la formalisation* (Document du travail, *Colloque interrégional tripartite sur l'économie informelle: Permettre une transition vers la formalisation*, Genève, 27–29 novembre 2007)
ILO, *Directrices sobre una definición estadística de empleo informal* (Adoptadas por la Decimoséptima Conferencia Internacional de Estadísticos del Trabajo, noviembre – diciembre de 2003)
ILO, *Rapport de la Commission de l'économie informelle* (Conférence internationale du Travail, 90e session, Genève, 2002a)
ILO, *Travail décent et économie informelle* (Conférence internationale du Travail, Rapport VI, 90e session, Genève, 2002b)
ILO, *Employment incomes and equality: A strategy for increasing productive employment in Kenya* (International Labour Office, Geneva, 1972)
Brien Keeley, *Income Inequality: The Gap between Rich and Poor* (OECD Insights, OECD Publishing, Paris, 2015)

D. Kucera and L. Roncolato, 'L'emploi informel: deux questions de politique controversées', *Revue internationale du travail*, 2008, Vol. 147, n° 4, pp. 347–377

Carlos Lacchini and Guillermo Zuccotti, *Importancia de la contributividad en el sistema de seguridad social. Elementos de análisis para la inclusión social en América Latina.* (Proyecto de seguridad social para organizaciones sindicales SSOS, primera edición, Centro Internacional de Formación de la ILO, España, 2009)

José Luis Monereo Pérez, *Manual de teoría de las relaciones laborales* (Editorial Tecnos, Madrid, 2011)

OECD, Inequality Update 2016 'Income inequality remains high in the face of weak recovery' (Centre for Opportunity and Equality, 24 November 2016)

OIT, *Panorama Laboral 2016*, (OIT / Oficina Regional para América Latina y el Caribe, Lima, 2016)

Marius Olivier, 'Work at the margins of social security: Expanding the boundaries of social protection in the developing world', in Wim Van Oorschot, Hans Peeters and Kees Boos (eds) *Invisible Social Security Revisited, Essays in Honour of Jos Berghman* (Lannoo Publishers, Lovaina, Belgium, 2014)

M. Queisser, 'Après le Chili, les réformes de la deuxième génération en Amérique Latine', *Revue internationale de sécurité sociale*, 1995, Vol. 48, n° 3–4, p. 29

J. Saavedra and M. Tommasi, 'Informalité, Etat et contrat social en Amérique latine: étude préliminaire', *Revue internationale du travail*, 2007, Vol. 146, n° 3–4, p. 301

J.-M. Servais, 'Secteur informel: un avenir pour le droit du travail', *Actualités du droit*, 1994, pp. 661–685

Víctor Tokman, *Informality: Exclusion and precariousness* (paper prepared for the Tripartite interregional Symposium on the Informal Economy: Enabling Transition to Formalization, ILO, Geneva, 27–29 November 2007a)

Víctor Tokman, 'Economie informelle, insécurité et cohésion sociale en Amérique latine', *Revue internationale du travail*, 2007b, Vol. 146, n° 1–2, p. 89

8. Structure and social protection of the self-employed society: an Eastern-European perspective based on Hungarian experience

Tamás Gyulavári

1. INTRODUCTION

The chapter focuses on the Hungarian social protection of self-employment; however, it also strives to draw some conclusions, which may be valid for the wider region of Central and Eastern Europe (CEE), particularly the European Union (EU) member states in this region. This analysis is supported by the fact that the labour and social law developments of the Central and Eastern European EU member states have been rather similar in the last decades as a consequence of common traditions, similar economic and social developments, as well as the effects of labour law harmonization. Therefore, the problems arising from the gradual restructuring of legal relationships aimed at work are rather analogous.

The chapter strives to map the social protection of self-employed workers. First, the categories and numbers of workers will be addressed, those in as well as out of employment, with special focus on different groups of self-employed persons, as they shed light on the structural problems and size of the issue of self-employment in CEE countries, with particular attention to Hungary. It will be followed by an overview of the general social security scheme in Hungary. Finally, the special social security schemes for self-employed will be explored through the lens of equal access.

2. LEGAL STATUS AND NUMBERS OF WORKERS IN AND OUT OF EMPLOYMENT

In CEE, employment relationship is still the most important legal relationship aimed at work; however, civil law contracts have also been playing an important role in the labour market. In this section, we will outline the legal framework of work relationships and the numbers of the various categories of the working population.

The typical employment relationship is still the dominant legal form of work in CEE, which is regulated by a separate law, the Labour Code in each of these countries.[1] Atypical forms of employment are far from being as widespread as in the western European Member States, as they still represent only a fraction of employees, such as part-timers, agency workers or teleworkers. The notable exception is fixed-term work, particularly in Poland, since cheap termination of fixed-term contracts seemingly attracts employers.[2] Therefore, the labour law heritage of CEE countries from the socialist period has proven to be stronger than the effect of EU labour law harmonization.

Beyond employment relationships, there are almost exclusively civil law contracts in CEE, which may provide a cheaper and less problematic alternative contractual framework for workers. This is a rather tempting option for both parties, as it regularly cuts employer expenses and maximizes employee income. The rocket like expansion of Polish fixed-term employment contracts[3] in the last decade (to the top of the EU league table in 2016 at 27.5%)[4] taught us an important lesson: it showed the high importance of cost cutting and easy termination rules in employers' decisions regarding the choice of the contractual form of work (e.g. employment contract or self-employment).

In CEE countries, civil law (service) contracts are regulated by the Civil Code as a legal relationship between two equal parties, without any cogent rules and employment protection. Thus, the parties may freely govern their relationship in the service contract within the remarkably weak regulatory framework provided by civil law. Civil law work contracts lack hierarchy among the parties, personal and economic subordination of worker and principal. The third legal category of economically dependent work (besides employment and civil law contracts), as it is known in several European legal systems,[5] has not been

---

1 Gyulavári (2014a) 267, 278.

2 Skupień et al. (2016).

3 Eichhorst (2014).

4 Employment statistics. Data from June 2017, <http://ec.europa.eu/eurostat/statistics-explained/index.php/Employment_statistics> accessed 19 September 2017.

5 See for example Countouris (2007); Casale (2011); Brodie (2005); Pennings and Bosse (2011); Davidov (2005); Deakin (2006).

regulated in CEE (except Slovenia[6]). There have been theoretically inspiring proposals on this third labour law category in Poland (2006) and Hungary (2011); however, without any effect on current legislation.[7]

We must clarify here, that self-employment covers three different groups of working people in the region. Genuine self-employment, economically dependent work and bogus (in other words, false) self-employment[8] all play a significant role in the labour markets of CEE. Genuine self-employment is used in this chapter as a notion covering independent contracts, where the relationship of the parties is not characterized by personal or economic dependence. Economically dependent work lacks personal dependence on the employer, but shows a high level of economic dependence on one client (quasi-employer). Bogus (false)[9] self-employment is an employment relationship with a high level of personal and economic dependence; however, the parties try to cut costs (by lower public burdens and fewer employer obligations) by concluding a civil law contract. We may refer here to the *FNV Kunsten* European Court of Justice (ECJ) judgment,[10] which interpreted the notion of 'false self-employed' in EU law.

The lack of legal clarification of the notions of self-employment and economically dependent work makes it difficult to draw a clear picture of the factual rearrangement of the legal framework. In practice, genuine and bogus self-employment and economically dependent work equally take the legal form of working individuals, individual entrepreneurship and membership in (one-man) companies[11] through civil law contracts. There is a sophisticated judicial test on the differentiation of bogus and genuine self-employment and on the national notion of an employment relationship. This test has been elaborated in the last decades by the courts.[12]

The real size of the three subgroups of the self-employed society is not revealed by available data, as statistics focus merely on the overall rate of

---

6 Senčur Peček (2017).

7 Swiatkowski (2011); Gyulavári (2014b).

8 Perulli makes a clear distinction between these categories: Perulli (2002).

9 Bogus and false self-employment are used in this chapter as synonyms.

10 C-413/13 *FNV Kunsten Informatie en Media v Staat der* Nederlanden [2014] ECLI:EU:C:2014:2411.

11 The working person may choose any of these legal qualifications to conclude a civil law contract to perform work as a natural person or through a company (usually set up for this very purpose).

12 ELLN and ILO (2013).

self-employment in the labour market. Therefore, we cannot even estimate the number of bogus self-employed and economically dependent workers. The proportion of self-employment is relatively high in CEE countries, particularly in Poland and Czech Republic, but regularly still does not exceed around one-seventh of all workers.

Hungary has a typical CEE labour market with an employment regulation based on a separate Labour Code and a Civil Code, a high proportion of typical employment relationships, scarcely used atypical forms (some fixed-term and agency work), and a remarkable volume of genuine as well as bogus self-employment. In Hungary, there is no commonly accepted and used definition of self-employed workers; however, it includes civil law contracts of individual entrepreneurs and members of companies, regardless of their having employees or not.[13] There are also some intermediate labour law categories, with some weak employment protection, but without real relevance and remarkable numbers, such as commercial agents[14] and security personnel.[15]

As for the rate of Hungarian self-employed workers, the numbers are low from a regional comparison perspective and they have even been decreasing in the last decade. Cooperatives are disappearing and self-employment is decreasing, except the use of contracting through a company, which is a popular form of bogus self-employment.

Consequently, various forms of (genuine and bogus) self-employment and also economically dependent work are present in the labour markets of CEE countries, even if these forms represent altogether only around 10–15% of workers. Therefore, the employment relationship and particularly the classic employment contract is still the basic pillar of labour and social law. Self-employment is almost exclusively regulated by the Civil Code, since economically dependent work (the third category between employment and self-employment) is missing from the employment legal framework, which was not changed by recent proposals on economically dependent work. Therefore, self-employment is still an exception in work relations. In the following section, the social rights of employees and self-employed persons will be highlighted.

---

13 Eurofound (2009).

14 Article 6:288 of the Civil Code.

15 Act 133 of 2005 on security guards and private detectives.

3. SOCIAL SECURITY OF WORKERS IN AND OUT OF EMPLOYMENT

This second part of the chapter will focus on the social security rights of employees and self-employed workers in Hungary. The contributions, coverage, range and level of social security services will be the key issues in this analysis. After the presentation of the general scheme, the cheaper and less protective special schemes will be highlighted. We will argue that the general scheme is very protective; however, the high total cost of employment drives workers towards cheaper and less protective options.

3.1 Social Security Contributions and Services: the General Scheme

In Hungary, the compulsory state social security system has traditionally included health, pension and unemployment insurance, which are financed by obligatory social security contributions.[16] On the one hand, health insurance provides all kinds of health services and also cash benefits, such as pregnancy-maternity benefits, child-care benefits, sick-pay, accident benefits and accident compensation.[17] On the other hand, the statutory pension insurance fund covers many more social risks apart from old age. Under this scheme, old-age pensions, disability benefits, accident-related disability pension, dependent relatives' benefits and rehabilitation benefits are covered as well.[18] Unemployment insurance provides job seeker's allowance and assistance.[19]

As for the pension system, Hungary was the pioneer in CEE in terms of introducing mandatory private funds into the pension system, following the model laid out by the World Bank in 1994.[20] In this model, the pay as you go (PAYG) scheme is the first pillar, mandatory private pension funds are the second, and voluntary private pension funds are the

16 Act 80 of 1997 on social security services.
17 Act 83 of 1997 on mandatory health insurance.
18 Act 81 of 1997 on social security pension.
19 Act 4 of 1991 on the promotion of employment and unemployment benefits.
20 World Bank (1994).

third pension pillar. The second pillar was created by diverting contributions from the first pillar (privatization).[21] As early as 1998, the Hungarian pension system was based on the above mentioned three pillars.[22]

As a result of the reform, 2.1 million workers – mostly under the age 40 and about 50% of the workforce – diverted part of their pension contributions (6% of payroll) to private pension funds in the first year (1999). It was compulsory for the career-starter employees to join a pension fund; for all others, including self-employed, it was only an option. However, the Orbán government nationalized the mandatory private pension pillar, and returned to the PAYG public scheme[23] in 2012.[24] Therefore, self-employed workers are compulsorily part of the PAYG public scheme and may also join a voluntary pension fund.

There is a statutory obligation to pay contributions, affecting employees, civil servants, public service employees, service providers and people with other legal working arrangements, and the self-employed working alone or in organisations. However, very high contributions are paid by employers and employees (altogether 40.5%). The employer's contribution is 22% of the monthly gross salary, which is paid in addition to the gross salary in 2017. Employees pay a total of 18.5% social security contributions, which are deducted from the gross salary: pension insurance contribution (10%), health insurance (7%) and labour market contribution funding unemployment benefits and services (1.5%).

The self-employed pay exactly the same high rates (altogether 40.5%) of social security contributions as those in employment relationships, although the detailed rules are quite complicated. The self-employed automatically become 'insured',[25] if their income exceeds 30% of the minimum wage.[26] A similar minimum income threshold is applied in all CEE countries.[27] As a general rule, the insured self-employed worker must pay a pension contribution (10%), health contribution (7% + 22%), and labour market contribution (1.5%). In addition income tax must be

[21] Drahokoupil and Domonkos (2014).

[22] The three Hungarian pillars: statutory pension fund (Act 81 of 1997), compulsory private pension funds (Act 82 of 1997) and voluntary private pension funds (Act 96 of 1993).

[23] Szikra (2014).

[24] Act 194 of 2011.

[25] There is health insurance and limited social benefits for the self-employed, who do not exceed this very low amount (Articles 15–16 of Act 80 of 1997).

[26] Act 80 of 1997, Article 5(1)g).

[27] Schoukens (2002) 224.

paid, which depends on the chosen taxation system (of several complicated options).[28] However, self-employed people pay higher contributions than employees, since they have to bear the social burden of the employer.

Self-employed persons must pay the above mentioned social security contributions calculated on the basis of their income, but it is subject to a statutory minimum ('expected') contribution basis. They cannot avoid the payment of a minimum contribution, even if their income is lower than the basis of the calculation (or not having an income at all). The 'expected contribution basis', which is a kind of expected or rather supposed income, is the minimum wage for pension contribution and 150% of the minimum wage for health and unemployment contributions.[29]

These figures are extremely high compared to other countries in the region, even though the employer's contribution was decreased by 5% in 2016 and further decreased year by year. Therefore, the total cost of employment, particularly the social security part of it,[30] is still very high especially regarding a low declared income, which is a basic characteristic of self-employment.

All contribution-payers are insured against all risks, without exception. Insured persons include employees in employment relationships and public administration, the self-employed, persons receiving income subsidy, job seeker benefit and so on. Everyone is automatically affiliated to the entire social insurance scheme as soon as he/she begins to work. In case of self-employed workers, there is an obligation to register at the social security authority in order to be entitled to all social services. For instance, in the unemployment insurance scheme, there is no special benefit for insured self-employed persons, who receive the same job seeker benefit as the employees.[31]

The general scope of the statutory social security scheme described above is a usual feature in CEE countries. The social security schemes for self-employed people are incorporated in the general social security systems. This system usually covers both wage earners and self-employed people for the risks of health care, sickness, maternity and parental leave, old age, invalidity and survivorship pensions, and in some countries also unemployment benefits and so on. However, there are

---

28 National Taxation Authority (NAV) (2017).

29 Act 80 of 1997, Article 27(2).

30 There is a low flat rate income tax of 15%.

31 European Commission (2013).

some exceptions, since several CEE countries provide self-employed persons with some or even all social security services on a voluntary basis.[32]

Thus, the large majority of CEE countries have incorporated 'self-employed entrepreneurs in the existing social security schemes that are in place for the employees and/or the whole population'.[33] Consequently, a general system of social insurances for income replacement benefits is applied both to employees and to self-employed people. There are also sufficient factors to differentiate between the eventual social protection available to the self-employed and that for wage-earners, such as the financing of the system, assessment of unemployment, and temporary and partial work incapacity.[34]

3.2 Cheap, Degraded Schemes for Self-employed Workers

As it has been elucidated above, social security contributions and taxes are extremely high in Hungary, but the potential social services represent a significantly low quality from the perspective of a western European comparison. Since the pension is regularly calculated on the basis of the minimum wage, expected future pensions will be closer to the present minimum pension (28 500Ft, 90 euros) than the present average pension[35] (around 120 000Ft, circa 400 euros). It may be even lower in the future, if the present level of pensions cannot be sustained, which is rather probable in the light of demographic trends. Similarly, job seeker's benefit is also calculated on the basis of the minimum wage, thus its amount is also quite low for a statutory maximum period of 90 days.[36] Usually self-employed workers do not pay more than the already very high minimum (39%!) contribution, based on the minimum wage (127 500 Ft, circa 410 euros).

Evidently, self-employed workers are far from being attracted by these services and do their best to avoid contributions. This has been a strong incentive to do undeclared work or at least to only pay tax through a sham company without social security contributions (and of course

32 'Social protection of the self-employed' <http://ec.europa.eu/employment_social/missceec/selfemployed_en.pdf> accessed 5 July 2017.

33 Schoukens (2002) 219.

34 Schoukens (2002) 220.

35 <http://napicsart.blog.hu/2017/02/24/igy_valtozott_a_magyar_atlagnyugdij_az_elmult_evekben> accessed 24 May 2017.

36 Article 27(3) of Act 4 of 1991 on the promotion of employment and job seeker's benefits.

rights) for the worker. Self-employed persons do not perceive that payment of a high contribution for poor services as a good deal, but rather as a waste of money, which is best to avoid. Certainly, the reduction of social security contributions has been on the public agenda for too long a time; however, it is very costly to reduce the general level of contributions.

As an exception to the traditional Hungarian fiscal policy of maintaining high contributions, 2017 started with a 5% decrease of employers' contribution from 27% to 22% and some further gradual reductions have been implemented.[37] Otherwise, legislation has been constantly providing cheaper special schemes for self-employed workers, which has been the main incentive of bogus self-employment. In these special schemes, the total cost of employment (taxes + social security contributions) is much lower, but social services are also limited. This is a special 'deal' between the state and the individual, where workers give up publicly financed social rights (future payments, services) for higher income (through lower contributions). The two main special schemes will be analysed below, in order to show the fragmentation of the Hungarian self-employed social security system: a) Small Taxpayer Entrepreneurs' Lump Sum Tax (KATA) and b) Simplified Public Burden Contribution (EKHO).

a) Small Taxpayer Entrepreneurs' Lump Sum Tax (KATA)

Small Taxpayer Entrepreneurs' Lump Sum Tax (KATA)[38] is the most popular, general taxation form, and has been providing a cheap option versus the general taxation and social security scheme since 2013. It may be chosen by individual entrepreneurs and companies with individual members. The worker/company has to pay only 50 000 Ft per month[39] (600 000 Ft/year, circa 2000 euros) up to a maximum income of 12 million Ft (circa 40 000 euros) in a year. This low lump sum tax includes all taxes and contributions, which must be paid by the worker and the company according to the law on the general.

If we suppose the maximum possible income of 12 million Ft, then it means 5% overall public burden. Moreover, the higher your income is, the lower the proportion of it paid due to the lump sum tax. This low lump sum tax is a shocking comparison with the 39% general social

[37] From 2018, the employers' contribution has been further decreased from 22% to 19.5% (Act 66 of 1998 on health contributions) and in 2019 to 17.5%.

[38] It was introduced by Act 147 of 2012 on Small Taxpayer Entrepreneurs' Lump Sum Tax and Small Company Tax.

[39] It is only half of that amount (25 000 Ft), if the person is insured elsewhere (second job).

security contribution (excluding tax). Consequently, this taxation form has become extremely popular amongst self-employed people in a very short time: its numbers jumped from 75 000 workers in the first year (2013) to almost double, 140 000 workers in 2016, and over 300 000 in 2017, which is around 8% of the total number of workers in Hungary.[40]

It must be emphasized that limited social security coverage and particularly pension rights are the price of this low public burden. The self-employed worker ('small taxpayer') is considered by social security as an insured person, and will have a pension, health and also unemployment insurance.[41] However, the basis of calculating any social security benefit will be a very small, reduced amount: only 90 000 Ft (circa 300 euros). Therefore, all social benefits accruing to these 'small taxpayer' self-employed persons will be very low, such as job seeker's benefit and old age pension.[42] If we take the example of a self-employed worker with a monthly income of 370 000 Ft (1200 euros), his/her net monthly income is 400 euros higher (!) than would be the case if he/she was an employee. However, his/her pension will be almost 400 euros less in a month, if we use the present pension regulation as the basis for our calculation.[43] We must see this phenomenon as a real time bomb in the pension system, as a high number of old people will remain without a real pension in the near future (when this group of self-employed retires).

b) Simplified Public Burden Contribution (EKHO)

Simplified Public Burden Contribution (EKHO)[44] is another cheap option for self-employed workers to pay lower taxes and contributions, and was introduced in 2006. It attracts a much lower number of workers than KATA,[45] since it was designed only for media workers and artists (professions listed by the law), working either in an employment relationship or as a self-employed person. The worker must pay 15% (pensioners

---

40 <http://www.uzletresz.hu/penzugy/20160202-kisadozo-vallalkozasok-teteles-adoja-kata-adozas-nav-adoszakerto.html> accessed 5 July 2017

41 A self-employed person is entitled to unemployment benefit, if he/she has paid the labour market contribution for one year in the last three years and does not have an employment relationship or other legal work relationship (article 25 of Act 4 of 1991 on the promotion of employment).

42 Articles 8–10 of Act 147 of 2012.

43 <http://bankmonitor.hu/cikk/vallalkozo-kata-s-igy-kerulheti-el-a-minimal-nyugdijat/> accessed 5 July 2017.

44 Act 120 of 2005 on simplified public burden contribution.

45 Unfortunately, there is no data available on the number of EKHO taxpayers.

only 11.1%) of all income up to a maximum of 60 million Ft per year, which burden includes all income taxes and social security contributions. In addition, the employer/client pays a further 20% of the worker's gross income.

As a result, the worker will be entitled to health care and pension; however, he/she is not entitled to cash benefits (e.g. sickness allowance, maternity allowance) and unemployment benefits.[46] Moreover, pension is calculated on the basis of only 61% of the taxed income.[47] As is clear from Table 8.1, EKHO provides workers with rather limited social security rights, even compared to KATA.

It must be mentioned here that similar tax exemptions may be found in other CEE countries as well. Currently many EU member states provide favourable fiscal treatment for the self-employed as regards income or social contributions, because entrepreneurship is beneficial for society or

Table 8.1 Contributions and social services: employees and self-employed persons

	Employees	Self-employed – General scheme	Self-employed – KATA scheme	Self-employed – EKHO scheme
Contributions	Employer: 22% Employee: total 18.5% – pension (10%), health (7%), labour market (1.5%) of gross income (average gross wage: 950 euros)	Pension (10%) and health contribution (7% + 22%), labour market contribution (1.5%), altogether 40.5%, based on at least 100%/150% of minimum wage (410 euros)	50 000 Ft/month, 600 000 Ft/year, (circa 2000 euros) up to a maximum income of 12 million Ft (circa 40 000 euros), including all taxes and social security contributions	Employer/ client: 20% Employee/ worker: 15% (9.5% income tax, 3.9% pension contribution, 1.6% health contribution)
Range of available social services	All health, pension and unemployment insurance services	All health, pension and unemployment insurance services	All health, pension and unemployment insurance services, calculated on the basis of 90 000 Ft	Health care and pension; not entitled to cash benefits or unemployment benefits

46 Articles 4–8 of Act 120 of 2005.
47 Act 81 of 1997, Article 22(1)g).

because self-employment is less secure and less well protected than employment. For example, in Slovakia, the self-employed pay contributions from a lower assessment base of income, and can deduct lump sum expenses of 40% or more; an 'own account' worker's net income is significantly higher than that of an employee.[48]

4. CONCLUSIONS: SOCIAL SECURITY RIGHTS OR HIGHER INCOME?

The traditional employment relationship, full-time employment for an indefinite term, is still the dominant form of employment in CEE. Atypical employment relationships have not played a significant role in these labour markets, despite the implementation of the related EU Directives. As a consequence of the traditional CEE binary model of work relations, self-employment has been and still is the only lawful alternative to employment relationships. Bogus self-employment has been increasing, as it provides employers and also employees with a cheaper alternative employment relationship. However, the overall official figure of self-employment is still around 10–20% of workers and it is slightly decreasing in several countries, including Hungary.

The Hungarian 'society' of self-employed persons is rather polarized and complex, consisting of several remarkably different groups, particularly the genuine self-employed, bogus self-employed and economically dependent workers. Hungary, as with all these new member states, does not have a legal definition of 'self-employed' in their labour and social law systems. Therefore, a legal and statistical clarification would be desirable, with special emphasis on the different groups of self-employed persons.

Hungarian self-employed persons pay basically the same contributions and are entitled to the same social security services as employees. Since the level of social security contributions is extremely high, even in a regional and EU context, self-employed workers do their best to avoid or minimize these payments. In addition to the high payments, the quality of the potential social services is very poor for all and particularly for the self-employed opting for a cheap scheme, in respect of the length and amount of unemployment benefits, old age pension and sickness benefits,

48 'Self-employment and social security. Effects on innovation and economic growth', Library Briefing: Library of the European Parliament 09/10/2013, 4, <http://www.europarl.europa.eu/RegData/bibliotheque/briefing/2013/130646/LDM_BRI%282013%29130646_REV1_EN.pdf> accessed 5 July 2017.

which are paid and calculated on the basis of the minimum wage. Thus, self-employed persons either pay high contributions, undertake the risks of undeclared work or opt for a special taxation scheme, such as KATA or EKHO.

These very popular reduced schemes are quite problematic, since they impose a much lower public burden on self-employed workers; however, the available social rights are also very limited. The most crucial disadvantage of these trends for the society as a whole lies in the low expected pension, as it will leave a large and increasing proportion of the working population without a real income after reaching their pensionable age. So the social security of self-employed workers is fully guaranteed on the surface, but more and more of them 'sell' their rights of a future pension income for a higher net income for now.

Therefore, a major revision of this statutory two-pillar (general and 'cheap' schemes for the self-employed) system is highly desirable. The high level of social burden is a key issue here, thus the high social contribution shall be gradually (further) decreased for employees and self-employed workers alike. At the same time, the cheap schemes should be converged to the general one regarding taxes and contributions. This policy would strengthen the labour market position and the attraction of employment relationships and employment law. However, the social rights of self-employed persons under the cheap schemes should also be developed, particularly as regards old age pension. This could be achieved by a higher contribution basis or the introduction of voluntary pension contributions, or incentivised membership in a voluntary pension fund. Therefore, there are several options to deactivate the 'self-employed pension bomb'.

BIBLIOGRAPHY

Brodie Douglas, 'Employees, workers and the self-employed' (2005) 34(3) Industrial Law Journal, 253–260

Casale Giuseppe, *The Employment Relationship. A Comparative Overview* (Hart Publishing, Geneva, 2011)

Countouris Nicolas, *The Changing Law of the Employment Relationship* (Ashgate Publishing, Aldershot, 2007)

Davidov Guy, 'Who is a worker?' (2005) 35(1) Industrial Law Journal, 57–71

Deakin Simon, 'The comparative evolution of the employment relationship' in Guy Davidov and Brian Langille (eds), *Boundaries and Frontiers of Labour Law: Goals and Means in the Regulation of Work* (Hart Publishing, Oxford, 2006, 89–108)

Drahokoupil Jan and Domonkos Stefan, 'Is the egg basket worth its price? The fiscal implications of pension privatization in Eastern Europe' in Benedict Clemens, Frank Eich and Sanjeev Gupta (eds), *Equitable and Sustainable Pensions: Challenges and Experience* (International Monetary Fund, Washington DC, 2014, 155–156)

ELLN and ILO: Regulating the employment relationship in Europe: A guide to Recommendation No. 198. ILO, Geneva, 2013, 28-5, <https://www.ilo.org/wcmsp5/groups/public/—ed_dialogue/—dialogue/documents/publication/wcms_209280.pdf> accessed 24 January 2019

Eichhorst Werner, 'Fixed-term contracts. Are fixed-term contracts a stepping stone to a permanent job or a dead end?' 2014, <https://wol.iza.org/articles/fixed-term-contracts/long> accessed 19 September 2017

Eurofound, 'Hungary: Self-employed workers', 2009, <https://www.eurofound.europa.eu/observatories/eurwork/comparative-information/national-contributions/hungary/hungary-self-employed-workers> accessed 23 May 2017

European Commission, 'Your social security rights in Hungary', 2013, 5, <http://ec.europa.eu/employment_social/empl_portal/SSRinEU/Your%20social%20security%20rights%20in%20Hungary_en.pdf> accessed 24 May 2017

Gyulavári Tamás, 'Trap of the past: Why economically dependent work is not regulated in the Member States of Eastern Europe' (2014a) 3–4, European Labour Law Journal, 267, 278

Gyulavári Tamás, 'A bridge too far? The Hungarian regulation of economically dependent work' (2014b) 1 Hungarian Labour Law E-Journal, <http://hllj.hu/letolt/2014_1_a/01.pdf> accessed 24 January 2019

National Taxation Authority (NAV), 'Az önálló tevékenység és az önálló tevékenységböl származó jövedelem (Income from independent economic activities)', 2017, <http://www.nav.gov.hu/nav/inf_fuz> accessed 24 May 2017

Pennings Frans and Bosse Claire (eds), *The Protection of Working Relations* (Kluwer Law International, The Netherlands, 2011)

Perulli Adalberto, 'Economically dependent/quasi-subordinate (parasubordinate) employment: Legal, social and economic aspects', European Commission, 2002, 6–29, <ec.europa.eu/social/BlobServlet?docId=2510> accessed 19 May 2017

Schoukens Paul, *The Social Security Systems for Self-Employed People in the Applicant EU Countries of Central and Eastern Europe* (Intersentia, Antwerp – Oxford – New York, 2002)

Senčur Peček Darja, 'The scope of labour law protection in Slovenia or who are employers obliged to grant the labour law protection to' (2017) 2 Hungarian Labour Law E-Journal, 16–29, <http://hllj.hu/letolt/2017_2_a/A_02_Sencur Pecek_HLLJ_2017_2.pdf> accessed 24 January 2019

Skupień Dagmara, Łaga Maciej and Pisarczyk Lukasz, 'Polish labour law: The impact of the economic crisis and demographic problems' (2016) 1 Hungarian Labour Law E-Journal, <http://hllj.hu/letolt/2016_1_a/A_01_Skupien_Laga_Pysarczyk_hllj_2016_1.pdf> accessed 6 July 2017

Swiatkowski Andrzej, 'The protection of working relationships in Poland' in Frans Pennings and Claire Bosse (eds), *The Protection of Working Relations* (Kluwer Law International, The Netherlands, 2011, 122–123)

Szikra Dorottya, 'Democracy and welfare in hard times: The social policy of the Orbán Government in Hungary between 2010 and 2014' (2014) 5 Journal of European Social Policy, <http://real.mtak.hu/21702/1/Journal%20of%20European%20Social%20Policy-2014-Szikra-0958928714545446%281%29.pdf> accessed 13 February 2017

World Bank, 'Averting the old age crisis: Policies to protect the old and promote growth', 1994, <http://documents.worldbank.org/curated/en/973571468174557899/Averting-the-old-age-crisis-policies-to-protect-the-old-and-promote-growth> accessed 5 July 2017

9. Informality and social insurance in East Africa: an assessment of the law and practice

Juliana Masabo

1. INTRODUCTION

This chapter examines social insurance systems in East Africa. It takes stock of reforms currently undertaken by individual countries in a bid to extend the scope of social insurance coverage to informal employees and persons previously excluded from the social insurance systems. It is observed that a certain degree of approval for extension of social insurance to informal workers and self-employed persons has been noted. Countries in the region are gradually transforming their legal frameworks to expand coverage beyond formal sector employees. In some of the countries, provisions are acknowledging social security as a basic human right to be enjoyed by all persons irrespective of employment status. This chapter will interrogate these reforms and assess their impact in improving the coverage base. The discussion in this chapter will only focus on four countries, namely Kenya, Rwanda, Tanzania and Uganda. The first three countries are founding members of the East African Community (EAC), the regional economic community for East Africa.[1] Their legal systems are more or less similar. They all follow the British common law system. Rwanda, on the other hand, is a relatively new entrant to the Community but has made notable developments in extending social insurance to persons previously excluded.

---

[1] The East African Community was formed in 1999. It has a total of six Partner States, namely Kenya, Uganda, Tanzania, Rwanda, Burundi and South Sudan.

2. THE STATE OF INFORMALITY

Informal employment in East Africa is predominately high and significantly contributes to the economy of the region by providing economic opportunities to those displaced from or who cannot be absorbed by formal employment. The International Labour Organization (ILO) estimates that informal employment accounts for 91.6 per cent of all employment in East Africa.[2] Although there are variations between countries the proportion of informal employment is consistently high and constantly on the rise. In 2015 Kenya was listed by the United Nations' Economic Commission for Africa (UNECA) as the country with the highest informal employment among the nine countries covered in its 2015 Economic Report on Africa.[3] According to this report, informal employment in Kenya accounted for 77.9 per cent of total employment while in Rwanda and Uganda it accounted for 73.4 and 59.2 per cent, respectively.[4] It was estimated further that three out of four workers in Kenya and Rwanda were employed in the informal sector.[5] Other reports have also consistently indicated higher proportions.[6] The situation in other countries is equally alarming. In Burundi the non-agricultural informal sector employment is estimated at 78 per cent[7] while in Tanzania the most recent Integrated Labour Force Survey has reported that three-quarters (75 per cent) of all paid and self-employed workers in non-agriculture have informal employment.[8] Available literature suggests

---

[2] International Labour Organization, 2018, p. 28.

[3] Other countries covered in this report are: Tanzania, Rwanda, Uganda, Egypt, Liberia, Madagascar, Mauritius and South Africa. See, United Nations Economic Commission for Africa (UNECA), Economic Report on Africa 2015: Addis Ababa: United Nations, 2015, p. 66.

[4] Ibid.

[5] Ibid.

[6] For example, a report submitted by Rwanda to the United Nations Human Rights Council in 2010 indicated that the informal sector "constitute 93,8% of the working population." See Republic of Rwanda: Rwanda National Report to the United Nations Human Rights Council (Submitted in Accordance with Paragraph 15(a) of the Annex to the Human Rights Council Resolution 5/1 in the Framework of the Universal Periodic Review). October, 2010.

[7] Danish Trade Council for International Development and Cooperation, Labour Market Profile 2015, <http://www.ulandssekretariatet.dk/sites/default/files/uploads/public/PDF/LMP/LMP2015/lmp_burundi_2015_final_version.pdf> accessed 13 August 2017.

[8] United Republic of Tanzania, The 2014 Integrated Labour Force Survey: Analytical Report Labour Force Survey, p. 46.

further that women tend to be overrepresented in this form of employment. The ILO statistics alluded to earlier estimate that the proportion of women in non-agricultural informal employment is 89.7 per cent whereas the proportion of men in the same category is 82.7.[9] In Tanzania, women are reported to have a significantly higher proportion, 81.7 per cent, in informal employment compared to men whose proportion is 71.7 per cent.[10] In Kenya the proportion of women is over 80 per cent.[11] As will be demonstrated later in this chapter, the majority of these are not covered by social insurance.

3. NATIONAL SOCIAL INSURANCE IN A NUTSHELL

Social insurance systems in East Africa, as elsewhere in the continent, comprise compulsory schemes financed unilaterally by the employer or by both employer and employee and voluntary or supplementary schemes in the form of occupational pension schemes and private schemes largely managed by employers and other private sector actors. The compulsory schemes, which are the focus of this study, have long been in existence. Most of these, mainly provident funds established primarily for civil servants, were inherited from the colonial governments. Over the years these schemes have been transformed into mandatory national pension schemes. The available schemes cover certain aspects of social insurance ranging from old age pension, invalidity pension, survivors benefits, maternity benefits, benefits in respect of occupational injury and health insurance.

In terms of regulation, the social insurance system in East Africa is sufficiently regulated. Each country has multiple laws through which social insurance schemes are established and governed. The multiplicity of schemes notwithstanding, social insurance coverage is significantly constrained. Until recently, eligibility for membership in these schemes was exclusively reliant on the existence of formal employment and therefore not available to workers in non-conventional employment relationships or to self-employed persons. The bias towards formal employment resulted in exceedingly high rates of exclusion from social insurance. In some of the countries, the total scope of exclusion was, until recently, as high as 95 per cent. In Tanzania, as of 2003, only 5.4 percent of the total labour force of over 16 million people was

9 Ibid.
10 Ibid.
11 United Nations Economic Commission for Africa, 2015 at 66.

insured.[12] Although there has been some slight improvement in the past decade, the level of coverage has remained persistently low. Currently, the average coverage size is as low as 10 per cent or slightly above 10 per cent of the labour forces as reports from Tanzania and Uganda show. At the end of 2016, only 12 per cent of Tanzania's total productive labour force was insured.[13] In Uganda the total coverage is only 11 per cent of the labour force.[14]

3.1 Kenya

Kenya's social insurance system is regulated by the Pensions Act,[15] the Public Service Superannuation Scheme Act, 2012,[16] the National Social Security Fund Act, 2013[17] and the Retirement Benefits Act, 1997.[18] The first two regulate provision of retirement benefit to public sector employees. The Pensions Act, which is the oldest legislation, came into being in 1946 and has since then been the subject of several amendments. It established the civil service pension scheme – a non-contributory scheme entirely financed by the state and managed by the Pensions Department within the Ministry of Finance. The scheme exclusively covered all permanent and pensionable civil servants. These were eligible for retirement benefits at the age 55 or 50 (early retirement) and survivor's benefit. The Public Service Superannuation Scheme Act is relatively new. It was adopted in 2012 and revised in 2014. This Act establishes the Public Service Superannuation Scheme (PSSS) whose effect is to replace the defined benefit scheme for public sector employees with a contributory defined scheme. The scheme is mandatory for all new public servants. Those who were on permanent and pensionable employment who have not attained the age of 45 years at the commencement of the Act were automatically transferred to the new scheme.[19] The new scheme

---

[12] United Republic of Tanzania, National Social Security Policy, 2003 at 8.

[13] United Republic of Tanzania, Social Security Regulatory Authority Annual Report 2015/016, p. 28.

[14] 13 million people out of Uganda's total labour force of about 14 million (an equivalent of 89 per cent of the 15.6 million labour force in the country) are not covered by any pension scheme. See Mark Keith Muhumuza "Uganda's Labour Force Get No Pension," *The Monitor* (Kampala, 1 August, 2016) 1.

[15] Cap 189.

[16] Cap 109.

[17] Operational on 10 January 2014.

[18] No. 3 of 1997 (Revised Edition 2016 [2013]).

[19] Section 5.

is jointly financed by the government and the employees. The contribution rate for each employee is 7.5% of the monthly pensionable emoluments. The government contributes 15% of the respective employee's pensionable emoluments. Members of this scheme are entitled to a retirement pension payable on a monthly or quarterly basis, annuity for life purchased from a life insurance company and survivor's benefits.

Persons employed in the private sector are covered by the National Social Security Fund (NSSF), which is a mandatory pension scheme for all private sector employees.[20] The NSSF has been operative since 1965. It has been reformed several times to respond to emerging issues and demands. At its inception it operated as a provident fund until 1997 when it was transformed into a pension scheme. Following the adoption of a new law in 2015, NSSF now operates two schemes, a pension scheme and a provident scheme.[21] The pension scheme is compulsory for all private sector employees.[22] Benefits payable to members under the Act include retirement pension; invalidity pension; survivors' benefit; funeral grant; and emigration benefit.[23] As of 2010, NSSF had 4.6 million members of which 1,175,000 were from the informal sector.[24]

The PSSS, NSSF and other retirement benefits schemes operative in Kenya are regulated by the Retirement Benefits Authority (RBA).[25] The RBA is mandated to regulate and supervise the establishment and management of retirement benefits schemes; protect the interest of members and sponsors of retirement benefits schemes; to develop and promote the retirement benefits sector; to advise the Government on matters relating to retirement benefits; and to implement all Government policies on retirement benefits.

Health insurance cover for salaried workers is provided by the National Hospital Insurance Fund (NHIF).[26] NHIF is a compulsory scheme for salaried workers. Eligibility for membership is also open to every Kenyan

---

20 The NSSF was established under the National Social Security Act, 2013.

21 The provident fund has been inherited from the predecessor Act.

22 Section 19. (1) Every employer who, under a contract of service, employs one employee or more shall register with the 'Fund as a contributing employer and shall, register his employee or employees, as members of the Fund'.

23 See section 34.

24 Danish Trade Council for International Development and Cooperation, Kenya Labour Market Profile 2015, <http://www.ulandssekretariatet.dk/sites/default/files/uploads/public/PDF/LMP/LMP2015/lmp_kenya_2015_final_version.pdf> accessed 1 February 2019: Copenhagen, at p. 15.

25 Established under the Retirement Benefits Act, No. 3 of 1997.

26 Kenya NHIF was established under the National Hospital Insurance Act, No. 9 of 1998 (Cap. 255).

of 18 years of age or above and with a minimum monthly income of 1000 Kshs. The Fund provides hospital cover for members and their dependants. NHIF's coverage has grown tremendously recently. In June 2017 the number of principal members of NHIF reached 6.5 million with approximately 24 million beneficiaries.[27] Insurance in respect of work related injuries and hazards for all salaried workers is regulated by the Work Injury Benefits Act, 2007. The Act requires employers to maintain an insurance cover for all their salaried employees.[28] Casual employees are, however, excluded from coverage.[29]

3.2 Tanzania

Tanzania has a unique arrangement. Social insurance, being a non-union matter, is regulated by two regimes, one for Zanzibar and another for Mainland Tanzania. The regime in Zanzibar does not differentiate between public sector and private sector employees. All employees are governed by the Zanzibar Social Security Fund Act, 2005, which establishes the Zanzibar Social Security Fund (ZSSF). ZSSF caters for virtually all categories of workers provided that they have an employer and receive remuneration. The only exception are the President of Zanzibar and the First and Second Vice Presidents of Zanzibar and Members of the Revolutionary Council, Minister, Deputy Minister, Speaker of the House of Representatives, Mayor of the Zanzibar Municipal Council, Regional Commissioner, and District Commissioner. The first three are covered by the Specified State Leaders Retirement Benefit Act, 1988, whereas the rest are catered for by the Pension (Political Appointees) Act, 1990.

The situation in Mainland Tanzania is different. In addition to having a separate regime for public sector and private sector employees, each cadre of public sector employees in the Mainland has a separate scheme. In total, there are five pension schemes. The Parastatal Pensions Fund (PPF) established under the Parastatal Pensions Act, 1978 covers employees in parastatal organizations and public institutions; all private companies in which the government owns shares; private companies that are

---

[27] See Stellar Murumba, Number of NHIF Members Hits 6.5 million, The Sunday News, 11 June 2017. For details of the labour force see, Kenya National Bureau of Statistics, The 2015/16 Kenya Integrated Household Budget Survey (KIHBS): Labour Force Basic Report (Kenya National Bureau of Statistics, 2018) p. 3.

[28] Section 7.

[29] Section 4(3).

not covered by any other social security fund; and all parastatal organizations.[30] The Public Service Retirement Benefits Act of 1999 established the Public Service Pensions Fund (PSPF) for permanent and pensionable employees in the central government and executive agencies. The Government Employees' Provident Fund (GEPF) was especially established for non-pensionable employees of the central government who were not covered by any other pensionable government social security scheme.[31] In 2013 it was transformed into a retirement benefit scheme.[32] The Local Authorities Pensions Fund Act, 2006 established a pension scheme for all categories of employees in local government employment (the Local Authorities Pensions Fund (LAPF)).[33] Private sector employees in Mainland Tanzania are covered by the National Social Security Fund Act, 1997, which establishes the National Social Security Fund (NSSF). Membership of NSSF is also open to government ministries, departments, and parastatal organizations employing non-pensionable employees; employees of faith based organizations; self-employed persons; persons working informally; and those not covered by any other social security scheme.

All of these schemes are defined contributory schemes offering an array of benefits to their members such as old age pensions, invalidity benefits and survivor's benefits. Some provide short-term benefits such as an education grant, maternity benefits, medical benefits and funeral grants. It should be noted that enrolment in these schemes is no longer sectorally defined. In 2013 the government passed regulations allowing new employees freedom of choice.[34] This has accorded all persons employed from 2014 onwards the liberty to enrol in any scheme of their choice. However, once enrolled in a particular mandatory scheme they cannot transfer their membership to another scheme.

Senior political leaders, including the President, Vice President, Prime Minister, ministers, deputy ministers, Speaker of the National Assembly,

---

30 The term 'parastatal' is commonly used in some African countries. It is defined in the *Oxford Dictionary* as an organization with some political authority and serving the state indirectly.

31 Established under the Provident Fund (Government Employees) Act, 1978.

32 The GEPF Retirement Benefit Fund Act, 2013.

33 This scheme covers almost all categories of workers including those in the local government authorities, the Local Government Loans Board, the Local Authorities Pensions Fund, any institution owned by a local government authority, and any institution that elects to contribute. See The Local Authorities Pensions Fund Act, 2006, section 2.

34 The Social Security Schemes (Membership Registration) Guidelines, 2013.

Deputy Speaker, members of parliament, and Regional and District Commissioners are covered by the Political Service Retirement Benefits Scheme (PSRB).[35] Employees of defence forces are regulated by a separate regime for defence forces established under the Defence Forces (Service Pensions and Gratuities) Regulations of 1966. Compensation in respect of permanent or partial disability emanating from occupational injury and diseases is regulated by the Workers' Compensation Fund which became operative in 2015. The Fund is financed by monthly contributions from employers. Public sector employers contribute 0.5 per cent of each employee's wages, whereas private sector employers contribute 1 per cent.[36] There is also a public health insurance scheme called the National Health Insurance Fund (NHIF).[37] NHIF is a mandatory contributory scheme for all public sector employees and serves as a voluntary scheme for private sector and self-employed persons. The contribution rate for NHIF is 6 per cent of the employee's salary shared equally between the employer and the employee. NHIF also manages the Community Health Insurance (CHI) programme which operates at grass-roots level.[38]

All of these schemes operate under the supervision of the Social Security Regulatory Authority (SSRA). The SSRA, which was established in 2008 in accordance with the Social Security Regulatory Authority Act, 2008, became operative at the end of 2010 and has since then played a significant role in regulating and supervising the social security sector.[39] For instance, in 2014/15 SSRA developed and rolled out Pension Harmonization Rules which substantially increased retirement benefits and provided room for indexation of pension benefits.[40] In 2009 it passed regulations regarding registration and management of social security schemes, which lowered the management cost of the schemes. It also spearheads the campaign for extension of social security to informal workers.

---

[35] Established under the Political Service Retirement Benefits Scheme Act, 1999.

[36] Established under the Workers Compensation Fund Act, 2008.

[37] Established and managed under the National Health Insurance Act, 1999.

[38] Established under the Community Health Insurance Act, 2001.

[39] Social Security (Regulatory Authority) Act, 2008.

[40] United Republic of Tanzania, Social Security Regulatory Annual Report 2014/2015, at 10.

3.3 Uganda

The public–private divide is also present in Uganda's social insurance system. Insurance arrangements for employees of central and local government are regulated by the Pensions Act, 1946, through which the Public Service Pension Scheme (PSPS) was established.[41] The PSPS is a non-contributory, defined benefit pay-as-you-go retirement scheme financed directly from tax revenues.[42] Benefits availed to members include old age pension, survivors' pension, invalidity pension and gratuities in respect of contract, death, short-term and marriage gratuities, and are paid from the consolidated fund.[43] Private sector employers are catered for by the National Social Security Fund (NSSF). Unlike PSPS, the NSSF is a contributory and mandatory scheme for all employers with five or more employees. The contribution rate for NSSF is 15 per cent of the employee's monthly emolument shared at 5 per cent and 10 per cent by the employee and employer, respectively.[44] The NSSF is not a pension scheme, it is a provident fund that pays out a lump sum benefit upon attaining the retirement age, which is 55 years (or 50 years in the case of early retirement), invalidity and survivors' benefit.[45] An emigration grant is also paid to non-Ugandans and Ugandans who emigrate from Uganda permanently. NSSF coverage is very limited. As of 2013 the total membership was 269,000 persons only.[46] There is also an exclusive scheme for Members of Parliament established under the National Parliamentary Pensions Act, 2007. This scheme is contributory whereby each member contributes 15 per cent of his/her pensionable emoluments which is matched by the government contribution of 30 per cent of the monthly pensionable emolument. Benefits in the form of a retirement pension is paid to a member who retires or ceases to be a member on or after attaining 45 years of age and having fulfilled the benefit eligibility requirement of ten years of service as Member of Parliament.[47] The Peoples' Defence Force and the Police Force have different pension

---

41 Cap 286.

42 Bukuluki and Mubiru, 2014, p. 60.

43 Ibid., 61.

44 Kasente et al., 2002.

45 Ibid., at 162.

46 Barya, 2011, p. 34.

47 Initially, the eligibility period was 5 years. The 10 year requirement was recently introduced by section 5 of the Parliamentary Pensions (Amendment) Act, 2015. Those who do not qualify receive a refund of their savings.

arrangements to cater for members in their respective units.[48] Insurance against work injury and hazards is covered by the Workers' Compensation Act, 2000.[49] In 2011, the Government established the Uganda Retirement Benefits Regulatory Authority (URBRA) with the mandate to supervise and regulate the establishment, management and operation of retirement benefits schemes while also protecting the interests of members and beneficiaries of retirement benefits schemes.[50]

Uganda, unlike Kenya and Tanzania, is yet to establish a public health insurance scheme although plans for the same started way back in 2006.[51] The Government had planned to launch a compulsory scheme which would initially cover about 2 million employed Ugandans, which is about 6 per cent of the population, and roll it out to the whole country.[52] The Bill for an enabling legislation was tabled before the Parliament of Uganda in March 2009 but could not sail through due to resistance from employers, trade unions and worker representatives. The process has since then been in stalemate.

3.4 Rwanda

Rwanda's social insurance system is comparably more advanced. Unlike the three EAC Partner States already discussed, Rwanda has only one pension scheme: the National Social Security Scheme (NSSS) established under the Law Governing the Organization of Pension Schemes which was passed on 30 March 2015 and gazetted on 18 May 2015.[53] This operates in two branches, namely a mandatory pension scheme and a voluntary pension scheme, both of which are governed by the Rwanda Social Security Board (RSSB). The mandatory pension scheme is a

---

48 These are governed by the Uganda Peoples Defence Force Act, 2005 and the Police Force Act, Cap. 303.

49 Cap. 225

50 Established under the Retirement Benefits Regulatory Authority Act, 2011.

51 Barya, 2011, p. 43.

52 Rosebell Kagumire Public Health Insurance in Uganda Still Only a Dream, 2009, <https://www.ncbi.nlm.nih.gov/pmc/articles/PMC2630345/> accessed on 11 August 2015.

53 Law Governing the Organization of Pension Schemes No. 5 of 2015.

contributory scheme for all employees in Rwanda regardless of nationality, type of contract, duration of the contract or the amount of wages.[54] The scheme is jointly financed by the employer and the employee whereby the employer and employees pay a premium equal to 6 per cent of the employee's gross salary (equally shared).[55] Members of the scheme are entitled to old-age benefits (paid to a person who is at least 60 years old (retirement age) and who has attained 15 years of contribution). Benefits are also paid in respect of early retirement and non-occupational disability.[56]

Rwanda is the only country in the region with a separate maternity scheme. This scheme is relatively new. It was established in 2016 in accordance with Law No. 003/2016 Establishing and Governing Maternity Leave Benefits Scheme. The maternity scheme is operated by the RSSB. The Scheme guarantees female employees 12 weeks' maternity leave with full pay. The scheme is part of Rwanda's distinguished commitment towards women empowerment and gender equality. The scheme is jointly financed by the employer and the employee through monthly contributions totalling 0.6 per cent of the employee's gross salary shared equally between the employer and the employee. The modalities for registration, remittance of contributions and procedures for payment of maternity leave benefits are regulated by the Ministerial Order Relating to the Maternity Leave Benefits Scheme.[57]

Rwanda's health insurance system is also comparatively advanced. It comprises the Rwanda Health Insurance Fund (la Rwandaise d'assurance maladie, RAMA), the Community Based Health Insurance (CBHI) scheme or *Mutuelle de Santé* as popularly known, and the Military Medical Insurance (MMI) scheme. The first two are managed by RSSB. RAMA was created in 2001 as a compulsory medical scheme for public

---

[54] Public servants and civil servants, political appointees, employees of international organizations, national non-governmental organizations, international non-governmental organizations, faith based organizations and employees of embassies accredited to Rwanda are mandatory members of this Scheme. See Article 4.

[55] The Government of Rwanda, Rwanda Social Security Board Strategic Plan, 2015–2020 at 14.

[56] The latter benefit is paid to an insured person, who becomes disabled before reaching retirement if he/she has contributed to the Scheme for at least three years (Article 24).

[57] Also see Ministerial Order No. 007/16/10/TC Relating to the Maternity Leave Benefits Scheme of 28/10/2016.

sector employees.[58] The scheme has extended its scope of coverage and currently covers civil servants, employees of government agents and private sector workers involved in the formal economy. Regarding financing, this scheme is financed generally by monthly contributions totalling 15 per cent of the member's salary, 7.5 per cent of which is paid by the employee and 7.5 per cent by the employer. The benefit package covers all medical services provided in public health centres, district hospitals and referral hospitals as well as private facilities. Members of the scheme and their dependants who include the member's legitimate spouse, legitimate or legally recognized children, children for whom the affiliated member is legally responsible, and legally adopted children enjoy unimpeded access to these services. As of July 2013, the coverage of the scheme was around 2.5 per cent of the national population.[59] The CBHI, which is also currently managed by the RSSB, is a relatively older system. Some of the first CBHI date back to the 1960s. The current CBHI came into being in 1999. This was introduced as pilot projects in three districts and later extended to all 30 districts in 2005. As of 2010, CBHI coverage was 91 per cent of Rwanda's population, which means that the majority of Rwandans have guaranteed access to drugs and medical services provided in health posts, health centres, district hospitals, province hospitals as well as referral hospitals. The MMI was created in 2005. It is managed by the Ministry of Defence. The scheme is also financed through a member's contribution, which at present accounts for 22.5 per cent of the base salary of its members, of which 17.5 per cent is paid by the Government and the remaining 5 per cent by the member.[60]

4. EXPANDING THE SCOPE OF COVERAGE

Extension of social insurance to informal workers and workers previously excluded is increasingly becoming a policy priority in East Africa and Africa in general. There are considerable strides in re-orienting national social insurance policies by widening the scope of social insurance coverage to include persons working informally, self-employed persons and others who work outside the confines of the traditional employer–employee relationship. This is to a large extent caused by a seemingly

---

58 Established by Law No. 24/2001 of 27/04/2001 on the Establishment, Organisation and Funding of Health Insurance Scheme for Government Employees.

59 RSSB presentation at p. 6.

60 Ruberangeyo et al., 2011, p. 343; Uwera, 2013, p. 10.

gradual recognition of the nexus between social insurance and development. The critical role of social insurance in providing economic security, alleviating poverty and helping people to cope with life challenges has increasingly yielded recognition in the region. This is evidenced, by among others, inclusion of statements relevant to social insurance in major national development agendas. For example, the Tanzania National Strategy for Growth and Reduction of Poverty (NSGRP II) considers provision of adequate social protection to the vulnerable and needy groups as one of the key strategies for improvement of quality of life and social well-being envisaged in Tanzania's Development Vision 2025.[61] To achieve this, the Government pledges its commitment to "increase the number of vulnerable economically active population reached with social protection in order to enable them to engage effectively in economic activities."[62]

Equally impressive is the recognition of social security as a human right and the corresponding drive towards universal coverage. Provisions recognizing social security as a human right to be enjoyed by all persons have gradually found their way into national constitutions. The Constitution of Kenya, 2010, which is the foundational legal instrument in Kenya, formally recognizes social security as a human right.[63] The Government pledges to provide appropriate social security to persons who are unable to support themselves, and their dependants are also provided for in the Constitution.[64] The Constitution of Uganda, 1995 contains several provisions relevant to social insurance. Paragraph XIV of the National Objectives and Directive Principles of State Policy states the will of the Government to fulfil the fundamental rights of all Ugandans to social justice and economic development and shall, in particular, ensure that all Ugandans enjoy rights and opportunities and access to education, health services, decent shelter, adequate clothing, food security, pension and retirement benefits. Article 254 is specifically focused on pensions for public sector employees. It provides inter alia that, "[a] public officer shall, on retirement, receive such pension as is commensurate with his or her rank, salary and length of service." It further provides that the pension so payable should not be subjected to tax and should be reviewed periodically on account of changes in the value of money. For efficiency purposes, it is directed that payment should be promptly and regularly

---

61 United Republic of Tanzania, National Strategy for Growth and Reduction of Poverty (NSGRP) II, (Government of Tanzania 2010) 63.

62 Ibid., 57.

63 See Article 43(1)(e).

64 See Article 43(3).

made to ensure that it is easily accessible to pensioners. Equally relevant is Article 40(4), which recognizes the importance of maternity protection for female employees and provides inter alia that, "[the] employer of every woman worker shall accord her protection during pregnancy and after birth, in accordance with the law."

Even in countries where the right to social security is yet to be formally incorporated in national constitutions, there are policy statements acknowledging the importance of social security as a fundamental human right to be enjoyed by every person irrespective of employment status. In Tanzania, the National Social Security Policy, 2003 contains a policy statement recognizing social security as a fundamental right. The Government's commitment to sensitize the society regarding the "importance of provision of social security services as a right" is also clearly stated.[65] Rwanda's commitments to extend social insurance coverage are firmer. Rwanda's Social Security Policy 2009 enshrines an unequivocal commitment by Government to develop all necessary programmes and mechanisms aimed at attaining the ideal situation of "*Social security coverage for all*".[66] The Government determination is to ensure that all Rwandans are ultimately covered with the maximum benefits possible for retirement and key pre-retirement provisions such as housing and education, professional risk benefits, sickness benefits, maternity benefits, health care, and unemployment benefits.[67] Regarding the extension of social insurance to informal workers, the Government pledges its commitment to reinforce measures for total adherence to pension schemes for all workers in the formal sector, for self-employed and for workers in the informal sector.[68]

There have been subsequent legislative reforms aimed at transforming these pledges into action. These have involved amendment of existing legislation as well as a total overhaul of the existing legislation and enactment of new laws. In Rwanda, the first reform took place in 2003 when the Organic Law N° 06/2003 of 22/03/2003 was passed to amend the Social Security Decree of 1974. Article 3 of this law allowed self-employed persons who are below the age of 45 to enrol in the mandatory pension scheme managed by RSSB. In tandem with this reform, the Social Security Act, 2015 imposes a mandatory registration by all employers with one or more employees.[69] To ensure that the scope

65 Paragraph 3.3.
66 Page 3.
67 Page 11.
68 Ibid.
69 See Articles 2(13) and 4(1).

of the Act does not exclude any worker the term "employee" for the purposes of this Act has been defined as "any person who performs an activity in exchange for payment" whereas an employer is defined as "any person that employs one or more people on a continuous or discontinuous basis."[70] Eligibility for membership of the mandatory pension scheme is also available to self-employed people who were not previously members provided they are not above 50 years of age.[71]

In Kenya the first reform took place in 2009 when the Government passed a Regulation extending mandatory coverage of the Kenya NSSF to employers with one to four employees.[72] Subsequently, the NSSF introduced voluntary membership and contributions. It also embarked on a rigorous marketing campaign to attract voluntary membership, particularly from the informal sector. The Social Protection Policy which was adopted three years later contains policy statements on extension of social insurance to informal workers. These include firm commitment by the Government to (among other things):

1. strengthen the existing social security regime and establish comprehensive social security arrangements that will extend legal coverage to all workers, whether in the formal or informal sectors, and their dependants;
2. undertake research into and consider viable options for extending coverage to those who work informally and their dependants;
3. extend the range of social security benefits to cover such key areas of need including unemployment and comprehensive pre-natal and post-natal care for mothers and babies;
4. re-establish the NHIF as a fully fledged comprehensive national health insurance scheme, which covers all Kenyans, and to which those who can afford it must contribute; and
5. establish a framework for enabling those who are not able to contribute, to access a core package of essential health services.[73]

The Government, subsequently, conducted a major review of the social protection sector which also, having noted the high rate of exclusion of informal workers by NSSF and NHIF, appealed for implementation of

---

70 Article 2 (12) read together with Article 4(1)). Also see Article 2(1) of the Law Establishing and Governing Maternity Leave Benefits Scheme, 2016.

71 See Article 5.

72 Kenya Gazette Notice No. 159 of 30 October 2009.

73 Republic of Kenya, Kenya National Social Protection Policy, 2011 pp. 19–21.

urgent and comprehensive measures for extension of coverage to the informal sector.[74] In line with this recommendation, the Parliament immediately repealed and replaced the NSSF Act with a new law, the NSSF Act, 2013 which became effective on 31 May 2014.[75] Cementing the changes already implemented by NSSF in 2009, the new law requires every employer who employs one or more employees to be compulsorily registered by NSSF as a contributing employer. However, unlike Rwanda, which makes no distinction of the eligible employment relationship, in Kenya this will only apply to employees under contract of service.[76] Employees under contracts other than contracts of service and the self-employed may opt to join the voluntary scheme; members contribute a minimum of 4800 Kshs a year.[77]

In Tanzania, the National Social Security Act, 1997 was the first to spearhead these reforms in accordance with its section 6 which permitted self-employed persons to be enrolled in the NSSF. The Act granted the Minister responsible for labour the discretion to expand NSSF coverage to workers who would otherwise not be eligible for enrolment. Building on NSSF's experience, other schemes such as LAPF and PPF followed suit. The enactment of the Social Security Regulatory Authority Act, 2008 concretized these reforms. Section 54(2) of this Act mandated the Minister responsible for labour to make regulations for extension of social insurance coverage to informal workers. Currently, almost all pension schemes have established voluntary schemes which enrol informal workers and workers who would otherwise be ineligible for membership.

Conversely, in Uganda these reforms did not take place until very recently. Although section 10 of the Uganda NSSF Act stipulates clearly that any employer who is not compulsorily required to register as a contributing employer may apply for voluntary registration as a contributing employer, arrangements for a voluntary scheme were not in place until 12 June 2017, when NSSF finally launched its long overdue voluntary scheme.[78] Employees of firms with fewer than five employees

---

[74] Republic of Kenya, Kenya Social Protection Sector Review June 2012, at p. 24.

[75] The NSSF Act, 2013. The Government also enacted the Public Service Superannuation Act, 2012.

[76] Section 19.

[77] Section 23.

[78] NSSF Launches Voluntary Membership Plan to Widen Coverage, <https://www.nssfug.org/256/NSSF_launches_Voluntary_Membership_Plan_to_widen_coverage> accessed 18 January 2019.

and self-employed persons can now register as members. Prior to this launch, the Uganda Retirements Benefits Regulatory Authority (URBRA) in 2016 licensed the first two private informal sector based pension schemes (Mazima Voluntary Individual Retirement Benefits Scheme (MVIRBS) and Kampala City Traders Association (KACITA)) to operate as retirement benefit schemes for informal workers.[79]

Remarkable achievements have been recorded with regard to health insurance. Public health insurance schemes operative in Kenya, Tanzania, and Rwanda currently enrol self-employed and informal workers. Although at inception these too were meant for public sector employees, they gradually extended their scope to private sector employees and very recently to informal employees, self-employed persons and to any other person willing to become a contributing member.[80] Each of these schemes operates a special scheme through which informal employees and self-employed persons and their dependants may access quality health care services at a moderate fee. There are also community health insurance schemes operative in almost all the countries. These operate at grassroots level. The Rwanda Community Based Health Insurance scheme, *Mutuelle de Santé*, is the best case in point. The scheme is jointly financed by the state and individuals' contributions. Members to the fund pay a premium of 2000 francs (for category 1 members), 3000 francs (for category 2 members), or 7000 francs (for category 3 members).[81] The Government,

[79] Uganda Gets Two Informal Pension Schemes, 20 June 2017, <http://www.monitor.co.ug/Business/Commodities/Uganda-gets-two-informal-pension-schemes/688610-3256838-qyjjrmz/index.html> accessed 18 January 2019. Also see, Bernard Busuulwa, Uganda's informal sector workers to access pension scheme, 25 June 2016, <http://www.theeastafrican.co.ke/business/Uganda-informal-sector-workers-to-access-pension-schemes-/2560-3267600-1oauqmz/index.html> accessed 18 January 2019.

[80] The Kenya National Hospital Insurance Fund launched insurance cover to cater for Kenyans working in the informal sector, 2014, <https://www.standardmedia.co.ke/health/article/2000107199/nhif-launches-health-cover-for-informal-sector> accessed 18 January 2019.

[81] Members are divided into three categories based on their economic situation. Category 1 members comprise the poorest group which accounts for 27 per cent of members. These pay a premium of RWF 2000 (USD 2.99) per person which is paid by the state. Category 2, which comprises members categorized as the middle group, constitutes 70 per cent of members and their annual premium is RWF 3000 (USD 4.35) per person per year. Category 3 members, indicated as the better off group, comprise around 3 per cent of members and they pay an annual premium of RWF 7000 (USD 10.34) per person.

on the other hand, contributes an equivalent of 13 per cent of its annual budget.[82]

Members became eligible for benefits, which include drugs and medical services at health posts, health centres, district hospitals, provincial hospitals and referral hospitals.[83] Membership is compulsory. Failure to enrol attracts a penalty of 5000 to 10,000 francs. Studies have indicated that CBHI has improved access to medicine and significantly lowered health care costs.[84]

Transformations taking place in labour and employment law have also had a positive impact on social insurance. Countries in East Africa and elsewhere in the continent have recently implemented major reforms in their labour and employment laws to align them with international labour standards and to respond to the changing patterns of the employment relationship. The reforms have resulted in replacement of the conventional definition of the term "employee" with an innovative construction through which the scope of labour law, and impliedly social insurance, is extended to persons previously excluded. An example can be cited from section 2 of [Tanzania's] Employment and Labour Relations Act, 2004. Under this provision an employee is defined as

> … (a) any person who has entered into a contact of employment or (b) any other contract under which he undertakes to work personally for the other party to the contract and the other party to that contract is not a client or customer of any profession, business, or undertaking carried on by the individual.

With this development, workers other than those under an employment contract have become eligible for labour law protection, and impliedly, social insurance cover if they undertake work under a contract with the qualities provided for under (b) above. In Rwanda, the term employer is liberally defined as "any physical or moral, public or private person that employs one or several workers, *even in a discontinuous way*" (emphasis

---

82 Article 15(2).

83 Members become eligible for benefits 30 days after their contribution. See Articles 8 and 9.

84 Management Science for Health, The Development of Community-Based Health Insurance in Rwanda: Experiences and Lessons, Technical Brief (Management Science for Health, 2016), <http://www.msh.org/sites/msh.org/files/the_development_of_cbhi_in_rwanda_experiences_and_lessons__technical_brief.pdf> accessed 13 August 2017.

mine).[85] An employee is defined as "any person who commits him/herself to put his/her professional activity in return for payment under the direction and authority of another person, natural, or public or private organisation."[86] These have automatically become eligible for social insurance cover for contingencies directly covered under labour laws such as paid maternity leave and other maternity-related benefits.

5. WHAT HAS BEEN ACHIEVED?

Extension of legal coverage to informal workers was expected to boost the coverage base. Conversely, coverage of social insurance has remained very low leading to the assumption that legislation alone does not necessarily boost enrolment. In some of the countries, the exclusion rate remains above 80 per cent of the active labour force. Tanzania serves as best case in point. As noted above, the legal avenue for informal workers to join social insurance has been in place for almost two decades, from 1998 when the NSSF Act was passed, but the exclusion rate has remained consistently high. As of 2016 the total number of persons covered by social insurance was 2,464,399 out of the 22,321,924 economically active population.[87] In Kenya, as of 2015, the NSSF, which caters for workers in the private sector, had 2,138,320 members only.[88] Given that the share of informal workers around the same period was 12.5 million (equivalent to 82.8 per cent of the total labour force of 15.1 million persons),[89] it cannot be overemphasized that the level of coverage has remained persistently low.

The mismatch between the proportion of workers in these schemes and their proportion in the total workforce means that the majority of workers in this group have no social insurance cover. There are a variety of

---

85 Article 1(32) of Law N° 13/2009 of 27 May 2009 Regulating Labour in Rwanda.

86 See, Article 1(33) of Law N° 13/2009 of 27 May 2009 Regulating Labour in Rwanda.

87 Social Security Regulatory Authority, Jarida la Hifadhi ya Jamii (Social Security Newsletter), (Social Security Regulatory Authority, 2016) p. 5. For the details on the labour force see, National Bureau of Statistics (NBS), Tanzania Integrated Labour Force Survey (National Bureau of Statistics 2014) p. 27.

88 National Social Security Fund [Kenya], Annual Report and Financial Statements for the year ended 30th June 2016 (National Social Security Fund, 2016) p. 17.

89 Kenya National Bureau of Statistics, Economic Survey 2016 (Kenya National Bureau of Statistics, 2016) p. 70.

impeding factors. The most common barriers as thoroughly discussed by Ackson and Masabo in respect of Tanzania, are (i) unwillingness on the part of the employers to contribute to social insurance so as to avoid increasing the labour cost coupled with a reluctance on the part of employees to allow the employer to deduct monies for contributions to the social security scheme as that would reduce their pay; (ii) irregularities, uncertainties and seasonality of income which significantly impair the collection of contributions and eligibility for benefits of informal workers; and (iii) mismatch between the real needs of informal employees and the benefits availed by mandatory social insurance schemes and, especially, the pension schemes.[90] These barriers are also present in other countries. Keizi, in her study of factors inhibiting extension of social security in Kenya, has observed that the major barriers to pension scheme participation by workers in the informal economy in Kenya include difficulty of collecting contributions from both the employee and the employer; inability of workers to contribute a certain percentage of their incomes to financing social security benefits; and workers' unwillingness to contribute when these benefits do not meet their immediate priorities.[91] There is also a strong feeling among many that pensions are less needed/relevant as old age appears very remote and the idea of retirement unreal. Unfamiliarity with social security schemes and distrust of the way the schemes had been managed in the past have also been cited among the key barriers compounding informal workers' reluctance to contribute to a retirement benefits scheme.[92]

To overcome these challenges various strategies have been adopted. These include establishment of specialized schemes and benefits geared towards meeting the specific needs of informal sector workers. The Voluntary Savings Retirement Scheme (VSRS) of the GEPF is one of the popular voluntary schemes in Tanzania. Launched in 2009, the VSRS provides coverage for informal employees, self-employed persons, farmers, fishermen, drivers, petty traders, food venders and organized groups such as VIBINDO, Saving Associations and Credit Co-operative Societies (SACCOS) and women groups.[93] Members of VSRS have two accounts, one a 50 per cent occupational account for meeting short-term needs and the other a 50 per cent retirement account for financing

---

90 Ackson, 2011, pp. 254–256. Also see, Ackson and Masabo, 2013.

91 Keizi, 2006, p. 11.

92 Ibid.

93 Ackson and Masabo, 2013. VIBINDO stands for Jumuiya ya vikundi vya wenye viwanda na biashara ndogondogo (literally translated as association of small scale industrialists and petty traders).

retirement contingencies. The scheme is highly flexible in terms of contributions. Payment of contributions depends on members' convenience. Deposits are payable on a monthly, weekly or daily basis or another period deemed appropriate, and could be made through banks, as cash payments at GEPF offices or through mobile phones.[94]

Tanzania's NSSF also operates specialized schemes for fishermen (Wavuvi Scheme), artisan miners (Madini (mineral) Scheme) and farmers (Wakulima Scheme). The Wakulima Scheme covers peasants and small scale farmers for social calamities while also extending social insurance for employees in the agricultural sector. Members of these schemes (and their families) are eligible for free treatment services. They also, in the case of Wavuvi and Wakulima Schemes, provide poverty reduction benefits in the form of cover for injury and disability, soft loans for agro or fishing inputs, school fees for members' children and other developmental activities. The Madini Scheme avails its members such benefits as access to credit and financial borrowing to boost their income so that they may access the local market and acquire the necessary equipment such as excavating machines.[95]

NSSF Kenya operates similar schemes. Members of the NSSF Voluntary Scheme pay an aggregate contribution of 4800 Kshs a year. Premiums are paid in instalments of a minimum of 200 Kshs paid directly to an NSSF office or by mobile money transfer through M-PESA.[96] These deposits go to the provident fund whose benefits include old age benefit in the form of a lump sum equal to the member's credit at the date of entitlement; survivors' benefit; invalidity benefit; withdrawal benefit; and emigration benefit.[97]

The VIKOA health insurance scheme operated by Tanzania's NHIF is yet another example of tailor-made programmes. The scheme is especially tailored for groups of entrepreneurs such as those in Savings and

---

94 SSRA, Overcoming the Challenges of Enforcement in the Informal Sector to Improve the Accessibility and Attractiveness of Social Security, paper presented at the Social Security & Pension Funds West Africa conference held in Accra, Ghana, 27–29 November 2014, p. 24.

95 NSSF, 50 Years Milestone Achievement: From Pension Provider to Social Security Service Provision and Mega Investment in Real Estate for Economic Development of Tanzania, pp. 16–17, <https://www.nssf.or.tz/index.php/publications/93-nssf-50th-years-anniversary-publication/file> accessed 18 January 2019.

96 NSSF, NSSF Guide Book, p. 6, <http://admin.theiguides.org/Media/Documents/NSSF%20GUIDE%20BOOK%20DOWNLOAD%20latest.pdf> accessed 2 April 2019.

97 See sections 41 to 46.

Credit Cooperative Societies (SACCOS), Agricultural Marketing Co-operative Societies (AMCOS), VIBINDO, Village Community Banking (VIKOBA) and special groups of registered entrepreneurs like motor cycle (bodaboda) drivers, food vendors or any other entrepreneurial group. Members of the VIKOA are required to contribute a total amount of TZS 76,800 on a yearly basis to qualify for an NHIF medical card to be used for medical treatment in over 6000 accredited health facilities in the country by the member, his/her spouse and four other legally recognized dependants who can be children, parents or spouse's parents.

6. CONCLUSION

This chapter has reflected on the state of social insurance in East Africa and the efforts towards extension of social insurance to informal workers. It is observed that social insurance systems in individual countries and the region at large have, until recently, operated to the exclusion of informal workers. Only a marginal section of society was protected. Efforts to narrow the coverage gap and extend social insurance to all workers have now become a priority and have taken many forms including policy and legal reform. An interrogation of the impact of these reforms has revealed that the reforms are yet to yield the desired impact as the exclusion rate has remained persistently high, leading to the adoption of specialized voluntary programmes geared towards the specific needs of informal workers. These measures are certainly commendable. However, for these to achieve the desired change, strategic marketing programmes should be put in place. Already, some of the schemes have launched rigorous marketing for their respective programmes which could be emulated by schemes/countries that are yet to launch similar programmes. Extension of mandatory membership to employers with one employee, as done by Kenya and Rwanda, is yet another commendable effort worthy of emulation by countries that are still limiting mandatory registration to employers with a minimum of five employees. Regarding health insurance, the approach taken by Rwanda's Community Based Health Insurance scheme, *Mutuelle de Santé*, presents good lessons worth exploring in improving accessibility of quality health care.

BIBLIOGRAPHY

Ackson, T, "Social Security for the Excluded in the United Republic of Tanzania: Legislative and New Policy Directives," *Zanzibar Yearbook of Law*, 1(2011) 249–264

Ackson, T, "Extension of Social Security Coverage to the Rural Population in Tanzania: Lessons from India and Iran," *Journal of African and International Law* (2009) 51, 70

Ackson, T and Masabo, J, Social Protection for the Informal Sector in Tanzania, presentation, SASPEN conference, Johannesburg, 2013, <http://www.saspen.org/conferences/informal2013/Paper_Ackson-Masabo_FES-SASPEN-16SEP2013-INT-CONF-SP4IE.pdf> accessed 1 February 2019

Barya, J, *Social Security and Social Protection in the East African Community* (Fountain Publishers, Kampala 2011)

Barya, J, Social Relations and Associations in the Informal Sector in Kenya, Social Policy and Development, Programme Paper No. 43/2010, <http://www.unrisd.org/80256B3C005BCCF9/(httpAuxPages)/E9CBDC63008BB214C12576DA00589211/$file/Kinyanjui-pp.pdf> accessed 1 April 2018

Barya, J, Interrogating the Right to Security and Social Protection in Uganda, HURIPEC Working Paper No. 23/2009, <http://huripec.mak.ac.ug/pdfs/working_paper_23.pdf> accessed 20 March 2018

Barya, J, Workers and the Law in Uganda, Centre for Basic Research Working Paper No. 17/1991, <https://idl-bnc-idrc.dspacedirect.org/handle/10625/50114> accessed 20 March 2018

Bukuluki, P and Mubiru, *The Status of Social Security Systems in Uganda: Challenges and Opportunities* (Konrad-Adenauer-Stiftung, Kampala 2014)

Dau, R K, "Trends in Social Security in East Africa: Tanzania, Kenya and Uganda," *International Social Security Review* (2003) 25, 27

Holmes, R and Scott, L, Extending Social Insurance to Informal Workers: A Gender Analysis, ODI Working Paper 438/2016, <https://www.odi.org/sites/odi.org.uk/files/resource-documents/10620.pdf> accessed 1 April 2018

International Labour Organization, *Women and Men in the Informal Economy: A Statistical Picture* (International Labour Office, Geneva 2018)

Kagumire, R, Public Health Insurance in Uganda Still Only a Dream, 2009, <https://www.ncbi.nlm.nih.gov/pmc/articles/PMC2630345/> accessed 11 August 2015

Kamuzora, P, "Extension of Formal Social Security Schemes in the United Republic of Tanzania" in Wouter van Ginneken (ed.) *Social Security for the Excluded Majority: Case Studies of Developing Countries*' (International Labour Organization, Geneva 1999)

Kasente, D et al., "Social Security Systems in Uganda," *Journal of Social Development in Africa*, 17, 2 (2002) 157–183

Keizi, L K, Barriers to Pension Scheme Participation by Workers in the Informal Economy (Retirement Benefits Authority, Nairobi, 2006)

Kinyanjui, M N, *Women and the Informal Economy in Urban Africa: From the Margins to the Centre* (Zed Books, London 2014).

Olivier, M, "Informality, Employment Contracts, and Social Insurance Coverage: Rights-Based Perspectives in a Developing World Context," *International Journal of Comparative Labour Law and Industrial Relations*, 27 (2011) 419, 433

Olivier, M P and Kalula, E R, "Regional Social Security" in Olivier, M P et al. (eds) *Social Security: A Legal Analysis* (LexisNexis Butterworths, Durban 2003)

Raichura, S K, Analytical Review of the Pension System in Kenya, <http://www.oecd.org/daf/fin/private-pensions/41564693.pdf> accessed 10 March 2018

Ruberangeyo, T et al., "Rwanda – Social Protection: An Ongoing Process" in Volume 18: Successful Social Protection Floor Experiences, *Sharing Innovative Experiences* (United Nations Development Programme, 2011) 333–358

Ruhara, M C, "Effect of Health Insurance on Demand for Outpatient Medical Care in Rwanda: An Application of the Control Function Approach," *Rwanda Journal* 3 (2016) 77, 100

Rwanda Civil Society Platform, Social Security in the Informal Sector in Rwanda, <http://www.rcsprwanda.org/IMG/pdf/Final_Report-CSP_II-2-_RCSP_doc.pdf> accessed 1 April 2018

Shimeles, A, Community Based Health Insurance Schemes in Africa: The Case of Rwanda, African Development Bank Working Papers Series No. 120/2010

Uwera, B Social Security and Pension systems in Rwanda: Limits and Alternatives (Masters Thesis, Tilburg University, 2013)

PART IV

Country case studies

10. Social protection for workers outside the traditional employment contract – a Swedish example

Annamaria Johansson Westregård

1. INTRODUCTION

Sweden's business structure has traditionally been built on large export companies in forestry, mining and metal industries. The country's labour law legislation and social insurance system have been adapted to this reality, and social insurance is designed with a focus on those permanently employed in large firms with regular working hours and incomes. However, changes are taking place. The number of self-employed people and small company employees has increased and the number of business owners in Sweden is about 9 per cent of the workforce (European Union (EU) average is almost 15 per cent) and 73 per cent of Swedish companies do not have any employees.[1] The number of fixed-term employees has also increased over the past 25 years and is now 16.7 per cent of the total number of employees in the 16 to 64 age group. The most common type of fixed-term employment is those 'employed by the hour with an agreed schedule for a specified period' (25 per cent of all fixed-term employees). Of the fixed-term employees 20 per cent work on an on-demand basis.[2]

In an era when different types of precarious work and employment are on the rise, and more people are willing to work in these forms, it is crucial to review and adapt the social insurance system to guarantee that these groups have basic economic security in the event of illness, unemployment, parental allowance and so on.

---

[1] <http://www.ekonomifakta.se/sv/Fakta/Foretagande/Naringslivet/Naringslivets-struktur/> accessed 28 June 2018.

[2] SOU 2017:24, 132 and 137 and the Statistics Sweden (SCB) statistics cited there.

Section 2 presents the concept of employment in Sweden and some untraditional work that has become common lately in Sweden. Section 3 provides a synoptic overview of the Swedish social security system with a focus on health insurance, parental allowance and unemployment insurance. The purpose is to analyse the differences in social security protection between different forms of employment and other performing parties, for example the self-employed, and the legislative amendments that have been put in place to provide self-employed and untraditional workers with similar protection. Section 4 presents a formal analysis of the deficiencies that still remain in the legislation, together with proposals for action and the unique problems connected with the collaborative economy. Section 5 contains some final remarks.

2. THE CONCEPT OF EMPLOYMENT AND THE 'NEW' FORMS OF WORK

Like most other countries, Sweden applies a binary system in which a working individual is either an employee or is self-employed. There is no general legal definition of the civil law notion of an employee in Community Law or national Swedish law.[3] The lack of a clear, well-established definition makes the concept of employee quite vague.[4] In Sweden the concept of employee is synonymous with the concept of worker. The legislation in the United Kingdom, unlike Sweden, separates employee from worker[5] and the concept of worker is broader and different from the concept of employee.[6]

The concept of employee is used to determine the application of legal rules and areas. The main purpose of the definition is to identify those who are covered by the labour legislation; those who should pay tax; and those who are covered by different social insurance rules.[7] In Sweden, the definition of the concept of employment in social insurance legislation is related to tax law and not labour law. The dividing line in social insurance is not between the employee and the self-employed, but between the two categories of self-employed. According to the Social

3 Westregård (2016).
4 Adlercreutz (1964) 15.
5 The Employment Rights Act 1996 s. 230 (1)–(3).
6 Kenner (2017) 153–83.
7 Källström (1999) 162.

Insurance Contribution Act,[8] persons deemed to be the owner of a business must pay the social contribution themselves. A principal, however, must pay social contribution for those who are self-employed and who do not carry out work independently, just as an employer must do for their employees.

The concept of employee is defined differently within labour law, tax law and social security legislation and different evidentiary facts have varying significance and meaning. Within labour law, for example, important evidentiary facts indicate that the work falls in the category of employment because the person performing the work has only one client, and most especially when this client is the person's former employer. In tax law (and social security law), on the other hand, the number of clients is less important and it is regarded as natural that a previous employer is the new company's first client. In a proposal for legal changes the commissioner was critical of the fact that a former employer can be a new company's only client. It is likely there will be some changes in the legislation suggested to avoid 'false self-employed'. Due to the different use of the concept of the employee, the same person could be regarded as self-employed in both tax and social security law but as an employee in labour law.[9]

In Swedish labour legislation, permanent, full-time employment of unspecified duration is still the most common form of employment.[10] Other forms, such as part-time work and fixed-term employment, are regarded as atypical or untraditional. Atypical work is also an arrangement under which the person doing the work is not an employee of the organisation on whose behalf the work is done, for example companies hiring out labour and other forms of contract work and self-employment. A large part of that atypical work could also be regarded as precarious work in the sense that the person doing the work does not have the same economic security as the typical employee has, evidenced through low wages and financial compensation, precarious conditions and limited social protection.

Atypical workers, outside the traditional employment contract, have emerged in Sweden since the turn of the millennium. Eurofound has

---

8 Chap 2 of the 2000 Social Insurance Contribution Act (Swedish Code of Statutes (SFS) 2000:980).

9 Westregård (2016); see also SOU 2018:49, 211 ff.

10 If nothing else is proved the employment is presumed to be of unspecified duration and a part-time employee is entitled to full-time employment if the employer is going to extend his business (section 4 and 25 a in 1982 Employment Protection Act (1982:80)).

mapped what they call new forms of employment and work.[11] Some of the forms are new because they exist thanks to new technology such as online platforms. Others are new in the sense that they are used more often today. Some of the workers outside the traditional employment contract are employees, some are self-employed and some are in a grey zone in-between. I focus here on the untraditional forms of work that have become more common in Sweden.[12]

One form is *intermittent work*: the employee is hired at regular or irregular intervals for fixed-term periods of a certain number of days at a time, and in a variant, *on-call work*, the employee has a continuous contract but the working hours are not specified; it can vary between a minimum and maximum time. This arrangement is also called a *zero-hours contract*. That means that the employer is not obligated to give the employee work. Another form is *portfolio work*. This is when sole proprietors work for many clients, carrying out small, short-term assignments for each client. A variant is *crowd employment*, in which many workers are gathered for an assignment via an online platform. It is important to note that there are many different kinds of crowdwork. This can be *work-on-demand by an app*, where the worker interacts with the client solely via an online platform. The platform can also have a business model with a much clearer organisation, where the online platform is paid by the client and distributes compensation to the worker. In a number of cases, the personal transport forum Uber has been found to be the drivers' employer.[13] A new business model that has become popular in Sweden is *umbrella companies* (*egenanställningsföretag*). They offer administrative services such as client invoicing and dealing with tax issues and are often connected with a collaborative platform. The business concept of an umbrella company is for a self-employed person, who does not own a company, to seek out an assignment and agree with the client how the work shall be performed and the amount of compensation.[14] Considering the extent of the concept of employee, it is possible that people using umbrella companies are regarded as fixed-term employees in labour legislation. On the other hand, they are not regarded as employees within unemployment insurance.[15]

---

11 See Eurofound (2015).

12 Eurofound (2015) chap 2–10; SOU 2017:24, chap 7,9,10 and 11.

13 *Uber BV and others v Mr Y Asiam & others* (2017) UKEAT/0056/17DA (EAT) 10 November 2017; *Berwick v Uber Technologies, Inc.*, 3 June 2015, where the court recognised the driver as an employee; Westregård (2017b).

14 SOU 2017:24, 161 ff.

15 SOU 2018:49, chap 8.

3. HEALTH INSURANCE, PARENTAL ALLOWANCE AND UNEMPLOYMENT INSURANCE

3.1 Introduction

How does the social security system function in relation to different forms of employees and the self-employed? In 2010, reforms were made to social security and tax regulations with the express ambition of encouraging all types of work, including work performed in non-traditional forms. Some complementary reforms were also made or have been initiated in 2018.[16]

In social insurance legislation, the self-employed, operating in different forms of company structure, are treated differently. This means that there are also consequences for the social insurance protection an individual receives, depending on the company structure they choose to operate in. A simple partnership (*enskild firma*), trading partnership (*handelsbolag*) and a limited partnership (*kommanditbolag*)[17] constitute one category.[18] Those working in a close company (*fåmansaktiebolag*) do not belong to this category; from a social insurance perspective, they are employed by their own company, and this has several consequences. The term close company here refers to small shareholder companies with only one employee, usually the owner.[19] The advantage of the close company structure is that the owners are not personally responsible for paying the company's debts; owners of simple partnerships are responsible for their company's debts.

The focus of the health insurance and parental allowance regulation, set out in the 2010 Social Insurance Code (2010:110), and the unemployment insurance regulation in the 1997 Unemployment Insurance Act (1997:238), set out as the legislative amendments in 2010 and proposals for new legal changes and inquiries for legislation in 2017 and 2018, is to create parity between traditional full-time employment

---

16 A legal change in SFS 2018:670 and prop. 2017/18:168; proposal for legal changes in SOU 2018:49; and inquiry for new legislation in Kommittédirektiv Dir. 2017:56; Kommittédirektiv Dir. 2018:8; Kommittédirektiv Dir. 2018:54.

17 Moberg (2010) 381.

18 SOU 2015:21, 969.

19 A close company (*fåmansaktiebolag*) is limited by shares in which four or fewer owners hold at least 50 per cent of voting shares (chap 56 Section 2 the 1999 Income Tax Law (1999:1229)). Companies listed on the stock exchange are not close companies.

and the 'new' untraditional employments and also between employed and self-employed.

The Swedish social insurance system also includes other areas of social insurance such as industrial injury insurance in the 1976 Industrial Injury Insurance Act (1976:380), and pension regulations in 1998 Earning-Related Retirement (1998:674), the Guarantee Pension Act (1998:702) and the Early Retirement Pension in chapter 35 of the 2010 Social Insurance Code. These regulations are not analysed in this chapter. There are collective agreements on a national level too, which contain supplemental compensation to social security insurance and pensions. In Sweden, healthcare is not connected to employment and, therefore, it is not relevant for inclusion here.

3.2 Content and Access – Health Insurance, Parental Allowance and Unemployment Insurance

This chapter gives a very brief overview of the social insurance system in Sweden. Some of the questions arising in this area seem particularly important for precarious workers and this section focuses, firstly, on access to social insurance and, secondly, the methods for calculating benefits.

Health insurance

In the last decade, health insurance in the 1991 Sickpay Act (1991:1047) has changed several times. In 2008 new regulations were introduced. An individual can have sickness benefits for 180 days but, subsequently, sickness benefit is only continued if the individual cannot work at all within the labour market. If the person can do some other work, but not with the present employer, the person must resign and apply for a new job and can seek unemployment benefits if necessary. If a person is too sick for any job at all, that person may seek sickness benefits until early retirement pension is available. After the recent change in legislation, early retirement pension is only permitted if it is obvious that the person will never be able to work again.[20]

Those working in a close company are obligated to pay out the first 14 days of sickness benefit themselves, just as employers pay sickness benefit to their employees.[21] There are disadvantages for owners of close companies compared to owners of other companies as small-business

20 Chap 27 and 35 Social Insurance Code; Westregård (2014).

21 Section 7 in the 1991 Sickness Payment Act (1991:1047).

owners of a simple partnership, trading partnership or limited partnership can determine their own number of qualifying days and pay a lower sickness benefit contribution.

After 14 days the sickness benefit paid is distributed for all employees by the Social Insurance Agency, 85 per cent of which is financed by mandatory employer contributions[22] (a health insurance labour market fee as part of the mandatory payroll tax) and the rest by the state taxes.[23]

Parental allowance

As soon as a child is born the parents are part of the parental insurance scheme. The amount is either work-based or housing-based if the work requirement cannot be fulfilled. Parental benefit is paid out at three different levels: *the income compensation level* (80 per cent of income) for those who work and have a sickness benefit qualifying income (see below), a *basic level* for parents insured on the housing-based benefit and those on *a lowest level.*

In addition, temporary parental benefit is available only for those on the income compensation level and only covers parents who work. In 2010, rules around allocation and calculation of temporary parental benefit were adjusted so that small-business owners would be on more of a par with employees.[24]

The parental allowance is 100 per cent financed by mandatory employer contributions (a parental insurance fee as part of the mandatory payroll tax), distributed by the Social Insurance Agency.[25]

Unemployment insurance

Both employees and the self-employed can be covered by Swedish unemployment insurance. The insurance includes basic insurance as well as loss-of-income insurance. *Basic insurance* provides the necessary amount to individuals who fulfil the basic and work requirements, but who have not been members of an unemployment insurance scheme for 12 months. Individuals who have been members for 12 months and who

---

[22] For 2018 the total employer contribution is 31.42 per cent of gross salary, <https://www.skatteverket.se/foretagochorganisationer/arbetsgivare/arbetsgivaravgifterochskatteavdrag/arbetsgivaravgifter> accessed 8 July 2018.

[23] The 2000 Social Insurance Contribution Act (2000:980) and Försäkringskassan *Socialförsäkring i siffror* (2017) 24.

[24] Chap 12 paragraphs 21–24 and chap 13 paragraphs 16, 20 and 21 in the 2010 Social Insurance Code.

[25] The 2000 Social Insurance Contribution Act (2000:980); Försäkringskassan *Socialförsäkring i siffror* (2017) 24.

fulfil the basic requirements receive *compensation from the loss-of-income* insurance scheme. Benefit is paid with some variation, that is, 80 per cent of an individual's income for the first 200 days or 70 per cent of their income for the following 100 days.[26]

Before the changes made in 2010,[27] problems arose with the 1997 Unemployment Insurance Act (1007:238) when a self-employed individual was to shift from working in his or her own company to unemployment insurance. To receive benefits before, the individual had to close down all business activity completely, making it difficult to start up the company again. A hiatus in operations can now be temporary or permanent; the only requirement is for the business owner to state that he or she is not operating the company. A temporary hiatus can occur so that the company owner does not need to close down the company to receive unemployment insurance.

Unemployment benefit insurance is administered by unemployment benefit associations in various sectors, according to the 1997 Unemployment Funds Act (1997:239). The benefit is financed approximately 90 per cent by employer contributions (a labour market fee as part of the mandatory payroll tax)[28] and around 10 per cent by membership fees.[29]

3.3 Calculation of Compensation

Sickness benefit qualifying income for health insurance and parental allowance

The amount of compensation naturally holds great significance for a person who is sick. Payment of income-based sickness benefit and parental benefit is based on sickness benefit qualifying income (*Sjukpenninggrundande inkomst*, SGI). This requires that the individual is covered by the employment-based insurance stipulated in chapter 6 of the 2010 Social Insurance Code or by the EU Regulation on the coordination of social security systems,[30] based on their annual income from working in Sweden. This work must be expected to last at least six months or be of

---

26 Sections 7 and 24 Unemployment Insurance Act. The basic amount is determined by the government, and for 2018 it is a maximum SEK 365 per day in the case of full-time work.

27 Section 35, a change of law (2010:445).

28 The 2000 Social Insurance Contribution Act (2000:980).

29 SOU 2015:21, 738.

30 Regulation (EC) No 883/2004—on the coordination of social security systems.

an annually recurring nature (seasonal work) and over a minimum level (decided every year, e.g. for 2018, just over 10 000 SEK).[31]

For employees and owners of a small close company, SGI A is calculated using predicted annual income as a basis. Previous income levels are not used; instead the individual's future income is predicted. Historical income shall be considered by way of a comparison and not as grounds for decision-making.[32] If a worker has irregular income, for example from sporadic work, the calculation will be based on information received from the individual themselves and their employer, as well as the estimate used for determining income tax. The method of forecasted income has been simple to use and easy to manage, because Sweden has traditionally had large workplaces where pay rises were controlled by collective agreements and thus were easy to predict.

If a person has received at least SEK 1000 for having performed work for someone else, this work is considered employment.[33] This also applies even when the person is not employed by the entity paying out the benefit. In the eyes of the 2010 Social Insurance Code, the compensating entity is considered to be the employer. This does not apply if the compensation is considered to come from some other gainful employment. This rule is significant for those receiving many small amounts of income for assignments from a variety of clients.

For those receiving income for other types of work, SGI B is calculated. This includes individuals operating small non-incorporated businesses, individuals approved for the Swedish Business Tax Certificate (*godkänd för F-skatt*[34]) and those who are self-employed.[35] SGI B is also calculated based on expected future income. Estimating future income for these persons is far more complicated than for employees and owners of close companies. To determine a basis for the calculation, the Social Insurance Agency asks the individual to provide a prediction of future income; the caseworker then compares this information with the worker's accounts and information from the accountant and from the Tax Agency.[36]

New calculation rules were introduced in 2010 to stimulate and facilitate the start of new businesses. During a start-up phase (now 36

---

31 It is 24 per cent of the price base amount (chap 25 Section 3 in the 2010 Social Insurance Code).

32 Ryberg-Welander (2014) 72.

33 Chap 25 Section 7 the 2010 Social Insurance Code.

34 Chap 13 Section 1 of the Income Tax Law (1999:1229).

35 Chap 25 Sections 8 and 10 the 2010 Social Insurance Code.

36 See Ryberg-Welander (2014) 80.

months) the owners of a simple partnership, trading partnership or limited partnership[37] are allowed to specify a fictitious income for the purposes of calculation. The comparison income shall correspond to the income that a comparable employee/self-employed individual would have earned. After a change in the legislation on 1 August 2018, the regulation also applies to close companies and is one way to create parity between different forms of company structures.[38] Before the changes in this regulation, there was a disadvantage for owners of close companies and significant consequences if the owner began with a small salary and subsequently became ill.[39] A parliamentary inquiry committee has been appointed to make proposals for new legislation to improve the protection for the self-employed and employees in their 'new' and changing working lives.[40]

Calculation of compensation from unemployment insurance

The income basis, according to the law on unemployment insurance, is calculated differently from SGI. Compensation for the basic amount is determined by the government. For employees, income-related benefits are based on earnings during the past 12 months, as documented in a so-called employer's certificate. The government sets a maximum amount each year for the daily benefit.

For the self-employed, the benefit level is determined based on the most recent decision on final tax, or if it is more advantageous for the individual, on an average taken from the past two years' taxation. The definition of company owners in the 1997 Unemployment Insurance Act has been related to the concept of economic activity in the 1999 Income Tax Law (1999:1229).[41] This means that, as distinct from the health insurance regulations, this regulation applies to all forms of companies including small close companies. In 2010, new rules were introduced for self-employed company owners who closed down their company within 36 months after establishment. In this scenario, the individual receives benefits based on income from previous employment. *Combiners*[42] receive benefits based on both employment and the operation of their

---

37 Chap 25 Section 9 the 2010 Social Insurance Code; SOU 2015:21, 966 f.

38 SFS 2018:670; prop. 2017/18:168, 20 f.

39 SOU 2015:21, 324.

40 Kommittédirektiv Dir. 2018:54. The result will be declared 30 June 2019.

41 This is a physical person who operates a business and who personally performs work over which he or she exerts significant influence.

42 A combiner receives income from both employment and clients, or employment and work on an assignment basis (SOU 2015:21, 941).

own businesses.[43] A parliamentary inquiry committee has also been appointed in this area and will make proposals for new legislation to adapt for new situations in working life.[44]

3.4 Conclusions

Of all the different categories of workers, permanent employees with regular, full-time work have the most protection given that insurance schemes were designed to fit this form of employment. For temporary employees, with irregular working times and incomes, and those with more than one employer, different problems arise.

The social insurance system is least adapted to *assignment workers*. These individuals take on assignment-based work without being employed or owning a company. Whether they are treated as employees or self-employed depends on the degree of independence in the working relationship.[45] This leads to uncertainty in applying the rules on a case-by-case basis. Those working in the new, precarious forms of employment are often assignment workers or combiners. The legislators' ambition is to improve social security for these workers and make it similar to what the social insurance system offers traditional employees. In the legislative reforms, the company owner perspective was taken into account, as well as the possibility to switch between and combine different forms of employment and business ownership.

Two types of amendments have been carried out: the introduction of measures to facilitate the shift from employment to company ownership, and measures to strengthen security and freedom of choice for small-business owners. Some of the special arrangements in the legislation for owners of a simple partnership, trading partnership or limited partnership have also lately been extended to close companies to create parity between different company structures.

---

43 Section 34, 37-7 b in the 1997 Unemployment Insurance Act.

44 Kommittédirektiv Dir. 2018:8. The result will be declared 31 January 2020.

45 SOU 2015:21, 944 and 969. In this case social insurance law and unemployment insurance rely on chap 13 Section 1 of the Income Tax Law (1999:1229).

4. THE OFFICIAL ANALYSIS OF DEFICIENCIES AND PROPOSALS FOR ACTION

4.1 Deficiencies

A parliamentary inquiry committee on social insurance carried out a review of the whole health and parental insurance system in 2015.[46] The findings of the investigation point to insufficiencies in the *calculation of compensation* with the SGI. For employees with a stable income, the method of 'income forecasting' works reasonably well. However, workers with many temporary employments are put at a disadvantage because they may find it difficult to demonstrate continuous employment. Estimates of future income for company owners, particularly those who combine employment with business activity, were found to have significant deviations when compared to estimates for permanent, full-time employees. Insufficiencies in the calculation methods make it difficult to predict which SGI will be set, and this is a source of uncertainty for the individual.[47] The calculation methods for unemployment insurance are also complicated. Company owners and workers with fluctuating employment find it hard to foresee the benefit that they would receive. It is particularly difficult to decide how to handle the situation of assignment workers.[48]

Earlier inquiries have suggested clearer rules for how assignment workers are defined, but this has not yet led to legislative reform.[49] The assignment workers therefore remain in a grey zone in the legislation between employees and self-employed. Neither have the parliamentary committee provided concrete proposals, such as flat-rate rules, to determine the classification of assignment workers. Owing to the variation in the group being so large, the investigators asserted that the circumstances of each individual case must be taken into account, and left it to the authorities to provide general recommendations.[50] Therefore, several new and *precarious forms of work remain in the grey zone* between employment and self-employed company ownership.[51] Unemployment benefit agencies find it especially difficult to handle the situation of those

---

46 The results were presented in the SOU 2015:21.

47 SOU 2015:21, 316 ff.

48 SOU 2015:21, 964 ff.

49 SOU 2011:52; SOU 1996:150.

50 SOU 2015:21, 966.

51 SOU 2011:52 Appendix 3 contains a description of assignment workers, such as bloggers, consultants, self-employed and others.

self-employed working through umbrella companies. The three-party relationship and the worker's significant level of independence has presented a challenge for classification processes.[52] The combiners are also in an uncertain position in this regard; for combiners, it is difficult to demonstrate continuous employment, and their SGI ends up being based purely on their employee income rather than their other income.

4.2 Proposals for Action

The proposal of the parliamentary committee is that the same concepts of income are used across unemployment insurance, health insurance and parental allowance. An individual's average income for the past 12 months, for which the employer has paid social insurance contributions, shall serve as the basis for calculating benefit. For owners of companies, the proposal is for actual income to correspond to the reported income for taxation (i.e. the surplus from economic activity). This would make it easier to predict the amount of compensation payable. The proposal would also eliminate a requirement on duration of employment. This would improve compensation for combiners and fixed-term employees with many small employments.[53] The committee's proposed changes have not yet been addressed in the legislative process, but as mentioned above, in 2018 new parliamentary inquiry committees were appointed.[54]

4.3 Precarious Work in the Collaborative Economy

The problems identified by the parliamentary committee inquiry are based on the idea that workers are 'in the system' and that taxes and social insurance contributions are correctly documented and paid. Unreported income is not included in the basis for calculation once income has been related to reported income. Thus the whole informal sector is excluded from the scope of unemployment and social insurance schemes.

In a report, the Tax Agency identified a number of tax law-related problems in the new collaborative economy. The primary challenge is determining who is responsible for payment of social insurance contributions and paying tax in the domestic services and personal transport

---

52 The Swedish Unemployment Insurance Board (2016:3, 15).

53 SOU 2015:21, 952, 976, 982–4 f; SOU 2012:47, 135.

54 Kommittédirektiv Dir. 2017:56; Kommittédirektiv Dir. 2018:8; Kommittédirektiv Dir. 2018:54; SOU 2018:49.

sectors.[55] In general, the rule is that the entity paying for the work shall pay social insurance contributions and tax, unless the worker owns a company and holds a Business Tax Certificate, and is responsible for paying his or her own contribution.

It can be difficult in collaborative economies[56] to determine whether the client/service consumer or the collaborative platform pays for the work. If the platform determines the nature of the work and the price, and is responsible for the contract between the worker and the client, then the worker can be considered subordinate to the platform. Therefore, the platform is the entity providing payment for the work and is responsible for payment of tax and social insurance contributions. If the worker decides when he or she will perform the work, as well as the price and other conditions, then the worker should be viewed as independent in relation to the platform. Therefore, the client/service consumer is the entity providing payment for the work, and is responsible for payment of tax and social insurance contributions. This can be difficult from an administrative perspective because often the platform is the only party that has the worker's personal data.

The Tax Agency has pointed out other problems with respect to tax reporting in collaborative economies. These include insufficient bookkeeping and inexperienced providers of information who are not accustomed to reporting income from various sources. The Tax Agency investigation also showed that unreported incomes are on the rise, and are higher in the collaborative economy than in comparable traditional sectors. For the Tax Agency, this problem is exacerbated by the large number of workers carrying out assignments for many clients, often for low, sporadic wages.

There is clearly a risk that income will remain unreported by both the client/paying party and the worker (who is responsible to pay if they have a Business Tax certificate).[57] The consequence is that this remuneration for work will not be included in the income on which the benefits of social insurance and unemployment is calculated and the benefits will be much lower for already vulnerable workers in the case of sickness, childbirth or unemployment.

55 Tax Agency Report (2016).
56 SOU 2017:26, 62; Westregård (2017a).
57 Tax Agency Report (2016, 25 and 29–34).

5. CONCLUSION

This chapter is about the Swedish legislators' ambition to create parity between different forms of employment, as well as between employees and those who operate companies, irrespective of company structure. Improvements have been made during the last decade but, so far, the proposals for improvement have been of little value in helping assignment workers – those occupying the grey zone between employment and company ownership – or in tackling the problem of unreported income in the collaborative economy. Work outside the traditional employment contract is often saddled with such problems.

The untraditional forms of work differ from the work performed by permanent employees who have regular, full-time work. They often involve fluctuating work and income. Some include many small and brief assignments delivered by business owners to many clients which can entail irregular work and uncertain income. In crowd employment without a company, it can be problematic to ensure that the entities ordering the work pay taxes and employer contributions on the many small fees they pay to suppliers. The individual's status as employee or business owner may be unclear; this can make it difficult to obtain access to social insurance.

Tax, social insurance and corporation law interact to achieve better conditions and security in social insurance. It is essential that changes and improvements are made consistently and simultaneously throughout the affected legal environments; so far, this has not always been the case in Sweden. Many persons in the untraditional forms of employment would surely be categorised as employees by the Labour Court, as Sweden has an extensive concept of the employee, but the tax law and social insurance law do not apply the labour-law concept of employment in their assessment.[58] The solution to precarity in working life is not only a question for labour legislation but also for regulation of social security. It is therefore important that labour legislation and social security insurance complement each other better than they do today. In Sweden social security legislation is linked more closely to tax legislation and payment of tax and social insurance contribution than it is to labour law. Managing the employment conditions of the growing numbers of precarious workers is a problem throughout the European Union as well. In the new proposal to a

---

58 Westregård (2016).

European Pillar of Social Rights, most of the protection is focused on workers, but also to some extent on the self-employed.[59]

Regardless of attempts to improve security in social insurance systems, a problem shared by many of the untraditional employment forms remains: they are uncertain, irregular and often with low wages. A type of company has emerged called the necessity start-up. This involves individuals who have started their own company because it is difficult to enter the Swedish labour market at all, for example without a high school degree or without speaking very good Swedish, and this prevents them from finding more traditional employment. Among small-business owners, 16 per cent are considered as economically vulnerable, earning less than 60 per cent of the average disposable income. In addition, large variations can be seen in annual salary over time.[60]

The Swedish example described in this chapter demonstrates the difficulty in covering all types of precarious forms of employment and self-employment, even when the ambition is to ensure equal security for these groups. Significant problems arising range from income fluctuations as well as occasional or short employments, to also dealing with the large number of stakeholders involved. Yet another challenge is the informal labour sector with its unreported incomes. Legislative efforts should focus on broad, technology-independent solutions for creating access to social insurance and calculation of benefits.

BIBLIOGRAPHY

Axel Adlercreutz *Arbetstagarbegreppet* (Norstedt & söners Förlag 1964)

Jeff Kenner 'Inverting the Flexicurity Paradigm: The United Kingdom and Zero Hours Contracts' in Ales et al. (eds) *Core and Contingent Work in European Union: A comparative analysis* (Hart Publishing 2017)

Kent Källström 'Employment and contract work' (1999) Comparative Labour Law & Policy Journal 21/1

Krister Moberg 'Company Law' in Michael Bogdan (eds) *Swedish Legal System* (Norstedts Juridik 2010)

Lottie Ryberg-Welander *Socialförsäkringsrätt Om ersättning vid sjukdom* (2nd edn Norstedts Juridik 2014)

Nina Sanadadji *Nödvändighetsföretagarna* (Timbro Report 8 May 2017)

---

[59] European Commission Brussels, 26.4.2017 COM (2017) 250 final Communication from the Commission to the European Parliament, the Council, the European and Social Committee and the Committee of the Regions Establishing a European Pillar of Social Rights (see chap III and pp. 21 and 50).

[60] Sanadadji (2017).

Annamaria Westregård 'Changes in the Swedish Sickness Insurance System and Labour Law due to influence of flexicurity' (2014) Europaeische Zeitschrift fur Arbeitsrecht/European Journal of Labour Law 1/2014

Annamaria Westregård 'The Notion of "Employee" in Swedish and European Union Law. An Exercise in Harmony or Disharmony?' in Laura Carson, Örjan Edström and Birgitta Nyström (eds) *Globalisation, Fragmentation and Employment Law – A Swedish Perspective* (Iustus 2016)

Annamaria Westregård 'Delningsplattformar och crowdworkers i den digitaliserade ekonomin – en utmaning för kollektivavtalsmodellen' in Birgitta Nyström, Niklas Arvidsson and Boel Flodgren (eds) *Modern affärsrätt* (Wolters Kluwer 2017a)

Annamaria Westregård 'Collaborative economy – a new challenge for the social partners' in Kerstin Ahlberg (ed.) *Vänbok till Niklas Bruun* (Iustus 2017b)

EU Legal Materials

Eurofound *New forms of employment* (Publications Office of the European Union 2015)

European Commission Brussels, 26.4.2017 COM (2017) 250 final Communication from the Commission to the European Parliament, the Council the European and Social Committee and the Committee of the Regions Establishing a European Pillar of Social Rights

Cases

Employment Appeal Tribunal: *Uber BV and others v Mr Y Asiam & others* (2017) UKEAT/0056/17DA (EAT), 10 November 2017 affirmed the Employment Tribunal's judgment

Labor Commissioner of the State of California, *Berwick v Uber Technologies, Inc.*, 3 June 2015

Swedish Preparatory Work for Legislation

Kommittédirektiv (Directive) Dir. 2010:48 *Hållbara försäkringar vid sjukdom och arbetslöshet*

Kommittédirektiv (Directive) Dir. 2017:56 *Trygghet och utveckling i anställning vad gäller arbetstid och ledighet*

Kommittédirektiv (Directive) Dir. 2018:8 *En ny arbetslöshetsförsäkring för fler, grundad på inkomst*

Kommittédirektiv (Directive) Dir. 2018:54 *Ett tryggare företagande i ett förändrat arbetsliv – för tillväxt och innovation*

Prop. (Legislative Bill) 2017/18:168 *Stärkt försäkringsskydd för studerande och företagare*

SOU (Government White Paper) 1996:150 *En allmän och sammanhållen arbetslöshetsförsäkring*

SOU (Government White Paper) 2011:52 *Uppdragstagare i arbetslöshetsförsäkringen*

SOU 2012:47 *Harmoniserat inkomstbegrepp – Möjligheter att använda månadsuppgifter i social- och arbetslöshetsförsäkringarna*

SOU (Government White Paper) 2015:21 *Mer trygghet och bättre försäkring*

SOU (Government White Paper) 2017:24 *Ett arbetsliv I förändring – hur påverkas ansvaret för arbetsmiljön*

SOU (Government White Paper) 2017:26 *Delningsekonomin På användarnas villkor*

SOU (Government White Paper) 2018:49 *F-skattesystemet – några särskilt utpekade frågor*

Other Materials

Försäkringskassan *Socialförsäkring i siffror* (2017)

SFS 2018:670 *Lag om ändring i Socialförsäkringsbalken*

The Swedish Unemployment Insurance Board (IAF) *Uppdragstagare i arbetslöshetsförsäkringen* 2016:3

Tax Agency Report (Skatteverkets Rapport) *Delningsekonomi. Kartläggning och analys av delningsekonomins påverkan på skattesystemet* 131 129 651-16/113 2016.

Electronic Sources

<http://www.ekonomifakta.se/sv/Fakta/Foretagande/Naringslivet/Naringslivets-struktur/> accessed 28 June 2018.

<https://www.skatteverket.se/foretagochorganisationer/arbetsgivare/arbetsgivaravgifterochskatteavdrag/arbetsgivaravgifter> accessed 8 July 2018.

11. The Netherlands: solo self-employment and labour on demand

Mies Westerveld

1. INTRODUCTION

In the Netherlands, social security is organised by means of employee insurance schemes for labour-related risks and national insurance schemes for social risks that concern all residents. This system was set up and expanded in the 1950s and 1960s and has endured several crises and societal changes. Nevertheless, it has been able to maintain its basic protective function against the most common risks. The latter are beginning to change, however. In particular the employee insurance schemes are increasingly failing to protect dependent or 'precarious' workers. This is caused by changes in the labour market. As in many other countries, the employment contract, traditionally the 'stepping stone' to employee insurance schemes, no longer constitutes a fixed, stable relationship between a worker and an employer. Employment contracts have become more flexible, and complex legal structures sometimes make it difficult to establish who the responsible other party with respect to the worker is. The advent of self-employed workers, too, sometimes 'employee-like workers', sometimes 'true entrepreneurs', has presented the government with difficult choices. This is not pre-eminently a Dutch phenomenon. Many European Union (EU) member states, but the US and Canada, too, have seen workers who are labelled 'self-employed workers without employees' (the Netherlands), 'solo self-employed' (the UK) or 'independent contractors' (the US) enter the labour market.[1]

[1] I. Hatfield (2015). See also Chapter 2 in this volume.

At the same time, solo self-employment (hereafter: SSE[2]) represents a broader development. Even more drastic, and certainly with respect to organising social security more complex, is the rise of Platform Enterprising as an exponent of what is also referred to as 'the third wave of globalisation'.[3] The term Platform Enterprise (hereafter: PE) includes different types of platforms but relevant to labour and labour law is the transaction type, which stands for 'a technology, product or service that acts as a conduit or intermediary facilitating exchange or transactions between different users, buyers, or suppliers'.[4] PEs originate for the most part from the US, China and a number of other Asian countries, but their impact on labour, labour relations and labour-related social security is worldwide. Hence, the rise of PEs has evoked strong reactions, often positive, with governments welcoming PEs as bearers of innovation. For labour law issues, however, PEs are considered disturbing, if not disruptive.[5] The way in which this development is referred to best illustrates the two approaches. Those in favour use terms such as 'creative' or 'sharing' economy; critics speak of the 'gig' economy or even the '1099' economy, spewing out a new 'Precariat'. For a contribution on labour-related social security I will use the term 'labour on demand', to emphasise that the issue here is not so much the enterprise that brings worker and consumer together, but the legal status of the individual carrying out the labour, such as the Uber driver and the Deliveroo bike courier. In order to gain better insight of the consequences of these developments for the social security protection of such workers, I will take 'the SSE case study' as an example, as this has been – more or less – crystallised in the Netherlands.

The chapter is structured as follows. In section 2, I will briefly discuss the concepts of 'employment' and 'self-employment' within the context of the Dutch legal system. Having done that, I will provide some facts and figures on the developments of the Dutch labour market, paying special attention to SSE. Section 3 will be devoted to the social security system, its structure and composition, and its development from an income protection system, for the most part, into an activating labour market policy tool. Section 4 will discuss the relevant developments with respect to SSE in tax law. The findings from sections 3 and 4 will come

---

[2] I use the abbreviation SSE for both the phenomenon (solo self-employment) and the worker (solo self-employed).

[3] Evans and Gawer (2016), p. 7, with reference to Rochet and Tirole (2003).

[4] Evans and Gawer (2016), pp. 7, 9.

[5] Kenney and Zysman (2016). For countries such as the Netherlands, where a major part of social security is connected with labour law, disruptive for labour law is equivalent to disruptive for social security law.

together in the final section where the actual questions as regards SSE and (among others) social security are discussed.

2. SSE WITHIN THE DUTCH CONTEXT

2.1 The Dutch Legal Framework and SSE: Introduction

Dutch labour law, at the outset, is binary. A worker is an employee – and consequently a target group of the employee insurances – or an SSE – and consequently not part of the individuals covered by this type of insurance. At the same time, the distinction is not fully black and white. Various schemes count non-employees among their personal scope and some employees are not insured under the employee benefit insurance schemes. I will discuss this topic in further detail hereafter. The concept of employee is legally defined in the Dutch Civil Code. The Netherlands is not an exception on this point, as many other EU countries have statutory definitions of an employee.[6] The central elements of this term are reasonably universal, that is, remuneration so that, for example, volunteer work falls outside the definition of employee; authority to give instructions on the part of the party providing the work; and having to personally carry out the labour, so that labour which may also be outsourced to someone else falls outside the scope of the definition of employee. Over the years, a wealth of jurisprudence has arisen regarding each of these elements. Such legal proceedings are generally implemented within the context of employment law and relate to subjects such as the right to a minimum wage or to continued payment of salary in the event of illness. Within social security, legal proceedings arise at the time that a 'fired' SSE claims that he was 'actually' an employee and thus, due to the unemployment, is entitled to unemployment benefit. The issue is also relevant within the context of tax law, but other interests play a role in that area of law. I will discuss this topic in further detail too.

2.2 The Flexible Labour Market and SSE: Facts and Figures

In the EU, the Netherlands is the front-runner in flexible labour: 20 per cent of its workforce is working under a flexible contract; another 16 per

[6] Sweden is an exception to this rule (see Chapter 10, section 2 of this volume) as well as France, Germany, Italy, Spain, Austria, Denmark, Belgium, Luxembourg, Bulgaria, the Czech Republic, Slovenia, and Cyprus (IAW, 2017). For more on this research group and its report see section 4 *infra*.

cent is SSE.[7] Both forms of work demonstrate a flexible labour market, yet they are not one and the same. Workers under a flexible contract at least have an employment contract, albeit a flexible one. Such a flexible contract may be a fixed-term contract, a zero hour contract, or a temporary employment contract.[8] Part-time labour, another form of work with the Netherlands topping the EU list, is not necessarily flexible. In the Netherlands, part-time labour often is a form of work with fixed working hours, and is usually a voluntary choice. In such a situation, the labour is not necessarily precarious either.

In the flexible workers category, SSE deserve specific mention as they, unlike workers under an employment contract, work at their own expense and risk, or are assumed to do so. After all, SSE may be true entrepreneurs, in which case they could actually make a profit. Or they may be dependent on one client, in which case they have the worst of two worlds: no chance of making a profit and a real risk of suffering a loss, and they are not protected under labour law.[9]

Over the last decade, the share of SSE in the Dutch labour market has steadily increased, in a manner that is, measured against European standards, exceptional.[10] But before jumping to conclusions, the SSE as an individual must be considered. Who is he/she, what type of labour does he/she perform and is this labour his/her main source of income? To start with the latter: in 2014, the Wetenschappelijke Raad voor het Regeringsbeleid (WRR; Scientific Council for Government Policy) classified 508,000 of the entire population of 1,349,000 SSE at the time into 'mainly SSE' and the rest into 'with an additional source of income'. This may be from employment, a partner earning an income or a retirement benefit of their own. A second relevant factor is whether opting for SSE is structural or rather a stage in an otherwise diverse career. For many SSE, the latter seems to be the case. The year 2013 saw approximately 207,000 SSE start-ups against 130,000 business discontinuations.[11] The work performed by SSE is very diverse, too. SSE work in Information and Communication Technology (ICT), health care, the cultural sector and construction. Hence, there are major differences in income, capital and the extent to which workers protect themselves

---

7 WRR (2017), p. 17.

8 WRR (2017), p. 20.

9 Deakin (2002); D'Amours and Crespo (2004).

10 Conen et al. (2016). In the period 1989–2014 Slovenia was the only other EU member state that experienced a similar increase of SSE labour (Grosheide and Barenberg, 2016, p. 208).

11 WRR (2017), pp. 23, 24, with reference to CBS (2016).

against social risks. Becoming SSE or employers having work performed by SSE is also driven by different motivations, one of which is, in the words of the Interdepartmental Policy Research (IBO), 'typically Dutch'. That motivation is institutional and connected to the legal system of social security and taxes.[12] The next two subsections will deal with these two areas of the law.

3. SOCIAL SECURITY LAW

3.1 A System of Three Compartments

Social security arrangements fall into three compartments. There is a 'Bismarckian' part for employees, a 'Beveridgean' compartment for residents and means-tested arrangements for (lawful) residents. This system originated at the start of the last century when the first employee insurance schemes emerged.[13] These were derived from the model that the German statesman Bismarck had introduced in his own country some years earlier. In that same period a provision was made to help self-employed with regard to the 'old-and-poor risk'. Self-employed, who were in an economically comparable position to that of employees, were given the possibility of purchasing a relatively cheap old age provision.[14] The provision was so cheap because the government paid a part of it. This made the scheme the first legal acknowledgement of the 'employee-like worker', or in German the *Arbeitnehmerähnlich*. Shortly afterwards, this employee-like worker also joined the employee insurance schemes. Case law from the Dutch High Court in Social Insurance (CRvB) made it clear that limiting employee-related benefits to those persons with an employment contract led to less fair outcomes.[15] This unfairness was removed with the introduction of the concept of 'deemed employment'. The facility was intended for the 'non-employee', who provided services on a regular basis for a person or company. That person or that company – not being his employer – was then required to pay social security premiums in order to insure this worker against the employee risks acknowledged at that time.

---

[12] IBO (Interdepartmental Policy Research) (2015), p. xi. Likewise WRR (2017).

[13] *Ongevallenwet* (Industrial Accidents Act) 1901, *Ziektewet* (Sickness Benefits Act) and *Invaliditeitswet* (Invalidity Act), both of 1913.

[14] *Ouderdomswet* (Old Age Act) 1919.

[15] Koopmans (1962), p. 39.

After the Second World War, the Beveridgean schemes were established. The late 1950s saw the introduction of (inter alia) the Old Age Pension Act (AOW) 1956,[16] which guarantees a flat-rate pension to all residents of 65 years and older who have lived in the Netherlands during their entire working lives. The pensions are financed by means of pay as you go (PAYG), to which all residents between the ages of 15 and 65 contribute according to their ability. Residents without any means of income are exempt from the obligation to pay the premium, but do build up a pension.

This statute put an end to a – long and sometimes stormy – discussion about compulsory insurance for employees or a free state pension. The outcome of that discussion was partly, but certainly not solely, determined by the fact that most self-employed persons had not purchased a subsidised pension. This might have been the case because, in the past, the government had already intervened, so that many assumed that this would happen again in their situation.[17]

In this period (1945–1970) the first post-war employee insurance schemes were established, such as the Unemployment Benefit Act and the Incapacity Benefits Insurance Act.[18] These are products of what later became known as the 'polder model'. This qualification ('polder model') stands for tripartite cooperation between employers' organisations, labour unions and the government. Van der Heijden points out that the International Labour Organization (ILO), too, had a tripartite organisational structure, long before the Dutch 'model' caused worldwide furore.[19] The European Commission (EC) points out, however, that this dialogue is gradually losing impact, due to the increasing flexibility of work and the trade unions' declining level of organisation. This is particularly visible in current debates on unemployment benefit duration and a number of recent strike announcements.[20] In addition, social security health insurance was established for employees below a certain salary threshold and residence insurance for long-term care costs.[21]

The third compartment contains means-tested benefits, the most important of which is the Social Assistance Act (now Participation Act)

16 *Algemene Ouderdomswet* (Old Age Pension Act) 1956.

17 Bossenbroek and Van den Berg (1952), p. 102.

18 *Werkloosheidswet* (Unemployment Benefit Act) 1949, *Wet op de Arbeidsongeschiktheidsverzekering* (Incapacity Benefits Insurance Act) 1967.

19 Van der Heijden (2018).

20 Dekker (2017).

21 *Ziekenfondswet* (Health Cost Act) 1964. *Algemene Wet Bijzondere Ziektekosten* (Residence Insurance Act on long-term Health Costs) 1965.

of 1963, which changed social assistance from a favour into a right.[22] Needy self-employed cannot claim this form of income support, with the odd exception, for example self-employed who wish to discontinue a loss-making business, or starters who are in need of assistance for an initial bridging period.

3.2 Privatisation and Activating Labour Market Policies (ALMPs)

Halfway through the 1990s many employees' insurances were reformed in accordance with the basic principles of the ALMP. The Sickness Act was 'privatised', which meant that income protection for sick employees was shifted from the social security system to the individual employer.[23] The act still exists as safety net for insured employees without an employer who can be held responsible, such as employees who have been hired on a flexible basis, for instance for temp work agencies, and the aforementioned worker who derives coverage from deemed employment.

In addition, activating elements were established in the system for levying premiums. The premium for long-term incapacity insurance is related to the degree of 'inflow' of (former) employees into this scheme: the more employees who claim disability benefit, the higher the premium of the (former) employer is and vice versa. This mechanism not only arises in relation to employees with whom the employer still has a contractual relationship, but also in relation to former employees who have fallen ill during a period of fixed-term employment.[24] The latter point in particular is unpopular among employers, because they feel they are being 'punished' for something that is beyond their control. After all, it is difficult to find alternative work for an employee who is no longer in their employ. At the same time, elements such as this contribute to a significant degree to the popularity of SSE, with regard to which such responsibilities do not exist.

---

[22] *Algemene Bijstandswet* (Social Assistance Act) 1963. It was State Secretary Klompé, defending the statute in Parliament at the time, who said that social assistance should not be a favour but a right.

[23] *Wet Uitbreiding Loonplicht bij Ziekte* (Extension of Obligation to Pay Salary (Sickness) Act) 1996, Bulletin of Acts and Decrees, 1996, 134. See for more Knegt and Westerveld (2008).

[24] An employee with an open-ended employment contract may not be dismissed in the first 104 weeks of illness. In that period, there are obligations of endeavour on the part of the employer and the employee geared to reintegration of the employee into his own or other suitable work.

Employers who think they can achieve a better result in finding alternative work for their (former) employees than the public administrator – and who have sufficient financial reserves to be able to bear the benefits costs – can opt for self-insurance. This qualification means that the employer leaves the public system and takes on responsibility himself for payment of disability benefits to his former employees. The evaluation as to whether the employee is entitled to the benefit remains a matter for the public administrator. This benefits risk is limited to the first ten years of incapacity for work and does not relate to employees who are fully and permanently incapacitated. For those two risks the employer continues to owe a (reduced) premium to the public General Invalidity Insurance Fund.

Also under the banner of 'privatisation' was the reform of the health insurance scheme (in 2006). The social security health insurance for employees up to a specific wage level made way for a residency-based insurance, which obliges all residents to take out health insurance.[25] Instead of a public insurer and a standard policy for everyone, a system has been established in which people can choose their own insurer and their own insurance package. Health insurers are obliged to admit every applicant on the same conditions, without making a distinction on the basis of individual risk factors. Insurers who have admitted an above-average number of 'bad risks' receive compensation from the Treasury.

3.3 Finance and Solidarity

This – necessarily succinct – description shows two things. Social security law is always law in flux, but the three-compartment approach can still be used to understand the system as a whole. Table 11.1 illustrates this.

Table 11.1 includes health care costs, both cure (GP, medicines, temporary hospital admission) and care (nursing home and other institutional health care), and a (basic) old age pension. For employees, this pension scheme serves as a 'floor' for the collective employee pension which social partners agree on (second-pillar pensions). The self-employed who wish to supplement their old age pension can make use of fiscal provisions for third-pillar products, such as insurance and annuities. That observation has also established a first link between social security and taxes.

---

25 *Zorgverzekeringswet* (Social Insurance Care Act) 2006. The system also has a social insurance scheme for long-term care; this will not be considered here.

Table 11.1 Social security by type of insurance

Type	Resident Insurance	Employment Benefit Insurance	Social Assistance Schemes
Who	Lawful residents	Employees and employee-like workers	Lawful residents
What	Flat-rate benefits or (partial) cost compensation	Income-related benefits (cap added)	Social assistance and provisions for the needy
Risk	Old age pensions Survivor's pensions Health costs	Illness (employees with liable employer excluded) Incapacity for work Unemployment	Minimum income Compensation for home help
Finance	Income-related contributions (cap added) Treasury	Income-related contributions (cap added). Possibility to opt out	Treasury

A second connection between the two relates to financing, in particular with regard to social insurance schemes. The premiums for employee insurance schemes are related to the average over the last year's salary, albeit that the insurance stops at a specific salary level (hence the words 'cap added'). No premium is charged over a certain salary level and there is thus no insurance. The system does generate certain risk solidarity. The premium for, for example, unemployment insurance is the same for all employees, regardless of the individual risk of becoming and remaining unemployed.

With regard to social residence insurance, the term 'cap added' has a different meaning. Under these schemes the benefits are flat rate and an income-related premium is charged. This system thus generates certain income solidarity, but this is, again, limited: no premium is charged above a certain income level. In addition, under these schemes income solidarity arises by way of taxation: both the old age pensions and the care and cure insurances are co-financed by the Treasury and income tax is income-related to a certain degree as well. At present, the contribution is approximately 15 per cent of the total expenditure, albeit that there are plans to gradually phase out the contribution.

4. SSE AND TAX LAW

4.1 The Taxation of Labour

The connection between social security and tax law will recur time and again in policy discussions regarding SSE. SSE after all do benefit from a relatively favourable tax regime, which means they pay far less tax on the profit they make than employees do on the salary paid to them. The effect at individual level is considerable: almost four out of ten SSEs pay no income tax or social insurance premiums at all. The system also has an effect on the premium charged for social insurance. SSEs with a taxable income up to €23,000 do not pay any old age pension premium, even though they do build up entitlement to an old age pension as a resident.[26]

At the time, the tax facilities for small SSEs were introduced for the following reasons: providing income support to small self-employment businesses, aligning the fiscal determination for profit to the specific characteristics of the entrepreneurial income and providing tax relief for the small and medium-sized enterprises (SME) sector, which would ultimately result in extra jobs. In practice the latter never materialised. Successful SSEs are more inclined to form partnerships with other SSEs than hire personnel.

The phenomenon was noted as a problem for the first time in 2012 by an advisory committee, which was supposed to flesh out scenarios for a more effective tax system.[27] This committee (hereafter: 'Van Dijkhuizen', after the chairman) established that the tax burden for entrepreneurs is substantially lower than for employees, across the board and particularly in the event of low profits. This is related to provisions such as the self-employed person's deduction and a tax exemption for the self-employed of the first 14 per cent of the annual profit. It is acknowledged in the report that entrepreneurs are a specific group within the working population. They work at their own expense and risk and are not insured under the employee insurance schemes.[28] Nevertheless, Van Dijkhuizen

---

26 Van Rooijen (representative for Party 50+), quoting tax expert Prof. L. Stevens, parliamentary debate House of Commons, 2016–17, 34036, nr 67, p. 3.

27 Commissie Inkomstenbelasting en toeslagen (2013) (now Van Dijkhuizen 2013).

28 The reference to the 'functions' of the self-employed person's deduction, in particular those mentioned under b): 'the compensation for the equity invested in the business, *including a risk premium for the entrepreneurial risk to be borne*', demonstrates that this element played a role in the considerations (Van Dijkhuizen 2013, pp. 86 83; emphasis mine).

believes, with reference to the Council of State, the Tax System Study Committee and the Netherlands Bureau for Economic Policy Analysis (Centraal Planbureau; CPB[29]), that the differential treatment is not justified (any longer) and that the self-employed person's deduction should disappear, albeit in time and in stages. The deduction has, in the words of this Committee, become a 'non-specific deduction for entrepreneurs, the amount of which is no longer justified in the current circumstances'.[30]

The Van Dijkhuizen report appeared at the time the second Rutte government came to power, a coalition of social democrats and liberals, which, because of its minority position in the Dutch Senate, was forced to enter into occasion-based coalitions for all controversial measures. That aspect and the fact that SSE field organisations had grown into an effective lobby group[31] ensured that the recommendation was never implemented. The self-employed person's deduction still exists, as does the difference between employees and self-employed in tax and premium burden.

In 2015 IBO made similar observations about the deduction. This working group was established by the Rutte II administration to make a detailed analysis, an inventory and policy options available for a public discussion on the income and financial position of SSE, their position on the labour market, the advantages and disadvantages of their fiscal treatment, the relationships to other groups and their connection to the social security system. In its report the IBO group made a distinction between more and less 'powerful' SSE. The first has a good negotiating position, and can 'price in', in his rate, the risks, provisions and benefits from several fiscal advantages (see subsection 4.2 below). A worker who does not have negotiating power, passes on the cost advantage[32] to the client, and in a situation where the negotiating position is more balanced, both parties could be better off with a client/SSE relationship.[33] The IBO group also visualised the budgetary consequences in the mid–long term in the event of what is called 'unaltered policy' (Figure 11.1).

---

[29] The CPB had pointed out in its 2012 policy brief that for some employees the choice to become self-employed is not so much based on the wish to become an entrepreneur but rather to avoid taxes (Centraal Planbureau 2012, p. 12).

[30] Van Dijkhuizen (2013), p. 85, table 4.5.4 and p. 89.

[31] Over time four organisations took on the role of SSE spokesperson: the SSE/FNV branch, the Platform for Self-employed Entrepreneurs, SSE-the Netherlands, an independent platform for and by SSE, and SSE Construction. Two of them (SSE/FNV and the Platform for SEE) have acquired a seat in the Socio-Economic Council (SER).

[32] The IBO group calculated that at the minimum wage level, an employee is up to 40 per cent more expensive than a self-employed person (IBO 2015, p. x).

[33] Ibid.

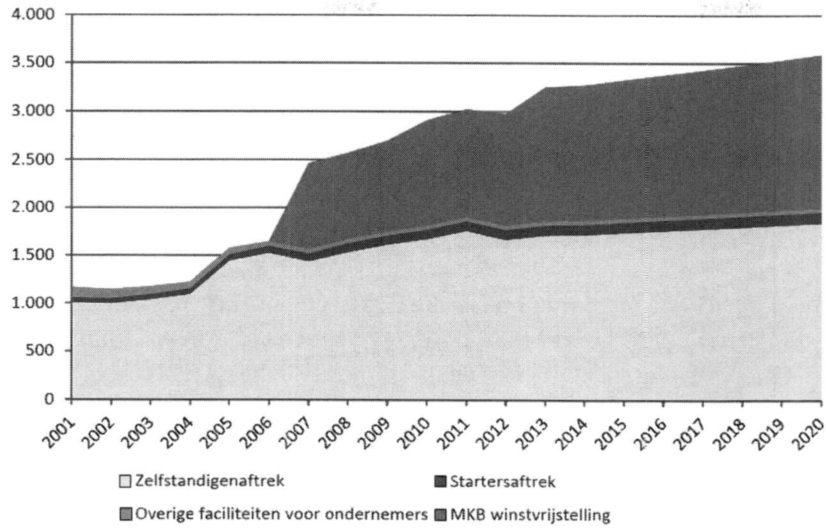

Notes:
Lower part: tax deduction for self-employed workers.
Upper part: profit exemption for small and medium-sized enterprises (SME).
Middle line, bottom: tax deduction for start-ups.
Middle line, top: other tax facilities for entrepreneurs.

Figure 11.1 Mid–long-term budgetary consequences

4.2 Conditions for SSE Tax Deduction

In order to understand the legal architecture at the time of the reports, one must go back to 2001. In that year the 'Declaration of Employment Status' (hereafter: Declaration) was introduced as an instrument for the SSE to show that he was 'entrepreneurial'. A prerequisite for obtaining this document was that the individual was registered as self-employed with the Chamber of Commerce and that he served at least three clients per year. With this Declaration the declaration holder was eligible for the above-mentioned tax facilities and he could show potential clients that they were doing business with a true entrepreneur and not with an employee in disguise. In the Dutch legal idiom such 'employee in disguise' is also referred to as 'false self-employed'.[34]

[34] In this idiom a 'false self-employed' is actually an employee. This is different in EU law, where the European Court of Justice (ECJ) introduced the term for self-employed workers who are 'dependent' on their clients and who

The Declaration did not, however, provide 100 per cent certainty. If an inspection brought to light that the SSE had only worked for one or two clients, the document would be revoked. When that happened, the SSE had to repay the tax deduction and the client could still receive a tax assessment for wage tax and employee insurance premiums. Both the assessment for the client and the demand for repayment from the SSE could go back several years.

This legal system encountered a lot of opposition. Employers/clients complained about the legal complexity, which entailed that they could not properly estimate their risks. SSE stated that this legal uncertainty discouraged potential clients from doing business with them. In response to the complaints the legal system was amended. Under the Statute 'Expanding the consequences of the declaration of employment status'[35] a client no longer had to fear for additional assessments, except in cases of apparent bad faith. The risk on the part of the SSE remained, however, but this risk would only be theoretical. There were barely any inspections of entrepreneurship and the possession of a declaration turned out to be sufficient to go to work as an entrepreneur with impunity, with all related facilities.

The effect of the expansion was enormous. The number of SSE claiming and receiving the deduction increased explosively and there were a lot of complaints – both from trade unions and from bona fide employers – regarding the use of false self-employed. As that situation was deemed undesirable, too, a proposal was sent to Parliament replacing the Declaration, which recorded the legal position for several years, by introducing a system of more temporary 'model contracts' between clients and SSE.[36] Such a contract can be approved in advance by the Tax and Customs Administration and after approval provides some certainty that there will be no additional assessments. This new scheme carried the name 'Deregulation Act' to illustrate that it was no longer the Tax and

---

may as such be excused from the restrictions of EU competition law. Under EU law a 'false self-employed' may, in other words, still be a self-employed worker, albeit with a precarious social economic position. See also Deakin (2002), footnote 10.

[35] *Wet Uitbreiding rechtsgevolgen verklaring arbeidsrelatie* (Statute expanding the legal consequences of employment relationship declarations), Bulletin of Acts and Decrees, 2004, 720.

[36] *Wet deregulering beoordeling arbeidsrelaties* (Dba Act; Assessment of Employment Relationships (Deregulation) Act), Bulletin of Acts and Decrees, 2016, 45.

Customs Administration that inspected whether a SSE is truly independent, but the parties themselves. At the same time, the guarantee is less hard than under the system of the expanded Declaration. The 'sting' – particularly for the client – lies in the fact that the working method between the parties must be laid down precisely and that, if it turns out afterwards that the work was not carried out in accordance with these rules, an additional assessment can follow, with all consequences mentioned above, including on the part of the client.

As had been the case with the first Statute, this proposal resulted in a lot of protest, both on the part of the SSE 'field parties' and on the part of the clients.[37] The complaints related to the bureaucracy of the new system and to the legal uncertainty on the part of, in particular, clients. The legislator pressed ahead with the law, though, and the bill entered into force as of 1 April 2016. The effect was as predicted. Employers refused to take on the role of 'client' in large numbers, and preferred giving the work to flexible employees rather than to SSE. And although this was the intention to a certain degree – fewer client/contractor relationships could mean fewer false self-employment – the resistance to the scheme increased significantly, not only among field parties and employers, but also among members of parliament, who had at the time agreed to the scheme. The Dutch House of Representatives forced the state secretary to promise a postponement of the enforcement of the scheme, a postponement that exists until this day.

This made the SSE dossier an issue for the Rutte III Cabinet, which was set up in October 2017. This coalition agreement shows a clear ambition to deal with the SSE file once and for all. In accordance with the intentions of the agreement, in future there will be three types of SSE workers. At the lowest level one finds SSEs who work at a low rate and carry out 'regular business activities', or who work for a period of three months or longer at a low rate. Such workers are granted the status of deemed employment. The top level will have an 'opt out' clause relating to salary tax and employee insurance premiums. This group is identified by the fact that they can and do agree a high rate for activities of a fairly short duration, or for activities which are not part of the regular business model of the company. For the middle group a 'principal's statement' will be introduced, along the lines of the one which exists in the UK. Contrary to the former scheme it is not the SSE worker but the principal that must apply for this statement by means of completing a web

[37] For more detail on these 'parties', see Westerveld (2012).

module.[38] The SSE tax deduction will be reduced in four yearly stages, starting in 2020. Remarkable with regard to the subject of social security is the intention of the cabinet to review in what way the uptake by SSEs of incapacity insurance can be increased. Toward this end the secretary of state intends to enter into a discussion with insurers in order to promote a better insurance offer for SSEs.

These plans, which were presented in the fall of 2017 and discussed with the most important field parties, did not meet with much enthusiasm. The state secretary of finance has expressed his willingness to discuss with social parties as well as SSE field parties a more sustainable system that meets the needs of precarious as well as entrepreneurial SSE workers. Given the average length of time of such reforms it looks like the target group must deal with the controversial 'Deregulation' statute for many years to come.

5. SOCIAL SECURITY FOR WORKERS OUTSIDE THE REALM OF THE EMPLOYMENT CONTRACT: LESSONS LEARNED?

The SSE work and social security case study shows a number of striking outcomes. First of all, this case study shows that the task of organising social security is not only dependent on sufficient financial resources and a reliable implementation apparatus. Just as important is the willingness of all parties concerned, the workers, their principals and ultimately the voters on whose favour governments depend. In the post-war period, the willingness to share risks was great, but over time it has decreased due to circumstances such as individualisation and what the law sociologist Schuyt calls the 'discourse of rights' ('if others can claim a right, why can't I?').[39] Another influential factor is the institutional framework itself. For example, the privatisation of health care has sent the message that taking out insurance against a risk that will probably never affect you personally is not only unnecessary but outright foolish as it comes down to 'throwing money out the window'. In addition, the privatisation of the sickness benefit scheme and the incentive in the social insurance premium system to avoid long-term disability has led to a deterioration of

---

[38] Rutte III Coalition Agreement, p. 26. The 'return' to the web module is striking. This version had been proposed at an earlier stage and was shot down by the SSE field parties as being unnecessarily bureaucratic and too cumbersome.

[39] Schuyt (2013).

the position in the labour market of work seekers with health problems. The SSE case study shows a comparable development. Workers in a strong socio-economic position have been tempted, partly on the basis of financial stimuli, to leave the public system and bear their own risks. The employers followed suit by exchanging fixed (and thus expensive) personnel on a large scale for SSEs, thus reducing their own responsibility for workers' risks.

Secondly, the SSE case study has caused a shift in the tried-and-trusted Dutch polder model. A third party has arisen in addition to, or perhaps in-between, the traditional employers and employees and this party has proven to be able to lobby effectively and forcefully as well. Because of the diversity of the SSE target group it is not always clear who these lobby groups represent and the support which they express for certain intentions is not always reliable either, but it is unmistakable that they can and do influence decision making relating to fiscal policy and social security.

This brings me to the relationship between social security and taxation. Fiscal stimuli, initially conceived to stimulate entrepreneurship and thus the growth of employment – an SSE will naturally turn into an SME, with one or more employees – have turned into an exemption from, inter alia, the social security premiums, without the expectation of growing into financially strong businesses having been realised. These facilities have also provided SSEs with a competitive advantage over workers in salaried employment, and they have thus initiated a competition relating to employment conditions – such as work-related social security. As the exemption particularly manifests itself at the bottom of the SSE market, this maintains a 'market', which does not deserve this qualification: without the exemption many of these self-proclaimed entrepreneurs would quickly go bankrupt.

The government is well aware of these effects, but if there is anything this case study has taught too, it is that it is much easier to hand out fiscal advantages than to reverse them at a later stage when the hoped for effect remains absent. This lesson should be heard loud and clear when the next challenge for labour law and social security presents itself – as it already has – that of labour on demand. The growth of this work type confronts governments, both in the Netherlands and elsewhere, with difficult questions relating to, inter alia, the organisation of social security. It is as yet too early in the day for funded predictions, let alone recommendations, but one observation stands out: the resemblance with the challenge for countries where a large proportion of workers is earning a living in the informal sector is striking. This observation underlines the importance of a constructive dialogue between countries with completely different architecture, in both the labour market and the institutional setting, with an eye open for differences as well as commonalities.

BIBLIOGRAPHY

Bossenbroek H. and J. Van den Berg, *Doel, grondslagen en geschiedenis der sociale verzekering in Nederland* (*Goal, foundation and history of the social insurance in the Netherlands*), zesde druk, 1952.

CBS (Central Bureau of Statistics) *Loopbaan of bijbaan als zzp'er?* (*Career or job on the side as solo self-employed?*) News bulletin, 27 January 2016.

Conaghan J., R.M. Fischl, K. Klare, *Labour law in an era of globalization*, Oxford University Press, 2002.

Conen W., J. Schippers and K. Schulze Buschoff, *Self-employed without personnel: between freedom and insecurity.* WSI Institute of Economic and Social Research, 2016, no 5.

D'Amours M. and S. Crespo, The dimensions of heterogeneity among own-account self-employed: elements for a typology, *Industrial Relations* 59, 3 (2004).

Deakin S., The many futures of the contract of employment. In: J. Conaghan R.M. Fischl and K. Klare, (eds) *Labour law in an era of globalization* Oxford University Press, 2002, pp. 177–197.

Dekker F., Challenges for the Dutch polder model, European Social Policy Network (ESPN) Flash Report 2017/40.

Evans P.C. and A. Gawer, *The rise of the platform enterprise. A global survey.* Centre for Global Enterprise, The Emerging Platform Economy Series No 1. http://thecge.net/wp-content/uploads/2016/01/PDF-WEB-Platform-Survey_01_12.pdf

Grosheide E. and M. Barenberg, Minimum fees for the self-employed: a European response to the 'Uber-ized' economy? *Columbia Journal of European Law* 22 (2016), 193–236.

Hatfield T., *Self-employment in Europe*, IPPR 2015.

Heijden, P. van der, The ILO Stumbling towards its Centenary Anniversary' *International Organizations Law Review* 15 (2018), 203–220.

Kenney M. and J. Zysman, The rise of the platform economy, *Issues in Science and Technology* 32, 3 (2016), 61–69.

Knegt R. (ed.) *The employment contract as an exclusionary device: an analysis on the basis of 25 years of developments in the Netherlands*, Social Europe Series, vol. 16, Intersentia, 2008.

Knegt R. and M. Westerveld, Sickness and disability: going Dutch as a cure for a 'Dutch disease', in: R. Knegt (ed.) The employment contract as an exclusionary device, an analysis on the basis of 25 years of developments in the Netherlands, Social Europe Series, vol. 16, Intersentia, 2008.

Koopmans, T. *De begrippen werkman, arbeider en werknemer* (*The concepts 'labourer', 'worker' and 'employee'*), Samson, 1962.

Rochet J.C. and J. Tirole, Platform Competition in Two-Sided Markets *Journal of the European Economic Association* 1, 4 (2003), 990–1029.

Schuyt K., *Noden en wensen. De verzorgingsstaat gezien als een historisch fenomeen.* Oratie bij de aanvaarding van de Van Doorn wisselleerstoel in Erasmus School of Social and Behavioural Sciences. Erasmus Universiteit Rotterdam, d.d. 24 juni 2013. *(Needs and Desires. The welfare state as a historical phenomenon.* Inaugural speech, Erasmus University Rotterdam, 24 June 2013).

Westerveld M. The 'new' self-employed, an issue for social policy? *European Journal of Social Security* 3 (2012) 3 156–174.

Policy Papers

Boot G., Commissie (Model)overeenkomsten, eindrapport (*Committee (Model)-contracts, Final Report*), November 2016.

Centraal Planbureau, *De fiscale behandeling van zelfstandigen, een kritische blik,* (*The fiscal treatment of self-employed: a critical review*) CPB Policy Brief 2012/02.

Commissie Inkomstenbelasting en toeslagen, *Naar een activerender belastingstelsel* (Committee of Income Tax and Allowances, *Toward a more activating tax system*) Tussenrapport (Interim Report), 2013.

EIM (P. Vroonhof, W. Verhoeven en M. Folkeringa), *Ondernemen makkelijker en leuker? Evaluatie zelfstandigenaftrek en enkele andere fiscale instrumenten gericht op het ondernemerschap* (*Being an entrepreneur, easier and more enjoyable? An evaluation of fiscal instruments directed at self-employment*), 2015,

IAW (Interdepartmental Civil Service Report) Onderzoek varianten kwalificatie arbeidsrelatie (Research Possible Qualifications of Labour Relations), 2017.

IBO (Interdepartmental Policy Research) *Zelfstandigen Zonder Personeel*, eindrapport (*Self-employed without employees*, Final Report), October 2015.

WRR (M. Kremer, R. Went en André Knottnerus, eds) *Voor de zekerheid. De toekomst van flexibele werkenden en de modern organisatie van arbeid* (*To be certain. The future of flexible workers and the modern organisation of labour*), 2017.

12. From a social protection regime to an income security agenda: Canada at the crossroads

Lucie Lamarche

In Canada, the debate about a guaranteed income is being revisited. In the wake of experiments such as the Finnish one, some provinces are piloting basic income projects aimed at lifting some households above the poverty line. This chapter suggests that such projects are in fact nothing more than the culmination of a deep transformation of the Canadian social protection regime. Nowadays, frontiers are blurred between workers and non-workers as well as between contributory and non-contributory schemes aimed at addressing different social risks. More and more, answers are to be found in social tax expenditures which correct the income of poor families without addressing the new reality of labour. The dissociation of the fight against poverty and of the one to provide decent work make labour law almost irrelevant for the poorest workers.

This chapter is divided in four sections built along the history of social security and social protection in Canada. A first section offers a constitutional overview of the Canadian federation and shows how social expenditures depend on both federal and provincial decisions. A second section rapidly explains how social security has been historically designed in Canada. As a Commonwealth country, Canada offers an interesting mix of universal and contributory social protection schemes. What was the strength of the system is about to become its problem as many programs are not strictly attached to work. The first two sections are useful in order to better understand the growing reliance in Canada on negative income tax devices in order to supplement poor wages. It all started in the 1970s with the first fight against poverty strategy. Nowadays, it is estimated that about 80 percent of non-contributory social benefits transit through non-refundable income tax credits. Often, those credits are made available after applying a clawback to benefits paid under contributory schemes and considered as income. And the combination 'poor households made of workers and non-workers' and 'low income' is the dominant one. This is what the third section of the chapter tends to illustrate. Finally, the last section addresses recent initiatives piloting basic income experiments in the form of negative income taxes and income supplement. Those raise the question of knowing what benefits can be amalgamated in a basic income and what will remain to be categorised as social security. At this point, we do not have answers. But we suggest that Canada is experiencing a vibrant moment of neoliberalism that will not leave untouched both labour law and social law.

A BRIEF OVERVIEW OF THE CANADIAN CONSTITUTIONAL CONTEXT

The Canadian federation celebrated its 150th anniversary in 2017. The first Canadian Constitutional Act was adopted in 1867.[1] It contains two articles aimed at establishing federal and provincial fields of jurisdiction, which remained markworthy unaltered until today. Article 92(13) of the Constitution provides for full provincial jurisdiction in the field of property and civil rights. It has been confirmed by the courts in numerous occasions that such enunciation includes social and labour law.[2]

Canada is a vast territory and from the start its economy has been rural in as much as it relied on natural resources. Until the end of the Second World War, social protection remained a desert of initiatives.[3] Two notable exceptions are to be mentioned. Firstly, Ontario and Quebec adopted respectively in 1914 and in 1909 an Act Respecting Industrial Accidents which provided for workers income replacement. This important regime was then and is still now totally funded by employers.[4] Secondly, the federal government, using its spending power, introduced in 1927 a basic pension scheme aimed at reimbursing provinces who implemented such scheme 75 percent of the costs.[5] This first pension

---

1 Constitution Act 1867, 30 & 31 Victoria c. 3 (U.K.).

2 *Attorney-General for Canada v Attorney-General for Ontario* [1939] A.C. 355.

3 For a detailed analysis of the history of social security in Canada, see Guest (1985) and Bureau et al. (1985) 79–147.

4 For a detailed analysis of the laws in relation to workers' compensation in Canada, see Lippel and Lefebvre (2005) and Lippel (1986).

5 Pension Act S.C. 1919 c. 43 as amended by S.C. 1937 c. 13.

plan was not universal and supported only the poor elderly male of 70 years and over. It was means tested and survived until 1951. In addition, only in 1940 did a constitutional amendment allow for the creation of a national and contributory unemployment benefits scheme.[6] Canadian provinces were simply not populated or rich enough to introduce their own.

During the first half of the 20th century, the Canadian debate about social security and social protection looked more like a constitutional than a social one. In 1942, the total population of Canada was estimated at 11 million and in 1939, only 5.6 percent of the General Domestic Product (GDP) was allocated to social spending. In the context of growing industrialisation and urbanisation as well as of a war economy, data showed that Canadian workers were poor and vulnerable. Fifty percent of them lived below the poverty line, described as a level of income under which basic needs cannot be properly addressed.

Nowadays, Canada can be described as an integrated market, internally as well as internationally. All Canadian provinces and territories recently renewed their commitment to an internal opened market by ratifying in 2017 the Canadian Free Trade Agreement (CFTA), which guarantees, among other topics, labour mobility (Chapter 7).[7] As far as labour laws are concerned, which in most cases fall under provincial jurisdiction,[8] the commercial residence of the employer determines which basket of labour laws are applicable: labour standards and determination of the minimum hourly wages; health and safety; workers' compensation for professional accidents; complementary pension regimes.

Finally, another characteristic of Canada as a sovereign state needs to be underlined. Although an active member of the International Labour Organization (ILO), Canada ratified only 21 conventions.[9] The classical

---

6 Constitutional Act, 1940, 3-4 George VI, c. 36 (U.K.)

7 The Canadian Free Trade Agreement (CFTA) entered in force in 2017 and was preceded by the Agreement on Internal Trade and its Protocols of Amendments. See https://www.ic.gc.ca/eic/site/ait-aci.nsf/vwapj/AIT_agreement_2007-05_en.pdf/$FILE/AIT_agreement_2007-05_en.pdf, accessed 6 August 2018 and https://www.cfta-alec.ca/wp-content/uploads/2017/06/CFTA-Consolidated-Text-Final-Print-Text-English.pdf, accessed 6 August 2018.

8 Federal jurisdiction in labour law applies to interprovincial matters such as railways, highway transport, pipelines, ferries, tunnels, bridges, canals, telephone and cable systems, intra-provincial and international trucking, air transport, radio and television broadcasting, banks and federal Crown corporations or agencies of the Crown.

9 See for detail of ratifications: http://www.ilo.org/dyn/normlex/en/f?p=1000:11200:0::NO:11200:P11200_COUNTRY_ID:102582, accessed 6 August

explanation for this low level of ratification is that a federation struggles to align with international labour standards all provincial and territorial legislations. In sum, Canada is a country that shows a low level of accountability towards international or regional human rights and social and labour law institutions. In fact, Canada actually tends to attach its labour and social policies to trade agreements much more than to human rights or labour standards treaties.[10]

EXITING THE SECOND WORLD WAR: TIME TO THINK ABOUT SOCIAL PROTECTION AND SOCIAL SECURITY

Foreseeing the end of a booming war economy, Premier Mackenzie King commissioned in 1943 the Marsh Report on social security.[11] Dr. Marsh's proposal was about building a social security regime (so far non-existent) on two guiding principles: (1) a decent level of wages replacement; and (2) a supplement to insufficient family income. Based on the analysis of the Canadian demography and economy as well as on the uneven development of regional economies, Marsh designed the different means to address those two goals: (a) demo grants (described as universal payments based on a single condition, such as the presence of children in family or a condition of age, which are not means tested) and (b) social insurance (where employers and employees, and even in cases, such as unemployment benefits, the State, would contribute to a mutualised fund). The proposal did not include at the time means-tested assistance measures, which clearly were seen as an exclusive provincial matter. Eventually, such assistance measures would be described as the third pillar of the Canadian social protection regime. Needless to say, the central figure of the Marsh model was the male industrial full-time

2018. Canada also ratified ILO Convention no 98 on the right to organise and collective bargaining. It entered in force in June 2018.

[10] For example, the North American Agreement on Labour Cooperation (NAALC), which entered in force in January 1994, see https://www.canada.ca/en/employment-social-development/services/labour-relations/international/agreements/naalc.html#naalc, accessed 6 August 2018.

[11] Government of Canada (1943a) (Marsh Report). Available at *Report on Social Security for Canada*, University of Toronto Press 1975. It is worth mentioning that at the same time a mandate was given to Dr. Heagerty, who was to explore a health insurance scheme for Canada. See Government of Canada, Advisory Committee on Health Insurance (1943).

worker and family breadwinner. Like in other countries, women were sent back home after the war. Clearly, the Marsh commission took its inspiration from the Beveridge Report implemented in the UK.[12]

In 1945, Premier Mackenzie King led an electoral campaign under the slogan *A New Social Order for Canada*, and won the election, although with a small majority. Mackenzie King, followed by Louis Saint-Laurent, adopted two major pieces of legislation: The Family Allowances Act in 1945[13] and the Old Age Security Act in 1951.[14] These two laws were demo grants. Eligibility to demo grants was based on a condition of residence in Canada (20 years in the case of old age security pension). To the contrary, eligibility for unemployment insurance was calculated according to a duration of attachment to the labour market (two years preceding the end of employment, in the original scheme of 1940).[15]

One can easily see from this short historical survey of social security in Canada what the missing piece is: health care. As of 1961, all provinces and territories had implemented a partial system of hospital costs coverage.[16] Canadians almost always refer to the universality of the health coverage program in Canada. By this they mean a public system accessible to all residents. This one system for all, clearly inspired by the British model, expanded to the point of including in all provinces out of hospital services, a coverage that was completed in 1967.[17] The Canadian Health Act was then adopted in 1984.[18] This important and highly symbolic piece of legislation corrected a major flaw in provincial systems which often allowed for fees to be charged either by hospitals or by private practitioners (everywhere in Canada doctors are independent professionals). The Canadian Health Act of 1984 accomplished two major changes: (1) the cost sharing of health expenses between the federal government and provinces and territories: and (2) the introduction of a general prohibition of care for fees.

Nowadays, health care expenses put an immense fiscal pressure on provinces that are constantly struggling with the federal government in order to get more financial support. In some provinces, such as Quebec, it is estimated that the health system has directly or indirectly privatised

---

12 Beveridge (1942).

13 Family Allowances Act S.C. 1944-1945 c. 40.

14 Old Age Security Act S.C. 1951 c. 18.

15 Unemployment Insurance Act S.C. 1940 c. 44.

16 Hospital Insurance and Diagnostic Services Act S.C. 1957 c. 28, aimed at reimbursing provinces for costs in the case of provincial coverage.

17 Medical Care Act S.C. 1966-1967 c. 64.

18 Canada Health Act S.C. 1984 c. 6.

up to 40 percent of the entire basket of services. And more and more, the federal government transfers subsidies to the provinces based on a targeted approach to issues, such as mental health or home care. Only those who can afford private care, a growing and booming market navigating in blurred regulatory waters, can still pretend that universal access to health care and services is guaranteed.

As the labour market relies more and more on temporary migrant workers, a new category of persons invites itself in the health care discussion: the documented temporary migrant workers, who are attached to an identified employer for a predefined period.[19] Although those workers have access to public health care, they are usually quickly sent back home by the employer following a work accident or a diminished capacity to work for other health reasons. These are the documented workers that can hardly exercise their right to health and to work mainly because they are refused the right to stay in Canada.

Like in the case of other Organisation of Economic Co-operation and Development (OECD) countries, Canada benefitted from the economic prosperity of the *Trente Glorieuses.*[20] In this context, both federal and provincial governments contributed in different ways to the consolidation of the social security system in Canada. The federal government created the Canada Pension Plan (CPP), a contributory and compulsory public pension regime for all workers, resident and non-residents as well as employed and self-employed.[21] The province of Quebec opted for the creation of its own pension regime, RRQ (Régie des Rentes du Québec),

---

[19] The number of migrant workers in Canada has increased by 70 percent in the last five years. Canada has been shifting towards a reliance on migrant labour. In 2008, for the first time, the number of temporary foreign workers in Canada exceeded the total number of permanent residents admitted in the same year. By the end of 2012, the gap had grown: there were 338 189 temporary foreign workers in Canada on 1 December 2012, compared to 257 515 new permanent residents (http://ccrweb.ca/en/increase-temporary-foreign-worker-numbers), accessed 6 August 2018. For a detailed analysis of this question see Lamarche (2016).

[20] *Les Trente Glorieuses* refers to the 30 years from 1945 to 1975 following the end of the Second World War in France. The term is derived from *Les Trois Glorieuses*, the three days of revolution on 27–29 July 1830 in France (http://dictionary.sensagent.com/trente%20glorieuses/en-en/, accessed 20 February 2018).

[21] Canada Pension Plan Act R.S.C. 1985 c. C-8. This codification has been altered by numerous amendments since 1985.

compulsory for all workers and contributory as well.[22] CPP and RRQ are often described as the second pillar of Old Age Security, following the universal Old Age Security Pension and Supplement. The third pillar of pensions is made up of private complementary schemes. More or less 40 percent of the labour market is unionised in Canada and this percentage includes the totally unionised public service. Although not exclusively, complementary pension plans serve first the unionised labour market. The debate about complementary pensions schemes is raging in Canada as employers and pension plans, regulated by a statutory framework, are now transiting from a defined benefits (DB) to a defined contributions (DC) regime.[23] The private sector employees are deeply affected by this transformation, especially in an era of precarious and non-continuous employment.[24]

The federal unemployment regime benefitted from a substantial improvement in coverage of insured workers in 1971.[25] It is often said that such improvement made the unemployment regime almost like a demo grant. To put it simply, one needed not more than ten weeks of work to collect almost a year of benefits at the time. This opening of the unemployment regime created for women, largely employed as civil servants and whose wages became insurable, a formidable opportunity to enter in the realm of social security benefits in their own right. In addition, it was decided to use the unemployment regime to create the first maternity benefits programs in Canada as well as a sickness benefit one. For a duration of 15 weeks of benefits, one did not have, if eligible, to demonstrate an active search for employment.

Finally, some provinces like Quebec, which always describes itself more as a social state than the rest of Canada, adopted in the 1970s *sui generis* laws aimed at providing answers to specific and contemporary social risks: no-fault income replacement Automobile Insurance Act at very low contributory costs for all drivers and automobile owners;[26] no-fault Crime Victims Compensation Act (for all residents – based on a workers compensation model – non-contributory);[27] and even legal aid

---

22 Quebec Pension Plan Act S.Q. 1965 c. 24. The initial legislation of 1965 has also been significantly amended since then.

23 For a detailed analysis of contemporary issues related to pensions in Quebec and in Canada, see Université du Québec à Montréal (2016).

24 For statistical information on the issue of contributory pensions in Canada and the risks they are exposed to see Cross (2014).

25 Unemployment Act L.C. 1970-1971-1972 c. 48.

26 Automobile Insurance Act 1977, c. 68.

27 Act respecting assistance for victims of crime 1988, c. 20.

(which is means tested).[28] A comparative inventory of all provincial initiatives of the 1970s would reveal a highly asymmetrical situation in regard to those secondary regimes.

But the real revolution of the 1970s in Canada was the introduction of a universal social assistance program, led by provinces, but cost-shared with the federal government. Under the Canada Assistance Plan (CAP),[29] a province could cost share its social assistance budget only if the program was based solely on a means-tested condition. Although with slightly different rates of allowances, all provinces adopted a social assistance scheme in the 1970s. Again, access to social assistance in a province depends on residence. And one can move from one province to the other and access in the host province social assistance benefits based on a condition of minimal residence. In theory, this includes the case of non-Canadian temporary migrant workers. But as they are attached to a labour contract, the end of such contract means that they have to leave the territory.[30]

It wasn't until the 1970s that what was then seen as a regime of social protection had been completed in Canada. It relied on three pillars: social security (contributory regimes); demo grants or universal programs; and finally, social assistance programs. Interestingly, the sparse literature on the topic usually isolates the health care program from such constellation. The probable reason for this special treatment could be the symbolic value of the universality of the health care system in Canada. It strangely makes it invisible – like in the case of other social tax expenditures – except in time of crisis, like more recently.

The Canadian social protection regime of the 1970s provided some security for precarious workers, although this was not the issue by then as poor and precarious workers were not synonymous. Many full-time workers of the formal sector were living under the national poverty line. Health coverage was not related to work and the same can be said about basic universal pension and family allowances. As for contributory regimes, they showed in Canada as much as elsewhere their genderised, racialised and other limits. If, as in the case of unemployment benefits, working income was replaced, in other cases, social protection benefits, in kind or in cash, were not subsidising low wages as much as they were maintaining the capacity of households to consume market goods. The shift of paradigm started at the end of the 1970s and, later on, the debate

---

28 Act respecting legal aid and the provision of certain other legal services, S.Q. 2010, c. 12 replacing L.R.Q. c. A-14, the initial Act of 1972.

29 Canada Assistance Plan, 1966-67, c. 45.

30 See supra note 19.

about the functions of social protection measures would clearly merge with the one about precarious work.

In conclusion, it can safely be affirmed that social protection in Canada is the result of pragmatic and economic decisions. In a sparsely populated country as large as Canada where the benefits of development were unevenly distributed, a mix of universal and contributory solutions to address social risks made sense. As a result, residency is often the qualifying factor to access some benefits, certainly in the case of the poorest households. But would such political and economic trade-offs survive the Welfare State era?

FROM SOCIAL PROTECTION TO THE WAR AGAINST POVERTY: THE NEOLIBERAL AGENDA … IN THE MAKING

The 1970 Croll Report on Poverty[31] raised the alarm: Canadian households were poorer than expected. Was it not the time to move towards a strategy of income security? It was in this context that the notion of a guaranteed basic income was raised in Canada. The input of social sciences clearly nourished this discussion based on concepts such as the poverty line, the market basket measure (MBM), low income cut offs measure (LICO) and so on. Pages of research have been published, focusing on the dynamic interactional understanding of poverty.

Of course, economists were at the time predicting not only a slowdown of the Canadian economy, but a transformation and a *precarisation* of the attachment to the labour market as well. In addition, workers and non-workers would have to adapt to a more open economy where labour costs play a significant role. Canada was engaging in a structured trade agreement with the USA which would lead in 1987 to the adoption of the first formal and global FTA,[32] followed by the North American Free Trade Agreement (NAFTA) in 1994.[33] The MacDonald Report of 1985[34] clearly was setting the stage for the posturing of a more competitive Canada in the context of global trade.

---

[31] Government of Canada, Report of the Special Senate Committee on Poverty (1970).

[32] Canada United States Free Trade Agreement 1988, c. 65, Annex Part A. http://www.international.gc.ca/trade-commerce/assets/pdfs/agreements-accords/cusfta-e.pdf Accessed 5 November 2017.

[33] North American Free Trade Agreement 32 ILM 289, 605 1993.

[34] Government of Canada, Privy Council (1985) (MacDonald Report).

These concerns were enough to encourage a historic change in outlook regarding social security in Canada. And politicians quite quickly started to associate the notion of basic or guaranteed income with another one that became toxic: labour activation, known in Canada as workfare programs. As in the case of the United States, the expression was firstly used to describe the pressure put on social assistance programs.[35] Poor and vulnerable workers (whatever the reason or the risk) would in terms thereof be divided into categories: the able and the unable to work persons. And many social programs would adjust and allow access to benefit according to this division.

In this context, the Canadian constitutional debate would experience a revival as for each dollar that the federal government clawed back from its contribution to some social protection regimes, such as social assistance, provinces would have to find answers to the needs of those made more vulnerable by such exclusionary categorisation. In Canada, the rule is quite simple: a worker losing a job will, if not eligible to unemployment benefits, often rely on last resort provincial social assistance benefits. And an insured worker – unable or unwilling to find or to accept a job with less pay nevertheless considered reasonable – would as well. Provinces were quick to subscribe to the idea that employment activation measures constituted the new rule of thumb. Insidiously, the purpose of social security benefits, excluding health coverage, was entering a transformation. From a risk by risk approach, social protection moved to a work at any price one. Supporting low wages and keeping the working poor households above the poverty line became the strategy. How did that happen?

Different techniques addressed the challenge of different types of social protection programs and at different times in the 1980s and 1990s. But for sure, they all moved in the same direction, which is relying on negative income tax credits. What followed provides some illustrations of the process.

Universal demo grants were put to an end. The federal government introduced a refundable tax credit for children of low-income families which decreased according to a revenue threshold schedule.[36] And later on, it abolished family allowances, focusing solely on tax credit for low- and middle-income families by submitting such credit to a clawback based on family income. An additional credit was made available for

---

35 Leman (1985); Lamarche and Girard (1998); Myles and Pierson (1995).

36 Income Tax and Children's Special Allowances Act S.C. 1992 c. 48.

families who incurred day care costs.[37] In the 2016 budget, the federal government merged all child credits in a single refundable non-taxable credit called the Canada Child Benefit (CCB).[38] It provides significant financial support: for example, $6 000 per year for an annual income of $30 000. Provinces who were offering family allowances followed the same path. Susceptible to variations on a budget to budget basis, those credits are now hidden in annual tax bills, hereby clearly departing from the predictability of social law benefits.

In the same breath, the federal government introduced at the very beginning of the 1970s a clawback mechanism in the basic universal Old Age Pension system and created a Supplement based on income.[39] The first clawback mechanism provided for a reduction of $1 for each $2 of income. Complementary pensions (private pensions) and CPP were considered as income.[40] Nowadays, Old Age Security can be totally clawed back based on the annual income.

The clawback method has also been applied to insurance schemes, such as the unemployment one.[41] Compulsory contributions to unemployment insurance are capped based on a determined maximum of yearly insurable earnings. In 1993, the Unemployment Insurance Act was amended in order to provide for the partial reimbursement of benefits. Such reimbursement equalled 30 percent of the lesser of total benefits paid in the year or of the amount by which the yearly income exceeded by 1.5 the maximum of yearly insurable earnings for that year.[42] In 1996, the federal government decided to turn the unemployment insurance program into an employment incentive one.[43] The program now requires between 420 and 910 worked hours in the reference period of one year and the income replacement level dropped from 66 percent to 55 percent. Consequently, only 40 percent of those contributing to employment

---

[37] Only Quebec adopted an affordable day care system. In other provinces, day care costs are at market price, except for the city of Toronto, which created a network of day care facilities comparable to the Quebec facilities. Canadian families are struggling to find and to pay day care. It is a huge burden on the family budget.

[38] For a detailed analysis of this new mechanism see Government of Canada (2018).

[39] Act to amend the Old Age Security Act, 1966-1967 c. 65.

[40] Act to amend Old Age Security Act S.C. 1984 c. 27.

[41] For a detailed analysis, see Canadian Centre for Policy Alternatives (2009).

[42] Act to amend the Unemployment Insurance Act 1993 S.C. c. 13.

[43] Employment Insurance Act S.C. 1996, c. 23.

insurance (EI) can now rely on benefits.[44] Repercussions for precarious workers are of course dramatic. Being the ones on whom more stringent eligibility conditions are imposed, they simply can never reach the required amount of worked hours. Clawback measures are still in force and the federal government who used to contribute to the Fund withdrew from it in 1990.[45] Although this is a topic by itself, it has to be said that the Unemployment Insurance Fund was successfully used as a regional stabiliser of the economy between 1950 and 2000. For example, the Fund was used to extend the period of benefits or to diminish the number of worked weeks (and then hours) in order to qualify.

Between 1985 and 2000, many social insurance programs were turned into work incentive programs. For example, an injured worker that partially recovered his working capacity (according to a workers' compensation act) was assigned, based on the residual working capacity, not only a type of employment he should look for but also a percentage of salary replacement rate associated with the assigned or presumed work he could theoretically do.[46]

In sum, a growing attachment to a predefined income threshold where clawback in contributory as well as non-contributory social programs is perceptible in Canada and, step by step, available income of all types is becoming the key operating concept for accessing residual social benefits. As well, poverty is defined in relation to income and not so much to wages as not only wages but all types of income are considered in a personal income tax report.

THE CONTEMPORARY SCENERY: TESTING BASIC INCOME (BI) HERE AND THERE IN CANADA

Canada is nowadays relying more and more on social tax expenditures to address one politically accepted risk – poverty – in replacement of classical and enumerated social risks. In terms thereof, it is more and more accepted that any person that works at any type of work or that receives a revenue from any kind of productive – and declared – activity can be poor. Governments would put it differently and say that the

---

[44] Mouvement autonome et solidaire des sans emploi MASSE, *Saviez-vous que* … , http://www.lemasse.org/index.php/13-saviez-vous-que/5-saviez-vous-que, accessed 6 August 2018; Macdonald (2014).

[45] Act to amend the Unemployment Insurance Act and the Act on the Employment and Immigration of Canada S.C. 1990 c. 40.

[46] Lippel and Lefebvre (2005).

purpose of social protection measures is to keep the working poor above the established poverty line.[47] One has to accept and look for any work and income coming from any source. Implicitly, this paradigm confirms the legitimacy of all forms of work: short-term contracts; independent; platform or gig economy, as examples.[48] The system will react to declared income shown in a personal income tax declaration more than it cares about the decency of the work from which one is receiving his or her wages. It is not that labour standards are vanishing. Complaint mechanisms for workers whose basic rights are violated are still in operation. It is not either that contributory regimes, such as unemployment or contributory pensions, are at risk. They are simply reserved for a growing elite in the workplace, unionised or not. The working poor are more and more living outside the sphere of labour law and relying on tax credits to keep their income above the poverty line. Such tax credits are available only to those who comply with the requirement of annually filling their income tax reports. Would space allow us to do so, we could demonstrate that this exercise is less and less escapable. Big Brother is controlling a growing amount of social data by relying on individual income tax reports.

In this modern vacuum of collective rights and of labour law, vulnerable parties find refuge in the human rights regime. The Canadian Charter offers a robust equality standard that applies to all legislation.[49] In addition, all provincial and territorial laws adopted a human rights

---

[47] The debate about the poverty line is a harsh one in Canada. See for an overview Government of Canada, Library of Parliament, Social Affairs division (2008).

[48] The concept of precarious work carries no legal definition in Canada and it is accepted that atypical work is not necessarily precarious. Thereof, precarity is a multifaceted situation that can be declared only by using a negative impact analysis method. For an interesting proposal, see Crawford and Vosko (2006) Figure 2.3 (Indicators of Precarious Work) at 57. Between 1993 and 2016, there was no significant variation in the percentage of temporary and part-time work in Canada (13.5 percent and 19.6 percent average). But some sectors (accommodation, services, recreation, education) and groups (mostly younger and older women) had been more affected by the precarity of work. See Fong (2018).

[49] Section 15(1) of the Canadian Charter of Rights and Freedoms, Canada Act 1982 (U.K.) c.11, reads as follows: 'Every individual is equal before and under the law and has the right to the equal protection and equal benefit of the law without discrimination and, in particular, without discrimination based on race, national or ethnic origin, colour, religion, sex, age or mental or physical disability.'

code over time.[50] An equality court case relies heavily on the comparison between an identified advantaged group and a disadvantaged one. More and more, workers are comparing amongst themselves: men and women; older and younger workers; short-term contracted workers and long-term ones; residents and migrants; and so on. As the academic literature demonstrates, litigating equality has not been useful at bringing to the centre of labour and social law protection of the more vulnerable workers.[51] Not only are domestic courts reluctant to interfere with the legislative process, but also, they prefer a hierarchical vision of all human rights that puts at the forefront the freedom to choose one's work, whatever it means. Capability, choice and empowerment are powerful ideological concepts that replace solidarity.

The ultimate frontier of the transformation of social programs into tax credits has now been moved to the social assistance laws (also called welfare laws). Being the last resort safety net for residents, welfare was under tremendous pressure in the 1980s and 1990s. Aggressive workfare measures were forced on beneficiaries as the legislature looked again and again for tax credits (refundable and non-refundable) that would keep them from returning to welfare by finding their way in the precarious employment labour market.[52] Again, the income for any productive activity, including work, matters more than the nature, the precarity and the risk attached to such activity.

Welfare or social assistance schemes are now under scrutiny and many believe that they will disappear. The social justice movement is generally in favour of this idea as research has abundantly documented the fact that welfare management cultivates multiple breaches of dignity among beneficiaries. Anything but … welfare, seems to be the goal. Among the centre right, the right and inside public administration, many are revisiting the well-known issue of the high cost of social assistance programs management. Accordingly, and like in Finland, Basic Income (BI), or guaranteed universal income, is back on the political agenda.

From a technical standpoint, Canada is well situated to experiment with BI as a negative tax credit answer to poverty. What we used to call social programs are now fiscally integrated to a significant extent. And it is estimated that 30 federal and provincial income support programs offering cash transfers already exist (sales tax credit; affordable living tax credit; solidarity credit; climate action tax credit; earned income tax

---

50 Day et al. (2014).

51 For an in-depth discussion, see Young (2013, 2006).

52 For a recent discussion, see Godbout and St-Cerny (2016) and Canadian Centre for Policy Alternatives (2016).

credit; etc.). Why not combine all those programs into a single BI one and at least, or at last, replace non-contributory welfare programs?

The experiment is now underway in the provinces of Ontario[53] and Quebec,[54] although the two provinces are not heading in the same direction. Nevertheless, both are working with a negative income tax model. About 60 percent of the Canadian population reside in Quebec and Ontario.

In June 2017, Ontario launched a pilot project in three districts of the province: rural, semi urban and urban. Persons between 18 and 64 are invited to participate. Following a tax credit model, the Ontario Basic Income Pilot will ensure that participants receive up to $16,989 per year for a single person, less 50 percent of any earned income, and up to $24,027 per year for a couple, less 50 percent of any earned income.

People with a disability will in addition also receive up to $500 per month. Participants currently receiving CCB and the Ontario Child Benefit (OCB) will continue to be eligible to receive such benefits during the pilot. Participants on EI or on the CPP will have their monthly basic income payment reduced dollar for dollar. Finally, people receiving support through Ontario Works (the social assistance program), who enter the pilot, will continue to benefit from the Ontario Drug Benefit,[55] and people on the Ontario Disability Support Program will continue to benefit as well from the minimal dental benefits program.

Combined benefits will provide participants with an annual income higher than the one they receive when on welfare but lower than the minimum wage. The purpose of this pilot project is to evaluate over a period of three years the impact of BI on the satisfaction of basic needs and on peoples' behaviour toward the labour market. Based on existing benefits and on the fiscal system (that remains unchanged), it is largely accepted that the Ontario formula is the only one that avoids bringing more people in poverty and that it may succeed in pulling some households above the poverty line. A clear dividing line is drawn here between contributory regimes that remain untouched but are considered

---

[53] Segal (2017); Government of Ontario (2017). Caution is recommended as the newly elected conservative Government of Ontario (April 2018) announced that it would put an end to the Basic Income Project prematurely. Canadian Broadcasting Corp (2018).

[54] Government of Québec, Ministère du Travail, de l'Emploi et de la Solidarité sociale et Ministère des Finances (2017).

[55] Except for in the province of Quebec, there is no public system of drug benefits or payment or reimbursement in Canada.

as income (such as EI and public contributory – CPP/RRQ – pension plan) and other programs.

The Ontario BI pilot is described as a fight against poverty measure. In addition, Ontario seems to believe that social assistance requires simplification and fewer social controls.[56] The Ontario BI project does not pretend to address the labour market failure nor does it tackle fiscal inequities amongst Canadians. In other words, it builds on the status quo of a neoliberal economy with one caveat: the minimum hourly salary in Ontario will reach the symbolic threshold of $15 in January 2019.[57]

Keeping in mind that Ontario is piloting a BI project and not implementing a full one, it can nevertheless be assumed that what is at stake is the idea of transforming social assistance in an income supplement program managed through the income tax report. Part of the anti-poverty movement is celebrating the near end of workfare measures that imply heavy social control by the state as well as the acknowledgment of a threshold of income that would put the poorest households above the poverty line at all times. Another part of the same movement is worrying about the initiative as they see in it a concretisation of increased structural inequalities in Canada. They believe that without revisiting both the efficiency of labour law to the benefit of precarious workers as well as the income tax structure, the BI pilot encourages precarity. The disabled beneficiaries are blowing hot and cold. Being the poorest in Canadian society, they celebrate the increase of their social assistance benefits. On the other hand, they realise that they are thereby trapped in the prison of disabilities; no money is invested in promoting a more inclusive labour market.

Quebec is taking a slightly different route[58] without considering a significant increase in the minimum wage. The political argument relies on the fact that, as opposed to the neighbouring province of Ontario, the industrial structure of the province of Quebec largely relies on small

---

[56] Government of Ontario, Income Security Reform Group (2017). It is worth noting that the expression 'income security' was never used in Canada when referring to provincial social assistance programs.

[57] An important and well-organised struggle aiming at raising the minimum hourly wage to $15 for all workers is fought across different jurisdictions of Canada and the United States. See *Why the Success of the $15 Minimum Wage Movement Has Surprised Its Leaders*, Los Angeles Times, 11 November 2015; Canadian Labour Congress (2016). See also for details of minimum wage scaling in Ontario https://www.ontario.ca/page/minimum-wage-increase, accessed 6 August 2018.

[58] See Government of Québec (2017).

businesses, which should not be overburdened with such an increase. As well, Quebec is different from Ontario as a social state. For example, Quebec is the only Canadian province that offers paid parental leave of one year (paid and contributory) as well as an accessible day care network. In addition, only in Quebec do we find in Canada a compulsory prescription drug insurance program that provides for contributions exemption for the poorest households.

Instead of embarking on a BI pilot project, Quebec decided to amend its social assistance legislation.[59] In a nutshell, this so-called income-support strategy relies on three different initiatives. Firstly, and like in Ontario, benefits for disabled persons will reach the MBM level by 2023.[60] Secondly, households actually benefitting from social assistance will be allowed to keep a larger portion of their working gains before being submitted to the clawback of their benefits. It is estimated that by 2023, this measure will allow the working poor households to rely on welfare assistance to cover 55 percent of the MBM.[61] Finally, newcomers to social assistance (mostly young single males) will have to register on a workfare program or suffer a major cut to their potential benefits.

The Quebec government clearly states that it does not believe in a BI program and decided instead to rely on a mix of social assistance adaptations and social tax expenditures. Like in Ontario, though, the actual labour law framework remains intact but for some minor adjustments and the income tax regime is untouched.

Looking at those two contemporary experiments, one can safely say that in Canada, the concept of income support is more appropriate than the one of basic or universal income in order to describe how social protection is being revisited.

CONCLUSION

What would Marsh think of the Canadian social security regime creation and transformation over the last 60 years? As the MacDonald Report suggested in 1985, is Canada finally adjusting itself to the global

---

59 Individual and Family Assistance Act, CQLR c. A-13.1.1 as amended by the Act to allow a better match between training and jobs and to facilitate labour market 2016 c. 25 (entered into force in November 2016).

60 The MBM is not as generous as the LICO used by Statistics Canada.

61 It is estimated that 70 percent of what is called the Income Support Program in Québec is actually covered by non-refundable and refundable tax credits for workers and working families.

economy? Transformations registered over the last two decades seem to suggest two conclusions calling for a positive answer to this question. Firstly, income, as in income security, is replacing wages and salary as the operative concept giving access to social protection in general. This not only has a serious chilling effect on labour law but as well acknowledges that in the era of precariat,[62] decent work is giving way to basic income security, even in a rich country. Social protection in Canada is more and more detached from wages and employment – which is easier to do in a country where the social security regime was designed as a mixed one (contributory and demo grants based on condition of residence). Secondly, a social protection system that depends on annual tax bills for adjusted refundable tax credits is much more adaptable to international economic competitiveness and much less susceptible of judicial overseeing. It may have taken over 30 years to turn the young Canadian social protection on its head, but it looks like MacDonald has the last word … for now.

BIBLIOGRAPHY

Beveridge W, *Social Insurance and Allied Services* (McMillan 1942)

Bureau R, Lippel K and Lamarche L, 'Développement et tendances du droit social au Canada, de la seconde guerre mondiale à nos jours (1940-1984)' in Ivan Bernier and Andrée Lajoie (eds), *Le droit de la famille et le droit social au Canada*, Royal Commission on the Economic Union and Development Prospects for Canada (Canada, Privy Council 1985)

Canadian Broadcasting Corp, *Ford Government Ditched Basic Income Pilot Project before Any Data Landed, Researcher Says*, 3 August 2018, https://www.cbc.ca/news/canada/basic-income-pilot-project-ford-cancel-1.4771343, accessed 6 August 2018

Canadian Centre for Policy Alternatives, *Canada's Declining Social Safety Net, the Case of EI Reform*, 2009

Canadian Centre for Policy Alternatives, *Basic Income, Rethinking Social Policy*, Alex Himelfarb and Trish Hennessy (eds), 2016, https://www.policyalternatives.ca/sites/default/files/uploads/publications/National%20Office%2C%20Ontario%20Office/2016/10/CCPA%20ON%20Basic%20Income_FINAL.pdf, accessed 6 August 2018

Canadian Labour Congress, *Minimum Wage Stats Show We Need $15 and Fairness across Canada*, 31 May 2016, http://canadianlabour.ca/news/news-archive/minimum-wage-stats-show-we-need-15-and-fairness-across-canada, accessed 6 August 2018

---

62 We have borrowed this expression from Standing (2011).

Crawford C J and Vosko L F, 'Conceptualizing Precarious Employment: Mapping Wage Work across Social Location and Occupational Context' in Leah F. Vosko (ed.), *Precarious Employment – Understanding Labour Market Insecurity in Canada* (McGill-Queen's University Press 2006)
Cross P, *The Reality of Retirement Income in Canada*, April 2014, https://www.fraserinstitute.org/sites/default/files/Reality%20of%20Retirement%20Income_web%20final.pdf, accessed 6 August 2018
Day S, Lamarche L and Norman K (eds), *14 Good Reasons for Human Rights Institutions in Canada* (Irwin Law 2014)
Fong F, *Navigating Precarious Employment in Canada: Who Is Really At Risk?* Chartered Professional Accountants Canada, 2018, https://www.cpacanada.ca/en/the-cpa-profession/about-cpa-canada/key-activities/public-policy-government-relations/economic-policy-research/rise-precarious-employment, accessed 6 August 2018
Godbout L and St-Cerny S, *Le point sur le soutien minimal de l'Etat: que reçoivent les ménages québécois?* Cahier de recherche no 2016-12, Université de Sherbrooke, Chaire de recherche en fiscalité et en finances publiques, https://cffp.recherche.usherbrooke.ca/wp-content/uploads/2016-12_Soutien-minimum.pdf, accessed 6 August 2018
Government of Canada, *Report for Social Security in Canada*, 1943a
Government of Canada, Advisory Committee on Health Insurance, *Report of the Advisory committee on health insurance appointed by order in council P.C. 836*, 1943
Government of Canada, Canada Child Benefit Overview, no date, https://www.canada.ca/en/revenue-agency/services/child-family-benefits/canada-child-benefit-overview.html, accessed 6 August 2018
Government of Canada, Library of Parliament, Social Affairs division, *Measuring Poverty: A Challenge for Canada*, PRB 08-65E, 2008, https://lop.parl.ca/content/lop/ResearchPublications/prb0865-e.htm, accessed 6 August 2018
Government of Canada, Privy Council, *Report – Royal Commission on the Economic Union and Development Prospects for Canada*, Vol. 1, 1985, http://publications.gc.ca/collections/collection_2014/bcp-pco/Z1-1983-1-1-1-eng.pdf, accessed 6 August 2018
Government of Canada, Report of the Special Senate Committee on Poverty, *Poverty in Canada*, Ottawa 1970
Government of Ontario, *Ontario Basic Income Project*, 2017 https://www.ontario.ca/page/ontario-basic-income-pilot, accessed 6 August 2018
Government of Ontario, Income Security Reform Group, *Income Security a Road Map for Change*, 2017 https://files.ontario.ca/income_security_-_a_roadmap_for_change-english-accessible_updated.pdf, accessed 6 August 2018
Government of Québec, *Government Action Plan to Foster Economic Inclusion and Social Participation 2017–2023* (French only), December https://www.mtess.gouv.qc.ca/publications/pdf/ADMIN_plan_action_2017-2023.pdf, accessed 6 August 2018
Government of Québec, Ministère du Travail, de l'Emploi et de la Solidarité sociale et Ministère des Finances, Comité d'experts sur le revenu minimum garanti, *Guaranteed Minimum Income in Québec: A Utopia? An Inspiration*

for Québec Final Report Volume 1 – Principles, Diagnosis and Recommendations, November 2017, http://www.gouv.qc.ca/EN/RevenuMinimumGaranti/Pages/Accueil.aspx, accessed 6 August 2018

Guest D, *The Emergence of Social Security in Canada* (2nd edn, University of British Columbia Press 1985)

Lamarche L, Hanley J, Noel D J and Christensen B, 'And when a worker's not working?' Income security (welfare and pensions) for mobile workers in Canada', July 2016, http://www.onthemovepartnership.ca/wp-content/uploads/2012/11/Welfare-and-Pensions-Lemarche-et-al-July-2016-for-circulation.pdf, accessed 6 August 2018

Lamarche L and Girard C, 'Evolution de la sécurité sociale au Canada: la mise à l'écart progressive de l'Etat Providence canadien' (1998) 13 Revue des lois et politiques sociales 95

Leman C, *The Collapse of Welfare Reform: Political Institutions, Policy, and the Poor in Canada and the United States* (MIT Press 1985)

Lippel K and Lefebvre M, *La réparation des lésions professionnelles: analyse jurisprudentielle* (Editions Yvon Blais 2005)

Lippel K, *Le droit des accidentés du travail à une indemnité analyse historique et critique* (MA thesis, Faculty of Law, University of Montreal 1986)

Macdonald D, *Behind the Numbers, EI is Not Actually Helping the Poor*, July 2014, http://behindthenumbers.ca/2014/07/14/ei-is-not-actually-helping-the-poor/, accessed 6 August 2018

Myles J and Pierson J, 'Friedman's Revenge: The Expansion of the Negative Income Tax in Canada and the United States' in Intégration continentale, recomposition territoriale et protection sociale, Colloque international du GRPTST, Montreal, October 1995 (unpublished, on file with the author)

Segal H D, *Finding a Better Way: A Basic Income Pilot Project for Ontario*, 2017, https://www.ontario.ca/page/finding-better-way-basic-income-pilot-project-ontario, accessed 6 August 2018

Standing G, *The Precariat: The New Dangerous Class* (Bloomsbury 2011)

Université du Québec à Montréal, XVIIème Journée en droit social et du travail, *Le droit humain à une retraite décente*, March 2016, https://www.youtube.com/watch?v=Rn9J6ftf9lY&list=PLbJC42QdNVtGGQd9lsvDAKfzZPekB8n8t, accessed 20 February 2018

Young M, 'Social Justice and the Charter: Comparison and Choice' (2013) 50 Osgoode Hall Law Journal 669

Young M, 'Blissed Out Section 15 at 20' (2006) 33 S.C.R.L. (2d) 45

Canadian Legislation

Act respecting assistance for victims of crime 1988, c. 20

Act respecting legal aid and the provision of certain other legal services, S.Q. 2010, c. 12

Act to allow a better match between training and jobs and to facilitate labour market L.Q. 2016 c. 25

Act to amend the Old Age Security Act, 1966-1967 c. 65

Act to amend Old Age Security Act S.C. 1984 c. 27

Act to amend the Unemployment Insurance Act 1993, c. 13
Act to amend the Unemployment Insurance Act and the Act on the Employment and Immigration of Canada S.C. 1990 c. 40
Automobile Insurance Act 1977, c. 68
Canada Assistance Plan, 1966–67, c. 45
Canada Health Act S.C. 1984 c. 6
Canada Pension Plan Act R.S.C. 1985 c. C-8
Canada United States Free Trade Agreement 1988, c. 65
Constitution Act 1867, 30 & 31 Victoria c. 3 (U.K.)
Constitutional Act, 1940, 3-4 George VI, c. 36 (U.K.)
Employment Insurance Act S.C. 1996, c. 23
Family Allowances Act S.C. 1944–1945 c. 40
Hospital Insurance and Diagnostic Services Act S.C. 1957 c. 28
Income Tax and Children's Special Allowances Act S.C. 1992 c. 48
Individual and Family Assistance Act, CQLR c. A-13.1.1
Medical Care Act S.C. 1966–1967 c. 64
North American Free Trade Agreement 32 ILM 289, 605 1993
Old Age Security Act S.C. 1951 c. 18
Pension Act S.C. 1919 c. 43 as amended by S.C. 1937 c. 13
Quebec Pension Plan Act S.Q. 1965 c. 24
Unemployment Insurance Act S.C. 1940 c. 44
Unemployment Act L.C. 1970-1971-1972 c. 48

Epilogue

Mies Westerveld and Marius Olivier

What attempts have been made to extend social security coverage to informal workers? What types of regulatory and normative frameworks are needed in countries with developed systems of labour law and social insurance? And what can we learn from attempts to make or keep social security all-inclusive? In this book, in addition to the introductory cross-cutting chapters, academics from countries with systems of social security at different levels of development reflected on such questions, using their own scientific or national affiliation as starting point. In this last chapter we look at commonalities and we look at the question of whether the analyses and exemplary reports – that were presented under the heading 'thematic', 'regional' and 'country case studies' – provide inspiration for future steps. Which questions appear unsolvable and for what questions might a suitable answer be available? With respect to the last element, 'availability' does not necessarily imply that such an answer will, at individual country level, be actually embraced. For that to happen, elements such as political will, a solid institutional framework, population's trust and financial resources, are – among many others – vital preconditions.

UNPROTECTED WORK: A FIRST ANALYSIS

A first and unsurprising conclusion is the observation that provided the rationale for this book. In countries with a large informal economy, at least until recently, social risks have been effectively shifted onto such workers and their families (Chapter 1 of this book). In recent times, however, conceptual, regulatory, institutional, operational and design measures have been adopted on a significantly comprehensive scale in a decisive attempt to extend social security to those working in the informal economy. In fact, the innovative nature of and the scale at which these coverage interventions have been developed and rolled out has been unprecedented, at least from the perspective of social security developments in the global south (see the contributions by Olivier and Ortiz).

In the global north, advanced welfare states witnessed a shift from protection to non-protection. This development – from 'typical' and as such solidly insured work to atypical, in many instances work without adequate coverage – took place even prior to, in the wording of Wynn and Paz-Fuchs, the 'trendy' gig economy. Social insurance adaptation to this development has been, as they put it, only piecemeal and not comprehensive. Li and Jianfei go deeper into the 'trendy topic', that is occurring for both global north and global south by pointing at 'extremely wealthy "Platform" owners' vis-à-vis online workers who are forced to bear labour risks they are hardly able to assume themselves (Chapter 5 of this book). This form of work in the 'collaborative economy' (terminology Westregård) is as a rule both precarious and hard to reach for contributory and taxation purposes.

A good illustration of the complexity for governments to react adequately was given in a local Dutch newspaper, reporting about the case of Seattle, home of the 'extremely wealthy Platform owners'. In this town the 'omnipresent Tech industry (Amazon, Facebook, Google)', in the wording of this article, is turning Seattle into a place that the predominantly progressive inhabitants do *not* want: a city for the super-rich, with nowhere for middle and lower class people to live. Affordable housing is scarce and efforts to levy more taxes on tech giants are met with threats to stop expansion and/or move away. This tech industry is not 'socially irresponsible', though. It just does not want government interference and prefers to solve such issues through philanthropic measures, in this case by offering temporary shelter, situated on company property, to homeless people. In the end the threat to withdraw their activities proved effective: the intended tax law was stricken.[1]

But it is not just tax law or tax authorities that are struggling with the question of how to respond to the rise of collaborative work. Several reports, both from the north and the south, indicate that the classic binary divide between employment and self-employment, and between formal and informal work, has become an obstacle for the organisation of workers' risks protection. And while labour relations have become more agile than ever, effective answers from labour *law*, as is the case with social security law, have yet to be found.

---

[1] Dutch newspaper, November 2018. *Dead poor in filthy rich Seattle*, https://www.nrc.nl/nieuws/2018/11/02/straatarm-in-steenrijk-seattle-a2753779

Taking a closer look at the person behind the qualification 'unprotected work', one inevitably stumbles on the issue of gender. After all, northern welfare states are gendered, as many labour law scholars have pointed out before[2] and work and workers in the informal economy are no exception to this rule. Fourie underlines this observation by pointing at the feminisation of poverty, the burden placed on women in respect of care and domestic work, and the fact that more women (than men) are prevalent in atypical work and have – more so than their male counterparts – limited access to resources. For the European Union (EU), Barnard and Blackham point out that women are less likely to be self-employed, less likely to employ others, and more likely to work in the services sector. And that sector is in turn more likely to be associated with low pay and high risk. The EU gender gap is enhanced by the fact that existing maternity and parental rights for self-employed workers are especially relevant for female workers, as women generally take on a larger share of caring responsibilities, and are biologically more likely to make use of maternity or parental leave (Chapter 4 of this book). For countries with a colonial past, a racial dimension enhances the gender disadvantage. Dias and Ogando point at an association 'between racial structures of oppression with such kinds of labour being allocated by gender, class, caste, race and ethnicity'. And it is in this area of intersection between gender and race, that women are exposed to cultural and social injustice at three levels, macro or societal, meso or enterprise, micro or inter personal (see the reflection on this in Chapter 3 of this book).

NORTH MEETS SOUTH: LESSONS LEARNED?

From the several country and regional case studies that have been presented, we want to highlight three observations.

First Observation. The Universality of the Theme: the Human Rights Dimension of Social Security

From an optimistic perspective, we conclude that the importance of a system of social protection against universally recognised social risks meets with wide acceptance. What's more, in a growing number of countries social security has been incorporated into the catalogue of

---

[2] See Sainsbury (1994 and 2008), Orloff (1996 and 2009), both in bibliography chapter 4 of this book.

human rights. This explains why countries all over the world are sensitive to the risk of having a social security system that is reserved for the privileged few.

Second Observation. Impressive Problem Analyses, No Universal Answers

Almost all chapters contain convincing arguments why social security is failing its main task. Without pretending completeness we want to underline three obstacles that were mentioned, or if one wishes, explanations of the lack of social coverage and why this turns out to be so hard to handle.

The first obstacle is especially relevant in the developed world and is, again, an explanatory factor for the 'fusion' of the issue in the developed and developing worlds. This obstacle is the individualisation of workers and the fragmentation of the labour market. This phenomenon has been mentioned many times before and does not need further explanation. It is, however, a trigger to another issue that is problematic in both the developed and developing worlds. This phenomenon concerns the dwindling of trade union membership, which is especially troublesome as trade unions are of origin carriers of social insurance schemes and allies for governments in the organisation of such schemes. The third problematic element is the aforementioned power shift between labour and capital as a result of the internationalisation and digitisation of labour. This shift puts the question of how to ensure a sufficient financial base to finance social security schemes even higher on the political agenda than it already was.

Third Observation. Acuteness Breeds Creativity

A somewhat surprising conclusion is that innovative initiatives to close the non-coverage gap that was mentioned in this book are from a global south region. Analyses from experiences in the 'north' are more often than not dominated by problem inventory and the observation that social security is in trouble. Innovative solutions or clear ideas about how to tackle the issues appear thus far to be lacking.

FINALLY: SOME CAVEATS

Taking an overall view of the topics that have been presented, we repeat the observation with which this book started out and that has been affirmed by the several country reports. Mass exclusion from social security, originally a challenge for the global south, threatens to become global. This calls for an exchange of ideas and practical solutions between countries with long experience of the matter and countries for whom this is relatively new. Such exchange may help to bring effective resolutions at nation state level within reach. For this exchange more research is needed than we have been able to present in this first effort to bring some countries and a selective group of scholars together in one book.

In this search for viable practices two caveats are in order, though. The first is that social security is, even more so than labour law, considered a matter of state sovereignty. This means that an approach that has proven its value in one state will not be easily adopted by another state. A good example of this affinity with the national system can be found in the history of the economic community that the EU is supposed to be. The moment the EU legislator or the EU Court only *appears* to be interfering with state sovereignty, significant opposition is raised. The second caveat is the one Ortiz gave in his analysis of methods in the Latin American region. Legislative measures or policy practices that are effective within one national context are not simply transportable to other countries. They will always need a certain 'translation' by academics or policy makers of the intended recipient country.

But when one takes these two caveats into consideration, the 'north' learning from the 'south' and vice versa might very well be considered the logical outcome.

Index

ECONOMIC ISSUES, PROBLEMS AND PERSPECTIVES

COLLAPSE AND BANKRUPTCY OF MF GLOBAL

TAO ZHU
EDITOR

nova publishers
New York

For permission to use material from this book please contact us:
Telephone 631-231-7269; Fax 631-231-8175
Web Site: http://www.novapublishers.com

Library of Congress Cataloging-in-Publication Data

ISBN: 978-1-62417-710-1

Published by Nova Science Publishers, Inc. † New York

CONTENTS

PREFACE

On October 31, 2011, MF Global, a large brokerage firm registered with the Securities and Exchange Commission (SEC) as a broker-dealer and with the Commodity Futures Trading Commission (CFTC) as a futures commission merchant (FCM), filed for bankruptcy. It appears that the firm failed as a result of losses from investments related to European sovereign debt. Normally, brokerage customers are protected from brokerage failure. On the securities side, investors may receive up to $500,000 from the Securities Investor Protection Corporation (SIPC) if the failed brokerage's assets are insufficient to meet customer claims. In futures markets, there is no insurance scheme comparable to SIPC, but customers are supposed to be protected by strict segregation rules. In the MF Global case, however, more than $900 million in customer funds were reported missing. This book provides information about MF Global, the rules for handling of customer funds, the enforcement of those rules, and the bankruptcy proceeding.

Chapter 1 – On October 31, 2011, MF Global, a large brokerage firm registered with the Securities and Exchange Commission (SEC) as a broker-dealer and with the Commodity Futures Trading Commission (CFTC) as a futures commission merchant (FCM), filed for bankruptcy. It appears that the firm failed as a result of losses from investments related to European sovereign debt.

Normally, brokerage customers are protected from brokerage failure. On the securities side, investors may receive up to $500,000 from the Securities Investor Protection Corporation (SIPC) if the failed brokerage's assets are insufficient to meet customer claims. In futures markets, there is no insurance scheme comparable to SIPC, but customers are supposed to be protected by strict segregation rules: customer funds entrusted to FCMs are required to be kept in separate accounts and the FCM is not allowed to use them for its own purposes.

In the MF Global case, however, more than $900 million in customer funds were reported missing. (Subsequent estimates of the shortfall range from $600 million to $1.2 billion.) The CFTC, SEC, Justice Department, and the bankruptcy trustee are investigating and trying to locate the missing funds. Violation of segregation rules, if it occurred, is subject to civil and criminal penalties.

MF Global had about 50,000 futures customers with active accounts. About 17,000 of those accounts with open futures positions have been transferred to other FCM firms, in order that those customers may regain use of their funds. Customers who had cash accounts with MF Global, but not open futures positions, have had their money frozen. On November 17, 2011, the bankruptcy court approved distribution of $520 million, or about 60% of frozen customer funds. On December 9, 2011, the court approved a third distribution of about $2.1 billion in customer funds. When completed, customers should have received about 72% of their funds.

In the future, there may be additional partial payouts. Because the customer funds in cash accounts were not guaranteed, however, the final distribution of cash to investors may not occur until the conclusion of the bankruptcy proceeding, and it is not certain that MF Global's futures customers will receive 100% of their money back.

This report provides information about MF Global, the rules for handling of customer funds, the enforcement of those rules, and the bankruptcy proceeding.

Chapter 2 – founded by James Man in London in 1783. In 1869, the business became known as E.D.&F. Man. It set up its first overseas operations in New York and Hong Kong in 1972, and began trading commodities futures. The company expanded its services in 1983 to include investment management, and by 1994, when it first listed on the London Stock Exchange, it had $1 billion in funds under management.

In 2000, E.D.&F. Man spun off its agricultural commodities business and changed its name to Man Group plc. Under the leadership of Kevin R. Davis, who joined the company in 1991 and rose to become the Chief Executive Officer (CEO) of Man Financial (Man Group's global brokerage businesses), the company sought to capitalize on the rapid growth in global derivatives markets by acquiring businesses offering new products, including futures, options, and other derivatives. Man Group acquired 17 companies in 18 years, including GNI Holdings Ltd. in 2002 and Refco Inc. in 2005. GNI was a leading European broker of futures and options, foreign exchange, and equity derivative products, and its acquisition established the Man Group, through Man Financial, as the world's largest independent futures broker. Refco was a regulated futures brokerage with client accounts and assets in the U.S., Singapore, Canada, and India, and its acquisition further expanded Man Financial's global brokerage services.

Following these acquisitions, and fueled by the growth of the derivatives industry, Man Financial became one of the leading brokers of exchange-listed futures and options in the world, providing execution and clearing services for exchange-traded and over-the-counter derivative products, as well as for non-derivative products and securities in the cash market. The company served more than 130,000 active client accounts, and held leading market share on the biggest exchanges in North America and Europe, including the Chicago Mercantile Exchange (CME), CBOT, the New York Mercantile Exchange, and Eurex. The company also had a global footprint, with 34 offices in cities such as New York, Chicago, London, Paris, Mumbai, Hong Kong, Singapore, and Sydney. Man Financial more than doubled its exchange-traded brokerage volume between 2004 and 2007, increasing both revenues and operating margins, and reported net income of $188 million on revenue of $5.7 billion for the fiscal year ending March 31, 2007.

Chapter 3 – This is the Statement of Jon S. Corzine, former CEO of MF Global. Hearing on "The Collapse of MF Global."

In: Collapse and Bankruptcy of MF Global ISBN: 978-1-62417-710-1
Editor: Tao Zhu

Chapter 1

THE MF GLOBAL BANKRUPTCY AND MISSING CUSTOMER FUNDS*

Rena S. Miller and Mark Jickling

SUMMARY

On October 31, 2011, MF Global, a large brokerage firm registered with the Securities and Exchange Commission (SEC) as a broker-dealer and with the Commodity Futures Trading Commission (CFTC) as a futures commission merchant (FCM), filed for bankruptcy. It appears that the firm failed as a result of losses from investments related to European sovereign debt.

Normally, brokerage customers are protected from brokerage failure. On the securities side, investors may receive up to $500,000 from the Securities Investor Protection Corporation (SIPC) if the failed brokerage's assets are insufficient to meet customer claims. In futures markets, there is no insurance scheme comparable to SIPC, but customers are supposed to be protected by strict segregation rules: customer funds entrusted to FCMs are required to be kept in separate accounts and the FCM is not allowed to use them for its own purposes.

In the MF Global case, however, more than $900 million in customer funds were reported missing. (Subsequent estimates of the shortfall range from $600 million to $1.2 billion.) The CFTC, SEC, Justice Department, and the

* This is an edited, reformatted and augmented version of the Congressional Research Service Publication, CRS Report for Congress R42091, dated December 12, 2011.

bankruptcy trustee are investigating and trying to locate the missing funds. Violation of segregation rules, if it occurred, is subject to civil and criminal penalties. MF Global had about 50,000 futures customers with active accounts. About 17,000 of those accounts with open futures positions have been transferred to other FCM firms, in order that those customers may regain use of their funds. Customers who had cash accounts with MF Global, but not open futures positions, have had their money frozen. On November 17, 2011, the bankruptcy court approved distribution of $520 million, or about 60% of frozen customer funds. On December 9, 2011, the court approved a third distribution of about $2.1 billion in customer funds. When completed, customers should have received about 72% of their funds.

In the future, there may be additional partial payouts. Because the customer funds in cash accounts were not guaranteed, however, the final distribution of cash to investors may not occur until the conclusion of the bankruptcy proceeding, and it is not certain that MF Global's futures customers will receive 100% of their money back. This report provides information about MF Global, the rules for handling of customer funds, the enforcement of those rules, and the bankruptcy proceeding.

BACKGROUND

MF Global Holdings, Ltd. was one of the world's leading brokers in markets for commodities and listed derivatives, providing clients with access to more than 70 exchanges globally. The firm was a leader by volume on many of the world's largest derivatives exchanges. MF Global was also an active broker-dealer in markets for commodities, fixed income securities, equities, and foreign exchange. It was one of 20 primary dealers authorized to trade U.S. government securities with the Federal Reserve Bank of New York. Headquartered in the United States, the firm had operations in Australia, Canada, Hong Kong, India, Japan, Singapore, the United Kingdom, and other countries.[1] In mid-2011, the firm reported total assets of $45.9 billion.

In the second quarter of 2011, MF Global reported total revenues of $611.2 million. Of this, $364.7 million (60%) was commissions and trading fees, $122.2 million (20%) was interest income (primarily net interest earned from customer margin funds held by the firm), and $116.8 million (19%) was attributable to principal transactions, or proprietary trading for the firm's own account. Although customer brokerage accounted for about 80% of MF Global's revenue, the firm's "strategic plan" called for a shift to an investment banking business model, in which proprietary trading and market making would become the principal sources of earnings.[2] It appears that proprietary trading losses drove the firm into bankruptcy.

The precise nature of the trades that caused MF Global to fail remains unclear. In October 2011, the firm published a fact sheet disclosing that it held $6.4 billion in sovereign debt of five European countries, and that this position was financed through repurchase agreements.[3] (A repurchase transaction, or repo, involves sale of a security with an agreement to buy it back later at a higher price. It is economically equivalent to a loan.) Some press reports suggest that the position was profitable to the extent that the interest rate MF Global paid on repos was lower than the rate paid by the sovereign bonds. If the cost of financing the bond position rose, MF Global would make a loss. In some versions, this is what happened: creditors insisted that MF Global post higher collateral against the position, either because the perceived credit risk of the bonds had increased or because MF Global's own credit rating had been downgraded (which happened on October 24, 2011).

Whatever the immediate causes of the failure, the markets appear to have taken a pessimistic view of MF Global for some time. Its stock price, which began 2011 at about $8 per share, began to decline in May and fell below $4 on October 3. On Monday, October 24, Moody's downgraded MF Global's long-term debt to Baa3, the rating just above junk bond status.[4] The next day, the stock price fell by 48%, from $3.55 to $1.86. On Friday, October 26, Standard & Poor's placed MF Global on "credit watch negative," meaning that a downgrade might be forthcoming. By that time, the press was reporting that some banks were refusing to deal with MF Global and that efforts were underway to sell the firm.[5] Over the weekend, MF Global notified the CFTC that more than $900 million in customer funds were unaccounted for, making a merger impractical and blocking a mass transfer of customer futures accounts to stable FCMs. On Monday, October 31, MF Global filed for bankruptcy.

How the System Was Supposed to Work

The failure of a brokerage does not necessarily expose customers to loss. Both futures and securities law and regulation provide safeguards to protect customer funds. Securities brokers regulated by the Securities and Exchange Commission (SEC) are subject to a net capital rule— they must cease operations before their assets fall below the level that allows customer claims to be met. In addition, broker-dealers must belong to the Securities Investor Protection Corporation (SIPC), which provides an insurance scheme whereby customers of failed broker-dealers may receive up to $500,000 from the SIPC fund.

There is no analog to SIPC in futures markets regulated by the Commodity Futures Trading Commission (CFTC). Instead, there are strict rules about the use of customer funds (in addition to net capital rules). Section 4d(a)(2) of the Commodity Exchange Act (CEA) requires that customer funds received by a futures commission merchant (FCM) to margin, guarantee, or secure a customer's futures contracts be held in segregated accounts, and not be commingled with the funds of the FCM itself, nor used to guarantee the trades or contracts of any person other than the customer.[6] Thus, any MF Global losses related to its own proprietary trading should not have affected customers. The shortfall of segregated customer funds is a rare event and represents a breakdown of the system. "This has been a significant blemish on the industry's reputation," said Dan Roth, president of the National Futures Association, an industry-funded self-regulatory organization.[7]

Moreover, customers were taken off guard because, as FCM bankruptcy is usually handled, they reasonably expected that their accounts would be transferred to another FCM, and that they would be able to access their funds. Customers expected this based on historical precedent and a feature of the bankruptcy code. Derivatives contracts, which include futures, are "qualified financial contracts" under bankruptcy law. This means futures contracts are not subject to the "automatic stay" that freezes other assets held by a bankrupt firm. One purpose of this exemption is to enable customers to avoid premature liquidation of futures positions whose value depends on often volatile movements of underlying commodities, as that could cause them to incur losses.[8]

On the weekend of October 29-30, before the bankruptcy filing, the CFTC was working to transfer MF Global customer accounts to another FCM. This attempt came to a halt with the disclosure at 2:30 a.m. on October 31 that segregated funds were missing—the second FCM would not accept futures positions without the associated margin.[9] The requirement that all traders post margin to cover potential and actual losses is essential to the financial integrity of futures markets.

Subsequent to the bankruptcy, as discussed below, some customer accounts were transferred to other FCMs.

Enforcement of Segregation Rules

Any shortfall in segregated accounts violates the CEA and CFTC regulations. Violations may result in CFTC administrative sanctions, such as fines or bans from the futures industry, CFTC civil suits, or referral to the Justice Department for criminal prosecution. The CEA provides for fines of up to $1 million or five years imprisonment for each violation of the law.

As noted above, Section 4d of the CEA requires segregation of customer margin funds and prohibits FCMs from using those funds for their own purposes. In addition, 17 C.F.R. Section 1.32 ("Segregated account; daily computation and record") requires FCMs to compute daily both the amount of segregated funds on hand and the amount required to be held. Any shortfall must be reported immediately to the CFTC by telephone.[10]

An FCM's duty to maintain adequate funds in segregated accounts is the subject of reporting obligations and inspection. According to a February 2011 CME Group publication,

> Every day, FCMs must submit a report to the National Futures Association (NFA) detailing the breakdown of their customer funds. This "Segregated Investment Detail Report" (SIDR) lists the actual and expected segregated funds in the FCM's accounts. In addition, every FCM must file monthly financial reports with the Commodity Futures Trading Commission's Division of Clearing and Intermediary Oversight (DCIO) within 17 business days after the end of the month. Finally, the FCM is subject to a yearly audit by the Joint Audit Committee, a consortium of U.S. futures exchanges and regulatory organizations.[11]

The front-line policeman monitoring MF Global's compliance was CME Group itself, acting as a self-regulatory organization. MF Global was a "clearing member" of the CME, meaning that it was part of the clearing house. According to a CME Group customer brochure,

> CME Group's Audit Department routinely inspects the books and records of clearing members to ensure, among other things, their compliance with segregation requirements. The integrity of segregation relies on the accuracy and timeliness of the information provided to CME Clearing by member firms. Violations by a clearing member of its segregation requirements are considered serious infractions and can result in major penalties imposed by the governing entity.[12]

The disappearance of customer funds raises questions about the adequacy of self-policing by FCMs and self-regulatory organizations (SROs), such as CME Group. In the securities markets, the Madoff Ponzi scheme led to calls for more active monitoring of customer accounts, including regular verification of the presence of customer assets by third parties, such as banks or depositories. Similar reforms might be considered in the futures area,[13] as well as a more direct inspection role by the CFTC itself.

Investment of Segregated Funds (Regulation 1.25)

A separate issue dealing with segregated funds is how those funds may be invested within the segregated pool. While segregated funds are thought of as "cash," they are not literally held in the form of currency. Traditionally, they have been invested in U.S. Treasury securities, in order that they generate interest income, which is shared between the customer and the FCM. In 2005, the CFTC broadened the range of permissible investments to include foreign sovereign debt, as well as other short-term debt instruments. In November 2010, the CFTC published a proposed regulation that would have tightened the definition of permissible investments. On December 5, 2011, the CFTC unanimously approved a final rule amending its Regulation 1.25 to prohibit investing customer margin funds in sovereign debt, in-house repurchase agreements, and certain forms of money market instruments.[14]

It is important to distinguish between investing customer funds in foreign sovereign debt and the investments MF Global made for its own account. The latter are not affected by the new Regulation 1.25. There is no evidence that investment losses *within the pool of segregated assets* were responsible for the shortfall in customer funds. Rather, it appears that funds were transferred out of the segregated pool and used for other purposes.

The Bankruptcy Process

Because MF Global was an SEC-registered broker-dealer, its bankruptcy process is overseen by SIPC as well as the bankruptcy court.[15] James W. Giddens, the SIPC trustee, will seek to identify and recover MF Global assets so that they may be distributed (with court approval) to customers and creditors. It does not appear that any client funds or securities were missing on the broker-dealer side of the firm. Instead, attention has focused on the futures customers, who may not recover all their funds.

According to press reports, MF Global had about 50,000 active futures customer accounts.[16] These included accounts with open futures contracts and accounts with cash only. (Many futures traders close all their positions before the market closes each day to avoid overnight price risk. The next day, they may enter new trades up to the limit of their margin accounts. In the meantime, the cash stays in the segregated account at the FCM.) A problem for customers with cash accounts is that while the CME clearing house guarantees payment on all futures contracts, it does not guarantee all customer funds held by FCMs.

During the first week in November 2011, about 17,000 customer accounts with open positions were transferred to other FCMs. This was accompanied by a release of about $1.55 billion in collateral associated with those positions.[17] According to the CME, "due to uncertainty over the amount of MF Global-held segregated funds to support customer trading, the Trustee only allowed CME Group to transfer customer positions to new clearing member firms with part, but not all, of their funds."[18]

Because of the possibility that futures customers may not receive 100% of the money that MF Global was supposed to have held in segregation, final distributions of cash to customers will be delayed until the trustee has a better understanding of the totality of creditor claims. A process for futures customers to file claims has been established. There may be several interim, partial distributions before the final payments are made.

The CFTC and the bankruptcy trustee are attempting to trace the missing customer funds. If they are able to identify specific transfers, out of segregated accounts and into other accounts, that money may be reclaimed exclusively for the benefit of the FCM customers. On the other hand, if no precise money trail can be established, FCM customers' claims may be weighed along with claims of MF Global's other creditors in the normal bankruptcy process.

The trustee has stated that he is unable to estimate when the investigation of the shortfall will be complete.[19] The investigation involves the Department of Justice, the CFTC, and the SEC, as well as the trustee.

On November 17, 2011, the bankruptcy court approved a distribution of $520 million, or 60% of the $869 million that has been frozen since the bankruptcy. The payout, affecting 21,000 customers, was expected to be made by November 21.[20]

The trustee next asked the court's permission to distribute another $2.1 billion, which was substantially all the property still under the trustee's control. The court approved this third distribution on December 9, 2011. When it is completed, futures customers are expected to have received about 72% of their assets.[21]

End Notes

[1] This description (and the financial results that follow) are based on MF Global Holdings' 10-Q quarterly report for the second quarter of 2011, filed with the Securities and Exchange Commission on August 3, 2011.

[2] Ibid., p. 55.

[3] MF Global, "Short-Term European Sovereign Portfolio," October 2011. Online: http://phx.corporate-ir.net/External.File?item=UGFyZW50SUQ9NDQ0MTE1fENoaWxkSUQ9NDY3MDg2fFR5cGU9MQ==&t=1.

[4] Moody's reported that it had "become increasingly concerned with MF Global's risk management and management's ability to prudently balance risk and reward as it undergoes a substantial re-engineering of the firm." Moody's Investors Service, "Rating Action: Moody's downgrades MF Global to Baa3; reviews for further downgrade," October 24, 2011.

[5] Jacon Bunge and Aaron Lucchetti, "MF Global Draws Interest as Tumultuous Week Ends," *Wall Street Journal*, October 28, 2011.

[6] However, §4d(f)(3)(A) of the CEA does provide an exception permitting commingling ''for convenience.'' It is unclear whether, and to what extent, this exception may have been invoked by MF Global. The funds that MF Global should have held in segregation were primarily margin payments. All traders must post a few thousand dollars per contract in margin before opening a futures position. The purpose of margin is to minimize the risk of default. Customers post margin with FCMs and the FCMs post margin with the clearing house, which guarantees payment on all contracts.

[7] As reported in Greg Meyer, " MF Global fallout revives regulatory calls," *Financial Times*, November 10, 2011.

[8] Details of how such transfers are permitted can be found in 17 C.F.R. §§ 190.01 through 190.10 (the "Part 190 Regulations"), and in Reg. 190.06(g). See "Emergency Motion Of James W. Giddens, Trustee For The Liquidation Of MF Global Inc., For An Order Approving The Transfer Of Certain Segregated Customer Commodity Positions And Extending The Trustee's Authorization To Operate The Business Of MF Global Inc. In The Ordinary Course," Case No. 11-2790 (MG) SIPA.

[9] CFTC, "Brief Description of Steps Taken by CFTC in MF Global," handout at briefing for Senate staff, November 14, 2011.

[10] 17 C.F.R. §1.12 ("Maintenance of minimum financial requirements by futures commission merchants and introducing brokers"). As noted above, MF Global did report the missing funds by telephone.

[11] "Safeguarding Customers Through Segregated Funds," *Managed Futures Today*, February 2011, available at http://www.cmegroup.com/managed-futures/Feb2011/safeguarding-customers-through-segregated-funds.html. (CME Group, formerly the Chicago Mercantile Exchange, is the largest futures exchange in the world. It has regulatory responsibilities as a "self-regulatory organization.")

[12] "CME Clearing Financial Safeguards," p. 10, http://www.cmegroup.com/clearing/files/financialsafeguards.pdf.

[13] In December 2010, the CFTC proposed a rule dealing with swap customer funds in bankruptcy, which appears to provide a stricter segregation standard for swaps than what now applies to futures. CFTC, "Protection of Cleared Swaps Customers Before and After Commodity Broker Bankruptcies," *Federal Register*, vol. 75 (December 2, 2010), p. 75162.

[14] Richard Hill, "CFTC Adopts Rule Tightening Investments Permissible With Client Funds," *BNA Daily Report for Executives*, December 6, 2011.

[15] CFTC does not have legal authority to force an FCM into bankruptcy.

[16] Jerry DiColo, Dan Strumpf, and Gina Chon, "Purgatory for MF Global Customers," *Wall Street Journal*, November 16, 2011, p. C2.

[17] According to the SIPC trustee, this represented about 60% of the collateral associated with those positions at the time of the bankruptcy, and was the "maximum relief available under the law and the circumstances, and it averts mandatory liquidation of the transferred positions under governing CFTC rules." See "Message to Former Customers of MF Global Inc.," November 7, 2011. Online: http://dm.epiq11.com/MFG/Project/default.aspx.

[18] CME Group Advisory Notice 11-415, "Update on Transfers of MF Global Inc. Customer Positions and Collateral -Revised – 11/15/2011."

[19] "Message To Commodities Claimants Of MFGI," November 10, 2011, at http://dm.epiq11.com/MFG/Project/default.aspx.

[20] "Judge OKs $520 Million Payout to MF Global Customers," Reuters, November 17, 2011, athttp://www.nytimes.com/reuters/2011/11/17/business/business-us-mfglobal-payout.html?_r=1&hp.

[21] "Statement from the Office of the Trustee for the Liquidation of MF Global Inc. On Judge's Approval of Third Transfer and Securities Accounts Sale," Press Release, December 9, 2011. (http://dm.epiq11.com/MFG/Project/default.aspx).

In: Collapse and Bankruptcy of MF Global ISBN: 978-1-62417-710-1
Editor: Tao Zhu

Chapter 2

THE COLLAPSE OF MF GLOBAL*

U.S. House of Representatives

> "The goal here is not to be a prop trader. ... I don't think that we will be in a risk-taking position, substantial enough to have it be the kind of thing that the rating agencies would say 'holy cow, these guys got a different business strategy' than what we told them we had."
>
> -Jon Corzine, May 20, 2010

MF GLOBAL PRIOR TO JON CORZINE'S ARRIVAL

Company Origin and Growth

MF Global traces its origin back 229 years to a sugar brokerage business founded by James Man in London in 1783. In 1869, the business became known as E.D.&F. Man. It set up its first overseas operations in New York and Hong Kong in 1972, and began trading commodities futures. The company expanded its services in 1983 to include investment management, and by 1994, when it first listed on the London Stock Exchange, it had $1 billion in funds under management.[1]

In 2000, E.D.&F. Man spun off its agricultural commodities business and changed its name to Man Group plc.[2] Under the leadership of Kevin R. Davis,

* This is an edited, reformatted and augmented version of the Subcommittee on Oversight and Investigations of the House Committee on Financial Services, dated November 15, 2012.

who joined the company in 1991 and rose to become the Chief Executive Officer (CEO) of Man Financial (Man Group's global brokerage businesses), the company sought to capitalize on the rapid growth in global derivatives markets by acquiring businesses offering new products, including futures, options, and other derivatives.[3]

Man Group acquired 17 companies in 18 years, including GNI Holdings Ltd. in 2002 and Refco Inc. in 2005.[4] GNI was a leading European broker of futures and options, foreign exchange, and equity derivative products, and its acquisition established the Man Group, through Man Financial, as the world's largest independent futures broker.[5] Refco was a regulated futures brokerage with client accounts and assets in the U.S., Singapore, Canada, and India, and its acquisition further expanded Man Financial's global brokerage services.[6]

Following these acquisitions, and fueled by the growth of the derivatives industry, Man Financial became one of the leading brokers of exchange-listed futures and options in the world, providing execution and clearing services for exchange-traded and over-the-counter derivative products, as well as for non-derivative products and securities in the cash market.[7]

The company served more than 130,000 active client accounts, and held leading market share on the biggest exchanges in North America and Europe, including the Chicago Mercantile Exchange (CME), CBOT, the New York Mercantile Exchange, and Eurex.[8] The company also had a global footprint, with 34 offices in cities such as New York, Chicago, London, Paris, Mumbai, Hong Kong, Singapore, and Sydney.[9]

Man Financial more than doubled its exchange-traded brokerage volume between 2004 and 2007, increasing both revenues and operating margins, and reported net income of $188 million on revenue of $5.7 billion for the fiscal year ending March 31, 2007.[10]

The Man Group Spins off MF Global

In 2007, Man Group decided to separate its brokerage businesses from its asset management businesses and announced that it would spin off Man Financial into an independent, Bermuda-incorporated company named MF Global.[11] In order to finance the spinoff, MF Global entered into a $1.4 billion unsecured committed revolving credit facility (bridge loan) with several institutions, the net proceeds of which the new company would use to repay its obligations to Man Group and third parties.[12]

On July 18, 2007, MF Global announced an initial public offering (IPO) of 97.38 million shares that would trade on the New York Stock Exchange (NYSE) under the ticker symbol "MF."[13] The offering, which was priced at $30 per share, generated $2.92 billion in capital, making it the second-largest NYSE-listed IPO of 2007.[14] Although share prices fell 15% in the first week of trading, they recovered by the end of the year to close at $31.47, with a corresponding market cap of nearly $3.8 billion.[15]

Unauthorized Trading Incident Shatters Investor Confidence

During the early morning hours of February 27, 2008, Evan Dooley, a registered trader in MF Global's Memphis office, began placing orders on wheat futures for his personal account through a home computer linked to the company's proprietary system.[16] Dooley accumulated a net short position in wheat futures totaling over 16,000 contracts, well in excess of his trading limits.[17] MF Global did not discover Dooley's trades until the price of wheat had increased, resulting in a loss of $141.5 million.[18] As a clearing member of the exchange through which Dooley had traded, MF Global was obligated to cover Dooley's losses.[19]

When the company announced the unauthorized trading the following day, share prices fell nearly 28% to close at $21.29.[20] On February 29, 2008, Fitch Ratings (Fitch) put MF Global on negative watch, citing deficiencies in its risk-management system, and Standard & Poor's (S&P) downgraded the company's credit rating to BBB with a "CreditWatch Negative" placement, indicating that it could lower the rating further based on its review of the company's risk management policies.[21]

On March 17, rumors of a liquidity crisis at the company sent share prices as low as $3.64 a share, prompting the CFTC to issue a statement indicating that "MF Global is currently in compliance with the agency's regulatory financial requirements."[22] The CME Group also issued a statement reflecting that "all clearing members, including MF Global … remain in good standing and continue to meet all of their obligations to the clearing house."[23] Although these statements helped stabilize MF Global's share price that day, the company's stock closed at $6.05, marking a 79% decrease in value in just three weeks.[24] Dooley's rogue trading and the resulting loss had shattered investor confidence in the company.

Efforts to Restore Investor Confidence Falter

In the aftermath of Dooley's unauthorized trading, MF Global was leveraged at almost 39-to-1, with $18.6 billion of its operating capital coming from short-term repurchase agreements, and would soon announce quarterly and fiscal year-end losses.[25] The company needed capital to repay the bridge loan maturing in December and sought ways to strengthen its capital structure. On May 20, 2008, MF Global announced that it entered into an agreement with a private equity fund controlled by J.C. Flowers & Co. LLC, in which the fund, J.C. Flowers II L.P., agreed to provide a backstop commitment of $300 million toward the sale of equity-linked securities.[26] MF Global planned to use the proceeds from the sale to repay a portion of its bridge loan.[27] Under the terms of the commitment, J.C. Flowers II L.P. would purchase a minimum of $150 million and a maximum of $300 million of perpetual convertible preferred shares.[28] Each preferred share paid a 6% annual dividend and was convertible at any time to common stock at an initial conversion price of $12.50 per share.[29] J.C. Flowers II L.P. also had the right to appoint up to two directors to MF Global's board of directors.[30]

At the time, M.F. Global's investors and its board welcomed the investment. J.C. Flowers & Co.'s managing director, J. Christopher Flowers, had a positive reputation on Wall Street.[31] Flowers had made partner at Goldman Sachs at the age of 30, and eventually headed the investment bank's financial services deals business.[32] Leaving Goldman in 1998, Flowers went on to orchestrate the buy-out of Long-Term Credit Bank of Japan — the first time foreigners had bought a Japanese bank — and then founded and managed several private equity funds.[33]

The J.C. Flowers deal appeared to momentarily calm investors. In June 2008, MF Global was able to enter into a five-year, $1.5 billion committed unsecured revolving credit facility (liquidity facility) with a syndicate of banks.[34] The company used proceeds from this liquidity facility to pay down $350 million of its bridge loan.[35] On June 18, the company announced that it would issue $150 million of convertible preferred shares and $150 million of convertible senior notes in two private offerings and use the proceeds to further pay down its bridge loan.[36]

However, in the press release announcing the offering, MF Global also disclosed for the first time that "the narrowing of short term credit spreads has had a negative impact on net interest income and overall pre-tax margins."[37] This news, which pertained to a major source of the company's revenue, renewed panic among investors and prompted Moody's Investor Service

(Moody's) to assign MF Global's credit rating a negative outlook.[38] On June 18, the day of the announcement, the company's stock fell more than 43%, to close at $7.83 a share, erasing nearly all of the previous three months' gains.[39] The Wall Street Journal noted that the announcement "left analysts and investors yearning for more information."[40]

MF Global continued to seek sources of capital and restore investor confidence throughout June and July 2008. It sold its previously-announced convertible preferred shares and senior notes on June 20, albeit with higher than anticipated annual dividend rates, reflecting the higher risk premium demanded by the market.[41] On July 18, the company sold an additional $150 million of convertible preferred shares to J.C. Flowers II L.P. paying an annual dividend of 9.75%, which it used to repay more of the bridge loan.[42] Also on July 18, the company entered into a credit agreement with several banks that provided for a two-year, $300 million unsecured term loan facility, which would enable it to repay the remaining balance on its bridge loan.[43] Finally, MF Global announced on July 29 that it had appointed David I. Schamis to its board and that he would serve on the company's audit committee.[44] J. Christopher Flowers had nominated Schamis, a managing director J.C. Flowers & Co. L.L.C., using the authority granted to J.C. Flowers II L.P. to appoint up to two directors under its investment agreement with MF Global.[45] Despite these efforts, the company's stock continued its precipitous fall, closing at just $4.34 on September 30, with a corresponding market cap of only $522.1 million.[46]

A New Strategy Stalls

With the company's efforts to restore investor confidence faltering, MF Global's board of directors sought a change in the company's leadership. On October 28, 2008, the company announced that its board had appointed Bernard W. Dan, the former President and CEO of the Chicago Board of Trade (CBOT), as CEO to replace the long-serving Kevin Davis.[47] Investors reacted favorably to Dan's appointment; the company's stock rallied 80% in the week following the announcement.[48] Dan immediately sought to further boost investor confidence by embarking upon a new strategy: in December, MF Global contacted the New York Fed to express interest in its U.S.-based subsidiary, MFGI, being designated as a "primary dealer."[49]

Primary dealers act as counterparties to open market operations executed by the New York Fed in furtherance of U.S. monetary policy as determined by the Federal Open Market Committee.[50] To be eligible for consideration as a primary dealer, a company must meet minimum capital standards and have the capacity to make markets for the New York Fed, regularly participate in treasury auctions, and provide market commentary and information and analysis.[51] Because of these requirements, the New York Fed historically has tended to select larger, well-established, and well-known financial institutions.[52] Over time, market watchers have come to regard a primary dealer designation as a "Good Housekeeping' seal of approval," enhancing the company's standing in the marketplace.[53]

By securing a primary dealer designation from the New York Fed for MFGI, MF Global hoped to capitalize on what it believed that market watchers would perceive as its enhanced franchise value — a value that could translate into new business lines and new customers. However, the company's strategy immediately ran into three problems. Two of the issues involved the company's incorporation in Bermuda. First, the Primary Dealers Act of 1988 prohibited the New York Fed from designating a subsidiary of a foreign-owned company as a primary dealer unless the country in which the parent was domiciled provided the same opportunities to U.S. companies as it did to domestic firms in the underwriting and distribution of government debt.[54] Because the New York Fed had not previously determined whether Bermuda met this requirement, it would have to study the country before it could designate MF Global's subsidiary as a primary dealer. This process would take time and had an uncertain outcome. Secondly, there were reputational concerns associated with Bermuda's well-known status as a tax haven.[55] When the New York Fed communicated this information to MF Global, the company indicated that it was considering switching jurisdictions.[56]

MF Global faced a third problem as well. In April 2009, the New York Fed contacted the CFTC and learned that MF Global was the subject of an investigation regarding the Dooley incident and one other matter.[57] In late April, the New York Fed informed MF Global that it had suspended consideration of MFGI's application pending resolution of the CFTC's investigation.[58] During this suspension period, MF Global executives tried to engage the New York Fed regarding the application, but were rebuffed and cautioned not to publicize its aspirations to be a primary dealer.[59] Concerned about, among other things, the public perception of designating any company as a primary dealer soon after regulatory action had been taken against the company, the New York Fed considered revising its primary dealer policy to institute a "cooling off" period beginning at the announcement of an enforcement action by a regulatory agency.[60]

On December 17, 2009, the CFTC issued its order against MF Global, citing the company for "risk supervision failures in four separate instances between 2003 and 2008," including the Dooley incident, and directing it to pay a $10 million fine and hire an outside consultant to review its risk management, supervision, and compliance programs.[61] The same day, MF Global contacted the New York Fed to express the company's eagerness to "re-engage" regarding MFGI's primary dealer application.[62] On January 11, 2010, the New York Fed released its revised primary dealer policy.[63] The revised policy required a two part application, established a formal application review procedure, and specified that the New York Fed would not designate as a primary dealer "any firm that is, or recently has been (within the last year) subject to litigation or regulatory action or investigation that [it] determines material or otherwise relevant to the potential primary dealer relationship."[64] MFGI formally submitted the first part of its primary dealer application on January 13, 2010, and submitted the second part on January 22.[65] In accordance with its new policy, the New York Fed determined that the CFTC order was material, and on January 26 informed MF Global that MFGI could not be named a primary dealer before December 17, 2010 (one year following the date of the CFTC order).[66]

The following day, Dan sent a letter to the New York Fed laying out MF Global's case for why a one-year delay would be unfair, asking the New York Fed to exercise its discretion to name MFGI a primary dealer before the expiration of the one-year period, and requesting a meeting to discuss the matter.[67] At the meeting on February 23, 2010, MF Global executives expressed concern about the length of time MFGI had been under consideration as a primary dealer and about the New York Fed's revised policy, which could further delay its designation.[68] New York Fed staff members reiterated that they had evaluated MFGI's application in accordance with the bank's revised primary dealer policy and that the company could not be designated as a primary dealer until after December 2010.[69] The New York Fed's decision thus stalled MF Global's primary dealer strategy — a strategy that the company had been pursuing since December 2008 — for at least another eleven months.

A Flawed Business Model Revealed

Unlike many of its competitors, MF Global was not affiliated with a larger financial institution, nor did it generally engage in non-brokerage businesses such as investment banking, asset management, or principal investment activity, including proprietary trading.[70] As an independent futures and options broker, MF Global generated most of its income from four sources: commissions from executing client orders on an agency basis; commissions from clearing services; mark-ups from client trades executed on a matched-principal basis; and interest income earned on cash and margin balances in client accounts as well as interest related to fixed income activities.[71] Accordingly, MF Global suffered from a fundamental flaw in its business model: because the company had not diversified its sources of revenue, it was vulnerable to a prolonged economic downturn affecting its areas of core profitability.

By the time MF Global learned that its primary dealer strategy had stalled, the financial crisis of 2008 had deepened into a global economic downturn which depressed both derivatives trading volume and interest rates and choked off MF Global's income. At the CME, average trading volume fell 20 percent and the total notional value of contracts traded on its exchanges fell by a third.[72] Additionally, monetary actions taken by several countries also resulted in ultra-low interest rates around the world.[73] In the United States, for example, the Federal Reserve System's Federal Open Market Committee reduced the target federal funds rate from 4.75 percent in 2007 to 0 to .25 percent by the end of 2008.[74]

MF Global's revenues collapsed in response to these developments. For fiscal years 2009 and 2010, the total volume of exchange-traded futures and options transactions that MF Global executed and cleared fell by 20 percent.[75] With fewer derivatives orders to execute and clear, MF Global's annual net commission revenue fell by 32 percent over the same time period (from $796 million to $544 million).[76] Additionally, the interest rate spreads that MF Global could realize by reinvesting client cash and margin balances shrunk significantly, resulting in declining interest revenue.[77] Over the five fiscal quarters between October 1, 2007, and December 31, 2008, for instance, MF Global's gross interest revenue decreased by 87 percent, from $1.26 billion to just $154 million.[78]

Credit rating agencies took notice of MF Global's shrinking revenues. On December 4, 2008, S&P changed the company's BBB credit rating outlook to negative because of its lower cash flows and a decline in customer payables.[79] On January 16, 2009, Moody's downgraded MF Global's credit rating to Baa2 from Baa1, noting a "weakening in MF Global's earnings generation ability" and predicting that MF Global's "revenues [would] continue to come under pressure over the coming quarters."[80] On February 25, S&P affirmed its BBB rating and negative outlook, noting that it expected MF Global to continue to face "revenue challenges and elevated competitive pressures."[81] On September 24, S&P again affirmed its BBB rating and negative outlook, noting that it expected MF Global would continue to have lower trading volumes and reduced interest income, which would likely reduce its revenue over the coming quarters.[82] Finally, on November 6, 2009, Moody's noted a "sharp increase in MF Global's balance sheet leverage" and assigned a negative outlook to its Baa2 ratings.[83]

The End of an Era

By 2010, MF Global faced serious financial difficulties. The company's stock, which had once traded above $30 per share, now traded for under $10, representing a reduction in market capitalization of over $2 billion.[84] The Dooley trading incident shattered investor confidence in the company, and its efforts to restore confidence, including its application to become a primary dealer, had faltered and stalled. MF Global was highly leveraged at above 35-to-1, and it lacked diversified revenue streams with which to combat the effects of the global economic downturn.[85] Additionally, the company had lost money three years in a row, reporting net losses of $69.54 million in fiscal year 2008, $48.61 million in fiscal year 2009, and $136.97 million in fiscal year 2010.[86]

On March 17, 2010, amid these financial difficulties, Bernard Dan resigned as CEO of MF Global, citing personal reasons.[87] His resignation came just 16 months into his term, and less than a month after the New York Fed delayed consideration of MFGI's primary dealer application. Dan's departure marked the end of an era for MF Global. The company's next Chairman and CEO would soon steer the company away from its roots as an independent futures and options broker and take the company in an entirely new direction.

THE JON CORZINE ERA

Corzine Appointed CEO of MF Global

MF Global's board moved quickly to replace Dan following his resignation. David Schamis immediately contacted J. Christopher Flowers to ask whether Jon Corzine would be interested in the position.[88] Securing an executive with Corzine's reputation and experience was viewed as a potential coup for MF Global. After a 23-year career at Goldman Sachs in which he rose from a bond trading desk to become the company's Chairman, Corzine served five years as a U.S. Senator and then four years as New Jersey's Governor.[89]

The timing for approaching Corzine was opportune: Corzine had lost his gubernatorial reelection bid only months earlier. Additionally, Schamis knew that Flowers would be ideal to approach Corzine with MF Global's offer. In addition to Flowers' private equity fund investing in MF Global, Flowers and Corzine were good friends.

Flowers and Corzine had worked together at Goldman Sachs, where Flowers had been instrumental in helping Corzine take Goldman Sachs public, and Flowers had later helped manage Corzine's blind trust after Corzine entered public service.[90] Additionally, Flowers had already been in contact with Corzine about the possibility of helping manage one of his company's private equity funds.[91]

Once Flowers approached Corzine with MF Global's offer, Corzine quickly accepted the position. On March 23, 2010, just six days after Dan's resignation, MF Global announced that Corzine would join the company as its Chairman and CEO.

The company agreed to pay Corzine a $1.5 million salary and a $1.5 million signing bonus, and established a $3 million target performance bonus for the year.[92] At the same time, J.C. Flowers & Co. LLC announced that Corzine would become a partner in its third private equity fund in a lucrative deal that significantly enhanced the compensation package offered by MF Global.[93]

Investors reacted favorably to Corzine's appointment as MF Global's CEO. MF Global's stock price jumped more than 12 percent the day after the company announced his appointment, and continued to rise thereafter, increasing 33 percent within three weeks.[94] The credit rating agencies also viewed Corzine's appointment favorably. An S&P analyst wrote that the company "[was] more credible and [had] a better chance to get where it wants to go with Corizine [sic] as CEO."[95]

Moody's discounted the abruptness of the transition between Corzine and Dan in light of "Mr. Corzine's decades of first-rate industry and leadership experience, as well as the reputational 'cache' [sic] and potential industry connections he would bring to MF Global."[96]

A New Environment for a Wall Street Veteran

MF Global was a new environment for Corzine. Although he had worked in the upper echelons of finance and politics, he had never worked in the futures industry, nor had he ever run a public company. The company's rapid expansion through acquisition had created nearly fifty direct or indirect subsidiaries located around the world, resulting in a disjointed corporate structure subject to supervision by multiple regulators with overlapping jurisdictions in multiple countries. As a holding company, MF Global derived 83 percent of its income from net revenue generated by six regulated subsidiaries, five of which were located outside of the United States.[97] MFGUK, for instance, was authorized and regulated by the United Kingdom's Financial Services Authority, but also had branch offices in the Netherlands and France authorized under the European Union's "passport" system, as well as a representative office in Switzerland licensed by the Swiss Financial Market Supervisory Authority.[98] MF Global Canada Co. was registered with the Investment Industry Regulatory Organization of Canada as well as with each of the regional securities commissions in the Canadian provinces and territories in which it operated.[99] MF Global Singapore Pte. was licensed by the Monetary Authority of Singapore, but also had a branch office in Taiwan licensed by the Financial Supervisory Commission, Executive Yuan, Republic of China and registered with another Taiwanese authority, the Chinese National Futures Association.[100] MF Global Australia Limited was registered with the Australian Securities and Investment Commission and authorized by the New Zealand Securities Commission.[101] MF Global Hong Kong Limited was licensed by the Securities and Futures Commission.[102]

MF Global's sixth regulated subsidiary, MFGI, was based in the United States.[103] Unlike most other jurisdictions, the United States regulates the securities and futures industries separately.[104] Because MFGI had both securities and futures customers, it was registered as a "broker-dealer" with the Securities and Exchange Commission (SEC) and as a "futures commission merchant" (FCM) with the CFTC.[105] As a registered broker-dealer, MFGI was also a member of the Financial Industry Regulatory Authority (FINRA), a self-regulatory organization (SRO) for the securities industry.[106] The Chicago Board Options Exchange (CBOE), another securities industry SRO, served as MFGI's "designated examining authority" for purposes of conducting yearly examinations of its finances and operations.[107] Similarly, as a registered FCM, the company was a member of the National Futures Association (NFA), a futures-industry SRO, and of all U.S. futures exchanges through which it cleared trades, including the CME Group, which served as its "designated self-regulatory organization." As such, the CME Group examined MFGI's records in accordance with protocols established by a group of futures-industry SROs, including examinations of MFGI's customer funds and its capital levels.

As a publicly-traded company, MF Global filed annual and quarterly reports with the SEC providing a comprehensive overview of the company's business and financial condition.[108] Because MFGI was also a broker-dealer and FCM, it was subject to the rules of the SEC and the CFTC that protect a registered company's customers, counterparties and creditors. Both the SEC and CFTC, for instance, have a "net capital" rule to ensure that registered companies have enough liquid assets on hand to pay off their liabilities quickly if they fail. Under both rules, a registered company must maintain a minimum level of "net capital," which, defined broadly, is the amount of current (liquid) assets the company holds in excess of its liabilities.[109] In calculating current assets, the rules impose "haircuts" on certain types of securities and futures, which are discounts from the present value of the assets to reflect the fact that they may have to be sold for less than market value in a rapid liquidation.[110]

Because MFGI was subject to oversight by both regulators, the company calculated its capital requirements according to both regimes, and complied with the higher capital requirement.[111] MFGI complied with the SEC's rule because, during the period in question, that rule provided a higher requirement than the CFTC's.[112] To ensure that it was properly capitalized, MFGI determined its level of net capital on a monthly basis and reported the amount to the SEC, the CFTC, and its SROs in a monthly report, known as the Financial and Operational Combined Uniform Single Report (FOCUS report).[113]

The SEC and CFTC each have separate rules governing the protection of customer property.[114] For securities customers, the SEC's "customer protection" rule requires a broker-dealer to maintain physical custody or control of all fully paid and excess margin customer securities and to segregate cash held on deposit in customer accounts to ensure that customer funds are not used as a source of capital for the company's operations.[115] To help ensure that a broker-dealer can readily return all customer property quickly in the event of failure, the broker-dealer must maintain a special reserve bank account holding an amount of cash or cash-equivalent securities greater than or equal to the amount of net obligations owed to customers as a result of daily trading activities.[116]

For futures customers, the CFTC had different "customer protection" rules for property held by an FCM for trading by customers on U.S. exchanges and property held for trading on foreign exchanges.[117] For customer property held for use on U.S. exchanges, an FCM must maintain a "segregated" account into which it deposits the property.[118] The balance of the segregated account must at all times be greater than or equal to the net liquidated value of all customer property.[119] An FCM may deposit its own funds into the segregated account as a cushion to prevent a shortfall of customer funds, but if it subsequently withdraws its funds from the account, the amount withdrawn cannot exceed the amount of this cushion.[120] For customer property held for use on foreign exchanges, an FCM must maintain a "secured" account that holds an amount that is greater than or equal to the "secured amount," which is defined as the aggregate amount of funds required to support each customer's open foreign futures and options positions, plus or minus gains or losses on those positions (the "Alternative Method").[121] Because the "secured amount" represents an FCM's minimum obligation under the rule, an FCM, if it chooses, may set aside funds equal to the net liquidated value of all customer property (the "Net Liquidation Method").[122] The difference between these two methods is that the Alternative Method does not require customer ledger or cash balance amounts to be included in the secured account, whereas the net liquidation method does.[123] The Alternative Method thus permits an FCM to maintain a lower minimum secured account balance than would be required under the Net Liquidation Method.[124]

On a daily basis, an FCM must determine (1) the account balances of its segregated and secured accounts, (2) the amounts required to be deposited by rule, and (3) the amounts of any excess it has deposited therein.[125] MFGI used the Alternative Method to calculate the amount required to be set aside in secured accounts, one of only five companies out of 55 FCMs that carried foreign customer funds to do so.[126] MF Global referred to the amount of its own funds maintained in MFGI's segregated and secured accounts as "Firm Invested in Excess."[127] Additionally, MF Global calculated the difference between the amount MFGI would be required to hold in its secured accounts under the Net Liquidation and Alternative Methods, and referred to the difference internally as "Regulatory Excess."[128]

Beginning in 2005, the CME Group required MFGI to report regulatory balances in the company's segregated and secured accounts on a daily basis; MFGI filed these statements with the CFTC, the CME Group, and the NFA.[129] Because MFGI used the Alternative Method to determine the minimum required balances in its secured accounts, MFGI did not report the amount of Regulatory Excess on its daily secured statements.[130]

Corzine Creates Strategic Plan for MF Global

When Corzine became CEO of MF Global, he initiated a comprehensive review to assess the company's challenges and opportunities.[131] Corzine quickly learned that MF Global had two options for returning to profitability. One option would be to cut costs and wait for the global economy to improve. Corzine rejected this option, telling colleagues: "By doing nothing, you're making one of the biggest bets, ever. You're betting on interest rates."[132] The second option would be to seek new sources of revenue by branching out into new business lines.[133] Corzine pursued this option.

Over the course of 2010, Corzine, along with his senior management, crafted a strategic plan to transform MF Global into a full-service global investment bank within three to five years.[134] This plan, which was described by financial journalists as creating a "mini-Goldman," contained several elements.[135] First, MF Global would reorganize its business lines to expand into new services.[136] Second, in tandem with its reorganization, the company would also recreate its employee base and compensation structure to better support its planned new activities.[137] Third, MF Global would finally secure MFGI's designation as a New York Fed primary dealer.[138] Fourth, the company would begin trading with its own funds as a means of generating profits to satisfy investors and avert further ratings downgrades while completing its transformation into an investment bank.[139]

Corzine Begins Implementing His Strategic Plan

Corzine lost no time in implementing his ambitious new strategic plan. He immediately began reorganizing MF Global's business lines by expanding its role in client facilitation, market-making, and principal activities; centralizing its retail services under a global brand; and consolidating its clearing and financing activities under one business group.[140] Additionally, he laid the groundwork for providing asset management, underwriting, structured finance, and advisory opinion services with a specialized focus on commodities and natural resources markets.[141]

To support these changes, Corzine also began to overhaul MF Global's employee base. The company laid off 10-15 percent of its 3,200 employees and began hiring new employees to undertake the company's planned services.[142] For these new hires, the company restructured compensation agreements by eliminating lockup provisions and tying bonuses to business unit profitability rather than broker performance alone.[143] Corzine also made significant changes to MF Global's senior management. On September 13, 2010, he hired Bradley Abelow as the company's Chief Operating Officer (COO).[144] Abelow had previously worked with Corzine at Goldman Sachs and later served as Corzine's Chief of Staff while he was governor of New Jersey.[145] Corzine also promoted Henri J. Steenkamp, the company's Chief Accounting Officer, to Chief Financial Officer (CFO), displacing the company's former-CFO, J. Randy MacDonald.[146]

Corzine also redoubled efforts to secure MFGI's primary dealer designation from the New York Fed, telling reporters that the designation was a "major part of his strategy to increase [company] revenue."[147] In April 2010, Corzine requested an opportunity to visit to the New York Fed's offices to discuss MFGI's candidacy.[148] New York Fed staff members had followed Corzine's appointment as MF Global's Chairman and CEO with interest, noting that his hiring was an indication that the company had "turned the corner on many fronts."[149] Even though officials at the New York Fed had found MF Global's Dan-era efforts to secure primary dealer designation "very aggressive (borderline obnoxious)" and had recently postponed approval of MFGI's application in response to the CFTC's regulatory action, the New York Fed agreed to Corzine's meeting request.[150]

Corzine visited with the New York Fed on June 1, 2010.[151] Following that visit, the New York Fed acted quickly on MFGI's application. Staff members discussed the company's candidacy with the CFTC on June 3, met internally for formal review sessions on August 5 and September 23, and visited the company's headquarters on November 4.[152] Following the visit, New York Fed staff members indicated that they "[d]o not see any showstoppers and expect we will escalate for more formal approval sometime in Dec [sic] with operationalization [sic] early in new year."[153] The New York Fed proceeded to approve MFGI's application soon thereafter, securing final approvals in January 2011 — just after the company's one-year waiting period had expired — and publicly announcing the company's designation as a primary dealer on February 2, 2011.[154]

While MF Global pursued the primary dealer designation for MFGI, the company also began using its own funds in an effort to generate additional revenues. In some cases, MF Global used its money to facilitate client transactions by taking the other side of a trade entered into by a client.[155] The company also used its funds to "make markets" in particular securities.[156] Although these principal transactions helped MF Global post a modest profit of $8.8 million for its fiscal quarter ending June 30, 2010, they did not produce the levels of revenue necessary to sustain long-term profitability and fund the company's transformation into an investment bank.[157] Increasingly, Corzine looked to proprietary trading — using MF Global's own funds to take positions from which the company hoped to profit, if the market moved as it expected — as a way to further boost revenues.

To achieve the kinds of gains that Corzine sought, new employees with trading experience would be needed. To that end, in June 2010, Corzine formed a new division known as the Principal Strategies Group and hired new employees tasked with identifying trading strategies for the company.[158] Corzine also maintained a portfolio within the Principal Strategies Group in order to personally execute proprietary trades.[159] MF Global's policies provided that an officer could make trades only if a more senior officer reviewed and approved the trades.[160] Because Corzine was the highest ranking officer at MF Global, he technically could not trade under this policy; however he reached a compromise whereby a subcommittee of the board of directors reviewed his trades, as well as any he directed others to place.[161]

The Principal Strategies Group soon identified what it thought was a promising trading opportunity. During the European debt crisis, sovereign bonds issued by several countries were trading at heavily discounted prices out of fear that these financially-troubled countries would default on their obligations.[162] On May 9, 2010, twenty-seven European nations created the European Financial Stability Facility (EFSF), a bailout fund meant to preserve financial stability in Europe by providing financial assistance to Eurozone countries experiencing acute economic difficulty.[163] Corzine and the Principal Strategies Group believed that this fund, which would not expire for several years, would protect the holders of short-maturity sovereign bonds against the risk of default.[164] They also believed that the bond markets had not fully incorporated this decreased risk into the price of the bonds, which created an opportunity to exploit the price dislocation and realize an unusually high return by acquiring the underpriced bonds and holding them to maturity.[165]

Despite Corzine's confidence in the profitability of an investment in the bonds, the investment — were MF Global to buy the bonds outright — would expose MF Global to volatility in its financial statements until the bonds reached maturity. Most of the bonds matured in either 2011 or 2012, which meant that MF Global would have to hold the bonds for a year or more before it realized profits on its investment.[166] Under the Generally Accepted Accounting Principles (GAAP) promulgated by the Financial Accounting Standards Board (FASB), the value of the bonds would have to be marked to market as assets daily and changes in value would have to be accounted for in the company's profits and losses.[167] If the bonds lost value before maturity, for instance, MF Global would have to report a loss until the company could redeem the bonds for par value at maturity.[168]

Because of this risk to the company's income statement and the time it would take to realize gains, a direct investment in the bonds themselves would not achieve Corzine's objectives. However, the company discovered that it could book quick profits by purchasing the bonds and then using them as collateral in a transaction known as a repurchase-to-maturity (RTM) agreement.[169]

Traditional repurchase agreements are frequently used by companies to secure short-term financing.[170] A company, for instance, might sign an agreement with a counterparty in which the company agrees to sell securities or other assets to the counterparty and to repurchase the same or similar assets from the counterparty at a future date for an agreed-upon price.[171] Usually, the amount of cash the counterparty gives to the company is less than the fair market value of the securities or other assets.[172] This difference is known as the initial margin or "haircut" and protects the buyer against a decrease in the value of the assets prior to their resale to the company, illiquidity of the assets, and counterparty credit risk.[173] The initial margin level varies depending upon the credit rating of the security sold.[174] The counterparty to a repurchase agreement also usually has the right to demand additional margin (in other words, make a "margin call") during the term of the agreement to maintain the value of the collateral in cases where the value of the underlying assets falls during the term of the agreement.[175] The counterparty can also require a company to post additional margin if it questions the company's creditworthiness.[176] These additional types of margin are known as "variation margin," and can expose a company that is a party to a repurchase agreement to liquidity risk if margin calls require the company to post cash and sell securities to cover its obligations.[177] Under FASB's accounting standards, traditional repurchase agreements are accounted for as a secured borrowing in which the company recognizes cash as proceeds from the transaction, together with a liability for the repurchase price specified in the agreement.[178] The collateral remains on the company's balance sheet as an asset, and any impairment to the collateral would be recognized in earnings over time.[179]

An RTM differs from a traditional repurchase agreement in one important respect. In a traditional repurchase agreement, the securities held by a counterparty are returned to the borrowing company before the securities collateralizing the borrowing reach maturity.[180] By contrast, in an RTM transaction, the counterparty keeps the pledged securities as collateral until they mature, whereupon the counterparty may either return the securities to the borrowing company or redeem them from their issuer at par value.[181] Under FASB's accounting standards, because a counterparty may redeem securities from an issuer at maturity rather than return them to the borrowing company, the borrowing company surrenders effective control of the securities when it transfers them as collateral to the counterparty.[182] Accordingly, FASB accounting standards require that the borrowing company account for the transaction as a "sale" of the securities coupled with a forward repurchase commitment, rather than a secured borrowing.[183] The forward repurchase commitment must be accounted for as a derivative at fair market value on the company's balance sheet, with changes in value recognized concurrently in income.[184] While the borrowing company retains the default and liquidity risks associated with the securities serving as collateral, the securities are "derecognized" from the company's balance sheet because they are deemed to be sold by the borrowing company at the time it enters into the RTM transaction with the counterparty.[185]

MF Global learned that by entering into RTM transactions collateralized with European sovereign bonds (European RTM trades) it could realize an immediate profit on the difference between the interest the issuer of the bonds paid to MF Global and the rate the company paid to its counterparty to repurchase the bonds, and that it could derecognize the bonds from its balance sheet.[186] Armed with an investment strategy that he believed could book instant profits for MF Global without affecting its balance sheet and a belief that the EFSF mitigated against sovereign default risk, Corzine ordered the company to place its first European RTM trades.[187]

In the late summer of 2010, MFGUK, on MFGI's behalf, bought approximately $1 billion of bonds issued by Ireland, Italy, Portugal, and Spain.[188] MFGUK then sold the bonds to MFGI, which used them as collateral in intercompany RTM transactions with MFGUK. MFGUK then entered into further RTM transactions, which cleared through LCH.Clearnet (LCHC).[189] This arrangement was necessary because only MFGUK maintained a trading relationship with LCHC.[190] At the time, all of the bonds serving as collateral were considered investment grade, so LCHC required margin as low as 3% to support the trades.[191] Once MF Global entered into the European RTM trades, it booked a profit on the difference between the interest paid by the issuer of the bonds and the repurchase rate specified in the RTM transactions that it cleared through LCHC, and then derecognized the bonds from its balance sheet.

Corzine Expands European Sovereign Debt Portfolio

Under MF Global's internal policies and procedures, the company's trades were normally subject to review by internal risk managers and multiple layers of management.[192] While MF Global's European RTM trades continued to be reviewed by the risk management department, the board of directors made decisions about the firm's risk appetite and whether the positions exceeded that risk appetite beginning after September 2010.[193] Staff from the Principal Strategies Group regularly updated Corzine on movements in the prices of trades supporting the company's European RTM trades.[194] Corzine, who had taken personal responsibility for the trades, communicated directly with MF Global personnel about the trades, and sometimes instructed them when to enter and exit various positions.[195] In setting the company's risk appetite regarding the European RTM trading strategy, the board normally relied upon the input of Corzine and the firm's chief risk officer, Michael Roseman.[196]

By September 2010, MF Global had increased its European RTM portfolio to between $1.5 billion and $2.0 billion.[197] As Corzine pushed for even more trades, Roseman began to question them based on liquidity risk concerns relative to the company's approved risk appetite.[198] Roseman met with Corzine to express his concerns, and the two agreed to consult MF Global's board of directors at its mid-September board meeting.[199] At the meeting, Corzine pushed for an overall exposure of $4 billion, which the board approved.[200] The same month, Corzine retained a search firm to find a new chief risk officer for the company.[201]

As MF Global's portfolio approached its $4 billion limit in late October of 2010, Roseman became further concerned about the liquidity risks and potential capital at risk of the European RTM trades, and again met with Corzine to express his views.[202] MF Global's board of directors met shortly thereafter, on November 8, 2010.[203] At the board meeting, Corzine sought, and the board approved, an increase in the company's European RTM portfolio limit to $4.75 billion.[204] Also in November, Corzine informed Roseman that he would no longer report directly to the board, but would report instead to Abelow, the company's COO and Corzine's long-time colleague.[205]

On November 5, 2010, MF Global announced a $38.7 million loss for the fiscal quarter ending on September 30.[206] That same month, LCHC imposed a 15% haircut on certain Irish bonds owned by MFGI, forcing the company to meet a margin call.[207] Later that month, S&P downgraded MF Global's rating to BBB-, just one notch above junk status.[208] S&P attributed MF Global's continued weak performance to lower volumes, low interest rates, and changes in the company's operating strategy.[209] S&P also noted that it expected Corzine's strategic plan to increase the company's risk profile and delay its return to profitability over the near- to medium-term.[210]

In January 2011, Corzine dismissed Roseman and replaced him with a new chief risk officer, Michael Stockman.[211] Like Roseman, Stockman reported to Abelow, the COO.[212] In preparing for his new position, Stockman met with Roseman, at which time the two discussed the European RTM trades as an item of interest to MF Global.[213] Stockman also reviewed minutes of board meetings from November and December at which risks associated with the European RTM trades were discussed.[214]

On February 3, 2011, MF Global reported another loss of $4.7 million for the fiscal quarter ending December 31, 2010.[215] The same day, Moody's noted MF Global's "weak" credit metrics and stated that it would evaluate "[o]ver the next four to six quarters...whether MF Global can 1) reengineer the franchise to generate annual pre-tax earnings in the $200M-$300M range, 2) keep balance sheet leverage in the 20x range, and 3) maintain the necessary liquidity and risk management discipline as it executes its...strategy."[216] At the end of February, Stockman met with Martin Glynn, a member of MF Global's board of directors, in part to discuss Glynn's background and visions for MF Global.[217] Before the meeting, Glynn informed Stockman that one of his concerns was the level of risk associated with MF Global's European RTM portfolio.[218] Glynn told Stockman that he would "be under tremendous pressure...to approve higher risk limits in non core areas to support earnings weaknesses elsewhere."[219]

Corzine continued to push forward with his European RTM trading strategy. In early March, MF Global's board of directors approved — with the newly-hired Stockman's support — a further increase in the company's portfolio limit to $5.8 billion until March 31, 2011, for the bonds of Ireland, Italy, Portugal, and Spain, at which time the limit for those countries would decrease to $5 billion.[220] In late March, the board of directors extended the temporary limit of $5.8 billion to September 30, 2011, including a separate $1 billion limit for Belgium.[221]

On May 20, MF Global reported its fiscal 2011 year-end results.[222] The company lost $81.2 million, $46.5 million of which came in the fiscal quarter ended March 31, 2011.[223] At the time, the value of MF Global's net European RTM portfolio was approximately $6 billion.[224] At a board meeting two weeks later, in early June, Corzine requested another portfolio limit increase to $8.4 billion.[225] When the board asked to meet without management present, Corzine said, outside the board's presence, that if the board didn't think he was the "right guy," maybe they "should find someone else [to run the company]."[226] After a discussion in which board members expressed concern about the company's European sovereign debt exposure, the board approved limits of $6.6 billion for Belgium, Italy, and Spain, and of $1.9 billion for Ireland and Portugal, for a total limit equaling $8.5 billion.[227] Stockman offered conditional support for the increase, provided that Henri Steenkamp, MF Global's CFO, ensured that the firm had adequate liquidity to meet stress scenarios.[228] MF Global's net exposure on its European RTM portfolio reached $6.4 billion at the end of June.[229]

By July 2011, as market conditions in Europe deteriorated, Stockman became concerned about an increasing risk of margin calls and bond default, and met twice with Corzine, Steenkamp, the company's sovereign debt and finance desk traders, and members of the company's Risk Department to discuss the European RTM portfolio.[230] During the meetings, Stockman provided detailed information about MF Global's daily sovereign risk report and liquidity stress scenarios and recommended that the company enter into "hedging" RTMs as a means of reducing the firm's net exposure.[231] Stockman advised that "Europe could get worse before it gets better," and recommended that the company develop a contingency plan to reduce MF Global's European sovereign debt exposure.[232] On July 30, 2011, Stockman memorialized his concerns and recommendations in an e-mail to Corzine, explaining that he did not support further increasing MF Global's European sovereign debt position, and recommended entering into more hedges to reduce the company's net exposure.[233]

By August 2011, the company's net European RTM position had reached approximately $7.4 billion.[234] This amount represented almost 14% of MF Global's assets and four-and-a-half times its total equity, and when measured as a percentage of equity or assets, the amount was significantly greater than its far larger competitors.[235] At the board's August 11 meeting, Corzine stated — this time in the presence of directors — that the board should consider replacing him as CEO if it no longer had confidence in his ability to run the company.[236] Stockman spoke about the continued risks to MF Global from its European sovereign debt positions and revealed that the company could need between $246 million and $930 million in additional funding to support margin calls and haircuts, if the value of the bonds further decreased.[237] Rather than using hedges as the primary means to reduce the company's exposure, which the board and Corzine deemed too costly, the board decided to cap MF Global's portfolio and allow the European RTM trades to "roll off" as the underlying bonds reached maturity, which would allow the company's net position to decrease over time.[238] The board also ordered management to prepare a "break the glass" plan, which outlined how the MF Global would respond to a credit downgrade and the liquidity demands arising from consequent margin calls.[239] The plan, which was distributed to the board in mid-October, noted that the European RTM trades were "the biggest draw on cash today" and that the company "need[ed] a clear strategy" for how to manage the trades in the event of a downgrade.[240] The plan estimated that MF Global had sufficient liquidity to "manage through one month under a severe stress event."[241]

MF Global's Independent Auditor Advises the Company to Enhance Disclosures about its European RTM Trades

When MF Global began entering into European RTM trades in September 2010, it accounted for the transactions as sales of the collateralized European sovereign bonds, which the company derecognized from its balance sheet, coupled with forward commitments to repurchase the bonds, which the company accounted for as derivatives. Because FASB's accounting standards require companies to mark-to-market the value of derivatives, MF Global sought to determine the fair value of the derivatives associated with the forward commitment.[242] The company used a valuation model that considered changes in value of the European bonds that collateralized the European RTM trades and changes in value of the forward repurchase commitments.[243] MF Global stated that in addition to these two factors, it further estimated the probability that the sovereign issuer would default on the bonds collateralizing the European RTM trades and then used the probability as a factor discounting the valuation of the derivatives.[244] The company determined that gains or losses attributable to the changing values of derivative were so small that they were immaterial for reporting purposes as of the end of September.[245]

On November 5, 2010, MF Global filed its unaudited quarterly 10-Q report with the SEC for the fiscal quarter ending on September 30, 2010.[246] The report did not specifically state that the company had entered into RTM transactions collateralized with European sovereign debt, but stated generally that "we also enter into certain resale and repurchase agreements that are accounted for as sales and purchases and accordingly de-recognize the related assets and liabilities from the unaudited consolidated balance sheet."[247]

Beginning in December 2010, PwC pressed MF Global to disclose more information about the European RTM trades in the company's regulatory disclosures.[248] In light of the requirement that companies value derivatives at fair value, PwC additionally advised MF Global that it should revise the methodology by which it valued the derivatives associated with the European RTM trades.[249] According to MF Global executives, PwC counseled that the company should not consider the probability of a default as a separate component in valuing the derivative, specifically, a change that could cause the company to recognize gains or losses.[250]

On December 23, PwC partners met with Corzine and other senior management at MF Global to discuss, among other things, the company's accounting of the European RTM trades, including its valuation of the derivatives.[251] In PwC's view, the meeting went poorly.[252] Corzine did not want to discuss accounting specifics and complained that he would not have entered into the European RTM trades if he had understood that marking the derivatives to market could result in volatility in the company's profits and losses.[253] PwC staff's impression of the meeting was that Corzine characterized the accounting and valuation requirements as a "PwC issue, and not [MF Global's]."[254] Additionally, PwC's staff described Corzine as feeling "ambushed," "bushwhacked," and extremely unhappy by PwC's advice.[255]

In January 2011, MF Global adopted a revised valuation methodology to better capture changes in the value of the derivative due to changes in the market value of the European bonds and repurchase agreement rates.[256] Pursuant to the revised valuation methodology, the company valued the derivative resulting from its European RTM trades at $60,000 for the quarter ended December 31, 2010, an amount that the company deemed immaterial for reporting purposes.[257] PwC tested the new methodology, which did not incorporate any discrete probability-of-default factor, and determined that it was appropriate given readily available information.[258] At the same time, MF Global told PwC that it was "in the process of enhancing their disclosures given the increased trading activity in the RTMs."[259]

On February 3, 2011, MF Global filed its 10-Q report for the quarter ended December 31, 2011.[260] In the report, MF Global disclosed that it "enters into securities financing transactions that mature on the same date as the underlying collateral" and that it "accounts for these transactions in accordance with the accounting standard for transfers and servicing and recognizes a gain or loss on the sale...of the collateral assets, and records a forward commitment [to repurchase the collateral]."[261] While the company did not state whether it accounted for the forward commitment as a derivative at fair value, it disclosed that it had "exposure to the risk of default of the issuer of the underlying collateral assets, such as U.S. government securities or

European sovereign debt."[262] Finally, MF Global disclosed the total value of all of the securities it had sold under agreements to repurchase during the quarter, but did not specifically disclose the amount that had been collateralized by European bonds.[263]

MF Global discussed its European RTM trades in detail in the fiscal year 2011 10-K report it filed with the SEC on May 20, 2011.[264] In a section of the 10-K report entitled "Off-Balance Sheet Arrangements and Risk," MF Global explained that it entered into "[c]ertain resale and repurchase transactions involv[ing] the sale and repurchase of the underlying collateral[,] which generally mature on the same date as the underlying collateral," and that some of these transactions were collateralized by the obligations of European sovereign issuers.[265] The company further disclosed that it retained exposure not only to the risk of default of the issuer, but also to the risk of margin calls to the extent the value of the collateral decreased.[266] MF Global also noted that market risks associated with the European RTM trades included, but were not limited to, "interest rate, credit spread, rating downgrade and issuer default risks."[267] Finally, the company reported that it had invested in the bonds of Belgium, Ireland, Italy, Portugal, and Spain, that these bonds matured not later than December 2012, and that its net position in European RTM trades was $6.3 billion.[268]

Elsewhere, in the fiscal year 2011 10-K, MF Global stated that it accounted for forward repurchase commitments as derivatives that are marked-to-market, and that changes in the value of the derivatives "may cause volatility" in its financial results.[269] In separate statements filed by MFGI with the SEC, FINRA, and CBOE, the company disclosed that losses associated with these derivatives were immaterial as of March 31, 2011.[270] As a result, MF Global neither recorded the derivatives as assets or liabilities on its consolidated balance sheet, nor did it reflect any losses or gains attributable to the derivatives on its income statement.[271]

Mounting Liquidity Strain

By the summer of 2011, it had become clear to MF Global that Corzine's strategic plan had increased the company's liquidity demands.[272] In June, MF Global's internal auditors assessed the processes and controls in place to manage the company's liquidity.[273] The auditors found numerous and significant gaps between the company's liquidity policies and existing practices. Among other problems, the internal auditors found that "existing liquidity reporting is manual in nature," that MF Global had never established a "formal liquidity management framework," and that "existing performance of formal stress testing and scenario analysis is not adequate to fully assess liquidity and capital needs."[274]

After observing MF Global's continuous losses and business changes, SEC staff requested a meeting with MFGI executives on June 14, 2011.[275] At the meeting, MF Global staff, including Corzine, discussed the company's organizational and managerial changes, its progress implementing its strategic plan, and its liquidity, market, and credit risk management practices.[276] MFGI also provided a presentation that depicted its financial health relative to that of MF Global's.[277] As liquidity demands increased, MF Global looked to additional sources of capital to support its operations. The company could draw from its $1.5 billion liquidity facility and could secure short-term financing through traditional repurchase agreements. Increasingly, however, the company began to turn to excess funds on deposit with its FCM accounts as a source of liquidity. In July, Henri Steenkamp discussed with Christine Serwinski, MF Global's North American CFO, whether the company's "Regulatory Excess" — the amount of futures customer funds deposited in secured accounts in excess of the regulatory requirement under the Alternative Method — could be loaned to the company to help meet its liquidity needs.[278] At the time, the amount of "Regulatory Excess" maintained by the company averaged about $1 billion.[279] After consulting with colleagues and the company's attorneys, Serwinski determined that the CFTC's rules did not prohibit MF Global from using the Regulatory Excess.[280] She advised Steenkamp, however, that she did not agree with using customer funds from the FCM to provide liquidity to the broker-dealer.[281] Serwinski advised Steenkamp that MF Global should consider only "Firm Invested In Excess" funds to satisfy its liquidity needs, which were the company's own funds deposited in the segregated and secured accounts.[282] From time to time, the company used this cushion for overnight and intraday transfers to help meet liquidity demands.[283] According to the trustee for MFGI's liquidation, however, the company also used a part of the Regulatory Excess at times for intraday funding during its last week of operation.[284] By September, LCHC required MF Global to post more than $400 million in margin to cover its positions.[285] In early October, Steenkamp informed Corzine that the company needed to address its sustained liquidity stress.[286] Steenkamp cautioned that reliance on excess funds on deposit in the FCM should be temporary, but was becoming permanent.[287] He noted that MFGI's broker-dealer business was unable to fund itself, in part, because of the "permanent pool of liquidity" needed for MF Global's European RTM trades.[288] Steenkamp tasked two MF Global employees with presenting options that MF Global could immediately take to alleviate the company's liquidity pressure.[289]

Dispute with FINRA

In light of the Eurozone debt crisis, FINRA adopted a heightened focus on the European sovereign debt exposure for firms it supervised.[290] In September 2010, FINRA contacted MF Global to determine whether the company had sovereign debt in its inventory.[291] MF Global answered that it did not, even though it had begun to enter into the European RTM trades.[292] FINRA first learned of the RTM trades shortly after reviewing MFGI's March 2011 FOCUS report.[293] In particular, FINRA observed that MFGI reported a $38 million loss for the month of March, which was considerably larger than the company reported in prior months.[294] When FINRA contacted MFGI to ascertain the reason for the large loss, it learned that the company had reallocated a portion of the revenue it earned from the European RTM trades to MFGUK in order to better reflect the market value of the services that MFGUK performed in managing the trades.[295] FINRA then reviewed MFGI's Annual Audited Financial Statements, filed in May 2011.[296] These statements contained written descriptions of the trades.[297]

After reviewing MFGI's disclosures, FINRA, in consultation with staff from the SEC and CBOE, concluded that the SEC's net capital rule required MFGI to take "capital charges" against its European sovereign bond positions as if they were on the company's balance sheet, notwithstanding that the bonds had been accounted for as "sold," in accordance with GAAP.[298] FINRA believed that for purposes of determining whether the company possessed sufficient liquid assets to satisfy its obligations in the event of liquidation, the SEC's net capital rule required the bonds collateralizing the European RTM trades to be considered in the calculation of MF Global's level of net capital, regardless of how they were treated for accounting purposes.[299] While recognizing the bonds as assets would not affect the company's equity, MF Global would have to treat the bonds as non-convertible debt securities for purposes of deducting haircuts in the company's net capital computation.[300]

MF Global pressed FINRA to demonstrate why the net capital rule required the company to take a capital charge on the European bonds that collateralized the RTMs.[301] In meetings with FINRA staff members, MF Global argued that the capital treatment of its European RTM trades should be governed by previous guidance issued by the SEC, which did not require companies to take haircuts or capital charges on U.S. Government securities used to collateralize RTMs, given that they present no risk of default and are highly liquid.[302] MF Global believed that this guidance should also govern the capital treatment of the European bonds that collateralized its RTMs because the risk that European nations would default on the bonds the company held was virtually non-existent.[303] MF Global additionally argued that it should not have to record a capital charge because GAAP rules allowed it to derecognize the bonds from its balance sheet.[304]

FINRA staff members responded by noting that MF Global had indicated in its regulatory filings that the company retained the default risk on its European bonds and that this risk was non-trivial.[305] FINRA pointed to the fact that LCHC, through which MF Global cleared its European RTM trades, required MF Global to post significant margin to support the positions.[306] In FINRA's view, the SEC's guidance for RTMs backed by U.S. Treasuries was inapplicable in determining the capital treatment of the European bonds.[307]

When FINRA refused to change its position, Corzine and other MF Global representatives took their case to the SEC, arguing that FINRA was re-interpreting the rule and that a capital charge was not required.[308] In MF Global's view, the extended discussions about the RTMs' capital treatment reflected the uncertainty surrounding a complex issue.[309] SEC staff members, however, were surprised to learn that MF Global had not taken haircuts on its European bonds, and found the company's representatives to be unfamiliar with published SEC guidance interpreting the net capital rule.[310] SEC staff believed that the capital charge was "cut and dry" and that there was never any doubt about what the net capital rule required.[311] In the SEC's view, MF Global should have, at a minimum, asked the agency about the regulatory net capital treatment of the European bonds before entering into the European RTM trades.[312] Accordingly, the SEC agreed with FINRA that MF Global was required to take a capital charge against its European RTM positions.[313]

THE COLLAPSE OF MF GLOBAL

FINRA Imposes Capital Charge

When it became clear to MF Global that the SEC agreed with FINRA's interpretation of the net capital rule, MF Global sought to negotiate the size of the capital charge that FINRA would impose.[314] In an August 11, 2011 memorandum to FINRA, MFGI requested that, for purposes of imposing haircuts under the net capital rule, the Belgian, Italian, and Spanish bonds collateralizing its RTM portfolio be treated as if they were U.S. bonds, and that its lower-rated Irish and Portuguese bonds be treated as if they were corporate bonds.[315] Additionally, MFGI argued that the standard haircuts set forth in the net capital rule encompassed several risk components such as default, settlement, market, liquidity, reputational, and legal risk, and because the only risk facing the company's bonds was default risk, the haircuts FINRA imposed on its Belgian, Italian, and Spanish bonds should be discounted by 80 percent to reflect only the default risk component.[316] Based on this requested treatment, MFGI calculated that the regulatory capital charge imposed by FINRA would total $55.8 million.[317]

FINRA rejected MFGI's proposed capital treatment, indicating that there was no justification for treating bonds within the company's portfolio as different types of securities based on either the country of issuance or credit rating, nor was there any justification for imposing haircuts smaller than those required under the net capital rule.[318] FINRA categorized the bonds collateralizing MFGI's European RTM portfolio as nonconvertible debt securities and calculated regulatory haircuts of approximately $257 million.[319]

In discussions with FINRA, Steenkamp indicated that infusing capital into MFGI could impede MF Global's growth opportunities, which FINRA understood to be a reference to the company's strategic plan.[320] Nevertheless, in anticipation of the charge, MFGI took steps to ensure that it would have net capital sufficient to exceed both the required minimum level and FINRA's early warning notification level.[321] MF Global increased MFGI's excess net capital by $183 million to $287 million as of August 24, 2011, which ensured that the subsidiary had adequate capital after accounting for the effect of FINRA's capital charge.[322] However, because FINRA applied the capital charge retroactively, FINRA rules required MFGI to amend its most recent FOCUS report to reflect a $150 million deficiency in net capital for the month of July.[323] As a result, the company was also required to file notices of net capital deficiency with the SEC and CFTC, and MF Global was required to amend its quarterly 10-Q filing for the quarter ended June 30, 2011.[324] In the amended 10-Q filed on September 1, MF Global disclosed that FINRA had required the company to "modify its capital treatment of certain repurchase transactions to maturity collateralized with European sovereign debt and thus increase its required net capital pursuant to SEC Rule 15c3-1" but that it had "net capital sufficient to exceed both the required minimum level and FINRA's early-warning notification level."[325] MF Global further stated that it did not believe that the increase in net capital would have a "material adverse impact on its business, liquidity or strategic plans" and that it expected that "its regulatory capital requirements will continue to decrease as the portfolio of these investments matures."[326]

The CFTC first learned of FINRA's capital charge on August 25, 2011 when MF Global sent its notice of net capital deficiency to the agency.[327]

Media Reports Capital Charge

Although FINRA's capital charge against MFGI became public on September 1, 2011, when MF Global filed its amended 10-Q, news of the charge did not become widely known until seven weeks later. On the morning of October 17, the Wall Street Journal published an article detailing the capital charge and noted that "the move underscores regulators' growing concerns about the exposure of financial firms to sovereign debt" and "highlights the potential perils surrounding the aggressive strategy employed by Mr. Corzine, the firm's chief executive."[328] Investors reacted to the news: MF Global's share prices fell 6 percent to close the day's trading at just \$3.71.[329]

The news came at an especially bad time for MF Global. The company was set to release its quarterly earnings report on October 27, which would announce a net loss of \$191.6 million, the company's worst performance ever, and had scheduled meetings with the ratings agencies that week to discuss its performance.[330] After meeting with Moody's on Friday, October 21, MF Global anticipated that Moody's would likely downgrade the company's credit rating.[331] Over the weekend, Steenkamp pleaded with Moody's not to downgrade the company, insisting that its "capital and liquidity has never been stronger" and that it "is in its strongest position ever as [a] public company."[332]

MF Global's Final Days

Monday, October 24, 2011

Steenkamp's weekend plea went unanswered. On October 24, 2011, Moody's downgraded MF Global's credit rating to "Baa3," one notch above junk status, explaining that "[t]he rating action reflects Moody's view that the current low interest rate environment and volatile capital markets conditions make it unlikely that MF Global, in the near term, will be able to achieve the financial targets that Moody's had previously specified were required for it to maintain its Baa2 rating."[333] Moody's also noted that MF Global's exposure to "European sovereign debt in peripheral countries and its need to inject capital into its broker-dealer subsidiary to rectify a regulatory capital shortfall highlights the firm's increased risk appetite and raises questions about the firm's risk governance."[334] Moody's analysts had recently discovered MF Global's position in European RTM trades when Moody's downgraded the company.[335] Moody's also placed MF Global's rating under review for possible further downgrade.[336]

Later that day, Corzine addressed MF Global employees in an e-mail stating: "While I am disappointed by this action, it bears no implications for our clients or the strategic direction of MF Global...Many of our peers are experiencing similar changes to their counterparty credit ratings...I believe in our strategy, our employees and our path ahead."[337] To calm worried investors, Corzine announced that the company would be moving up Thursday's planned earnings announcement to Tuesday morning at 7:30 a.m.[338]

Tuesday, October 25, 2011

During the earnings call on Tuesday morning, Corzine and Steenkamp disclosed the company's quarterly loss and sought to reassure analysts about MF Global's prospects. Corzine said that although there were "no excuses" for the company's performance, he remained committed to his strategic plan, and that "the long-term return profile of an investment bank is attractive."[339] Additionally, he minimized the significance of FINRA's capital charge, stating that the action was not specific to MF Global in relation to capital and that the company was "dealing with an actual regulatory reinterpretation of the haircuts [the regulators] apply" to European sovereign debt holdings.[340] Corzine also sought to clear up "clouded perceptions" about the company's European RTM portfolio, asserting that the trades had "relatively little underlying principal risk" and had realized "zero" loss.[341] "On a personal note," Corzine added, "our positions and the judgment about risk mitigation steps are my personal responsibility and a prime focus of my attention."[342] Regarding the Moody's credit downgrade, Corzine stated that "we are disappointed with the action quite obviously" but that "we think we can grow our earnings" and that MF Global was continuing to work with Moody's in its credit assessment by "walking through with them...some of the strategic actions we're thinking about," including increasing capital through "asset sales of non-core holdings."[343] Steenkamp closed his explanation of the company's financial condition by stating, "I'm proud to say that our capital structure has never been stronger," and that "despite these uncertain and volatile times, we feel good about…our liquidity position as well as the strategic direction and progress against the plan."[344]

Corzine's and Steenkamp's assurances to analysts, however, did little to quell investor panic. When the NYSE opened for trading that morning, the trading volume for MF Global's stock surged to more than eleven times the volume of the day before. The stock, which opened at $3.31, traded as low as $1.75 during the day and closed at just $1.86, marking a decline of approximately 44 percent.[345]

MF Global's customers and counterparties also reacted to the earnings news, and as the crisis deepened, MF Global faced a liquidity drain of crisis proportions.[346] Several of the company's biggest securities and futures customers closed their accounts or withdrew funds.[347] MF Global's counterparties to its European RTM trades began to demand additional margin and deeper haircuts on bonds posted as collateral.[348] One counterparty, HSBC pulled MF Global's line of credit and ordered the company to wind up its business with the bank by the end of the year.[349]

Wednesday, October 26, 2011

On October 26, 2011, S&P placed MF Global's BBB- credit rating on "CreditWatch Negative," noting that "continued volatility in the capital markets and low interest rates could further harm MF Global's ability to generate capital."[350] S&P also noted that the company's exposure to European RTM trades was "very high compared to the company's loss absorbing capital base," though S&P mistakenly asserted that the European RTM trades were "entered…as a means to facilitate client trades," rather than proprietary investments.[351] S&P believed that MF Global's future business plans "could entail increased risk taking as it transforms itself into a full-service investment bank."[352]

That day, consistent with the Alternative Method, MFGI reported excess funds of approximately $1 billion in segregated and secured accounts as of the close of business on Tuesday, though the company's internal records showed that it had only $21.5 million of its own funds in the accounts. Edith O'Brien, the company's assistant treasurer, authorized $615 million in intraday transfers from the company's FCM customer accounts.[353] Because these transfers exceeded the amount of MFGI's "Firm Invested in Excess" funds, the difference came from customer funds.[354]

The SEC advised MFGI that it wanted to meet with the company's managers the next day to discuss liquidity, funding, financial statement condition, and regulatory computations, and that the CFTC would also participate in the meeting.[355] MF Global also held a conference call with FINRA and CBOE to discuss similar issues.[356]

Thursday, October 27, 2011

On Thursday, Moody's and Fitch both downgraded MF Global's credit rating to junk status.[357] Moody's cited "weak core profitability" that had "contributed to [MF Global] taking substantial risk in the form of its exposure to European sovereign debt in peripheral countries."[358] Fitch cited continued challenges in reducing the company's leverage and achieving sustained profitability, especially because low interest rates reduced the revenue generated by MF Global's commodity business.[359] Fitch also stated that "significant headwinds" made it more difficult for the company to complete its "strategic transformation from a pure broker to a broker-dealer and, longer term, to a full investment bank without [taking on] outsized incremental risk."[360] Additionally, Fitch said that "increased risk taking activities" had left the company "vulnerable to potential credit deterioration and/or significant margin calls."[361]

These downgrades sparked increasing margin calls and further contributed to an exodus of customers. MF Global had to draw $805 million from its liquidity facility, leaving the credit line totally depleted.[362] LCHC demanded an additional $211 million in margin to cover the company's European RTM trades.[363] The Depository Trust & Clearing Corporation, another clearing house used by MFGI, reduced the amount of credit it extended to the company to settle trades by $234 million.[364] Similarly, the Fixed Income Clearing Corporation increased MFGI's margin requirement and withheld cumulative excess margin of approximately $108.9 million.[365] Counterparties also increased haircut demands, and some counterparties stopped trading with MFGI altogether, leaving $606 million of the company's securities "in the box," meaning that the company could not find a counterparty to lend it money against these securities in a repo transaction.[366] Customers began withdrawing funds from the company's customer accounts.[367]

On Thursday, the SEC and the CFTC met with MF Global executives to conduct a risk review.[368] The CME Group also sent members of its audit department to review the segregated and secured account balance statements that MFGI had filed as of close of business on Wednesday.[369] The CME Group sent a letter to Serwinski, instructing her that "effective immediately," any equity withdrawals "must be approved in writing by CME Group's Audit Department."[370]

Late on Thursday evening, JPMorgan Chase bank (JPMC) began putting all of MF Global's accounts on "debit alert."[371] Once on debit alert, JPMC would execute funds transfers as instructed by MF Global only after determining funds present in the account to be debited were adequate to support the requested transfer.[372] As part of the debit alert process, JPMC terminated its uncommitted intraday credit lines to MF Global.[373] The bank's intraday credit lines to MF Global were similar to overdraft protection, and provided unsecured liquidity to the company in support of different types of funds transfers from MF Global's cash accounts at JPMC.[374] The debit alert "caused significant delay in the settlement of [certain cash] transactions" instructed by MF Global, "even when [JPMC] ultimately determined that MFGI had 'good funds' on deposit to permit the transaction to settle."[375] JPMC also sent a team to MF Global's New York headquarters to aid the company's efforts to unwind its securities lending arrangements in order to generate liquidity.[376]

Friday, October 28, 2011

In the prior day's confusion, MFGUK overdrew several of its accounts with JPMC by approximately $175 million.[377] MF Global was trying to sell roughly $5 billion in bonds with the help of JPMC to shrink the company's balance sheet and generate liquidity, but JPMC informed Corzine that "they would not engage in those transactions until the overdrafts in London were cleaned up."[378] Corzine therefore contacted MF Global's Chicago office and asked them to resolve the overdrafts.[379]

To cover the overdrafts, O'Brien approved and processed a $200 million wire transfer from one of MFGI's customer segregated accounts to one of the company's "house" accounts.[380] O'Brien then authorized a $175 million transfer from the same "house" account to an MFGUK account at JPMC in London.[381] O'Brien noted in an e-mail that the $175 million transfer to pay the JPMC overdraft was "per [Jon Corzine's] direct instructions."[382] When O'Brien authorized the $200 million wire transfer, she had not yet received the segregation statement detailing customer fund balances for the previous day because Matthew Hughey, MF Global's Regulatory Capital Controller, was still preparing them.[383]

Because JPMC was the depository bank for certain of MF Global's customer funds, it subsequently observed that MF Global had moved $200 million from one of the company's customer accounts to its "house" account just before MF Global transferred $175 million from that "house" account to cover the overdraft.[384] JPMC's Chief Risk Officer, Barry Zubrow, called

Corzine to seek an assurance that the money transferred from the customer segregated account did not represent customer funds.[385] The bank then sent Corzine a letter, to be signed by O'Brien, that sought an assurance that all transfers from MF Global's segregated customer accounts complied with the CFTC's customer protection rules.[386] In response to requests from MF Global, JPMC revised the letter twice to narrow its focus to the transfers in question.[387] However, despite MF Global staff's oral assurances to JPMC that O'Brien would sign the narrowed version of the letter, neither O'Brien nor any other representative of MF Global ever did so.[388]

Hughey completed his preliminary review of the segregated and secured calculations as of the close of business on Thursday. He was surprised to find that the company was deficient in its segregated accounts by over $300 million. Hughey initially believed the apparent deficiency resulted from a failure to account for several wire transfers. He contacted representatives of MF Global's Treasury department to reconcile the numbers, but found them to be atypically unresponsive. Given the fast-approaching noon deadline for submitting the MFGI's segregated and secured statements to regulators and the concern surrounding the large deficiency in segregated accounts, Hughey and his colleague, Philip Cooley, approached O'Brien to discuss the problem. When Hughey and Cooley arrived at O'Brien's office to discuss the matter, she said that she was very busy. The two men found O'Brien to be aloof and non-responsive to their concerns about the deficiency in the segregated customer accounts. O'Brien asked Jason Chenoweth, an accountant who worked for her, to handle the matter.[389]

Chenoweth ushered Hughey and Cooley into a separate room where they worked to reconcile the deficiency. After reviewing the wire transfers, Chenoweth determined the deficiency was a result of five transactions – totaling $540 million – that were booked incorrectly. Hughey and Cooley manually adjusted the segregated statement by $540 million, which resulted in a reported excess of $200 million in the segregated statement.[390]

Shortly after Hughey made the manual adjustment, he contacted Serwinski, who was on vacation, to inform her that Chenoweth had reconciled the deficiency in the segregated account, but stated that he had not yet received backup documents to support Chenoweth's conclusions.[391] After speaking with Serwinski, Hughey filed the company's segregated and secured statements showing the excess balance of roughly $200 million.[392] Serwinski then told Hughey that he and his team must report to the office early Saturday morning to get a head-start on preparing the Friday close of business segregated and secured statements.[393]

At approximately 6:00 p.m. on Friday night, the New York Fed suspended MF Global from conducting new business as a primary dealer.[394]

Saturday, October 29, 2011

On Saturday morning, Hughey and his team prepared initial drafts of the segregated and secured statements for Friday that showed a deficit in segregated customer funds of over $900 million.[395] MF Global's Treasury Department assured Serwinski's staff that the shortfall must have resulted from reconciliation errors and that the customer accounts were not undersegregated.[396] The company did not inform its regulators about the apparent shortfall in segregated customer funds and its efforts to reconcile the shortfall.[397]

Meanwhile, MF Global's senior management was attempting to sell all or part of the company and to unwind its proprietary investments, including the European RTM trades.[398] At 5:30 p.m., Corzine updated regulators about the company's negotiations with potential purchasers and the company's asset sales.[399] Corzine had identified Interactive Brokers, LLC as a potential buyer, and executives for both companies worked through the weekend to negotiate the terms of a deal.[400]

Sunday, October 30, 2011

Throughout the weekend, CFTC Chairman Gary Gensler and CFTC staff expressed concern that the amounts on deposit in MF Global's foreign secured accounts were less than what the company owed to commodity customers who traded on foreign exchanges.[401] Because MF Global used the "Alternative Method" of calculating funds to set aside in those accounts, it did not have to deposit all customer money in the accounts. As a consequence, officials from the CME Group encouraged the company to move more funds into the accounts.[402]

The concern that there would be a shortfall in amounts owed to customers, despite the fact that MF Global was technically in compliance with the rules, prompted Chairman Gensler to remark that the CFTC should consider whether to abandon the Alternative Method.[403] On Sunday, Chairman Gensler wrote to a colleague that he had spent too much of the weekend focused on gaps in part thirty customer funds.[404] He stated MF Global gave him "more reasons…to consider proposals to modify part 30 rules," which governed the safekeeping of funds deposited by customers for trading abroad.[405]

Also on Sunday, CFTC staff recognized that most funds that were held in foreign secured accounts were located with MFGUK and other foreign entities.[406] Of the funds held by MFGUK, CFTC staff wanted to know the amount of the funds, how they were being held by the UK affiliate, if the funds were safe and secure, and the issues with getting the funds back to U.S. customers.[407]

CFTC staff set a 1:00 p.m. deadline on Sunday afternoon for MF Global to provide information on its customer-segregated funds statement for Friday.[408] As of 2:57 p.m., MF Global staff was working to determine the balances and liabilities for the accounts.[409] The CFTC insisted that MF Global submit information on the segregated statement by 3:00 p.m.[410] The CFTC's Chief Counsel for Clearing and Risk e-mailed MF Global's offices of Treasury and General Counsel stating that the lack of data and supporting documentation was driving adverse inferences.[411] Separately, the CFTC's Chief Counsel wrote to colleagues, "This is NOT good."[412] In an e-mail to the director of the SEC's Division of Trading and Markets, SEC Chairman Mary Schapiro related Chairman Gensler's view that MF Global had not been forthcoming with the CFTC and that, as a result, "they face enforcement."[413]

Around 3:00 p.m., CFTC staff in MF Global's Chicago office saw a draft of the company's customer-segregated funds statements for Friday showing that there was a deficiency in customer accounts.[414] The CFTC staff informed CME Group staff of the apparent shortfall.[415] Throughout the afternoon and evening, MF Global staff and MF Global's regulators worked to obtain more information on the shortfall.[416]

Around 7:00 p.m., MF Global staff spoke with the CFTC and the CME Group.[417] During that discussion, the company attributed the deficiency in the segregated account to an accounting error.[418] Serwinski arrived at the company's Chicago office around 9:00 p.m.[419] As late as 10:00 or 11:00 p.m., Serwinski and O'Brien continued to convey their belief to regulators that the shortfall was due to an accounting error.[420] By midnight, however, neither the CME Group's auditors nor MF Global staff had been able to identify any error that could explain the deficiency.[421]

Monday, October 31, 2011 and Tuesday, November 1, 2011

At 12:40 a.m. on Monday, October 31, 2011, a CME Group audit-team member e-mailed his colleagues to inform them that Serwinski would "look into coming up with additional funds to transfer into segregation as a contingency" if the accounting error was not identified.[422] Soon thereafter, O'Brien informed Serwinski that she believed that the shortfall in customer segregated funds calculated by the company was not the result of an accounting error and that customer funds were in fact missing from the segregated accounts.[423] O'Brien provided a document that showed the deficiency to be the result of three types of transactions: (1) intra-day loans between MF Global's FCM and its broker-dealer; (2) the funding of client withdrawals from the broker-dealer; and (3) the $175 million transfer to cover MFGUK's overdrawn JPMC account on October 28.[424] Together, these transactions totaled $909 million.[425]

At approximately 2:00 a.m. on Monday morning, O'Brien and Serwinski informed the CME Group that customer funds were missing from segregated accounts.[426] During a conference call at approximately the same time, MF Global's senior management also informed the company's regulators of the deficiency.[427]

Before the markets opened on Monday morning, Serwinski sought to identify assets that MFGI could deposit in the company's customer segregated accounts in order to mitigate any shortfall.[428] Among other assets, Serwinski identified approximately $220 million in excess company funds deposited in a reserve account, which the company maintained for its securities customers.[429] Though the SEC had expressed concern to MF Global about the calculation of excess funds in the reserve account and cautioned the company against transferring these funds, MFGI transferred the full amount of the perceived excess to its segregated FCM customer accounts.[430]

On Monday, Matthew Hughey considered whether the $175 million transfer from MFGI to MFGUK affected MFGI's net capital levels.[431] MF Global staff had not consulted with staff from the company's Finance Department, including Serwinski and Hughey, before making the transfer the previous Friday.[432] Upon review, however, Hughey determined that the $175 million transfer was a "non-allowable asset" for purposes of computing MFGI's net capital.[433] Hughey concluded that MFGI's equity (and thus its net capital level) would be reduced to the extent that MFGI could not perfect a security interest in collateral owned by MFGUK equal to the value of the transfer.[434] After consulting with colleagues, Hughey concluded that MFGI could assert a lien against MFGUK assets valued at $120 million, and reduced the amount of the "nonallowable asset" accordingly.[435] There is no indication that MF Global staff consulted with MFGI's regulators or SROs before executing the transfer, despite the fact that it potentially affected MFGI's regulatory capital level. There is also no indication that MF Global staff consulted with the CME Group in order to determine whether the transfer constituted an "equity withdrawal" within the meaning of CME's instruction that the company not make any such withdrawal, except with CME's express written permission.[436]

On Tuesday, November 1, an SEC staff member informed a colleague that MFGI had withdrawn the full amount of the perceived excess from the securities reserve bank account.[437] Separately, a FINRA staff member informed colleagues that he understood MF Global to have ignored an instruction from an SEC official not to transfer the funds.[438] In a follow-up e-mail to Chairman Schapiro and others, the director of the SEC's Division of Trading and Markets related that an SEC staff member had heard from MF Global's General Counsel, Laurie Ferber, that the CFTC had pressured MF Global to make the transfer.[439] Chairman Schapiro responded, "Without telling us? That is unacceptable."[440]

Bankruptcy Filing and Liquidation

When MF Global informed Interactive Brokers of the shortfall of customer funds, the company withdrew from negotiations.[441] With no other alternatives available, MF Global filed for reorganization under Chapter 11 of the Bankruptcy Code in the United States Bankruptcy Court for the Southern District of New York.[442]

Following MF Global's filing, the Securities Investor Protection Corporation commenced a proceeding to liquidate MFGI under the Securities Investor Protection Act.[443] A federal district court judge appointed James W. Giddens as trustee for the liquidation of MFGI.[444] Giddens then hired his law firm, Hughes Hubbard and Reed, LLP as counsel and retained Ernst & Young and Deloitte as consultants and forensic accountants to aid him in investigating the collapse of MFGI and the shortfall in customer funds.[445] Giddens released a report in June 2012 indicating that the shortfall in segregated property is approximately $900 million in domestic accounts (both commodities and securities), plus approximately $700 million in secured accounts related to trading by customers on foreign exchanges.[446] To date, Giddens has recovered approximately 80 percent of the segregated customer property missing from domestic securities accounts and between 60 and 90 percent of the segregated customer property missing from domestic futures accounts.[447] However, he has only recovered approximately five percent of the funds missing from the accounts of customers who traded on foreign exchanges.[448] Most of the remaining shortfall for these customers involves secured property that is being withheld by the Joint Special Administrators of MFGUK. Giddens has filed a claim to recover those funds.[449] However, Giddens and the MFGUK administrators disagree about whether, under U.K. law, Giddens is entitled to have his claim satisfied from the disputed funds before other creditors.[450] The resolution of the disagreement depends on whether, when MFGI deposited funds into MFGUK's account to support client trades, it also transferred ownership of those funds to MFGUK.[451] If it did, the trustee's claim will be satisfied only after the funds have been used to pay certain other creditors.[452] A trial is scheduled for April 9, 2013, in the U.K. to resolve the dispute.[453]

Whether MF Global's customers get all of their property back depends on whether the MFGI trustee can recover funds held by MFGUK; what he can recover through litigation and negotiation with third parties; and on the ability to allocate the property of the MFGI estate to the company's former customers.[454] Because MFGI's other creditors normally would be entitled to have their claims satisfied from MFGI's estate, diverting MFGI property to make customers whole will diminish any recovery that the company's creditors otherwise would realize.[455]

Ongoing Criminal and Civil Investigations and Litigation

MF Global is currently the subject of multiple civil and criminal investigations in jurisdictions around the world. In the U.S., the company and its former employees remain the subject of an investigation by the Department of Justice, led by U.S. Attorneys in Chicago and New York. Additionally, the company is under investigation by both the SEC and the CFTC. MF Global's customers, shareholders, and former employees have commenced litigation against the company and its executives in multiple jurisdictions.[456] Those actions filed pre-petition against the company have been stayed pursuant to the U.S. Bankruptcy Code.[457] However, several post-petition actions filed against Corzine by MF Global's customers and shareholders are currently pending before the United States District Court for the Southern District of New York.[458]

FINDINGS AND RECOMMENDATIONS

The Subcommittee's yearlong investigation into MF Global's collapse involved over fifty interviews and held three hearings at which it considered the testimony of nineteen witnesses, including MF Global's former senior managers and its principal regulators. Additionally, the Subcommittee examined more than 243,000 documents produced by MF Global, the company's federal commodities and securities regulators, the company's auditor, credit rating agencies, the New York Fed, the self-regulatory organizations, exchanges, and clearing houses to which the company belonged. The following findings and recommendations are based on information gathered by the Subcommittee during the course of its investigation.

Jon Corzine Caused MF Global's Bankruptcy and Put Customer Funds at Risk

During his nineteen-month tenure as Chairman and CEO of MF Global, Jon Corzine made several fateful decisions, the cumulative effects of which caused MF Global's bankruptcy and jeopardized customer funds.

Soon after joining MF Global, Corzine decided to turn the company into a full-service investment bank. This decision charted a radical new course for the financially troubled company. By expanding MF Global into new business lines without first returning its core commodities business to profitability, Corzine ensured that the company would face enormous resource demands and exposed it to new risks that it was ill-equipped to handle. According to the head of a rival company, Corzine's idea of taking a broker and making it into an investment bank was "an utter impossibility… They do not have the deep culture that Goldman has of handling risk. You cannot leap with a single bound into proprietary trading and hope to survive intact."[459]

In order to generate much-needed revenue to fund MF Global's transformation, Corzine decided to invest heavily in the sovereign debt of struggling European countries. These investments carried significant default and liquidity risks. Although Corzine firmly believed that the existence of the EFSF mitigated default risk, he did not develop a strategy for managing the liquidity risks that would result if a credit downgrade prompted margin demands from counterparties. As Corzine built the company's European bond portfolio, counterparty margin demands became a major draw on MF Global's cash reserves, further exacerbating the company's liquidity strain.

These risks were compounded by the atmosphere that Corzine created at MF Global, in which no one could challenge his decisions. He hired his former gubernatorial chief of staff, Bradley Abelow, to serve as the company's COO. When Michael Roseman, the company's CRO, disagreed with Corzine about the size of the company's European bond portfolio, Corzine directed Roseman to report to Abelow rather than to MF Global's board of directors. This change effectively sidelined the most senior individual charged with monitoring the company's risks and deprived the board of an independent assessment of the risks that Corzine's European RTM trades posed to MF Global, its shareholders, and its customers. Additionally, by acting as the de facto chief trader for the company, Corzine insulated his trading activities from the company's normal risk management review process. He negotiated the size of the company's European bond portfolio solely with MF Global's board of directors, which he chaired. Consequently, Corzine quickly built the company's European bond portfolio well in excess of prudent limits without effective resistance.

Rather than hold the European bonds on MF Global's books, which could expose the company to earnings volatility, Corzine chose to use these bonds as collateral in European RTM trades, permitting the company to book quick profits and "derecognize" the bonds from its balance sheet. As a result, MF Global did not initially disclose the full extent of its holdings in discussions with FINRA or in its public SEC filings, which meant that regulators and the investing public were not aware of all of the risks facing the company. By October 2011, MF Global had accumulated considerable exposure to European debt. The company's net European RTM portfolio was $6.3 billion, which amounted to 14 percent of MF Global's total assets and was orders of magnitude greater than the relative exposure of its larger competitors. The revelation of the surprising size of the company's portfolio, coupled with poor earnings news, prompted the credit rating agencies to downgrade the company's rating to junk status and set off a "run on the bank" by MF Global's investors, customers, counterparties, creating extraordinary demands upon the company's capital and liquidity reserves.

As MF Global's chief executive, Corzine was responsible for ensuring that the company maintained integrated systems and controls for managing the company's liquidity and protecting customer funds. However, under Corzine's tenure, the company's cash management, liquidity monitoring, and regulatory compliance functions remained fragmented among several of the company's departments. MF Global lacked any formal liquidity management framework, and the company could not fully assess and anticipate its liquidity needs. Under Corzine's leadership, the company failed to address concerns raised in an internal audit suggesting that MF Global's liquidity tracking and forecasting capabilities lagged behind the firm's evolving business needs. Consequently, MF Global was unable to coordinate its activities during the liquidity crisis in its final days of operation. As the company struggled to find additional liquidity, company employees identified excess company funds held in customer accounts. However, because they did not have an accurate accounting of the amount of customer funds the company held, they withdrew customer funds as well as company funds. Prosecutors and MF Global's regulators will determine whether the company or its employees violated laws or regulations when these withdrawals were made. However, the responsibility for failing to maintain the systems and controls necessary to protect customer funds rests with Corzine. This failure represented a dereliction of his duty as MF Global's Chairman and CEO.

Recommendation:

The futures market cannot function unless customers are confident that FCMs will safeguard their funds. To restore investor confidence in the futures markets and help ensure that an FCM does not misuse customer funds in the future, the Subcommittee recommends that Congress consider enacting legislation that imposes civil liability on the officers and directors that sign a FCM's financial statements or authorize specific transfers from customer segregated accounts for regulatory shortfalls of segregated customer funds.

The SEC and the CFTC Failed to Share Critical Information about MF Global with One Another, Leaving Each Regulator with an Incomplete Understanding of the Company's Financial Health

Following MF Global's collapse, the Subcommittee requested that the SEC and the CFTC produce all documents relating to each agency's regulatory oversight of MF Global during the twenty months leading up to its bankruptcy. These documents show no record of meaningful communication between the regulators regarding MF Global before the company's final week of business, even though MFGI was registered with both agencies. The SEC's and the CFTC's failure to coordinate regulatory oversight of the company meant that the agencies missed several opportunities to share critical information with one another.

The SEC did not include the CFTC or the commodities SROs in the meeting it held with MF Global in June 2011 to examine the company's global operations and subsidiaries. That meeting, prompted by MFGI's continued losses and change in business strategy, would have been relevant to the CFTC's oversight of the company's FCM business.[460] Additionally, the SEC did not include the CFTC in its discussions with FINRA about the capital charge imposed on MF Global that resulted from its failure to take regulatory haircuts on the value of its European sovereign bonds, even though the decision to impose a capital charge would affect the regulatory capital the company would be required to maintain under both SEC and CFTC rules.[461] The CFTC, for its part, did not inform the SEC that MFGI was using the Alternative Method to calculate its obligations to its commodities customers trading on foreign exchanges, and that as a result the company could use the "excess margin funds" in secured customer accounts as a source of liquidity for its broker-dealer operations. Staff at the SEC's Division of Trading and Markets was surprised to learn MF Global was using the Alternative Method.[462] In their view, the Alternative Method allowed MF Global to "us[e] the FCM as an ATM."[463] Even when the SEC and the CFTC finally began communicating with one another during MF Global's last week of operations, the agencies often worked at cross-purposes.[464] When MF Global reported that it had set aside $220 million above the amount it was required to hold for its broker-dealer customers, the SEC instructed the company not to transfer any of these funds without prior approval. Nonetheless, the CFTC later instructed the company to transfer the funds to the FCM side of its business. When informed of the transfer, SEC Chairman Mary Schapiro stated that the transfer was "unacceptable" and that the CFTC should not have ordered the transfer without telling the SEC.[465] Had the SEC and the CFTC coordinated their supervision of MFGI and had they shared critical information about MF Global, they might have gained a more complete understanding of the company's deteriorating financial health, and they might taken action to better protect the company's customers and investors before it collapsed.

Recommendation:

When Congress established the CFTC in 1974, the CFTC and the SEC each had a clearly delineated jurisdiction over distinct markets.[466] But as financial markets evolved and financial products were developed that had attributes of both futures and securities, the jurisdictional dividing line between the CFTC and the SEC began to erode.[467] As a result, market participants found themselves subject to the regulatory authority of both the SEC and the CFTC.[468] Exchanges that list and trade securities futures are subject to the jurisdiction of both regulators, as are financial intermediaries, like MF Global, that serve investors who trade both securities and futures.[469]

As financial products, markets, and market participants have converged, the SEC's and the CFTC's regulatory jurisdictions have increasingly overlapped. In response to this convergence, the regulators have pledged to work together in various areas. In 2004, the SEC and the CFTC signed a memorandum of understanding (MOU) under which they agreed to share information regarding securities futures regulated by both agencies.[470] The regulators signed another MOU in 2008 intended to create a formal structure for improved coordination and communication between the two agencies.[471] That MOU expressly directed the regulators to inform each other in advance of issues that might impact each others' jurisdiction, including supervisory developments and decisions, material events that may have a significant impact on the operations or activities of an entity or market, and enforcement actions, investigations, or sanctions.[472] A SEC press release touted the agreement as creating "a permanent regulatory liaison between the agencies" and establishing "a framework that will facilitate discussions and coordination regarding issues in…areas of common regulatory interest between the two agencies, such as…the oversight of firms registered with both agencies."[473] In 2009, the SEC and the CFTC met to discuss regulatory harmonization and later released a joint report recommending the creation of joint agency task forces on enforcement and information technology.[474]

None of these efforts, however, resulted in meaningful cooperation between the SEC and the CFTC regarding MF Global. The apparent inability of these agencies to coordinate their regulatory oversight efforts or to share vital information with one another, coupled with the reality that futures products, markets and market participants have converged, compel the Subcommittee to recommend that Congress explore whether customers and investors would be better served if the SEC and the CFTC streamline their operations or merge into a single financial regulatory agency that would have oversight of capital markets as a whole.

MF Global Was Not Forthright with Regulators or the Public about the Degree of Its Exposure to Its European Bond Portfolio, nor Was the Company Forthright about Its Liquidity Condition

When MF Global first entered into European RTM trades in September 2010, the company neither acknowledged the exposure it had to European sovereign debt when questioned by its regulators, nor did it clearly describe the size and nature of its portfolio to the public in the company's regulatory filings. When FINRA contacted MF Global in September 2010 to determine whether the company had exposure to European sovereign debt, the company responded that it had no such exposure even though it had already acquired between $1.5 and $2 billion of bonds. FINRA believes the MF Global's response was "negligent" or "misleading."[475]

MF Global did not mention the net value of its European RTM trades in its September 2010 10-Q filing, even though the company had acquired between $1.5 and $2 billion worth of bonds, or in its December 2010 10-Q, when its bond holdings reached $4.5 billion. MF Global did not provide a more complete discussion of its European RTM trades, their accounting, and their risks until it filed its FY 2011 10-K report in May 2011. That report, filed over six months after MF Global began amassing its European RTM portfolio, was the first public filing to state the aggregate notional value of the trades, which by then had grown to $6.3 billion. In contrast to previous filings, the May 2011 10-K also identified the European nations whose sovereign bonds collateralized the European RTM trades. Finally, MF Global's September 2011 amended 10-Q provided no information to investors beyond noting that FINRA had required the company to increase its required net capital for certain RTM transactions collateralized with European sovereign debt.[476]

Had MF Global been more forthright about the size of its European bond portfolio as it amassed those positions, MFGI's regulators could have protected investors by requiring MF Global to take a capital charge commensurate with the risk posed by its portfolio.[477] Investors also could have decided for themselves whether the company's investments were sound. MF Global's failure to be fully transparent about the size of its European bond portfolio denied regulators and the public the opportunity to inform themselves about the extent of MF Global's European RTM trades and to respond accordingly. As a result, the company's investors, customers and counterparties were stunned when the Wall Street Journal reported the size of the company's European bond portfolio in October 2011. The ensuing panic precipitated the company's rapid collapse.

In addition, certain public statements asserted by MF Global executives in the week leading up to the company's bankruptcy appeared to have painted a more optimistic picture of MF Global's financial condition than what may have been understood privately. On October 6, 2011, Steenkamp informed Corzine that one of MF Global's subsidiaries was again undergoing significant liquidity stress after having experienced a couple of "better days" in the first week of October.[478] In particular, Steenkamp characterized MFGI's liquidity as being in a state of "sustained stress," writing that its broker-dealer was "currently unable to fund itself," and that its need for cash injections from the FCM was becoming permanent because funds from other sources were insufficient to meet the broker-dealer's needs. Steenkamp also cautioned Corzine that the broker-dealer's liquidity demands were in part due to the margin required to cover MF Global's European RTM trades — which at the end of September totaled more than $400 million — and that it could be more challenging for MFGI to draw down its revolving credit line as a result of its liquidity condition.[479] Nineteen days later, on an October 25, 2011 earnings call, Steenkamp and Corzine discussed MF Global's overall financial condition for the fiscal quarter ended September 30. Steenkamp described the ways in which MF Global had "improved [its] capital and liquidity positions" that quarter and expressed his optimism that despite "uncertain and volatile times, we feel good about [MF Global's] capital structure and liquidity positions."[480] Corzine backed Steenkamp's claim by stating that MF Global's actions had put the firm in a "much, much stronger liquidity position" as of September 30.[481] As a result of these public statements, investors were not aware of MFGI's liquidity issues and could not asses their impact on MF Global's overall condition.

Recommendations:

Federal securities laws and SEC rules are intended to protect investors by ensuring that public companies disclose sufficient information for individuals to make informed investment decisions. The Subcommittee recommends that the SEC investigate whether MF Global violated these laws or rules in connection with its disclosures about the European RTM trades and the firm's overall financial health.

MF Global's ability to amass more than $6.3 billion in European sovereign debt without fully disclosing the size and nature of its European RTM portfolio raises concerns about the sufficiency of off-balance sheet reporting requirements under GAAP and SEC rules. In May, FINRA proposed a rule requiring member companies to disclose the gross contract value of European RTM trades that are derecognized from their balance sheets in a supplementary schedule for quarterly FOCUS reports.[482] FASB has also tentatively voted to amend its accounting guidance to require RTM transactions to be accounted for as secured borrowings rather than sales, which would result in transferred financial assets being treated as if the assets were used as collateral for borrowed funds, instead of recording the assets as being sold.[483] The Subcommittee understands that FASB intends to release an exposure draft of its proposal for public comment by the end of this year. The Subcommittee views these rules as a positive development and recommends that the SEC consider enhancing its own disclosure and accounting rules to better ensure that investors have timely information about off-balance sheet transactions, including RTM trades.

Moody's and S&P Failed to Identify the Biggest Risk to MF Global's Financial Health

While Moody's and S&P acknowledged that MF Global's transformation into an investment bank would increase the company's risk profile as it took on greater proprietary trading positions, the credit rating agencies did not sufficiently review MF Global's public filings to identify these risks when they did emerge. Beginning in May 2011, MF Global disclosed in its fiscal year 2011 10-K, and in a subsequent quarterly filing, that it had over $6 billion in net exposure through European RTM trades; that it bore default risk on the bonds that collateralized them; and that it could be subject to margin calls until the trades concluded. MF Global's September 2011 amended 10-Q also cited FINRA's concerns about the company's exposure to European sovereign debt.

Despite the information that was available to them for a period of five months, Moody's and S&P did not factor MF Global's European sovereign debt exposure into its public credit assessments until one week before MF Global filed for bankruptcy. It was not until October 24, 2011, that Moody's identified MF Global's "outsized … exposure to European sovereign debt" as a reason for a ratings downgrade.[484] S&P similarly placed MF Global on "credit watch negative" on October 26, 2011, partly because MF Global's European RTM trade exposure was "very high compared to the company's loss absorbing base."

Moody's and S&P also did not understand the nature of MF Global's European sovereign exposure. Both firms believed that the European RTM trades were client-driven transactions, and that MF Global hedged the risks of these transactions. But, their understanding was inconsistent with MF Global's public filings, which stated that the company maintained exposure to the underlying sovereign issuer and that mark to market movements associated with the European RTM trades could cause volatility in MF Global's financial results. MF Global's CFO also stated in a May 2011 earnings call that MF

Global entered the European RTM trades because it identified principal trading opportunities.[485]

In the case of MF Global, Moody's and S&P's failures are notable because they suggest an absence of due diligence. Both firms received substantive information about MF Global's financial health and discounted its significance or altogether failed to identify or understand it. Additionally, documents reviewed by the Subcommittee demonstrate that neither Moody's nor S&P probed MF Global's European exposure until eleven days prior to the firm's bankruptcy. As a result, MF Global's credit ratings were not based on a complete examination of all relevant information that affected the company's long-term health.

Recommendation:

Given the significant and market-wide impact of credit ratings, investors expect Moody's and S&P to perform a careful and searching inquiry into the companies they rate. Their failure to do so in the case of MF Global raises questions about the role that credit rating agencies should play in financial markets. Whether it is faulty ratings on Worldcom, Enron, structured financial products, or MF Global, the failures of rating agencies to exercise due diligence have significantly affected markets. Given the credit rating industry's concentration – Moody's, S&P, and Fitch account for 98% of all ratings – the market impact of inaccurate ratings is magnified.[486]

In 2010, the House Committee on Financial Services (Committee) drafted reforms enacted in Section 939A of The Dodd-Frank Wall Street Reform and Consumer Protection Act (P.L 111-203) to reduce the reliance on the Nationally Recognized Statistical Rating Organizations (NRSROs). Section 939A received overwhelming bi-partisan support and was an important first step in the reform process. As such, the Committee must continue to hold regulatory agencies accountable for meeting the statutory objectives and deadlines established by Section 939A. The Subcommittee recommends that the Committee consider whether other legislative alternatives to promote greater competition in the credit rating industry are warranted.

The opinions and ratings that Moody's and S&P issued for MF Global exemplify a familiar pattern the three dominant rating agencies follow, in which ratings are "good" until a sudden event results in a precipitous downgrade that leaves investors and creditors stunned and scrambling. The Subcommittee believes that some form of periodic review could instill a greater level of scrutiny and diligence in the ratings process and give the investing public more confidence that the ratings they receive are current. To address the problems raised by sudden downgrades, the Subcommittee recommends that the Committee review whether the SEC should require each NRSRO to establish and enforce written policies and procedures reasonably designed to provide for periodic monitoring of credit ratings and periodic communications to the market about the NRSRO's monitoring practices.

MF Global's Use of the "Alternative Method" Allowed the Company to Use Some Customer Funds as a Source of Capital for the Company's Day-to-Day Operations, Which Subjected Customers to the Risk that MF Global Would Not be Able to Return Those Funds to Customer Accounts upon the Company's Insolvency

The "Alternative Method" of calculating the amount of funds to set aside in secured accounts for customers trading on foreign exchanges allowed MF Global's executives to use certain customer funds to meet the company's liquidity needs. MF Global's executives determined that the Alternative Method did not require the company to set aside excess margin funds in secured accounts and as a result, MF Global used these funds for its own purposes. MF Global therefore subjected customers who traded on foreign exchanges to the risk that during a period of financial distress, the company would not be able to set aside funds in secured accounts equal to what MF Global owed them.[487] The risk was evident to commodities regulators, however, and in the last week of October 2011, staff from the CFTC and the CME Group actively encouraged MF Global to move funds into its secured accounts.[488]

In addition, MFGI's use of the Alternative Method contributed to the $900 million shortfall in the company's *segregated* accounts. The substantial excess funds in secured accounts under the Alternative Method made customer accounts a more attractive source of liquidity for the company's day-to-day activities. In MFGI's hectic final days, the company repeatedly transferred funds into and out of segregated accounts, amplifying the risk that it would miscalculate account balances for regulatory purposes. The Alternative Method, combined with the risk that such a miscalculation would occur, increased the chance that transfers made by MFGI would result in a deficiency of customer funds.

Recommendation:

By permitting FCMs to exclude a customer's excess margin funds from the amount that must be set aside in secured accounts, the Alternative Method is inconsistent with the Commodity Exchange Act's "bedrock" customer protection principle, which "ensure[s] that property entrusted by customers to their brokers will not be subject to the risks of the broker's business."[489] Staff from the CFTC and the CME Group recognized that MF Global's use of the Alternative Method posed precisely this risk and, in the company's final days, devoted significant resources to ensure that the company set aside more funds in the secured accounts. On October 23, 2012, the CFTC announced that it would be proposing new rules to enhance customer protections by, among other things, amending Part 30 of its regulations to no longer permit FCMs to use the Alternative Method.[490] Instead, FCMs would be required to hold sufficient funds in secured accounts to meet their total obligations to customers computed under the net liquidation method.[491] This rule change would echo actions already taken by the NFA earlier this year to strengthen the protection of customer funds held by its members.[492] The Subcommittee welcomes the CFTC's announcement of proposed rules and will follow their development with great interest.

The New York Fed Should Have Exercised Greater Caution in Determining whether to Designate MF Global as a Primary Dealer, Given the Company's Prior Risk Management Failures, Chronic Net Losses, and Evolving Business Strategy

Under its primary dealer program, the New York Fed grants financial companies the privilege of acting as counterparties to open market operations executed by the New York Fed. These open market operations are undertaken in furtherance of U.S. monetary policy pursuant under the direction of the Federal Open Market Committee. Over time, market watchers have come to regard a primary dealer designation as a "Good Housekeeping seal of approval," enhancing a company's standing in the marketplace.[493] The New York Fed has attempted to eliminate this market perception by stating in its primary dealer application that the designation neither constitutes an endorsement of the company nor replaces prudent counterparty risk management and due diligence. Written testimony and letters from the New York Fed's General Counsel echo the same warning. Nonetheless, despite its admonitions to the contrary cautioning otherwise, the New York Fed is aware that the financial services industry views primary dealer designation as conferring prestige on firms that are so designated. The New York Fed's General Counsel conceded that the market may view a primary dealer designation as a sign of a company's capabilities and that the perception may encourage companies to apply to the program. A former Executive Vice President of the New York Fed commented that the New York Fed's practice of pre-approving counterparties as part of the primary dealer program results in an "irreducible minimum Good Housekeeping Seal of Approval."[494]

During the course of MFGI's application to be designated a primary dealer, the New York Fed was made aware of several issues regarding the questionable financial health and stability of MF Global. First, the CFTC informed the New York Fed of four separate instances of risk management failures by MF Global. As a result of these compliance failures, the CFTC fined MF Global $10 million and required it to strengthen its risk monitoring procedures and to undertake an independent review and assessment by a risk management and regulatory compliance consulting firm. Second, MF Global reported net losses that doubled in size from fiscal years 2008 to 2010. Finally, MF Global's new CEO, Jon Corzine, announced that he would embark on an aggressive and risky business strategy to turn the company into a full-service global investment bank within three to five years.

The New York Fed was also aware that MF Global's leadership counted on MFGI being designated a primary dealer to carry out its business strategy, even though the New York Fed cautioned MF Global not to do so. MF Global's former CEO Bernie Dan and then Corzine both violated the New York Fed's explicit warning by speaking openly with the press about the company's desire for MFGI to become a primary dealer. MF Global's General Counsel informed New York Fed employees that the company had spent resources and hired individuals specifically for the purpose of MFGI becoming a primary dealer. The actions of MF Global's leadership and the concerns about the company's financial health led one New York Fed employee to suggest that his colleagues focus on "well known and respected firms" for primary dealer designation, rather than "spending so much time with MF Global, a firm that clearly brings a high degree of risk to the New York Fed."[495] MF Global's risk management failures, chronic net losses, and untested business strategy, combined with the New York Fed's internal concerns that MF Global posed reputational risks, should have given the New York Fed pause before conferring primary dealer status on MFGI. Even though the subsidiary met the basic requirements to become a primary dealer, the New York Fed should have, at a minimum, placed MFGI's application on hold until MF Global's new business strategy had been successfully implemented.

Recommendations:

The New York Fed is aware that the financial services industry views a primary dealer designation as carrying the "Good Housekeeping Seal of Approval" and that the New York Fed's disclaimers have not been effective in removing that perception. As a consequence, and in contravention of the New York Fed's directives, applicant companies may incorporate becoming a primary dealer into their business strategy or tout their application to the media. In order to further discourage companies from utilizing a primary dealer designation beyond its intended purpose, the Subcommittee recommends that the New York Fed examine strengthening its application guidelines to expressly forbid companies from speaking to publicly about their application status during the pendency of the application unless required for regulatory disclosure purposes. If an applicant company ignores the disclosure prohibition, the New York Fed should consider instituting a cooling-off period, similar to the one-year delay for material regulatory actions. The Subcommittee further recommends that the New York Fed consider re-examining its primary dealer selection process to provide for greater scrutiny of companies with questionable financial health, risk management histories, and ambitious business strategies. If a company has experienced multi-year losses, chronic regulatory failures, or is in the process of implementing a dramatic change in business strategy – red flags that were clearly present during MFGI's application – the New York Fed should consider prolonging the application process to better assess how these factors will affect the company's overall suitability as a counterparty.

Differences between Foreign and U.S. Law Gave Rise to the Potential That MFGI Global Customers Trading on Foreign Exchanges Would Experience a "Shortfall" in Funds Owed to Them, Despite the Fact That Such Funds Were Set Aside in Accounts Designated as Secured Accounts

MFGI customers who traded abroad faced the risk that the funds set aside in secured accounts would not readily be available to satisfy their claims upon

MFGI's bankruptcy and subsequent liquidation. Customers who traded foreign futures and options executed and cleared trades on foreign exchanges, which were beyond the jurisdiction of the U.S. authorities. MFGUK acted on behalf of MFGI when the latter's customers instructed MFGI to place a trade on a foreign exchange with which MFGUK maintained a trading relationship. To effectuate those trades, MFGI maintained a secured account with MFGUK, into which MFGI deposited funds to margin its customers' futures and options positions. The disposition of funds in MFGUK's account was subject to British law when MFGUK entered into administration following the collapse of its U.S. affiliates and parent on October 31, 2011. In a mandatory disclosure made by MFGI to customers when they opened their accounts, the company had cautioned that funds margining foreign futures transactions "may not be provided the same protections as funds received to margin futures transactions on domestic exchanges."[496]

When MFGI collapsed, the assets in its secured accounts exceeded the company's liabilities to customers who traded abroad by approximately $4 million. Nonetheless, the trustee liquidating MFGI determined that there was a shortfall of $700 million in funds available to satisfy these customers' claims. This shortfall arose because MFGI placed a "significant percentage" of customer funds in a secured account at MFGUK; and MFGUK has disputed whether MFGI is entitled to these funds in preference to other creditors of MFGUK under British law. As a result, MFGUK will not return these funds to MFGI (for subsequent distribution to customers who traded on foreign exchanges) until this question is resolved in a trial scheduled to take place in the summer of 2013 in the United Kingdom. Because a substantial portion of customer funds were in MFGUK's secured account, as of June 2012, MFGI's trustee was able to make a limited distribution to foreign-trading customers equal to approximately ten percent of their claims.

Recommendation:

The Subcommittee recommends that the Committee on Agriculture consider whether to direct the CFTC to study whether it can better mitigate the risks that FCM customers face when customer funds are placed in secured accounts subject to the law of a foreign jurisdiction. In conducting any such study, the CFTC should consider whether the rules that govern trading on foreign exchanges should be amended to establish protections comparable to those that govern domestic transactions. In particular, the CFTC should consider whether any potential rule change could impose costs on FCMs and their customers that would place foreign futures and options trading at a competitive disadvantage to similar products and services.

End Notes

[1] Man website, http://www.mangroupplc.com/about-man/heritage/index.jsf (last visited July 19, 2012).
[2] *Id.*
[3] From 2001-2007, the compound annual growth rates in contract volumes in exchange-traded and over-the-counter derivates were 22% and 32%, respectively. Form 10-K for MF Global Holdings Ltd. (fiscal year ended Mar. 31, 2008) at 12-13 (citing Bank for International Settlements Quarterly Review) [hereinafter FY08 10-K].
[4] MF Global IPO Prospectus [hereinafter IPO Prospectus], at 122 and 49.
[5] *Man Group Acquires Derivative Brokerage GNI*, INVESTORS OFFSHORE, Oct. 24, 2002, (http:// www.taxnews.com/news/Man_Group_Acquires_Derivatives_Brokerage_GNI____9774. html) (last visited Nov. 14, 2012).
[6] IPO Prospectus, *supra* note 4, at 2 and 122; FY08 10-K, *supra* note 3, at 138, note 19; Standard & Poor's Rating Services [hereinafter S&P] Ratings Outlook for MF Global, July 13, 2007 [hereinafter S&P July 2007 Ratings], at 4.
[7] IPO Prospectus, *supra* note 4, at 1.
[8] *Id.* The Chicago Mercantile Exchange and the Chicago Board of Trade officially merged to form the CME Group Inc. on July 12, 2007. http://www.cmegroup.com/company/history/ magazine/Summer2007/FromWaterStreetToTheWorld.html (last visited Sept. 25, 2012).
[9] IPO Prospectus, *supra* note 4, at 1; S&P July 2007 Ratings, *supra* note 6, at 3.
[10] Form 10-K for MF Global Holdings Ltd. (fiscal year ended Mar. 31, 2007).
[11] Jacob Bunge, *MF Global: History From IPO to Bankruptcy*, WALL ST. J., Oct. 31, 2011 (http://blogs.wsj.com/deals/2011/10/31/mf-global-history-from-ipo-to-bankruptcy/) (last visited Oct. 3, 2012).
[12] IPO Prospectus, *supra* note 4, at 51. Although MF Global planned to replace its bridge loan with debt offerings following its IPO, market conditions frustrated the company's efforts to do so. Instead, MF Global renegotiated its bridge loan with existing lenders to extend the loan maturity to Dec. 12, 2008 in exchange for paying higher interest rates on the $1.05 billion balance.
[13] IPO Prospectus, *supra* note 4.
[14] Form 10-Q for MF Global Holdings Ltd. (quarterly period ended Sept. 30, 2007) [hereinafter FY08 Q2 10-Q], at 13.
[15] MF Global Holdings Ltd. (MFGLQ) Stock Chart, Yahoo Finance, Mar. 23, 2010 – Mar. 24, 2010 [hereinafter Mar. 23-24, 2010 MFG Stock Chart] http://finance.yahoo.com/echarts?s= MFGLQ+Interactive (last visited July 20, 2012).
[16] Form 10-K for MF Global Holdings Ltd. (fiscal year ended Mar. 31, 2010) [hereinafter FY10 10-K], at 35; Press Release, U.S. Commodities Futures Trading Commission [hereinafter CFTC], CFTC Sanctions MF Global Inc. $10 Million for Significant Supervision Violations between 2003 and 2008 (Dec. 17, 2009), *available at* http://www.cftc.gov/PressRoom/ PressReleases/pr5763-09 (last visited Oct. 15, 2012).
[17] Form 8-K for MF Global Ltd. (Feb. 27, 2008).
[18] *Id.*
[19] *Id.*
[20] Mar. 23-24, 2010 MFG Stock Chart, *supra* note 15.
[21] Letter from Craig Parmelee, Managing Dir. and Lead Analytical Manager for North American Fin. Institutions Ratings, S&P, to Randy Neugebauer, Chairman, Subcomm. on Oversight

and Investigations [hereinafter O&I Subcomm.] (Jan. 17, 2012) at 3. [hereinafter S&P Jan. 17, 2012 letter]; Jennifer Yousfi, *Unauthorized Trades Cost MF Global $141.5 Million*, MONEY MORNING, Feb. 29. 2008 (http://moneymorning.com/2008/02/29/unauthorized-trades-cost-mf-global-1415-million/) (last visited Oct. 15, 2012).

[22] Press Release, CFTC, Statement on MF Global (Mar. 17, 2008) http://www.cftc.gov/PressRoom/PressReleases/cftcmfglobalstatement031708 (last visited Sept. 25, 2012).

[23] Press Release, CME Group, Statement on MF Global in Good Standing at CME Clearing (Mar. 17, 2008) http://cmegroup.mediaroom.com/index.php?s=43&item=708&page template=article (last visited Sept. 25, 2012).

[24] Mar. 23-24, 2010 MFG Stock Chart, *supra* note 15.

[25] FY08 10-K, *supra* note 3.

[26] Press Release, MF Global, MF Global Reports Record Fourth Quarter and Fiscal Year 2008 Results (May 20, 2008), at 2 http://www.sec.gov/Archives/edgar/data/1401106/000119312508118826/dex991.htm (last visited Sept.25, 2012).

[27] *Id.*

[28] *Id.*

[29] *Id.* As a result of the issuance of additional convertible preferred shares on June 20, 2008, MF Global paid J.C. Flowers a make-whole payment of 26.7 million and increased the dividend rate on its existing preferred shares to10.725%.

[30] *Id.*

[31] *Id.*

[32] Ryan Dezember, *Private-Equity Investor J.C. Flowers Could Lose Nearly $48 million on MF*, WALL ST. J., Nov. 1, 2011 (http://online.wsj.com/article/SB10001424052970204394804577010181017063466.html).

[33] *Id.*

[34] Form 10-Q for MF Global Ltd. (quarterly period ended June 30, 2009), at 16-17. JP Morgan [hereinafter JPMC] and Bank of New York Mellon were the primary lenders.

[35] Form 10-K for MF Global Holdings Ltd. (fiscal year ended Mar. 31, 2009) at 78 [hereinafter FY09 10-K].

[36] Press Release, MF Global, MF Global to Offer $150 million of Convertible Preference Shares and $150 Million of Convertible Senior Notes (June 17, 2008) http://www.sec.gov/Archives/edgar/data/1401106/000119312508135379/dex991.htm (last visited Sept. 25, 2012).

[37] *Id.*

[38] Ratings Action, Moody's Investors Service [hereinafter Moody's] confirms MF Global's Baa1 rating; assigns negative outlook, June 18, 2008.

[39] Mar. 23-24, 2010 MFG Stock Chart, *supra* note 15.

[40] *MF Global Tries to Temper Selloff*, WALL ST. J. (June 18, 2008).

[41] Form 8-K for MF Global Ltd. (June 20, 2008).

[42] Form 8-K for MF Global Ltd. (July 18, 2008).

[43] *Id.*

[44] Form 8-K for MF Global Ltd. (July 29, 2008).

[45] Investment Agreement between MF Global Ltd. and J.C. Flowers II L.P. (May 20, 2008), at 21, *available at* http://www.sec.gov/Archives/edgar/data/1401106/000119312508133184/dex1048.htm (last visited Oct. 15, 2012).

[46] O&I Subcomm. staff analysis of data obtained from MF Global's 10-K and 10-Q filings [hereinafter MF Global Fin. Performance]; O&I Subcomm. staff analysis of data obtained from historic share price data obtained from Yahoo Fin. [hereinafter MF Global Stock Prices].

[47] Form 8-K for MF Global Ltd. (Oct. 28, 2008); Press Release, MF Global, MF Global Appoints Bernard W. Dan as Chief Executive Officer (Oct. 28, 2008).

[48] MF Global Stock Prices, *supra* note 46.

[49] E-mail from Donald Galante, Senior V.P., MF Global Inc., to Debby Perelmuter, Senior V.P., Markets Group, Federal Reserve Bank of N.Y. [hereinafter NYFRB] (Dec. 19, 2008, 03:34 p.m.).

[50] NYFRB Operating Policy Administration of Relationship with Primary Dealers Jan. 11, 2010 http://www.newyorkfed.org/markets/pridealers_policies.html (last visited Sept. 25, 2012) [hereinafter NYFRB New Primary Dealer Policy]; *Hearing on the Collapse of MF Global Before the Subcomm. on Oversight and Investigations of the House Comm. on Fin. Services,* 112th Cong. 93 (2011) [hereinafter Dec. 15, 2011 Hearing](statement of Thomas C. Baxter, Jr., Gen. Counsel, NYFRB).

[51] *Id.*

[52] NYFRB Primary Dealers List http://www.newyorkfed.org/markets/pridealers_current.html (last visited Sept. 25, 2012).

[53] The New York Fed took steps to eliminate this perception, specifically warning that primary dealer designation neither constitutes an endorsement of the company nor a replacement for prudent counterparty risk management and due diligence, NYFRB New Primary Dealer Policy, *supra* note 50, and going so far as to eliminate its surveillance activities over primary dealers in 1992, stating that the action "should be viewed merely as confirmation of the long-standing reality that the Bank does not have – nor has it ever had – formal regulatory authority over the Government securities market or authority over the primary dealers in their capacity as such." NYFRB Operating Policy Administration of Relationship with Primary Dealers, Jan. 22, 1992, http://www.newyorkfed.org/markets/pridealers_policies_920122.html (last visited September 25, 2012) ; Letter from Thomas C. Baxter, Jr. Gen. Counsel, NYFRB, to Randy Neugebauer, Chairman, O&I Subcomm. at 6 (June 22, 2012); Dec. 15, 2011 Hearing, *supra* note 50, at 3 (testimony of Thomas C. Baxter, Jr., Gen. Counsel, NYFRB). Nevertheless, the perception remained.

[54] *See* 22 U.S.C. §§5341-5342.

[55] E-mail from Debby Perelmuter, Senior V.P., Markets Groups, FRBNY, to Jennifer Wolgemuth, Counsel & Ass't V.P., NYFRB, et al. (Apr. 1, 2009, 8:45 a.m.) [hereinafter Perelmuter E-mail]; *see also* Large U.S. Corporations and Federal Contractors with Subsidiaries in Jurisdictions Listed as Tax Havens or Financial Privacy Jurisdictions, GAO-09-157 (Dec. 18, 2008) http://www.gao.gov/assets/290/284522.pdf (last visited Sept. 25, 2012).

[56] Perelmuter E-mail, *supra* note 55. MF Global later confirmed that it would be switching jurisdictions, and reincorporated in Delaware on Jan. 4, 2010. E-mail from Perelmuter to Wolgemuth, et al. (June 11, 2009, 03:57 p.m.); E-mail from Perelmuter, to Wolgemuth, et al (June 30, 2009, 03:37 p.m.); FY10 10-K, supra note 16, at 1, 34, 44.

[57] E-mail from Wolgemuth, to Richard Dzina, Market Operations Monitoring and Analysis, Markets Group, NYFRB, et al. (Apr. 30, 2009, 02:42 p.m.).

[58] Dec. 15, 2011 Hearing, *supra* note 50, at 6 (testimony of Thomas C. Baxter, Jr., Gen. Counsel, NYFRB); E-mail from Wolgemuth, to Dzina, et al. (Apr. 30, 2009, 02:42 p.m.); E-mail from Perelmuter, to Wolgemuth, Dzina, et al. (Apr. 30, 2009, 02:57 p.m.).

[59] E-mail from Michael Silva, Chief of Staff, FRBNY, to Laurie Ferber, Gen. Counsel, MF Global (July 30, 2009, 05:38 p.m.); E-mail from Dzina, to Perelmuter (July 31, 2009, 07:04 p.m.); E-mail from Wolgemuth, to Dzina (Oct. 13, 2009, 06:17 p.m.).

[60] E-mail from Wolgemuth, to Thomas Baxter, Gen. Counsel, NYFRB (Sept. 1, 2009, 12:26 p.m.); E-mail from Joshua Frost, NYFRB, to Dzina (Oct. 12, 2009, 6:17 p.m.).

[61] Press Release, CFTC, CFTC Sanctions MF Global, Inc. $10 Million for Significant Supervision Violations between 2003 and 2008 (Dec. 17, 2009) http://www.cftc.gov/PressRoom/PressReleases/pr5763-09 (last visited Sept. 25, 2012); In the Matter of MF Global, Inc., CFTC Docket No. 10-03 http://www.cftc.gov/ucm/groups/public/@lrenforcementactions/documents/legalpleading/enfmfglobalorder12172009.pdf (last visited Sept. 25, 2012).

[62] E-mail from Peter McCarthy, Exec. V.P., Global Head of Fixed Income, MF Global, to Dzina (Dec. 17, 2009, 03:58 p.m.).

[63] Press Release, NYFRB, New York Fed Publishes Revised Policy for Administration of Primary Dealer Relationships (Jan. 11, 2010) http://www.newyorkfed.org/newsevents/news/markets/2010/ma100111.html (last visited Oct. 15, 2012).

[64] NYFRB New Primary Dealer Policy, *supra* note 50.

[65] NYFRB Memorandum, Chronology of FRBNY's Actions Relating to MF Global (Dec. 13, 2011), at 14, 15 [hereinafter NYFRB Chron].

[66] *Id.* at 15.

[67] *Id.*

[68] E-mail from James P. Bergin, NYFRB, to Wolgemuth (Feb. 24, 2010, 04:41p.m.).

[69] *Id.*

[70] FY08 10-K, *supra* note 3, at 4, 10.

[71] *Id.*

[72] Matt Koppenheffer, *J. Christopher Flowers: Corzine's Kingmaker*, THE MOTLEY FOOL, Dec. 16, 2011 (http://www.fool.com/investing/general/2011/12/16/j-christopher-flowers-corzines-kingmaker.aspx) (last visited Nov. 14, 2012) [hereinafter Koppenheffer article].

[73] Joellen Perry, *ECB Cuts Rates to 2%, Matching '05 Low*, WALL ST. J., Jan. 16, 2009 (http://online.wsj.com/article/SB123201496350385293.html) (last visited Nov. 14, 2012).

[74] FRBNY, Historical Changes of the Target Federal Funds and Discount Rates, http://www.newyorkfed.org/markets/statistics/dlyrates/fedrate.html (last visited Sept. 25, 2012).

[75] *See* FY09 10-K, *supra* note 35, at 50; FY10 10-K, *supra* note 16, at 44.

[76] *Cf.* FY09 10-K, *supra* note 35 to FY10 10-K, *supra* note 16.

[77] See FY10 10-K, *supra* note 16, at 18.

[78] FY08 Q2 10-Q, *supra* note 14; Form 10-Q for MF Global Ltd. (quarterly period ended Dec. 31, 2008).

[79] S&P Jan. 17, 2012 letter, *supra* note 21, at 3.

[80] Letter from Steven R. Ross, Partner, Akin Gump Strauss Hauer & Feld, to Randy Neugebauer, Chairman, O&I Subcomm. (Jan. 17, 2012), at 2 [hereinafter Moody's Jan. 17, 2012 letter].

[81] Global Credit Portal: Ratings Direct, MF Global Ltd. research update, S&P, Feb. 25, 2009.

[82] S&P Jan. 17, 2012 letter, *supra* note 21, at 3.

[83] Moody's Jan. 17, 2012 letter, *supra* note 80, at 2.

[84] MF Global Fin. Performance, *supra* note 46. MF Global Stock Prices, *supra* note 46.

[85] MF Global Fin. Performance, *supra* note 46.

[86] FY08 10-K, *supra* note 3; FY09 10-K *supra* note 35; FY10 10-K, *supra* note 16.

[87] Form 8-K for MF Global Ltd. (Mar. 23, 2010) [hereinafter Mar. 23, 2010 8-K]; Press Release, MF Global, MF Global Appoints Jon S. Corzine Chairman and Chief Executive Officer (Mar. 23, 2010) [hereinafter MF Global Mar. 23, 2010 Press Release] http://sec.gov/Archives/edgar/data/1401106/000119312510064637/dex991.htm (last visited Oct. 15, 2012).

[88] Peter Elkind and Doris Burke, *The Last Days of MF Global*, CNN MONEY, June 4, 2012 (http://finance.fortune.cnn.com/2012/06/04/the-last-days-of-mf-global) (last visited Nov. 14, 2012) [hereinafter Elkind Burke article].

[89] Dec. 15, 2011 Hearing, *supra* note 50, at 127 (statement of Jon S. Corzine, CEO, MF Global).

[90] Koppenheffer article, *supra* note 72.

[91] *Id.*

[92] Mar. 23, 2010 8-K, *supra* note 87; MF Global Mar. 23, 2010 Press Release, *supra* note 87.

[93] J.C. Flowers & Co. offered Corzine a 3.5% carried interest in the fund's profits. *See* "Jon S. Corzine Contract with J.C. Flowers & Co. LLC" *and* "Jon S. Corzine Employment Agreement," accompanying Mar. 23, 2010 8-K, *supra* note 87.

[94] Mar. 23-24, 2010 MFG Stock Chart, *supra* note 15.

[95] S&P Rating Summary Record for MF Global Holdings Ltd. (Nov. 24, 2010), at 8.

[96] Press Release, Moody's, Moody's comments on MF Global's CEO change (Mar. 23, 2010) http://www.moodys.com/research/Moodys-comments-on-MF-Globals-CEO-change--PR_196823 (last visited Sept. 25, 2012).

[97] MF Global, Presentation to the Securities and Exchange Commission [hereinafter SEC], at 17 (June 14, 2011) [hereinafter MF Global SEC Presentation]. The company derived 15 percent of its income from interest earned on held-to-maturity investments, with the remaining two percent coming from all other sources.

[98] *See* "Part II to the Application of MF Global Inc., a subsidiary of MF Global Holdings Ltd. to become a primary dealer," at 11 (Jan. 22, 2010) [hereinafter MFGI Primary Dealer App. Part II] http://www.newyorkfed.org/markets/MFG_part_II.PDF (last visited Sept. 25, 2012).

[99] *Id.*

[100] *Id.* at 12.

[101] *Id.*

[102] *Id.*

[103] Before Jan. 1, 2008, MF Global had conducted its U.S.-based securities and derivatives brokerage businesses through two separate legal entities. However, it merged these two entities on Dec. 31, 2007, and changed the name of the surviving entity to MF Global Inc. *See* MFGI Primary Dealer App. Part II, *supra* note 98, at 10.

[104] The Dept. of Treasury Blueprint for a Modernized Financial Regulatory Structure (Mar. 2008).

[105] Dec. 15, 2011 Hearing, *supra* note 50, at 107 (statement of Dan M. Berkovitz, Gen. Counsel, CFTC); *Id.* at 115 (statement of Robert Cook, Dir., Div. of Trading and Markets, SEC).

[106] *Id* at 52 (statement of Robert Cook, Dir., Div. of Trading and Markets, SEC).

[107] *Id.* at 56 (statement of Richard Ketchum, Pres., Chairman and CEO, FINRA).

[108] 17 C.F.R. §240.13a-1 (filing of annual report) *and* 17 C.F.R. §240.13a-13 (filing of quarterly report).

[109] 17 C.F.R. §240.15c3-1 (net capital requirements for broker dealers); 17 C.F.R. §1.17 (minimum financial requirements for futures commission merchants [hereinafter FCMs]).

[110] *Id.* The haircut percentage to apply is set by rule and depends on the type of asset and its maturity date.

[111] *See, e.g.*, 17 C.F.R. §1.17(a)(1) (requiring FCMs to maintain capital equal to or in excess of the greatest of one off our measures, including the amount of net capital specified by SEC rule).

[112] Dec. 15, 2011 Hearing, *supra* note 50, at 118 (Statement of Robert Cook, Dir., Div. of Trading and Markets, SEC).

[113] 17 C.F.R. §240.17a-5 (requiring broker dealers to submit monthly reports); 17 C.F.R. §1.18 (allowing FCMs to submit FOCUS report in lieu of CFTC Form 1-FR in certain circumstances).

[114] 17 CFR 1.20 (establishing protections for customers trading on domestic futures exchanges), 30.7 (protections for customers trading on foreign futures exchanges), and 240.15c3-3 (protections for securities customers).

[115] 17 CFR §240.15c3-3.

[116] *Id.*

[117] *Cf.* Rule 1.20 and 30.7. Although the Commodity Exchange Act requires that FCMs segregate customer funds used for trading on U.S. exchanges, the Act does not expressly require FCMs to segregate funds used for trading on foreign exchanges. *See, e.g.*, 76 FR 78776, 78777 (2011). Instead, the Act grants the CFTC the discretion to write rules governing trading on foreign exchanges. *Id.* When it published the rules, the CFTC recognized that there were "inherent limitations on its ability to provide U.S. residents trading on foreign exchanges [with] identical protections available to U.S. contract markets" because those funds may become subject to foreign law governing the disposition of customer funds upon the insolvency of the customer's broker. *Id.*; *see also* Foreign Futures and Foreign Options Transactions, 52 Fed. Reg. 28,980, at 28,984-85 (Aug. 5, 1987) (to be codified at 17 C.F.R.

pts. 1, 30, 32, and 166) [hereinafter Foreign Futures and Options Rulemaking]; Interview by O&I Subcomm. staff with CFTC personnel, in Wash., D.C. (July 2, 2012) [hereinafter Interview with CFTC].

118 17 C.F.R. §1.20.

119 *Id.*

120 17 C.F.R. §1.23.

121 17 C.F.R. §30.7; 17 C.F.R. §1.3(rr) (setting forth definition of "Foreign Futures and Options Secured Amount"). In addition, when a foreign futures or options customer opens an account, an FCM must give written warning of the risks inherent in trading on a foreign exchange. 17 C.F.R. §30.6; *see also* 17 C.F.R. §1.55 (providing that disclosure must state, in part, that "funds received from customers to margin foreign futures transactions may not be provided the same protections as funds received to margin futures transactions on domestic exchanges").

122 Foreign Futures and Foreign Options Rulemaking, *supra* note 117 at 28, 984.

123 Rep. of the Trustee's Investigation and Recommendations, *In re MF Global Inc..*, No. 11-2790 (MG) SIPA, at 38 (Bankr. S.D. N.Y. June 4, 2012) [hereinafter MFGI Trustee Report].

124 MFGI Trustee Report, *supra* note 123, at 38, fn. 23. ("For example, if a customer deposits $100,000 in cash into her "30.7" Foreign Secured account on Day 1, in order to start trading on UK exchanges, but has no open positions, there is no maintenance margin requirement, and therefore, under the Alternate Method, there would be a $0requirement for MFGI to set aside her deposited funds. Conversely, under the Net Liquidating Method, there wouldbe a $100,000 requirement.")

125 Rule 1.32 (requiring computation of balances by noon on the next business day).

126 Following MF Global's collapse, one firm changed to the net liquidation method in Nov. 2011, and the remaining three changed in Jan. and Feb. 2012, after discussions with CFTC staff. Interview with CFTC, *supra* note 117. Further, FCMs were prohibited from using the alternative method as of Sept. 1, 2012, under rules proposed by the National Futures Association [hereinafter NFA] and approved by the CFTC.

127 MFGI Trustee Report, *supra* note 123, at 11.

128 *Id.*

129 Dec. 15, 2011 Hearing, *supra* note 50, at 82 (Testimony of Terrence A. Duffy, Executive Chairman, CME Group Inc.); MFGI Trustee report, *supra* note 123, at 41.

130 MFGI Trustee Report, *supra* note 123, at 39, 108; Interview by O&I Subcomm. staff with CME Group personnel, in Wash., D.C. (June 18, 2012) [hereinafter Interview with CME Group].

131 Elkind Burke article, *supra* note 88; Form 10-K for MF Global Holdings Ltd. (fiscal year ended Mar. 31, 2011) [hereinafter FY11 10-K]

132 Elkind Burke article, *supra* note 88.

133 *Id.*

134 FY11 10-K, *supra* note at 131.

135 *See, e.g.*, Andrew Ross Sorkin, *It's Lonely Without the Goldman Net*, N.Y. TIMES, Oct. 31, 2011 (http://dealbook.nytimes.com/2011/10/31/its-lonely-without-the-goldman-net/) (last visited July 20, 2012).

136 FY11 10-K, *supra* note 131, at 6-7.

137 MF Global Ltd. F4Q10 (Qtr End 03/31/10) Earnings Call Transcript (May 20, 2010) [hereinafter FY10 Q4 MF Global Earnings Call].

138 Corzine describe this as "one of his top priorities." See Terrence Dopp and Matthew Leising, *Corzine Returns to Wall Street as CEO of MF Global*, BLOOMBERG, Mar. 23, 2010 [hereinafter Dopp Leising article] (http://www.bloomberg.com/apps/news?pid=newsarchive &sid=akA2OHOzoQ2M&pos=4) (last visited Oct. 16, 2012).

139 FY11 10-K, *supra* note 131, at 16.

140 *Id.*, at 6-7.

[141] *Id.*

[142] FY10 Q4 MF Global Earnings Call, *supra* note 137. MF Global turned over nearly 46% of its workforce during Corzine's tenure, releasing 1,400 of its 3,200 workers and hiring 1,100 new employees. See Elkind Burke article, *supra* note 88.

[143] FY10 Q4 MF Global Earnings Call, *supra* note 137.

[144] MF Global Holdings Ltd. Schedule 14A Proxy Statement (July 7, 2011), at 32.

[145] FY11 10-K, *supra* note 131, at 13.

[146] *Id.* at 13-14.

[147] Dopp Leising article, *supra* note 138.

[148] E-mail from Dzina, NYFRB, to Wolgemuth, NYFRB (Apr. 16, 2010, 03:01 p.m.).

[149] *Id.*; E-mail from Joshua Frost, NYFRB, to Dzina, NYFRB (Mar. 23, 2010, 05:46 p.m.); E-mail from David G. Sewell, NYFRB, to Dzina, NYFRB (Mar. 24, 2010, 09:00 a.m.).

[150] E-mail from Dzina, NYFRB, to Wolgemuth, NYFRB (Apr. 16, 2010, 03:01 p.m.); E-mail from Dzina, NYFRB, to Michael Schetzel, NYFRB (Apr. 22, 2010, 08:24 p.m.).

[151] NYFRB Chron, *supra* note 65, at 23.

[152] *Id.* at 23-25.

[153] E-mail from Dzina, NYFRB, to Brian P. Sack, Fed. Reserve System (Nov. 12, 2010, 09:12 p.m.).

[154] Press Release, NYFRB, Primary Dealers List (Feb. 2, 2011) http://newyorkfed.org/newsevents/news/markets/2011/an110202p.html (last visited Oct. 23, 2012).

[155] FY11 10-K, *supra* note 131, at 16.

[156] *Id.* at 6-7.

[157] Form 10-Q for MF Global Holdings Ltd. (quarterly period ended June 30, 2010) at 41 (noting $8.8 million profit).

[158] FY11 10-K, *supra* note 131, at 7.

[159] *See, e.g.*, MF Global Capital Markets Weekly Management Meeting (week ending Oct. 19. 2011), page 12; E-mail from Spencer Salovaara, MF Global, to Jon Corzine, CEO, MF Global (Oct. 25, 2011, 09:46 p.m.); Elkind Burke article, *supra* note 88 (noting that Corzine "wasn't just trading RTMs…He was also trading oil futures and T-bills and foreign currencies" and that "Corzine tracked his positions…on his Bloomberg terminal, on his Blackberry, on his iPad")

[160] MFGI Trustee report, *supra* note 123, at 68, Footnote 61.

[161] *Id.*

[162] David Cottle, *Euro Sovereign Woes Bubble Back Up*, WALL ST. J., July 19, 2010 (http://blogs.wsj.com/source/2010/07/19/euro-sovereign-woes-bubble-back-up/) (last visited Oct. 23, 2012); Dec. 15, 2011 Hearing, *supra* note 50, at 132 (testimony of Jon Corzine, CEO, MF Global) (noting that spread in European sovereign debt securities appeared to be favorable).

[163] Press Release, Council of The European Union, European Stabilisation Mechanism to Preserve Fin. Stability (May 9, 2010).

[164] Dec. 15, 2011 Hearing, *supra* note 50, at 133 (testimony of Jon Corzine, CEO, MF Global).

[165] *Id.* at 131-132.

[166] MF Global, Board of Directors European Sovereign Portfolio (Aug. 11, 2011) [hereinafter MF Global Euro Sovereign Portfolio].

[167] *See* MFGI Trustee Report, *supra* note 123, at 66 (noting that MFGI classified European bonds as "securities owned subject to MtM" before entering into intercompany repos with MFGUK). FASB is "the designated organization in the private sector for establishing standards of financial accounting that govern the preparation of financial reports by nongovernmental entities." *See* "Facts about FASB," available at http://www.fasb.org/jsp/FASB/Page/SectionPage&cid=1176154526495. While the SEC has authority to establish accounting standards for publicly held companies pursuant to the Securities and Exchange Act of 1934, *see* Exchange Act, Section 13b, the SEC generally has deferred to the private sector with respect to the formulation of accounting standards. *See* "Facts about FASB."

[168] *See* MFGI Trustee Report, *supra* note 123, at 66.

[169] Dec. 15, 2011 Hearing, *supra* note 50, at 132 (testimony of Jon Corzine, CEO, MF Global).

[170] The Repurchase Agreement Refined: GCF Repo, Current Issues in Economics and Finance, New York Fed, at 1 (June 2003), available at http://www.newyorkfed.org/research/current_issues/ci9-6.pdf (last visited Nov. 14, 2012).

[171] For example, a securities dealer may borrow $100 from its client for a week in exchange for a security worth $100. A week later, the securities dealer will return $105 to the client, and the client returns the security to the dealer. *See Regulating Wall Street: The Dodd-Frank Act and the New Architecture of Global Finance* at 321 (Viral V. Acharya et al., eds. 2011). Repos are functionally similar to a secured loan. Thus, the five dollars paid by the securities dealer in the foregoing example is interest on the $100 loan principal. *Id.*

[172] *Id.* at 321.

[173] *See* Richard Comotto, Haircuts and Initial Margins in the Repo Market, European Repo Council, at 5-6 (Feb. 8, 2012), available at: http://www.icmagroup.org/assets/documents/Maket-Practice/Regulatory-Policy/Repo-Markets/Haircuts%20and%20initial%20margins%20in%20the%20repo%20market_8%20Feb%202012.pdf; *see also* CFTC Glossary, "Haircut," available at: http://www.cftc.gov/consumerprotection/educationcenter/cftcglossary/glossary_h (last visited Oct. 24, 2012).

[174] *Id.*

[175] Dec. 15, 2011 Hearing, *supra* note 50, at 132 (Statement of Jon Corzine, CEO, MF Global).

[176] *Id.*; *see also* MFGI Trustee Report *supra* note 123, at 89 (noting that if MF Global were downgraded below investment grade, "that event would trigger a margin call as high as 200% under LCHC rules and higher margin at other exchanges like Euroex").

[177] Memorandum from Andrea Kennedy, Mike Bolan, Pallavi Rayan, MF Global to MF Global files (Mar. 31, 2011) [hereinafter MF Global RTM Memo].

[178] FASB, Transfers and Servicing, Topic 860 [hereinafter FASB Topic 860].

[179] *Hearing on The Collapse of MF Global: Part 3 Before the Subcomm. on O&I of the House Comm. on Fin. Services,* 112th Cong. 10 (2012) [hereinafter Mar. 28, 2012 Hearing] (testimony of Susan M. Cosper, Technical Dir., Chairman, Emerging Issues Task Force, FASB).

[180] *Id.*

[181] *Id.*

[182] FASB Topic 860, *supra* note 178, 860-10-40-5.

[183] *Id.*

[184] FASB, Derivatives and Hedging, Topic 815 [hereinafter FASB Topic 815]; *see also* FASB, Fair Value Measurement, Topic 820 [hereinafter FASB Topic 820].

[185] FASB Topic 860, *supra* note 178.

[186] Dec. 15, 2011 Hearing, *supra* note 50, at 131 (Statement of Jon Corzine, CEO, MF Global).

[187] *Id.* at 133.

[188] Elkind Burke article, *supra* note 88.

[189] MFGI Trustee Report, *supra* note 123, at 124. The London Clearing House Ltd. merged with Banque Centrale de Compensation SA (then trading as Clearnet) in Dec. 2003 to form the LCH.Clearnet Group Ltd. See LCH.Clearnet Annual Report 2003, at 4, available at: http://www.lchclearnet.com/Images/RA%202003_tcm644282.pdf (last visited Oct. 23, 2012).

[190] MF Global RTM Memo, *supra* note 177.

[191] Dec. 15, 2011 Hearing, *supra* note 50, at 133 (Statement of Jon Corzine, CEO, MF Global); MFGI Trustee Report, *supra* note 123, at 67; First Rep. of Louis J. Freeh, Chapter 11 Trustee of MF Global Holdings Ltd., et al., for the Period Oct. 31, 2011 through June 4, 2012, at 35, *In re MF Global Holdings Ltd.*, Case No. 11-15059 (MG)(June 4, 2012) [hereinafter Freeh Report].

[192] MF Global Holdings Ltd., Board of Directors Delegations of Authority for Risk (Sept. 27, 2007), at 2, 9-10.

[193] Dec. 15, 2011 Hearing, *supra* note 50, at 133-134 (Statement of Jon Corzine, CEO, MF Global).

[194] *Id.*, at 37, 41-42, 132, 134. Corzine characterized the trades as "my personal responsibility and a prime focus of my attention." Matthew Leising, *MF Global Drops by Most Since 2008 on Biggest Quarterly Loss,* BLOOMBERG BUSINESSWEEK, Oct. 25, 2011 (http://www.businessweek.com/news/2011-10-25/mf-global-drops-by-most-since2008-on-biggest-quarterly-loss.html#p2) (last visited July 21, 2012); E-mails from Lauren Cantor, MF Global, to Jon Corzine, CEO, MF Global (Oct. 24, 2011). In Jan. 2011, Corzine began acting, on an "interim" basis, as the head of the company's institutional capital markets division, in which the Principal Strategies Group was housed. MF Global Holdings Ltd. Board of Directors Meeting Minutes, at 3 (Jan. 28, 2011). Shortly after the Jan. board meeting, Munir Javeri was hired as MF Global's Global Head of Trading; Elkind Burke article, *supra* note 88. Javeri left MF Global in June 2011, however, reportedly "after expressing discomfort with the RTMs." *Id.*

[195] *See, e.g.*, E-mail from Jon Corzine, CEO, MF Global, to Lauren Cantor, MF Global (Mar. 9, 2011, 10:30 a.m.) (instructing Ms. Cantor to "work" Italian RTM trades); MFGI Trustee Report, *supra* note 124, at 68.

[196] Michael Roseman timeline provided to O&I Subcomm. (July 17, 2012) [hereinafter Roseman timeline].

[197] *Id.*

[198] *Id.*

[199] *Id.*

[200] *Id.*

[201] Elkind Burke article, *supra* note 88.

[202] Roseman timeline, *supra* note 196.

[203] MF Global Holdings, Ltd. Board of Directors Meeting Minutes (Nov. 8, 2010).

[204] *Id.* at 2.

[205] Letter from Samuel F. Abernethy, attorney for Michael K. Roseman, to Randy Neugebauer, Chairman, Subcomm. on O&I, at 1 (Feb. 24, 2012).

[206] Form 10-Q for MF Global Ltd. (quarterly period ended Sept. 30, 2010), at 1 [hereinafter FY11 Q2 10-Q]

[207] MF Global RTM Memo, *supra* note 177, at 4.

[208] S&P, *Research Update: MF Global Holdings' Rating is Lowered to 'BBB-'; Outlook Stable*, Nov. 24, 2010.

[209] *Id.*

[210] *Id.*

[211] Letter to Michael Roseman from Thomas F. Connolly, Global Head of Human Resources, MF Global (Feb. 24, 201), at 1; Michael Stockman timeline provided to O&I Subcomm. (June 21, 2012), at 4,6 [hereinafter Stockman timeline]. Stockman had been contacted about applying for the position on Sept. 16, 2010.

[212] Stockman Timeline, *supra* note 211, at 5.

[213] *Hearing on The Collapse of MF Global: Part 2 Before the Subcomm. on O&I of the House Comm. on Fin. Services,* 112th Cong. 37 (testimony of Michael Stockman, Global CRO, MF Global Holdings Ltd.) [hereinafter Feb.2, 2012 Hearing].

[214] *Id.*

[215] Form 10-Q for MF Global Ltd. (quarterly period ended Dec. 31, 2010) [hereinafter FY11 Q3 10-Q].

[216] Press Release, Moody's, Moody's affirms MF Global's Baa2 rating, maintains negative outlook (Feb. 3, 2011).

[217] E-mail from Michael Stockman, CRO, MF Global, to Martin Glynn (Feb. 24, 2011, 07:44 p.m.).

[218] *See* E-mail from Martin Glynn, to Michael Stockman, CRO, MF Global (Feb. 25, 2011, 03:00 p.m.).

[219] *Id.*

[220] Memorandum from Michael Stockman, CRO, MF Global, to MF Global Board of Directors (Mar. 2, 2011). In the memo, Stockman wrote that the "European sovereign trade is a unique opportunity in the capital markets to earn reasonable to high reward to risk returns relative to other available strategies." Despite the fact that the "transactions [had] default or restructuring risk," those risks were "not the focus" of Stockman's "current market risk analysis" because, "[b]ased on current spreads, the market is pricing in a very small probability of this scenario." In the memo, however, Stockman estimated that the RTM positions could subject the company to margin calls and haircuts of between $297 million and $761 million. *Id.*

[221] MF Global Holdings Ltd., Executive Committee of the Board of Directors, Meeting Minutes, at 2 (Mar. 23, 2011); Stockman timeline, *supra* note 211, at 1.

[222] FY11 10-K, *supra* note 131.

[223] *Id.*

[224] Stockman timeline, *supra* note 211, at 1.

[225] *Id.*

[226] *Id.*

[227] *Id.*

[228] *Id.*

[229] Form 10-Q for MF Global Ltd. (quarterly period ended June 30, 2011), at 90.

[230] Stockman timeline, *supra* note 211, at 1-2.

[231] *Id.* at 2.

[232] *Id.*

[233] E-mail from Michael Stockman, CRO, MF Global, to Jon Corzine, CEO, MF Global (July 30, 2011, 02:33 p.m.); Stockman timeline, *supra* note 211, at 3.

[234] MF Global Euro Sovereign Portfolio, *supra* note 166, at 6.

[235] Memorandum from MF Global Investor Relations to MF Global Board of Directors (Oct. 2011).

[236] Stockman timeline, *supra* note 211, at 4. Stockman informed O&I Subcomm. staff that his recollection of Corzine's statement to the board of directors is based on a conversation that Stockman had with another MF Global employee after the Aug. 2011 board meeting.

[237] Stockman timeline, *supra* note 211, at 3; MF Global Euro Sovereign Portfolio, *supra* note 166, at 2.

[238] Telephone Interview by O&I Subcomm. staff with Michael Stockman, in Wash., D.C. (June 13, 2012); Feb. 2,2012 Hearing, *supra* note 213, at 3 (statement of Michael Stockman, Global CRO, MF Global Holdings Ltd.).

[239] Mar. 28, 2012 Hearing, *supra* note 179, at 92 (testimony of Henri Steenkamp, CFO, MF Global Holdings Ltd.);Feb. 2, 2012 Hearing, *supra* note 213, at 76 (testimony of Mr. Michael Stockman, Global CRO, MF Global Holdings Ltd.); MF Global, Stress Scenario Analysis—Downgrade Potential Impact on MF Global (Oct. 13, 2011).

[240] MF Global, Stress Scenario Analysis—Downgrade Potential Impact on MF Global (Oct. 13, 2011).

[241] *Id.*

[242] FASB Topic 820, *supra* note 184.

[243] Telephone Interview by O&I Subcomm. staff with PricewaterhouseCoopers [hereinafter PwC] personnel, in Wash., D.C. (Oct. 10, 2012) [hereinafter Telephone Interview with PwC].

[244] Telephone Interview by O&I Subcomm. staff with MF Global executive, in Wash., D.C. (Oct. 4, 2012) [hereinafter Telephone Interview with MF Global Exec.]. PwC, MF Global's independent auditor, described the model differently; in their view, the model did not incorporate a separate probability-of-default input, and it did not independently consider the value of the repurchase agreement. Telephone Interview with PwC, *supra* note 243.

[245] In addition, when MF Global revised its valuation methodology in Jan. 2011, the company reassessed the value of the derivative as of Sept. 30, 2010 and determined that, under the revised method, the value of the derivative was immaterial. Telephone Interview with MF Global Exec., *supra* note 244.

[246] FY11 Q2 10-Q, *supra* note 206.

[247] *Id.*

[248] PwC Two-Legged Repo to Maturity Audit Memorandum (Dec. 31, 2010), at 3 [hereinafter PwC Dec. 31, 2010 Audit Memo].

[249] Telephone Interview with PwC, *supra* note 243.

[250] Telephone Interview with MF Global Exec., *supra* note 244. According to PwC staff, PwC counseled that MF Global adopt a methodology that incorporated additional market factors and that independently considered the bond and repurchase agreement values. Telephone Interview with PwC, *supra* note 243.

[251] *Id.*

[252] E-mail from George C. Gallagher, Partner, Banking and Capital Markets, PwC, to Peter M. Messana, PwC (Jan. 3, 2011, 06:34 a.m.).

[253] *Id.*

[254] *Id.*

[255] PwC Memorandum (Dec. 23, 2010). In an interview with O&I Subcomm. staff, one of MF Global's executives recounted his belief that PwC was aware of, and did not object to, MF Global's use of the "probability-of-default" valuation approach. The executive further recounted that PwC was present at a meeting of the audit committee of MF Global's board of directors during the fall of 2010, at which the audit committee discussed the probability-of default approach. As a result, the executive indicated, MF Global's management did not anticipate that PwC would advise the company in Dec. 2010 that it should change the way it valued the derivative associated with the forward repurchase commitment. Telephone Interview with MF Global Exec., *supra* note 244. On the other hand, PwC stated in an interview with O&I Subcomm. staff that it never approved or otherwise opined on a valuation method that incorporated an explicit "probability-of-default" input. Telephone Interview with PwC, *supra* note 243. Further, PwC stated that it did not recall being present at an audit committee meeting at which the committee discussed such a valuation methodology. *Id.*

[256] PwC Test Forward Repurchase Commitment Audit Memorandum (Dec. 31, 2010), at 2.

[257] *Id.*

[258] *Id.*

[259] PwC FY11 Q3 MF Global Update Meeting Minutes (Jan. 25, 2011); *see also* PwC Dec. 31, 2010 Audit Memo, *supra* note 248, at 3 (noting "Management has added additional disclosures beginning in the 3rd quarter 10Q").

[260] FY11 Q3 10-Q, *supra* note 215.

[261] FY11 Q3 10-Q, *supra* note 215, at 14, 80.

[262] *Id.* at 14.

[263] *Id.*

[264] FY11 10-K, *supra* note 131.

[265] *Id.* at 71. In 2003, pursuant to a mandate contained in the Sarbanes-Oxley Act of 2002, the SEC adopted rules requiring the disclosure of a company's off-balance sheet arrangements. *See* Sarbanes Oxley Act of 2002, Pub. L. No. 107-204 (July 30, 2002), §401. As a result, MF Global was required to explain its off-balance sheet arrangements in a specially captioned part of its regulatory filings. Disclosure in Management's Discussion and Analysis About Off-Balance Sheet Arrangements and Aggregate Contractual Obligations, 2003 WL 175446 (SEC Jan. 28, 2003).

[266] *Id.* at 49.

[267] *Id.* at 76.

[268] *Id.* at 77-78.

[269] *Id.* at 71.
[270] MFGI, Annual Audited Financial Statement, Note 4 (March 31, 2011).
[271] *See, e.g.*, PwC Partner notes, meeting with Jon Corzine (Apr. 27, 2011) (noting that RTM volatility was as yet "not material" but that Corzine "understood the fwd was at fair value and could *introduce* volatility into the P&L") (emphasis added).
[272] MF Global, Global Liquidity and Capital Management, Internal Audit Report, at 2 (June 2011).
[273] *Id.*
[274] *Id.*
[275] E-mail from Kari Jin, Broker Dealer Risk Office, SEC, to Bob Larson, CBOE, and Jeffrey Fortune, Fin. Industry Regulatory Authority [hereinafter FINRA] (June 7, 2011, 10:56 a.m.). The meeting was part of the SEC's 17-H program, which authorizes regulators to analyze "financial dependencies and unregulated business activities which could potentially affect the net capital, liquidity, financing or profitability of [MFGI]." SEC Risk Assessment Program. http://www.sec.gov/divisions/marketreg/bdriskoffice.htm (last visited July 19, 2012). MF Global's losses and changing business model had caused "concerns" at the SEC, prompting SEC staff members to request the June meeting. E-mail from Melanie Chan, SEC, to Jeffrey Fortune, FINRA (June 14, 2011, 12:29 p.m.). The SEC previously met with MF Global executives in Jan. 2010 and held a conference call on Apr. 6, 2011 pursuant to the 17-H program. See E-mail from Matt McGarvey, Branch Chief, 17-H Broker Dealer Operations, Div. of Trading and Markets, SEC, to Robert W. Cook, Dir., Div. of Trading and Markets, SEC (Dec. 9, 2011, 05:05 p.m.).
[276] MF Global 17-H Meeting Agenda (June 14, 2011).
[277] MF Global SEC Presentation, *supra* note 97.
[278] *See* E-mail from Edith O'Brien, Ass't Treasurer, MF Global, to Christine Serwinski, North American CFO, MF Global (July 19, 2011, 2:37 p.m.) (asking about Serwinski's call with Steenkamp regarding use of excess funds). Inan interview with O&I Subcomm. staff, Christine Serwinski stated that, to her belief, Jon Corzine initiated the request that Steenkamp discuss with Serwinski whether the Regulatory Excess could be used for this purpose. Telephone Interview by O&I Subcomm. staff, with Christine Serwinski, North American CFO, MF Global, in Wash., D.C. (July 23, 2012) [hereinafter Telephone Interview with Serwinski].
[279] MFGI Trustee Report, *supra* note 123, at 38.
[280] E-mail from Christine Serwinski, North American CFO, MF Global, to Henri Steenkamp, CFO, MF Global (July27, 2011, 04:25 p.m.).
[281] E-mail from Christine Serwinski, North American CFO, MF Global, to Edith O'Brien, Ass't Treasurer, MF Global (July 19, 2011, 02:46 p.m.).
[282] In the event that the aggregate assets on deposit in customer segregated and secured accounts were less than MF Global's liabilities to customers under the Net Liquidation Method, Serwinski and her colleagues determined that MFGI would have to "lock up" funds equal to the difference in the *securities* customer reserve account that the company maintained pursuant to Rule 15c3-3. MFGI Trustee Report, *supra* note 123, at 77. MF Global's employees made this determination after consulting guidance issued by FINRA interpreting Rule 15c3-3. E-mail from Matthew Hughey, Controller, Fin. Regulatory Group, MF Global, to Christine Serwinski, North American CFO, MF Global (July 28, 2011, 12:47 p.m.). Under the rule, MF Global determined the amounts to set aside in the 15c3-3 account as of the close of business each Fri. and at the end of the month.
[283] *See, e.g.,* MFGI Trustee Report, *supra* note 123, at 77-78. Because MF Global was transferring funds within the same legal entity, the "loans" that MF Global referred to were not loans in any legal sense, but rather were merely transfers of funds.
[284] *Id.* at 103 (noting transfers exceeding firm invested in excess on Wed., Oct. 26, 2011).
[285] MFGI Trustee Report, *supra* note 123, at 88, Annex F, at 7.

[286] E-mail from Henri Steenkamp, CFO, MF Global, to Jon Corzine, CEO, MF Global (Oct. 6, 2011, 9:05 p.m.) [hereinafter Steenkamp E-mail].
[287] *Id.*
[288] *Id.*
[289] *Id.*
[290] Dec. 15, 2011 Hearing, *supra* note 50, at 155 (statement of Richard G. Ketchum, Chairman and CEO, FINRA).
[291] Interview by O&I Subcomm. staff with FINRA personnel, in Wash., D.C. (June 27, 2012) [hereinafter Interview with FINRA].
[292] *Id.*; Dec. 15, 2011 Hearing, *supra* note 50, at 155 (statement of Richard G. Ketchum, Chairman and CEO, FINRA).
[293] Interview with FINRA, *supra* note 291.
[294] *Id.* MF Global reported $6.7 million and $2.9 million losses in Jan. and Feb. respectively.
[295] *Id.* MFGI did not record the expense associated with allocating RTM revenue to MFGUK as a discrete, expressly captioned line-item on the income statement in the company's March 2011 FOCUS report. Rather, after performing a "variance analysis" at line 14145 of the report, FINRA determined that MFGI incurred over $59 million in increased expenses for "Commissions and Clearance Paid to All Other Brokers" in Mar. as compared to Feb. This increase represented the majority of the overall increase in the expenses that MFGI incurred in Mar.
[296] PwC, Annual Audited Financial Statement, at 9 (quarter ended Mar. 31, 2011).
[297] Annual Audited Financial Statements are filed by broker-dealers pursuant to SEC Rule 17a-5, though they are similar in many respects to 10-K annual reports, which are filed by all public companies. Interview with FINRA, *supra* note 291.
[298] Dec. 15, 2011 Hearing, *supra* note 50, at 155 (statement of Robert Cook, Dir., Div. of Trading and Markets, SEC).
[299] Interview with FINRA, *supra* note 291.
[300] *Id.*
[301] *Id.*
[302] See SEC Staff Guidance to NYSE, Repurchase Transactions to Maturity (No. 97-6, Oct. 1997).
[303] Interview with FINRA, *supra* note 291; Dec. 15, 2011 Hearing, *supra* note 50, at 155 (statement of Richard G. Ketchum, Chairman and CEO, FINRA).
[304] Interview with FINRA, *supra* note 291.
[305] *Id.*
[306] *Id.*
[307] *Id.*
[308] Because it was unusual for the CEO to personally present his company's position on such a matter, SEC staff were "surprised" that Corzine personally attended the meeting. Interview by Subcomm. on O&I staff with SEC personnel, in Wash., D.C. (June 29, 2012) [hereinafter June 2012 Interview with SEC]; *see also* E-mail from Neil Hatton, MFGUK, to Henri Steenkamp, CFO, MF Global (Sept. 1, 2011, 01:00 p.m.) (characterizing MF Global's position that regulators were reinterpreting the net capital rule).
[309] E-mail from Laurie Ferber, Gen. Counsel, MF Global, to Laurie Ferber (Sept. 6, 2011, 09:32 a.m.).
[310] June 2012 Interview with SEC, *supra* note 308.
[311] *Id.*
[312] *Id.* News of the exposure, without haircuts on the bonds, "raised [the] eyebrows" of some SEC staff members.
[313] *Id.*
[314] Interview with FINRA, *supra* note 291.
[315] See Memorandum from MFGI to FINRA (Aug. 11, 2011). Under the net capital rule, the haircuts imposed on U.S. bonds ranges between 0 and 1.5 percent, depending on the

maturity date, and the haircuts imposed on corporate bonds is two percent for bonds with a less than one year to maturity and three percent for bonds with between one and two years to maturity. MFGI's Belgian, Italian, and Spanish bonds were rated AA+, AA-, and AA+, and its Irish and Portuguese bonds were rated BBB+ and BBB-, the latter being the lowest investment grade category.

[316] *Id.*

[317] *Id.*

[318] Interview with FINRA, *supra* note 291.

[319] E-mail from Edith O'Brien, Ass't. Treasurer, MF Global, to David Dunne, MF Global (Aug. 25, 2011, 06:34 a.m.).

[320] Interview with FINRA, *supra* note 291.

[321] Letter from Michael Bolan, Global Product Controller, MF Global Inc., to Michael Macchiaroli, Assoc. Dir., Div. of Trading and Markets, SEC, at 1 (Aug. 25, 2011) [hereinafter MFGI letter to SEC].

[322] *Id.*

[323] Interview with FINRA, *supra* note 291.

[324] MFGI letter to SEC, *supra* note 321 *and* Dec. 15, 2011 Hearing, *supra* note 50, at 156 (statement of Richard G.Ketchum, Chairman and CEO, FINRA).

[325] MF Global Holdings Ltd., Amendment No. 1, Form 10-Q/A for the Quarter Ended June 30, 2011 at 1 (Sept. 1,2011).

[326] *Id.*

[327] Interview with CFTC, *supra* note 117; E-mail from Jill Sommers, Commissioner, CFTC, to O&I Subcomm. staff (Sept. 7, 2012, 11:32 a.m.).

[328] Aaron Lucchetti, *MF Global Told to Boost Capital*, WALL ST. J., Oct. 17, 2011 (http://online.wsj.com/article/SB10001424052970203658804576635361082548304.html) (last visited Oct. 24, 2012) [hereinafter Lucchetti Article].

[329] MF Global Stock Prices, *supra* note 46.

[330] *See* Lucchetti Article, *supra* note 328; MF Global Fin. Performance, *supra* note 46.

[331] E-mail from Henri Steenkamp, CFO, MF Global, to Al Bush, Moody's (Oct. 22, 2011, 11:33 p.m.).

[332] *Id.*

[333] Press Release, Moody's, Moody's Rating Action: Moody's downgrades MF Global to Baa3; reviews for further downgrade (Oct. 24, 2011).

[334] *Id.*

[335] Moody's Compliance – Rating Committee Addendum (Oct. 27, 2011).

[336] Press Release, Moody's, Moody's Rating Action: Moody's downgrades MF Global to Baa3; reviews for further downgrade (Oct. 24, 2011).

[337] E-mail from Jon S. Corzine, CEO, MF Global, to MF Global staff (Oct. 24, 2011, 06:26 p.m.).

[338] Shannon D. Harrington and Matthew Leising, *MF Global May Be Lowered to Junk by Moody's as Corzine Adds Trading Risk*, BLOOMBERG, Oct. 24, 2011 (http://www.bloomberg.com/news/2011-10-24/mf-global-may-belowered-to-junk-by-moody-s-as-corzine-adds-trading-risk.html) (last visited Oct. 24, 2012); MF Global Holdings Earning Call FY12 Q2 (Oct. 25, 2011).

[339] MF Global Holdings Earning Call FY12 Q2 (Oct. 25, 2011).

[340] *Id.*

[341] *Id.*

[342] *Id.*

[343] *Id.*

[344] *Id.*

[345] MF Global Holdings, Ltd. stock prices for Oct. 25, 2011. http://finance.yahoo.com/q/hp?s=MFGLQ&a=09&b=25&c=2011&d=09&e=25&f=2011&g=d (last visited Oct. 24, 2012).

[346] MFGI Trustee Report, *supra* note 123, at 90.

[347] MFGI Trustee Report, *supra* note 123, at 145-46, 153.

[348] Dec. 15, 2011 Hearing, *supra* note 50, at 141 (testimony of Jon S. Corzine, CEO, MF Global).

[349] E-mail from Victoria Foster, European Head of Equity Finance, MFGUK, to Mark Whitehead, MFGUK, et al. (Oct. 25, 2011, 03:51 p.m.).

[350] S&P, Research Update: MF Global Holdings Ltd. Rating Placed on CreditWatch Negative (Oct. 26, 2011) [hereinafter S&P Research Update].

[351] S&P Jan. 17, 2012 letter, *supra* note 21, at 6; S&P Research Update, *supra* note 350, at 2. The CreditWatch action signaled to the market that S&P believed there was a substantial likelihood of a rating action for MF Global within 90 days. *See* S&P, General Criteria: Use of CreditWatch and Outlooks, at 3 (Sept. 14, 2009).

[352] S&P Research Update, *supra* note 350, at 2.

[353] MFGI Trustee Report, *supra* note 123, at 102-03.

[354] *Id.* In addition, an MF Global employee gave three computer discs to a CFTC employee at 5:30 p.m. on Fri., Oct. 28, which contained information relevant to the computation of balances in MFGI's segregated accounts. While the CFTC did not comprehensively review the disks when it received them, it later examined MFGI's records, including the data on the disks, and determined there was a deficiency in customer funds in segregated accounts as of Wed., Oct. 26. "Implementing Derivatives Reform: Reducing Systemic Risk and Improving Market Oversight," Senate Committee on Banking, Housing and Urban Affairs, 112th Congress, 2d Session, May 22, 2012 (CFTC Responses for the Record to Senator Shelby).

[355] Mar. 28, 2012 Hearing, *supra* note 179, at 6-7 (statement of Laurie Ferber, Gen. Counsel, MF Global); Interview by O&I Subcomm. staff with SEC personnel, in Wash., D.C. (Mar. 15, 2012) [hereinafter Mar. 2012 Interview with SEC].

[356] Mar. 28, 2012 Hearing, *supra* note 179, at 6-7 (statement of Laurie Ferber, Gen. Counsel, MF Global); E-mail from Matt McGarvey, Branch Chief, 17H Broker Dealer Operations, Trading and Markets Div., SEC, to Robert Cook, Dir. Trading and Markets Div., SEC (Dec. 9, 2011, 02:21 p.m.).

[357] Press Release, Moody's, Ratings Action: Moody's downgrades MF Global to Ba2; reviews for further downgrade (Oct. 27, 2011); William Spain, *Fitch Ratings Downgrades MF Global*, WALL ST. J. MARKET WATCH, Oct. 27, 2011 (http://articles.marketwatch.com/2011-10-27/news/30903166_1_fitch-ratings-downgrades-issuerdefault-ratings) (last visited July 21, 2012) [hereinafter Spain Article].

[358] Spain Article, *supra* note 357.

[359] *Id.*

[360] *Id.*

[361] *Id.*

[362] MFGI Trustee Report, *supra* note 123, at 94.

[363] *Id.* at 96.

[364] *Id.*

[365] *Id.*

[366] *Id.*

[367] Elkind Burke article, *supra* note 88. By the end of the week, customers had withdrawn $1 billion in funds from the company's customer accounts.

[368] Dec. 15, 2011 Hearing, *supra* note 50, at 67 (testimony of Dan M. Berkovitz, Gen. Counsel, CFTC); *Id*, at 119 (statement of Robert Cook, Dir., Div. of Trading and Markets, SEC).

[369] *Id.*

[370] Letter from Michael A. Procajlo, Director, Audits, CME Group, to Christine Serwinski, CFO, MFGI (Oct. 27, 2011).

[371] Mar. 28, 2012 Hearing, *supra* note 179, at 4 (statement Diane M. Genova, Deputy Gen. Counsel, JP Morgan Chase [hereinafter JPMC]).

[372] *Id.*

[373] *Id.*

[374] Interview by O&I Subcomm. staff with JPMC representatives, in Wash., D.C. (Mar. 9, 2012) [hereinafter Interview with JPMC]; *see also* MFGI Trustee Report, *supra* note 123, at 128.

[375] MFGI Trustee Report, *supra* note 123, at 128.

[376] Mar. 28, 2012 Hearing, *supra* note 179, at 4 (statement Diane M. Genova, Deputy Gen. Counsel, JPMC).

[377] E-mail from Vinay Mahajan, Global Treasurer, MF Global, to Russell Haley, MF Global, Edith O'Brien, Ass't. Treasurer, MF Global, cc: Jon Corzine, CEO, MF Global (Oct. 28, 2011, 08:27 a.m.).

[378] Dec. 15, 2011 Hearing, *supra* note 50, at 11 (testimony of the Hon. Jon Corzine, CEO, MF Global). In an e-mail to two MF Global employees, Vinay Mahajan explained that JPMC was "holding up vital business in the U.S. as a result" of the overdrawn UK account. E-mail from Vinay Mahajan, Global Treasurer, MF Global, to Jon Ferber, MF Global, Russell Haley, MF Global (Oct. 28, 2011, 01:35 p.m.). The employees were to confirm that the overdraft had been covered. *Id.*

[379] Dec. 15, 2011 Hearing, *supra* note 50, at 11 (testimony of the Hon. Jon Corzine, CEO, MF Global).

[380] E-mail from Edith O'Brien, Ass't. Treasurer, MF Global, to Laurie Ferber, Gen. Counsel, MF Global (Oct. 28, 2011, 05:37 p.m.) [hereinafter O'Brien E-mail Oct. 28, 2011, 05:37 p.m.]. A company's house account is an account designated for a company's own funds.

[381] E-mail from Edith O'Brien, Ass't Treasurer, MF Global, to Laurie Ferber, Gen. Counsel, MF Global (Oct. 28, 2011, 09:43 p.m.).

[382] E-mail from Edith O'Brien, Ass't Treasurer, MF Global, to Russell Haley, MF Global (Oct. 28. 2011, 01:34 p.m.).

[383] O'Brien E-mail Oct. 28, 2011, 05:37 p.m., *supra* note 380; Interview by O&I Subcomm. staff with Matthew Hughey, Controller, Fin. Regulatory Group, MF Global, in Wash., D.C. (May 29, 2012) [hereinafter Interview with Hughey]. The most recent statement reported excess funds of approximately $116 million in segregated accounts as of Wednesday and, on Thursday, the company had returned a total net amount of approximately $375 million to the accounts. *See* MFGI Trustee Report, *supra* note 123, at 107, fn. 117, at 109, fn. 79. In fact, balances in the company's segregated accounts were not as O'Brien may have understood; subsequent analysis by the MFGI trustee determined there was a deficiency in customer funds on deposit in segregated accounts as of the close of business on Wednesday and Thursday. *Id.* at Annex D (detailing $298 million deficiency as of Wednesday and $413 million deficiency as of Thursday).

[384] Mar. 28, 2012 Hearing, *supra* note 179, at 7 (statement of Diane Genova, Deputy Gen. Counsel, JPMC).

[385] Interview with JPMC, *supra* note 374.; *see also* Mar. 28, 2012 Hearing, *supra* note 179, at 7 (statement of Diane Genova, Deputy Gen. Counsel, JPMC).

[386] E-mail from Donna Dellosso, Managing Dir., TSS Risk Management, JPMC, to Jon Corzine, CEO, MF Global(Oct. 28, 2011, 02:28 p.m.).

[387] *Id.*

[388] Mar. 28, 2012 Hearing, *supra* note 182, at 139 (testimony of Dianne Genova, Deputy Gen. Counsel, JPMC). *See Id.* at 51 (testimony of Laurie Ferber, Gen. Counsel, MF Global) ("My understanding was JPMorgan confirmed that they were interested in two transfers…and on inquiry, [I] thought it would be better if [the letter] was limited to that. We would be able to make that [representation]. I…asked them to…limit the letter to what they needed and we would get it signed"); *Id.* at 139 (testimony of Dianne Genova, Deputy Gen. Counsel, JPMC) ("I personally had conversations with both Ms. Ferber and her deputy…who gave me oral assurances that they knew the rules, they were in compliance with the rules, and that—and when we finally revised the letter to only refer to the two transfers that I…really had some concerns about, that in fact the letter would be signed"); E-mail from Dennis Klejna, MF Global, to Laurie Ferber, Gen. Counsel, MF Global (Oct. 28, 2011, 08:08 p.m.).

[389] Interview with Hughey, *supra* note 383.

[390] *Id.* Chenoweth's determination that the five transactions were incorrectly booked later turned out to be erroneous. MFGI Trustee Report, *supra* note 50, at 112.

[391] *Id.*

[392] Telephone Interview with Serwinski, *supra* note 278.

[393] Interview with Hughey, *supra* note 383.

[394] Dec. 15, 2011 Hearing, *supra* note 50, at 13 (testimony of Thomas C. Baxter, Jr., Gen. Counsel, NYFRB).

[395] Mar. 28, 2012 Hearing, *supra* note 179, at 48 *(*testimony of Christine Serwinski, North American CFO, MF Global).

[396] *Id.* at 3 (statement of Christine Serwinski, North American CFO, MF Global).

[397] *See id.* at 48-49 (testimony of Christine Serwinski, North American CFO, MF Global); Mar. 28, 2012 Hearing, *supra* note 179, at 7 (testimony of Laurie Ferber, Gen. Counsel, MF Global).

[398] Dec. 15, 2011 Hearing, *supra* note 50, at 141-142 (testimony of Jon Corzine, CEO, MF Global, Inc.).

[399] E-mail from Grace Vogel, FINRA, to Richard Ketchum, FINRA, et al (Oct. 29, 2011, 07:10 p.m.).

[400] *Id.* JPMC told MF Global's financial advisor that it was not interested in purchasing the company, but might be interested in particular assets or securities portfolios.

[401] *See* E-mail from Gary Gensler, Chairman, CFTC, to Bart Chilton, Commissioner, CFTC (Oct. 30, 2011, 08:05p.m.); E-mail from Gary Gensler, Chairman, CFTC, to Mark Metjen, CFTC (Oct. 30, 2011, 08:13 p.m.) [hereinafter Gensler E-mail].

[402] *See* E-mail from Michael Procajlo, CME Group, to Thomas Smith, CFTC, et al (Oct. 28, 2011, 12:01 p.m.).

[403] *See* Gensler E-mail, *supra* note 401.

[404] *Id.*

[405] *Id.*

[406] E-mail from Robert Wasserman, Chief Counsel, Div. of Clearing and Risk, CFTC, to Gary Gensler, Chairman, CFTC (Oct. 30, 2011, 02:19 p.m.).

[407] *Id.*

[408] E-mail from Gary Gensler, Chairman, CFTC, to Ananda Radhakrishnan, CFTC, Gary Barnett, CFTC (Oct. 30, 09:56 a.m.); E-mail from Melissa Hendrickson, CFTC, to Thelma Diaz, CFTC, Robert Wasserman, CFTC (Oct. 30, 2011 at 02:54 p.m.).

[409] E-mail from Melissa Hendrickson, CFTC, to Thelma Diaz, CFTC, Robert Wasserman, CFTC (Oct. 30, 2011, 02:57 p.m.).

[410] *Id.*

[411] E-mail from Robert Wasserman, Chief Counsel, Div. of Clearing and Risk, CFTC, to Edith O'Brien, Ass't Treasurer, MF Global, Matthew Hughey, Controller, Fin. Regulatory Group, MF Global, et al (Oct. 30, 2011, 03:40 p.m.).

[412] E-mail from Robert Wasserman, Chief Counsel, Div. of Clearing and Risk, CFTC, to Melissa Hendrickson, CFTC, et al. (Oct. 30, 2011, 02:59 p.m.).

[413] E-mail from Mary Schapiro, Chairman, SEC, to Robert W. Cook, Dir., Div. of Trading and Markets SEC (Oct. 30, 2011, 02:12 p.m.).

[414] *See* CME MF Global Chronology, Week of Oct. 24-31, 2011 [hereinafter CME Chron], at Oct. 30, 2011(stating that at approximately 2:00 p.m. U.S. Central Time CFTC staff member Melissa Hendrickson called Michael Procajlo and told him she had seen a draft of 10/28 segregated statement and that it showed a deficiency in segregated customer funds.).

[415] *Id.*

[416] *See id.* at 5-8.

[417] *Id.* at 6-7, 6:00 p.m.

[418] *Id.*

[419] *Id.* at 7, 8:00 p.m. to 9:00 p.m.

[420] *Id.*

[421] *Id.* at 8, 9 p.m. to 10 p.m.

[422] *Id.*

[423] Mar. 28, 2012 Hearing, *supra* note 179, at 4 (statement of Christine Serwinski, CFO for North America, MF Global).
[424] Telephone Interview by O&I Subcomm. staff with Christine Serwinski, North American CFO, MF Global, in Wash., D.C. (Jan. 5, 2012).
[425] *Id.*
[426] CME Chron, *supra* note 414, at 8, approximately 1 a.m. – 2 a.m.
[427] Dec. 15, 2011 Hearing, *supra* 50, at 50 (statement of Robert Cook, Dir., Div. of Trading and Markets, SEC); *Id.,* at 54 (statement of Terrence A. Duffy, Exec. Chairman, CME Group); E-mail from Robert Wasserman, CFTC, to Gary Barnett, CFTC, and Thelma Diaz, CFTC (Oct.31, 2011, 01:58 a.m.).
[428] E-mail from Christine Serwinski, North American CFO, MF Global, to Mike Bolan, MF Global, Henri Steenkamp, CFO, MF Global (Oct. 31, 2011, 10:25 a.m.).
[429] MFGI Trustee Report, *supra* note 123, at 119.
[430] Mar. 2012 Interview with SEC, *supra* note 355; Telephone Interview by O&I Subcomm. staff with FINRA personnel, in Wash., D.C. (Feb. 29, 2012); Telephone interview by O&I Subcomm. staff with FINRA personnel, in Wash., D.C. (Apr. 25, 2012). In an interview with O&I Subcomm. staff, Christine Serwinski stated that, to her recollection, no one communicated to her an instruction or caution from regulators that MF Global not transfer excess funds from the securities customer account.
[431] E-mail from Matthew Hughey, Controller, Fin. Regulatory Group, MF Global, to Dennis Klejna, MF Global, Kemper Cagney, MFGUK (Oct. 31, 2011, 12:50 a.m.) [hereinafter Hughey E-mail].
[432] Interview with Hughey, *supra* note 383; Mar. 28, 2012 Hearing, *supra* note 179 (testimony of Christine Serwinski) (stating that Serwinski would not have made the transfer had she been consulted).
[433] Hughey E-mail, *supra* note 431.
[434] *See id.*
[435] E-mail from Matthew Hughey, Controller, Fin. Regulatory Group, MF Global, to Dennis Klejna (Oct. 31, 2011, 08:02 p.m.).
[436] Interview with CME Group, *supra* note 130. The transfer may have been an "equity withdrawal" to the extent it constituted an unsecured loan.
[437] E-mail from Ethan Allfree, SEC, to Robert Sollazzo, SEC (Nov. 1, 2011, 01:14 p.m.).
[438] E-mail from Jeffrey Fortune, FINRA, to Grace Vogel, Executive V.P., FINRA (Nov. 1, 2011, 02:00 p.m.).
[439] E-mail from Robert W. Cook, Dir., Div. Trading and Markets, SEC, to Mary Schapiro, Chairman, SEC, et al. (Nov. 1, 2011, 02:16 p.m.).
[440] E-mail from Mary Schapiro, Chairman, SEC, to Robert W. Cook, Dir., Div. Trading and Markets, SEC (Nov. 1, 2011, 02:18 p.m.) [hereinafter Schapiro E-mail].
[441] Felix Salmon, *What happened at MF Global?*, REUTERS, Nov. 1, 2011 (http://blogs.reuters.com/felixsalmon/2011/11/01/what-happened-at-mf-global/) (last visited Oct. 24, 2012).
[442] Freeh Report, *supra* note 191. On Nov. 28, 2011, the bankruptcy court approved the U.S. bankruptcy trustee's appointment of Louis J. Freeh as the trustee of MF Global's estate.
[443] *Id.* at 29, 30; *see also* 15 U.S.C. §78aaa et seq.
[444] Order Granting App. to Liquidate MF Global, Inc. pursuant to Securities Investor Protection Act, *Securities Investor Protection Corp. v. MF Global Inc.*, No. 11-02790, at 1 (S.D.N.Y. entered Oct 31, 2011).
[445] Freeh Report, *supra* note 191, at 34.
[446] MFGI Trustee Report, *supra* note 123, at 2.
[447] *Id.* at 8.
[448] Update Regarding June 20, 2012 Interim Distribution, http://dm.epiq11.com/MFG/Project#Section2_35 (last visited July 23, 2012).
[449] MFGI Trustee Report, *supra* note 123, at 157.

[450] *See, e.g.,* Witness Statement of Richard Heis at 7, *In the Matter of MF Global UK Limited*, No. 9527 (2011).
[451] *Id.* at 9.
[452] *Id.* at 8.
[453] Update to 30.7 Customers Regarding UK Legal Proceedings, June 1, 2012, *available at* http://dm.epiq11.com/MFG/Project#Section2_31 (last visited July 23, 2012).
[454] MFGI Trustee Report, *supra* note 123, at 3.
[455] *See In re Griffin Trading Company*, 245 B.R. 291, 296 (N.D. Ill. 2000) (vacated 270 B.R. 882 (N.D. Ill. 2001)).
[456] Freeh Report, *supra* note 191, at 87.
[457] *Id.*
[458] *Id.* at 87, 88, 109-111.
[459] John Gapper and Izabella Kaminska, *Downfall of MF Global*, FIN. TIMES, Nov. 4, 2011 (http://www.ft.com/intl/cms/s/0/2882d766-06fb-11e1-90de-00144feabdc0.html#axzz290FsXI68) (last visited Oct. 24, 2012).
[460] E-mail from Kari Jin, Broker Dealer Risk Office, SEC, to Bob Larson, CBOE, Jeffrey Fortune, FINRA (June 7, 2011, 10:57 a.m.); In an email to FINRA personnel about the June 14, 2011 17-H meeting, SEC personnel stated that "[t]he SEC has concerns with MF Global." E-mail from Melanie Chan, SEC, to Jeffrey Fortune, FINRA (June 14, 2011, 12:25 p.m.).
[461] A CFTC senior staffer informed the O&I Subcommittee that, in hindsight, he wished that FINRA and the SEC had discussed the capital charge with the CFTC sooner. Had they done so, the staffer stated that the CFTC would have learned why FINRA was worried about the valuation of the European bonds for regulatory capital purposes, would have learned more about the nature of RTMs, and would have known in advance that MFGI was going to restate its capital. The staffer stated that he would like to know when a company enters into highly risky proprietary trades, even if it executes them through its securities broker-dealer. Interview with CFTC, *supra* note 117.
[462] June 2012 Interview with SEC, *supra* note 308.
[463] *Id.*
[464] In an Oct. 30, 2011, email exchange between SEC's Director of the Division of Trading and Markets, Robert Cook, and SEC Chairman Mary Schapiro, the two acknowledged that there were three conference calls between securities and commodities regulators scheduled for 10 a.m. Chairman Schapiro commented, "Ahhhh, coordination in action!" To which Cook responded, "If we were really coordinated, we wouldn't have 3 calls at 10am!!" Chairman Schapiro responded, "Exactly!!" E-mail from Mary L. Schapiro, Chairman, SEC, to Robert W. Cook, Dir.of the Div. of Trading and Markets, SEC (Oct. 30, 2011, 09:54 a.m.).
[465] Schapiro E-mail, *supra* note 440.
[466] *A Joint Report of the SEC and the CFTC on Harmonization of Regulation*, at 15 (Oct. 16, 2009) (http://www.cftc.gov/ucm/groups/public/@otherif/documents/ifdocs/opacftc-secfinaljointreport101.pdf).
[467] *Id.*
[468] *Id.* at 16.
[469] *Id.*
[470] Memorandum of Understanding Between the SEC and the CFTC Regarding Oversight of Security Futures Product Trading and Sharing of Security Futures Product Information (Mar. 17, 2004) (http://www.cftc.gov/ucm/groups/public/@internationalaffairs/documents/file/moubetweencftcandsec031704.pdf) (last visited Oct. 17, 2012).
[471] Memorandum of Understanding Between the SEC and the CFTC Regarding Coordination in Areas of Common Regulatory Interest (Mar. 11, 2008) (http://www.sec.gov/news/press/2008/2008-40_mou.pdf) (last visited Oct. 17, 2012).
[472] *Id.* at 3.

[473] Press Release, SEC, SEC, CFTC Sign Agreement to Enhance Coordination, Facilitate Review of New Derivative Products (Mar. 11, 2008) (http://www.sec.gov/news/press/2008/2008-40.htm) (last visited Oct. 17, 2012).

[474] SEC and CFTC Joint meetings on Harmonization of Regulation (Sept. 2, 2009) http://www.sec.gov/rules/other/2009/34-60539.pdf; CFTC and SEC, A Joint Report of the SEC and the CFTC on Harmonization of Regulation (Oct. 16, 2009), at 14-15 http://www.cftc.gov/ucm/groups/public/@otherif/documents/ifdocs/opacftc-secfinaljointreport101.pdf

[475] Interview with FINRA, *supra* note 291.

[476] Specifically, the amendment represented that MFGI could comply with its capital requirements as a result of the charge, but it did not state the value of the European bond holdings by which MFGI calculated "haircuts" under the capital rule. The size of the capital charge imposed upon the company was directly proportional to the value of its European bond holdings. The Sept. 1, 2011 10-Q/A amended MF Global's quarterly report for the period ended June 30, 2011. The original filing disclosed that the notional value of MFGI's net exposure to European sovereign debt at the end of June. In Aug. 2011, MFGI transferred European RTM trades in Italian sovereign debt with a notional value of $4.2 billion to a non-regulated affiliate, thus reducing haircut charges by approximately $120 million.

[477] *Id.* Additionally, SEC staff was surprised to learn that MF Global had entered into the European RTM trades without taking haircuts on the European bonds. They believed that the capital rule was "cut and dry" and that, at a minimum, MF Global's executives should have asked the SEC to confirm whether the company's interpretation of the net capital rule was correct when they began entering into the European positions. June 2012 Interview with SEC, *supra* note 308. By contrast, MF Global's executives believed that the trades would not impose a capital cost on the company, relying, among other things, on guidance that held that the SEC's net capital rule did not require firms to take haircuts on U.S. Treasuries underlying European RTM trades. *See infra* at 50.

[478] In his e-mail to Corzine, the O&I Subcomm. believes that Steenkamp referred to a liquidity condition that existed before Oct. 2011. *See* Steenkamp E-mail, *supra* note 286 ("There remains a significant stress on liquidity—this week, after a couple of better days since quarter-end [on Sept. 30, 2011], the stresses have *returned*") (emphasis added).

[479] *Id.* ("Of most concern, is the sustained levels of stress and the lack of signs this will reduce soon. It makes drawdowns of the revolver more challenging, as we cannot guarantee certainty of immediate repayment. The revolver is not meant as a source of permanent liquidity").

[480] MF Global Holdings Ltd., F2Q 2012 Results (Qtr End Sept. 30, 2011) Earnings Call Transcript (Oct. 25, 2011).

[481] *Id.*

[482] Supplemental FOCUS Information: FINRA Requests Comment on Proposed Supplementary Schedule for Derivatives and Other Off-Balance Sheet Items, FINRA Regulatory Notice 12-23.

[483] Summary of Board Decisions, FASB (Oct. 3, 2012).

[484] Moody's Jan. 17, 2012 letter, *supra* note 80, at 12.

[485] MF Global Ltd. F4Q12 (Qtr End 03/31/11) Earnings Call Transcript (May 19, 2011). Though MF Global defined principal trading to include both proprietary trading as well as trading that facilitated client business, Steenkamp suggested the European RTM trades were proprietary positions when he described how the firm had reduced its "matched repo" book while entering into more European RTM trades, because the RTMs yielded greater revenues. The "matched repo book" referred to market making that facilitated client trades. Also, for the first quarter of FY12 the European sovereign positions accounted for about 12% of MF Global's revenues; another indication, by virtue of its relative size, that the trades were proprietary in nature. MF Global Ltd. F2Q12 (Qtr End 09/30/12) Earnings Call Transcript (Oct. 25, 2011).

[486] Gary Shorter and Michael V. Seitzinger, Cong.Research Serv., Report R40613, Credit Rating Agencies and Their Regulation 1 (2010). http://www.crs.gov/Products//r/pdf/R40613.pdf (last visited Oct. 9, 2012).

[487] The risk faced by MF Global's foreign secured customers was relatively low in the months leading up to the company's failure because MF Global usually maintained a positive "Firm Invested in Excess," meaning that the company deposited funds in secured and segregated accounts (which were for customers' domestic trading) that exceeded, in the aggregate, the company's liabilities to customers. On certain days in the last week of Oct. 2011, however, the risk that customers faced became greater. Internal statements prepared by MF Global reflected a negative Firm Invested in Excess, which indicated that the company's liabilities to its customers were greater than the aggregate assets on deposit in secured and segregated accounts.

[488] Despite the risks faced by MF Global's secured customers, and the regulators' concerns, by the time the company filed for bankruptcy, funds in the accounts exceeded MF Global's liabilities to foreign-trading customers by approximately $4 million.

[489] *In re Stotler & Co.*, 144 B.R. 385, 387 (N.D. Ill. 1992) (quoting S. Rep. No. 989, 95th Cong. 2d Sess. (1977)).

[490] Press Release, CFTC, CFTC Proposes New Regulations and to Amend Existing Regulations to Enhance Protections for Customers and Customer Funds Held by FCMs and Derivatives Clearing Organizations (Oct. 23, 2012).

[491] *Id.*

[492] Press Release, CFTC, CFTC Approves New Financial Rules Submitted by the NFA to Strengthen the Protection of Customer Funds Held by FCMs, CFTC (July 13, 2012); Letters from Thomas W. Sexton, Sr. V.P. and Gen. Counsel, NFA, to David A. Stawick, Office of the Secretariat, CFTC (May 29, 2012 and Aug. 21, 2012).

[493] Dec. 15, 2011 Hearing, *supra* note 50, at 94. The NYFRB has used the term the "Good Housekeeping Seal of Approval" as a description that industry sees primary dealer status as an endorsement by the NYFRB.

[494] Telephone Interview by O&I Subcomm. staff with Peter Fisher, former Exec. V.P. of NYFRB, in Wash., D.C. (July 23, 2012).

[495] Email from Krevolin, NYFRB, to Wolgemuth, NYFRB (Apr. 6, 2009, 07:26 p.m.)

[496] 17 C.F.R. §30.6; *see also* 17 C.F.R. §1.55 (prescribing text of disclosure statement).

In: Collapse and Bankruptcy of MF Global
Editor: Tao Zhu
ISBN: 978-1-62417-710-1

Chapter 3

STATEMENT OF JON S. CORZINE, FORMER CEO OF MF GLOBAL. HEARING ON "THE COLLAPSE OF MF GLOBAL"*

Chairman Neugebauer, Ranking Member Capuano and Distinguished Members of the Subcommittee:

Recognizing the enormous impact on many peoples' lives resulting from the events surrounding the MF Global bankruptcy, I appear at today's hearing with great sadness. My sadness, of course, pales in comparison to the losses and hardships that customers, employees and investors have suffered as a result of MF Global's bankruptcy. Their plight weighs on my mind every day–every hour. And, as the chief executive officer of MF Global at the time of its bankruptcy, I apologize to all those affected.

Before I address what happened, I must make clear that since my departure from MF Global on November 3, 2011, I have had limited access to many relevant documents, including internal communications and account statements, and even my own notes, all of which are essential to my being able to testify accurately about the chaotic, sleepless nights preceding the declaration of bankruptcy. Furthermore, even when I was at MF Global, my involvement in the firm's clearing, settlement and payment mechanisms, and accounting was limited.

The Members should also understand that the Subcommittee turned down my request to testify voluntarily in January. I had hoped that, by that time, I

* This is an edited, reformatted and augmented version of the testimony given on December 15, 2011 before the House Committee on Financial Services, Oversight and Investigations Subcommittee.

would have obtained and reviewed relevant records so that I could be more helpful to the Subcommittee.

As a consequence of my situation, not every fact of which I am or may have been aware that may be relevant to your inquiry is contained in this statement. While I intend to be responsive to the best of my ability today, without adequate time and materials to prepare, I may be unable to respond to various questions members might pose. Other questions, given my specific role in the company, will be questions for which I simply have no personal knowledge. Many of your questions may well be ones I myself have.

Considering the circumstances, many people in my situation would almost certainly invoke their constitutional right to remain silent a fundamental right that exists for the purpose of protecting the innocent. Nonetheless, as a former United States Senator who recognizes the importance of congressional oversight, and recognizing my position as former chief executive officer in these terrible circumstances, I believe it is appropriate that I attempt to respond to your inquiries.

My Background

I was born in 1947 and raised in the rural community of Taylorville, Illinois. After high school graduation in 1965, I attended the University of Illinois, from which I graduated in 1969. In the summer of 1969, I joined the United States Marine Corps Reserve, in which I served until 1975. In 1970, I enrolled in the University of Chicago Business School. I took classes at night while working at a bank during the day, and I and received my MBA in 1973.

In 1975, after working for a short time for a regional bank in Ohio, I took a job as a bond trader at the investment banking firm Goldman Sachs in New York. I remained at Goldman Sachs until January 1999, rising to the position of Senior Partner.

In 2000, I was elected to serve in the United States Senate representing New Jersey. I served in the Senate until January 2006, when I became the Governor of New Jersey. I was elected to one term as Governor, serving from January 2006 to January 2010.

Approximately three months after I left the governorship, I was recruited to become the chief executive officer of MF Global, whose prior chief executive had resigned abruptly after serving for 17 months. Prior to being approached about this position, I had no involvement with MF Global, and my only financial tie to it was extremely remote I was an investor in the private equity fund J.C. Flowers, which had an investment in MF Global and a seat on the board of directors. My connection to J.C. Flowers led to my introduction to MF Global.

MF GLOBAL BEFORE I JOINED

Before I joined the company in late March 2010, MF Global was primarily a brokerage which provided execution and clearing services for products traded in derivative markets on exchanges around the world. MF Global was primarily a voice-based broker, which means that it took and placed orders largely over the telephone and had not yet made significant use of electronic trading technology. As stated in MF Global's annual Form 10-K filing for the fiscal year ended March 31, 2009, the company's revenues derived principally from commission fees generated from execution and clearing services and from interest income on cash held in customer accounts.[1]

By 2010, however, online brokerages and high-frequency traders had begun exerting downward pressure on commissions. Interest rates were at historic lows and were expected to remain so for an "extended period," according to Federal Reserve policy statements. As a consequence of these developments among others, revenues were in decline. MF Global was accordingly experiencing substantial losses. The firm had reported losses in five consecutive quarters before I arrived, including the final quarter of the fiscal year ended March 31, 2010 (just as I was arriving),[2] and it had lost money in each of the previous three years, including the fiscal year that ended on March 31, 2010, for which the company posted a net loss to common shareholders of $167.7 million.[3] (MF Global's fiscal year ran from April 1 to March 31; the fiscal year ended on March 31, 2010 was MF Global's 2010 fiscal year.)

I took the job at MF Global even though the company was in a weak financial position because it had several positive attributes such as memberships on multiple derivative exchanges around the globe, solid market shares on those exchanges, and an extensive set of client relationships. I saw the possibility of taking part in the transformation of a challenged company by restructuring existing businesses and capturing opportunities available in the post-2008 financial environment.

Upon my arrival at MF Global, management and the board initiated a strategic review of our business. We engaged an outside consultant, the Boston Consulting Group, to help the firm define a business strategy that would lead it to profitability. Management, the board of directors, and the consultant came to the common conclusion that MF Global had to change its business strategy and diversify its revenues.

The new business plan provided, in substance, that MF Global would evolve into a broker-dealer, and ultimately into an investment bank, which would provide broker, dealer, underwriting, advisory and investment management services. The implementation of the plan was expected to take three to five years. This new strategic plan was communicated to the public.[4]

During my tenure as chief executive officer, MF Global made both structural and personnel changes in an effort to implement the strategic plan. One of the first priorities was to reduce the level of compensation as a percentage of MF Global's revenues. The company paying over 60% of its revenues to its employees, and sought to reduce this figure. Many employment contracts were restructured to increase the amount of pay that was dependent on MF Global's performance. My own pay was structured to include a substantial component determined by MF Global's performance, as discussed below.

Before my tenure at MF Global, Promontary Financial Group ("Promontory"), a prominent financial consulting firm run by Eugene Ludwig, the former United States Comptroller of the Currency, had been retained pursuant to a settlement with the CFTC to review and assess MF Global's implementation of the settlement.[5] During my tenure, we retained Promontory to review various of MF Global's compliance systems.

I was hopeful about the prospects for the company, and I invested in it personally. Much of my compensation was in the form of options to purchase stock, which would have value only if the company prospered. When the company made a public equity offering in June 2010, I purchased almost $2.5 million worth of stock. In 2011, I bought approximately $500,000 more stock in the company.[6]

MF Global's Leverage

One of the recurrent themes in the media has been that MF Global took on too much risk during my tenure, in particular the amount of leverage that MF Global bore at the time of its bankruptcy. In fact, MF Global reduced leverage. In the quarter ended March 31, 2010, MF Global's leverage was 37.3. During my tenure, it was consistently around 30.[7]

THE RTMs

A. Description of RTMs

There has been extensive comment about a series of positions entered into by MF Global that involved "repurchase transactions to maturity," known colloquially as "RTMs." I would like to address those here.

As relevant here, repurchase transactions (also known as "repos") worked roughly as follows: MF Global would purchase a debt security (such as sovereign debt) from a seller and would sell the same security to another party (the "Counterparty"), with an agreement to repurchase the security from the Counterparty at a later date. The agreement between MF Global and the Counterparty to sell and buy back the debt security was the repurchase agreement, and it served, in effect, as a loan from the Counterparty to MF Global. The Counterparty would hold the debt security as collateral for the loan.

An RTM is a particular kind of repurchase transaction in which the purchaser (MF Global) agrees to buy back the underlying debt security on its maturity date.

The economic benefit of RTMs to MF Global was the difference (or "spread") between (a) the interest rate paid by the issuer of the debt security to MF Global, and (b) the repurchase rate (referred to as the "financing rate") paid by MF Global to the Counterparty. It is my understanding – and I do not claim to be an accountant – that under the applicable accounting principles, MF Global was required to recognize its profit immediately in RTMs, and the asset (the debt security) and the liability (the money owed to the Counterparty) must be "de-recognized," *i.e.*, removed from MF Global's balance sheet. I want to note here that I believe that accounting issues with respect to the RTMs would have been reviewed by MF internal auditors, outside auditors (PricewaterhouseCoopers), and its audit committee.

B. Risks Related to RTMs

Financing the purchase of debt with RTMs allowed MF Global to reduce certain kinds of risk. Because RTMs financed MF Global's purchase of the debt security to the security's maturity, the RTMs eliminated the risk (referred to as "financing risk") that at some point during the life of the security MF Global would not be able to find additional financing for the security, and would therefore be forced to sell the security, potentially at a loss. Elimination of the financing risk meant that MF Global's market risk (arising from the fluctuation of the price of the underlying debt security) was significantly reduced.

MF Global retained, however, the risk that the debt securities might default or be restructured. If the debt securities defaulted or were restructured, then MF Global would not be paid in full at their maturity, even though MF Global would still have the obligation to buy back the debt securities from the Counterparty in full (at par).

Also, the clearing house through which the repurchase transaction was executed (typically, the London Clearing House, or "LCH") could demand that MF Global increase its margin. It might do so for at least two reasons: (a) if it determined that MF Global itself was not credit-worthy, or (b) if it determined that the underlying debt security – which was the collateral for the loan from the Counterparty to MF Global – decreased in value. The possibility of such margin calls from LCH meant that MF Global retained liquidity risk.[8]

To mitigate some of the risk of the RTMs, on some occasions MF Global took short positions in the underlying debt securities or in similar securities.[9]

C. The Decision to Engage in RTMs Involving European Sovereign Debt

Even before I joined MF Global, the firm traded European sovereign debt securities. For instance, for the year ending March 31, 2010, the company reported that it was carrying over $9 billion in foreign government securities, including both foreign securities owned outright and those sold to counterparties under repurchase agreements.[10] The company also reported that it had used RTM agreements to purchase some securities, although not specifically foreign government debt.[11]

In the summer of 2010, I met with MF Global's senior traders to discuss ways to improve the company's profitability. One of the ideas discussed was for MF Global to purchase European sovereign debt using RTMs. Such transactions were attractive for the reasons stated above – the reduction of finance risk and market risk – and the spread on the European sovereign debt securities appeared to be favorable. MF Global could engage in RTMs with these securities much as it had already done with other securities. Through these discussions, I became an advocate of purchasing European sovereign debt using RTMs.

At the time that MF Global entered into the transactions, I believed that its investments in short-term European debt securities were prudent. MF Global invested in RTMs with respect to the debt of Belgium, Italy, Spain, Ireland and Portugal. The first three of these – Italy, Spain and Belgium – were rated AA or better when MF Global invested in them. Even today, they are all at least A rated, and some of them are AA rated.[12] All of the sovereign debt of these three countries that MF Global held in RTMs matured no later than December 2012. Ireland and Portugal were lower rated, but for most of the time that MF Global held these securities they were backed by financing offered through the European Financial Stability Facility (EFSF) and the IMF, which made it highly likely that Ireland and Portugal would be able to roll over their outstanding debt before June 2013, when the funding facility expired. All of the sovereign Irish and Portuguese debt that MF Global held in RTMs matured no later than June 2012. Furthermore, because the European debt instruments that MF Global purchased did not all mature at the same time, there was an additional level of risk mitigation. As time went on and as the instruments matured, MF Global's risk would decrease.

D. Participants in the Decision to Engage in RTMs Involving European Sovereign Debt

MF Global's involvement in RTMs involving European sovereign debt securities was the subject of internal discussions with the company's traders, senior managers, and the board of directors.

The RTM transactions were reported to the board of directors. There were discussions at board meetings, at which the transactions were described, analyzed and debated. Although some people complain that boards of directors are "rubber stamps" for the decisions of company management, MF Global's board was not a rubber stamp. The members of the board of directors were independent and sophisticated, and they asked hard questions and raised concerns about the RTMs. All of the members had been on the board of directors before I joined MF Global. The board met without management on some occasions, and it is my understanding that the RTM portfolio was a topic of discussion during at least some of those meetings.

The directors approved sovereign risk limits up to which MF Global could invest in the RTM trades. Ultimately, the limits were specified on a country-by-country basis. MF Global attempted to adhere to those limits, and generally did so. On a few occasions, however, the chief risk officer reported that the firm had exceeded its limits with respect to a particular country. I recall, for example, one occasion on which the limit was exceeded because the Euro gained value against the dollar, and the risk limits were set in dollars. On the occasions on which the firm exceeded the country limits, it nonetheless remained within the overall limit and took appropriate steps (such as entering a reverse-RTM or shorting the same security) to bring its level of exposure back within the country limits. At the time of the bankruptcy, MF Global was within the risk limits set by the board of directors.

I accept responsibility for the RTM trades that MF Global engaged in from the time that I arrived at MF Global until my departure, on November 3, 2011, and I strongly advocated the trading strategy that I have described here. It is important to recognize, however, that MF Global's involvement in RTM trades was disclosed to the board of directors, the senior officers of the company, the company's accountants and numerous outsiders.

E. The Public Disclosures of the RTMs

The RTM trades were also publicly disclosed, both in the periodic financial statements and in other public statements, including press releases and earnings calls.

MF Global's annual filing (Form 10-K), dated May 20, 2011, for the fiscal year ended March 31, 2011, stated that MF Global invested in the sovereign debt of Italy, Spain, Belgium, Portugal and Ireland, and that the final maturity for any of these securities was no later than December 2012, which, it noted, was "prior to the expiration of the European Financial Stability Facility."[13] The filing also reported that "[a]t March 31, 2011 securities . . . sold under agreements to repurchase of $14,520,341[,000] at contract value, were de-recognized, of which 52.6% were collateralized with European sovereign debt."[14]

On July 28, 2011, the company announced its results for the first quarter of fiscal year 2012 (which ended on June 30, 2011), and its disclosures about the RTMs were again extensive. Its filing (Form 10-Q) stated that as of June 30, 2011, "securities purchased under agreements to repurchase of $16,548,450[,000] . . . were de-recognized, of which 69.3% . . . were collateralized with European sovereign debt, consisting of Italy, Spain, Belgium, Portugal and Ireland."[15] The Form 10-Q also stated that the net notional value of the Italian, Spanish, Belgian, Irish and Portuguese sovereign debt securities that MF Global held was $6.4 billion.[16] In a conference call that

MF Global held on July 28 to announce its results, the RTMs collateralized with European sovereign debt were discussed.[17]

F. The Fate of the RTMs

As of today, none of the foreign debt securities that MF Global used in the RTM trades has defaulted or been restructured. All of those securities that reached maturity while they were part of the RTM position paid in full.

COMMUNICATIONS WITH REGULATORS

A. FINRA's Position Regarding the Capital Treatment of the RTMs Involving European Sovereign Debt Securities

In approximately the first week of August 2011, I recall becoming aware that officials from FINRA were considering whether to require that MF Global modify its capital treatment under SEC Rule 15c3-1 of the RTMs involving European sovereign debt instruments. I believe that FINRA officials may have raised this issue with others at MF Global earlier than August 2011, but to the best of my recollection, I did not focus on the issue until approximately early August. I had not met with FINRA officials, to the best of my recollection, although I spoke briefly at a meeting at MF Global's offices on or about June 14, 2011, that was attended by officials from the SEC, the CFTC, FINRA and perhaps other regulators. I believe that I spoke about RTMs at that meeting. I believe that other members of the management of MF Global spoke at that meeting about several topics, although I did not attend those others members' presentations.

On or about August 15, 2011, I went with others from MF Global to the SEC in Washington to question FINRA's interpretation of SEC Rule 15c3-1. We met with Michael Macchiaroli, the Associate Director in the Division of Trading and Markets, and others from the SEC, and presented our argument that the capital treatment of the RTMs involving European sovereign debt securities should not be changed in the way that FINRA proposed. Some days after the meeting, MF Global was apprised by FINRA that FINRA would not change its position. I thereafter made a telephone call to Mr. Macchiaroli who told me, in substance, that there was no further appeal and that MF Global had to comply with FINRA's direction. He noted, however, that other companies in similar positions had sent letters of objection to the SEC, although he was clear that such a letter would make no difference to FINRA's or the SEC's position.

Although MF Global disagreed with FINRA's position, the firm promptly complied with the demand that its United States subsidiary increase its net capital. On September 1, 2011, we made a Form 10-Q/A public filing disclosing FINRA's ruling. It stated:

> As previously disclosed, the Company is required to maintain specific minimum levels of regulatory capital in its operating subsidiaries that conduct its futures and securities business, which levels its regulators monitor closely. The Company was recently informed by the Financial Industry Regulatory Authority, or FINRA, that its regulated U.S. operating subsidiary, MF Global Inc., is required to modify its capital treatment of certain repurchase transactions to maturity collateralized with European sovereign debt and thus increase its required net capital pursuant to SEC Rule 15c3-1. MF Global Inc. has increased its net capital and currently has net capital sufficient to exceed both the required minimum level and FINRA's early-warning notification level. …[18]

B. My Communications Regarding Proposed CFTC Rules Changes

Sometime in late 2010 or early 2011, the CFTC proposed certain changes in 17 C.F.R. §1.25 ("Rule 1.25"). As far as I understand, roughly speaking, Rule 1.25 outlines the permissible investments and uses for customer funds, as that term is defined in the CFTC Rules and Regulations, held by a Futures Commission Merchant ("FCM").

The proposed rule change was the topic of substantial discussion among regulated entities, industry organizations, associations, committees and even designated self-regulatory organizations. I understand that there were numerous letters received by the CFTC opposing various aspects of the proposed rule change.[19] MF Global submitted a letter, along with Newedge, which was one of the largest FCMs in the United States, opposing the proposed amendments to the rule.

The proposed rule change was also the topic of the conference call in which I took part on July 20, 2011, in which CFTC Chairman Gary Gensler participated. As best as I can recall, there were others from MF Global who took part in the conference call, and the CFTC's own records state that in addition to CFTC Chairman Gensler, four other officials from the CFTC were on the call. According to the CFTC's records, I was not the only representative of the industry that had calls with members of the CFTC, including Chairman Gensler, regarding the proposed changes.

The principal topic of discussion was whether Rule 1.25 should be changed to prevent FCMs from engaging in repurchase transactions with related broker-dealers. As I understood it, the then-current version of Rule 1.25 permitted such transactions but the proposed version would not, or would somehow limit such transactions. Consistent with the letter that we had submitted with Newedge, I argued, in substance, that such transactions should continue to be permitted because such transactions could be beneficial to the FCMs.

On the same afternoon, I spoke with another CFTC commissioner, Mr. Bart Chilton, to discuss the same matter. Mr. Chilton, who, according to the CFTC's records was accompanied by another CFTC official, listened to the arguments. I was joined on the phone by the general counsel for MF Global.

Later, I came to understand that the CFTC deferred consideration of the new rule.

C. Further Contacts

From the time that I joined MF Global through October 30, 2011, to the best of my recollection, I spoke with Chairman Gensler on only limited occasions. In addition to those contacts set forth above, I had a meeting with him in or about May 5, 2010, and I also met with him in or about December 2010. Those meetings were at the CFTC in Washington, and on those occasions there were other officials from the CFTC present.

In addition, Chairman Gensler and I had a few brief interactions at which there was, to the best of my recollection, no private discussions about the CFTC's regulation or oversight of MF Global. For example:

(a) He was a guest lecturer on government regulation at my class at Princeton on or about November 22, 2010. When he spoke at Princeton, there was another person from the CFTC present, and we did not discuss professional matters, except in the context of the class.
(b) I also attended a conference that was sponsored by the investment firm of Sandler & O'Neill on or about June 9, 2011. Chairman Gensler was there, as were others from the CFTC. I gave a

presentation about MF Global at the conference, and Chairman Gensler gave the luncheon speech. I do not recall that I discussed any business with Chairman Gensler other than a question that I put to him before the full audience during a question and answer session following his presentation. To the best of my recollection, the question was about proposed changes to Rule 1.25.

(c) In addition, on or about September 14, 2011, Chairman Gensler and I attended the wedding celebration of mutual friends. On that occasion, Chairman Gensler was not accompanied by anyone from the CFTC, but, again, we did not discuss business or regulatory matters so far as I recall.

On various occasions during my tenure at MF Global, I met or communicated with others at the CFTC about a variety of issues.

Until my final days at MF Global, to the best of my recollection, I never spoke about business with Chairwoman Shapiro of the SEC, another of our regulators, or any other SEC Commissioner. (I may have greeted Chairwoman Shapiro at a conference.) During the days preceding the filing of the MF Global bankruptcy, there were a number of conference calls with various regulators, and I now believe Ms. Shapiro was on at least one, and perhaps more than one, of the calls in which I also participated. There were typically several people on the conference calls during those final days. During my tenure at MF Global, to the best of my recollection, I never communicated with Secretary of the Treasury, Timothy Geithner. During my tenure at MF Global, to the best of my recollection, I never spoke with the President of the New York Federal Reserve William Dudley until approximately the week preceding the bankruptcy of MF Global, other than on one occasion (on or about April 13, 2011) when he and I attended a speech at Princeton by Chairman Bernanke of the Federal Reserve. To the best of my recollection, Mr. Dudley and I greeted each other on that occasion, but did not engage in substantive conversation. During my tenure at MF Global, to the best of my recollection, I did not speak with any governor of the Federal Reserve other than to greet Chairman Bernanke after his presentation at Princeton.

THE EVENTS OF OCTOBER 2011

The late summer and fall of 2011 were extraordinarily difficult times in the financial markets for almost all market participants. Like many comparable firms, MF Global was experiencing poor earnings principally on account of diminished revenues, and highly correlated volatility in many markets.

On October 17, 2011, the *Wall Street Journal* published an article that described the FINRA ruling that MF Global had disclosed on September 1. Other news stories followed, and some of MF Global's counterparties decided to reduce their exposure to the company, requiring some adjustment in our financing. MF Global's stock began to perform relatively poorly.

On or about October 21 and 22, 2011 – in anticipation of a disappointing earnings announcement, and concerned that the ratings agencies would downgrade MF Global – I and several of my colleagues made presentations to the ratings agencies to put the earnings announcement in context. The firm customarily made presentations to the ratings agencies shortly before the firm's quarterly earnings announcements.

On Monday, October 24, 2011, Moody's cut MF Global's rating from Baa2 to Baa3, followed by another downgrade to Ba2, on October 27. Fitch followed suit, cutting the company's rating from BBB to BB+. On October 26, S&P placed MF Global on its "credit watch negative" list, although it did not downgrade its rating below investment grade.

MF Global announced its quarterly earnings on October 25, 2011. The announcement was made two days ahead of schedule so that the firm could get full information to the public in light of Moody's downgrade. The announcement revealed that MF Global had lost $191.6 million in the quarter that ended September 30, 2011.

In light of the attention that has been given to RTMs, and the press reports that attributed MF Global's loss to RTMs involving European debt securities, it is important to make clear here that the loss was *not* related to those positions. The lion's share of the quarterly loss was a write- off of approximately $119.4 million that reflected a valuation adjustment against a deferred tax asset. That asset had been created by years of (non-RTM) tax losses cumulated (mostly before I arrived at MF Global) in the firm's United States and Japanese subsidiaries, which had allowed MF Global to recognize as an asset potential tax benefits – equal to $119.4 million – in future years. Under applicable accounting rules, by the second quarter of MF Global's 2011 fiscal year (*i.e.*, the quarter ending September 30, 2011) the firm was no longer permitted to recognize those tax benefits as assets, and therefore, with the advice and knowledge of its external auditor, it recognized a loss in that amount.

In addition, approximately $16.1 million of the quarterly loss resulted from the retirement of debt arising out of MF Global's purchase of certain of its 9% senior notes due 2038. Another approximately $10.0 million was for "restructuring charges," which included the closure of our Japanese securities business. The remainder was miscellaneous matters including reserves for litigation, much of it arising out of events before I arrived at MF Global. Approximately $18 million was operating losses (again, not related to the RTMs).

Shortly following the earnings announcement and the ratings downgrades, some clients and counterparties withdrew their business from the firm; others required increased margins. The firm's stock traded at sharply higher volumes and lower prices.

During the week of October 24-28, 2011, MF Global undertook extraordinary steps to ensure that it was able to honor customers' requests to withdraw funds or collateral. To the best of my recollection, during that week the firm unwound hundreds of millions of dollars worth of RTMs, and sold the underlying sovereign debt instruments; it also sought to draw down its revolver loans from a consortium of banks led by J.P. Morgan. On October 27, MF Global sold, to the best of my recollection, $1.3 billion in commercial paper instruments for same-day settlement, and over $300 million in corporate securities, also for same-day settlement. The next day, I believe that MF Global sold approximately $4.5 billion in United States agency securities. Over the course of the week, MF Global reduced the size of its match book by, to the best of my recollection, approximately $10 billion. Despite our best efforts to sell assets and generate liquidity, the marketplace lost confidence in the firm.

The firm was in regular contact with its regulators, including the CFTC, the Federal Reserve Bank of New York, the SEC and the U.K's Financial Services Authority, and the Chicago Mercantile Exchange (CME), the firm's designated self-regulatory organization.

The firm was also engaged in efforts to sell the FCM part of its business. It had been contemplating, for some time prior to the week of October 24, a strategic partnership involving the FCM business. On or about Tuesday, October 25, the firm retained an investment bank, Evercore, to explore selling that business. By the next day, MF Global instructed Evercore also to explore selling the entire firm. MF Global was in negotiations to sell the firm through the weekend of October 29-30. The sale did not take place when it was discovered that customer accounts could not be reconciled at that time.

THE UNRECONCILED ACCOUNTS

Obviously on the forefront of everyone's mind – including mine – are the varying reports that customer accounts have not been reconciled. I was stunned when I was told on Sunday, October 30, 2011, that MF Global could not account for many hundreds of millions of dollars of client money. I remain deeply concerned about the impact that the unreconciled and frozen funds have had on MF Global's customers and others.

As the chief executive officer of MF Global, I ultimately had overall responsibility for the firm. I did not, however, generally involve myself in the mechanics of the clearing and settlement of trades, or in the movement of cash and collateral. Nor was I an expert on the complicated rules and regulations governing the various different operating businesses that comprised MF Global. I had little expertise or experience in those operational aspects of the business.

Again, I want to emphasize that, since my resignation from MF Global on November 3, 2011, I have not had access to the information that I would need to understand what happened. It is extremely difficult for me to reconstruct the events that occurred during the chaotic days and the last hours leading up to the bankruptcy filing.

I simply do not know where the money is, or why the accounts have not been reconciled to date. I do not know which accounts are unreconciled or whether the unreconciled accounts were or were not subject to the segregation rules. Moreover, there were an extraordinary number of transactions during MF Global's last few days, and I do not know, for example, whether there were operational errors at MF Global or elsewhere, or whether banks and counterparties have held onto funds that should rightfully have been returned to MF Global. I am sure that the trustee in bankruptcy, the SIPC receiver, and the regulators are working to answer these questions and to understand precisely what happened during the firm's last days and hours.

As the chief executive officer of MF Global, I tried to exercise my best judgment on behalf of MF Global's customers, employees and shareholders. Once again, let me go back to where I started: I sincerely apologize, both personally and on behalf of the company, to our customers, our employees and our investors, who are bearing the brunt of the impact of the firm's bankruptcy.

That concludes my prepared statement. I am willing to answer the Subcommittee's questions.

End Notes

[1] *See* FY 2009 Form 10-K (for fiscal year ended March 31, 2009) (filed on June 10, 2009), at pp. 3-4 ("Description of Business").

[2]

Quarter	*Profit/(Loss)*	*Source*
4Q 2010	($96.5 million)	News Release, "MF Global Reports Fourth Quarter and Fiscal Year 2010 Results," May 20, 2010, at p. 1 (filed with Form 8-K on May 20, 2010)
3Q 2010	($22.3 million)	News Release, "MF Global Reports Third Quarter 2010 Results," Feb. 4, 2010, at p. 1 (filed with Form 8-K on Feb. 4, 2010).
2Q 2010	($16.0 million)	News Release, "MF Global Reports Second Quarter 2010 Results," Nov. 5, 2009, at p. 1 (filed with Form 8-K on Nov. 5, 2009).
1Q 2010	($32.8 million)	News Release, "MF Global Reports First Quarter 2010 Results," Aug. 6, 2009, at p. 1 (filed with Form 8-K on Aug. 6, 2009).
4Q 2009	($119.4 million)	News Release, "MF Global Reports Fourth Quarter and Fiscal Year 2009 Results," May 21, 2009, at p. 7 (Consolidated & Combined Statements of Operations) (filed with Form 8-K on May 21, 2009).

[3]

Quarter	*Profit/(Loss)*	*Source*
FY 2010	($167.7 million)	News Release, "MF Global Reports Fourth Quarter and Fiscal Year 2010 Results," May 20, 2010, at p. 1 (filed with Form 8-K on May 20, 2010).
FY 2009	($69.2 million)	News Release, "MF Global Reports Fourth Quarter and Fiscal Year 2009 Results," May 21, 2009, at p. 7 (Consolidated & Combined Statements of Operations) (filed with Form 8-K on May 21, 2009).
FY 2008	($71.1 million)	News Release, "MF Global Reports Record Fourth Quarter and Fiscal Year 2008 Results," May 20, 2008, at p. 1 (filed with Form 8-K on May 20, 2008)

[4] *See, e.g.*, FY 2011 Form 10-K filing (for fiscal year ended March 31, 2011) (filed May 20, 2011), at p. 6 ("Growth Strategy"); *id.* at 15.

[5] In February 2008, MF Global suffered a loss of $141.0 million, following an unauthorized trading incident involving wheat futures ("Dooley Trading Incident"). Criminal charges were brought against the trader, Evan Dooley. MF Global, among other things, entered into a settlement with the CFTC, under which the company agreed to specific undertakings relating to risk management, including the engagement of an independent outside consultant (Promontory). *See* FY 2010 Form 10-K (for fiscal year ended Mar. 31, 2010) (filed May 28, 2010), at p. 35.

[6] *My Equity Acquisitions in MF Global*

04/07/2010	Granted 2,500,000 stock options (granted as part of my initial compensation)
06/03/2010	Bought 352,100 common shares at $7.10, in a public offering
05/20/2011	Granted 1,600,000 stock options (granted at the time of my contract extension)
06/09-11/2011	Bought 36,100 common shares at between $6.85 and $6.92, on the market
08/08/2011	Bought 33,960 common shares at $5.71 and $5.91, on the market
08/10/2011	Bought 1,000 common shares at $5.41, on the market
08/18/2011	Bought 18,800 common shares at $5.25, on the market

I never sold any shares or options.

[7] Leverage is calculated by dividing (a) the reported total assets, by the sum of (b) total equity and (c) preferred shares. The relevant data can be found in MF Global's consolidated balance sheets, which are contained in the firm's quarterly (Form 10-Q) or annual (Form 10-K) financial statements.

[8] These risks were described in, for example, MF Global's Form 10-Q for the period ending June 30, 2011 (filed August 3, 2011), at p. 76:

Under the Company's repurchase agreements, including those repurchase agreements accounted for as sales, its counterparties may require the Company to post additional margin at any time, as a means for securing its ability to repurchase the underlying collateral during the term of the repurchase agreement. Accordingly, repurchase agreements create liquidity risk for the Company because if the value of the collateral underlying the repurchase agreement decreases, whether because of market conditions or because there are issuer-specific concerns with respect to the collateral, the Company will be required to post additional margin, which the Company may not readily have. If the value of the collateral were permanently impaired (for example, if the issuer of the collateral defaults on its obligations), the Company would be required to repurchase the collateral at the contracted-for purchase price upon the expiration of the repurchase agreement, causing the Company to recognize a loss. Also, margin funds that are posted by the Company cannot be used by it for other purposes, which may limit the Company's ability to deploy its capital in an optimal manner or to effectively implement its growth strategy. For information about these exposures and forward purchase commitments, see "—Off Balance Sheet Arrangements and Risk" and "Item 3. Quantitative and Qualitative Disclosures about Market Risk—Disclosures about Market Risk—Risk Management."

[9] *See, e.g.*, FY 2011 Form 10-K, at p. 78 ("From time to time, and in addition to short positions in our non-trading book, we also take short positions in our trading book to mitigate our issuer credit risk further.").

[10] *See* Notes 5 & 7 to Consolidated & Combined Financial Statements, FY 2010 Form 10-K, at p. 112-13.

[11] *See id.* at pp. 100, 112 (describing accounting treatment of RTMs).

[12] The current ratings are as follows:

Belgium:	AA negative (S&P)	AA+ negative(Fitch)	Aa1possible downgrade (Moody's)
Italy:	A negative (S&P)	A+ negative (Fitch)	A2 negative
Spain:	AA- negative (S&P)	AA- negative(Fitch)	A1 negative

The credit ratings above were obtained from the websites of the three major credit rating agencies on December 6, 2011. See http://www.standardandpoors.com/ratings/en/us/; www.fitchratings.com; www.moodys.com.

[13] FY 2011 Form 10-K, at pp. 77-78; *see also id.* at pp. 99-100.

[14] *Id.* at p. 100.

[15] Note 3, to Consolidated & Combined Financial Statements, 1Q FY 2012 Form 10-Q, at pp. 13-14 (filed Aug. 3, 2011).

[16] *Id.* at p. 90 (table).

[17] Earnings call, "MF Global Holdings' CEO Discusses F1Q2012 Results," July 28, 2011, at p. 4.

[18] "Additional Information," Q1 FY 2012 Form 10-Q/A, at p. 2.

[19] The CFTC received over 30 comment letters related to topics covered by the proposed changes. Many of these letters commented on the same proposed changes on which MF Global commented. As examples, both the CME and the Futures Industry Association ("FIA") in conjunction with the International Swaps and Derivatives Association ("ISDA"), Inc. challenged, among other things, the proposed amendments regarding permissible investments and internal repurchase transactions. The comments provided by the CME, FIA and ISDA advocated that an FCM should be permitted to invest in certain types of foreign sovereign debt and also advocated that FCMs should be able to engage in repurchase transactions and reverse repurchase transactions with affiliates and to engage in in-house transactions. Both JP Morgan Futures, Inc. and Morgan Stanley took similar positions.

INDEX

A

B

C

D

E

F

G

H

I

T

U

V

W